# Unity® Virtual Reality Development with VRTK4

## A No-Coding Approach to Developing Immersive VR Experiences, Games, & Apps

Christopher Coutinho

Apress®

*Unity® Virtual Reality Development with VRTK4: A No-Coding Approach to Developing Immersive VR Experiences, Games, & Apps*

Christopher Coutinho
GameWorks, Mumbai, Maharashtra, India

ISBN-13 (pbk): 978-1-4842-7932-8
https://doi.org/10.1007/978-1-4842-7933-5

ISBN-13 (electronic): 978-1-4842-7933-5

Managing Director, Apress Media LLC: Welmoed Spahr
Acquisitions Editor: Spandana Chatterjee
Development Editor: Spandana Chatterjee
Coordinating Editor: Divya Modi
Copy Editor: Jana Weinstein

Cover designed by eStudioCalamar

Cover image designed by Pixabay

Distributed to the book trade worldwide by Springer Science+Business Media New York, 1 New York Plaza, New York, NY 10004. Phone 1-800-SPRINGER, fax (201) 348-4505, e-mail orders-ny@springer-sbm.com, or visit www.springeronline.com. Apress Media, LLC is a California LLC and the sole member (owner) is Springer Science + Business Media Finance Inc (SSBM Finance Inc). SSBM Finance Inc is a **Delaware** corporation.

For information on translations, please e-mail booktranslations@springernature.com; for reprint, paperback, or audio rights, please e-mail bookpermissions@springernature.com.

Apress titles may be purchased in bulk for academic, corporate, or promotional use. eBook versions and licenses are also available for most titles. For more information, reference our Print and eBook Bulk Sales web page at http://www.apress.com/bulk-sales.

Any source code or other supplementary material referenced by the author in this book is available to readers on GitHub via the book's product page, located at https://github.com/Apress/VR-Development-with-Unity-VRTK. For more detailed information, please visit http://www.apress.com/source-code.

Printed on acid-free paper

*To all VR enthusiasts . . .*
*wherever you are*

# Table of Contents

# About the Author

 **Christopher Coutinho** is the founder of GameWorks, a Mumbai-based game development studio specializing in VR and virtual product development using Unity and VRTK 4. GameWorks provides development services to clients in game creation, Unity tools creation, and VR simulation-training development. Christopher is highly active on the VRTK's Discord channel. He is also known for his highly acclaimed online virtual reality courses on Udemy using Unity and VRTK 4.

# About the Technical Reviewer

 **Dr. Kevin Tan** is an associate professor at the Game School, which is part of Inland Norway University of Applied Science in Norway. He is also the course leader for the Augmented and Virtual Reality add-on program at the Game School.

Before Kevin joined the Game School in 2019, he received a Bachelor of Science degree with Honors in computer science, with a concentration in software engineering, from the University of Greenwich; a Master of Science degree in computer vision, visual, and virtual environments from the University of Leeds; and a PhD in bimanual interaction in virtual environments from the University of Salford, all in the United Kingdom.

After receiving his PhD, Kevin served as a postdoctoral research assistant at the Materials Science Center at the University of Manchester and went on to become a senior lecturer and course leader in the Computer Games Development course at Manchester Metropolitan University.

Kevin's research interests lie in developing Extended Reality (XR) for crossdisciplinary enterprise applications. In the past, he was involved in neural networks and artificial intelligence for gaming. He is now researching the emotion and personality of AI and the use of emotional traits to represent facial expressions in digital learning with VR. Besides that, Kevin also researches the achievement of realistic interactions with physical objects in VR environments.

Kevin's research focuses on the following areas:

- The use of Augmented Reality (AR) and VR technology in using game engines such as Unity3D and Unreal Engine.

- The research applications of the hybrid versions of augmented and virtual reality for health care, art, and tourism.

- The use of deep-learning algorithms for the prediction of microfacial expressions in simulation and games.

- Human-oriented cognitive issues that are integrated into neural network systems in the human-computer interaction environment.

Kevin is also a Unity-certified associate programmer.

# Acknowledgments

I want to thank Apress publishing for allowing me to write this book. The experience of working with the editors Spandana Chatterjee and Divya Modi has been a true pleasure from inception to completion.

A big thank you must also go to Kevin Tan, my technical reviewer, whose frank and precise comments made this a much easier-to-understand book. I also would like to thank the developer of the VRTK, Harvey Ball, also known as "the stone fox," whose insightful explanations have always been helpful and whose perspicacious ability is commendable. Additionally, I want to thank the VRTK community that I often frequent to learn from others and answer questions.

Last, I'd like to recognize the people who have made my experience with Unity a fruitful one. That, of course, starts with those at Unity Technologies, the company that makes the game engine at Unity.

# Introduction

## Who Is This Book Written For?

This book is for game developers interested in developing immersive virtual reality (VR) experiences, games, apps, and tool kits using Unity and the VRTK. It uses a no-coding approach, so you don't need to know C# programming and you won't be called upon to launch Visual Studio even once.

The book is aimed at beginner-to-intermediate Unity game developers who want to know get know their way around the Unity editor for basic scene editing. A basic knowledge of how Unity prefabs function, of how its events work in general, and of programming logic would be beneficial. You don't need to be able to write any event code to do the exercises in this book. However, if you're an absolute beginner to Unity, this is not the book for you.

## What Are We Building?

This book is structured for building a complete VR framework over the course of 22 chapters. You'll learn to set up state-of-the-art VR mechanics as part of the VR framework you build.

It uses version 4 of the VRTK, which is free to download. This makes understanding VRTK 4 super easy, and the framework you develop will be one massive, cohesive, lean and mean machine. By the end of this book, you'll have an advanced VR framework that you can even publish yourself.

Using Unity and VRTK 4, we'll build an advanced VR framework from scratch that can be used as the foundation for creating any VR game or experience. In the last chapter, you'll utilize the VR framework you built to create your very own minigame, without writing a single line of code.

# What Is Required for This Book

To do the exercises in this book, you'll need access to a six-DOF (degrees of freedom) headset of Steam VR or Oculus. A three-DOF headset won't work, as you need to be able to move around within your world.

You could use a Steam VR headset like the HTC Vive, an Oculus headset like the Oculus Rift, or the Oculus Quest (both 1 and 2 will work fine). These are some of the more popular six-DOF headsets available, and the ones this book's content has been tested with. The content of this book hasn't been tested with a Windows Mixed Reality headset, so you'll need to use one of the headsets just mentioned.

If you intend to use the Oculus Quest, it would be advisable to have a link cable, as deploying a build to the headset each time you test is not very practical and would be time consuming. You aren't required to get the Oculus-approved link cable, as several cheaper options are available online from Anchor, Belkin, and Amazon.

You need to have a computer running Windows 10 and the 2020 version of Unity LTS (Long Term Support). Your computer hardware should be compatible with your VR headset in terms of the graphics card it uses and the amount of RAM it requires. If you can play VR games while being tethered to your computer without any issues, your computer should already be compatible for development.

Both Oculus and Steam VR provide system tools that allow you to check whether your computer meets the minimum requirements to be VR ready. Head over to `www.vive.com/eu/setup/` or `www.oculus.com/setup/`, and go through the guided installation and setup process listed on either site. Last, ensure that you have your VR headset set to Developer Mode.

# Downloadable Content

Most chapters in this book include some form of downloadable content that lets you experiment with and implement the advanced VR mechanics taught here. Most of this downloadable content has been provided to you as Unity package files and a single manifest.json file. The book's chapters explain how these files are to be used.

In addition, you've been provided with the complete working VR framework and minigame as a .rar file download (VR_Playground.rar) so that you can quickly examine how various individual VR mechanics have been set up as part of this framework. Upon decompressing the VR_Playground.rar file, you need to ensure that you load this project using version 2020.3.15f2 of Unity LTS only, as this is the version the project was created in. Unity 2020 is notorious for breaking a project if used with a version different from the one in which the project was created. If you intend to use the provided VR_Playground project, it must be launched using version 2020.3.15f2 to be functional. Launching the project with any other version of Unity will result in colliders missing and many other issues cropping up.

All downloadable content for this book can be accessed on the following page: https://github.com/Apress/VR-Development-with-Unity-VRTK.

# CHAPTER 1

# Introduction

In this introductory chapter, you will get acquainted with Unity virtual reality development, a no-coding approach that you can use to create immersive virtual reality (VR) experiences. You will find out two ways that you can approach the material covered in the book. I will also discuss the other alternatives available for VR development and point out the advantages of using the no-coding approach. Finally, I will list the VR hardware required to follow along with this book.

## A No-Coding Approach to VR Development

The goal of this book is to show you everything you need to know to develop truly immersive VR experiences using Unity without the need to write a single line of code.

This no-coding approach is made possible by version 4 of the Virtual Reality Toolkit (VRTK) by Extend Reality Ltd. VRTK is available for free and licensed by MIT (Massachusetts Institute of Technology).

Every VR developer knows that getting their VR framework right is fundamental to having a great VR experience. The proper framework involves a mix of the latest and greatest VR mechanics you see within VR games and experiences today. In this book, you will learn to build your own VR framework from scratch, using some advanced VR mechanics. The VR framework you build can be transferred from one VR project to another, using as few or as many VR mechanics as you require. Using the VR framework you built, you will be able to create almost any type of VR game or experience you desire.

By the end of this book, you will have not only implemented some exciting game mechanics but will have also created your very own minigame.

© Christopher Coutinho 2022
C. Coutinho, *Unity® Virtual Reality Development with VRTK4*, https://doi.org/10.1007/978-1-4842-7933-5_1

# Two Ways to Approach the Material Covered in This Book

Every chapter in this book utilizes a practical, hands-on approach for implementing the content in your Unity project. Learning by practice is the ideal way to get to know VR development.

There are two ways to approach the material covered in this book; namely, a top-down approach and a bottom-up approach.

Beginners in VR development should use the top-down approach, starting with Chapter 1 and proceeding sequentially through the chapters in the book, implementing the concepts taught within their project. Using this approach, you will utilize several provided Unity packages, which you will download and import, as explained in each chapter. In my opinion, this is the best way to get the most out of this book, especially if you are a beginner in VR development or version 4 of the VRTK. I suggest that you first review each chapter to get an overall idea of the concepts and then review the chapters a second time to implement the content in your Unity project.

If you're not a beginner in VR development or version 4 of the VRTK, you're probably looking to jump right into working with the VR framework and use it to build your very own game, app, or experience. In this case, I would suggest the bottom-up approach, where you directly download the complete VR framework ZIP file and then launch it using Unity's latest LTS (Long Term Support) version 2020.3.x. With this, you can browse through chapters that interest you and explore how the various prefabs have been set up. It would help to quickly learn how to use the framework. You can always go back through the chapters sequentially when you have the time.

# Advantages of VRTK over Alternative Solutions

Version 4 of the VRTK is not the only solution available for getting started with VR development. Unity, Oculus, and Steam VR also provide their SDKs (Software Development Kit) for VR development. It is also possible to purchase assets from the Unity asset store to achieve the VR-specific functionality you desire.

Unity's Extended Reality (XR) Interaction Toolkit is another high-level component-based interaction system for creating VR experiences. Oculus and Steam VR, on the other hand, provide SDKs for their respective platforms.

However, the most significant advantage of version 4 of the VRTK is that it provides a simple yet extensible framework that works across multiple platforms. It is also both free and open source.

The VRTK is a VR development tool kit that provides a wide range of built-in support for the core components of VR, such as locomotion, interaction with 3D objects, and 2D and 3D controls. It reduces the amount of code you need to write to get started with VR development, allowing you to concentrate on developing the parts of your game or application without having to worry about input management , character controllers, locomotion methods, climbing and grabbing mechanics, UI interactions, and a lot of other fundamentals you probably have come to expect from a VR framework.

Building this whole extensive VR framework by yourself from scratch will give you a much deeper level of understanding of how to put it to use in building different VR games and experiences. By the end of this book, you will have built an extremely sophisticated VR framework, way better than you would get with most other free and paid VR frameworks and tool kits out there.

## Summary

In this introductory chapter, you learned about the no-coding approach that you find with version 4 of the VRTK. You have also been introduced to the two ways you can approach the material covered in this book. You then explored the other solutions available for VR development and some of the advantages that version 4 of the VRTK provides over them. Lastly, the VR hardware that you will need to follow along with the content matter in this book was discussed.

# CHAPTER 2

# A New Reality through Virtual Reality

In this chapter, I will explain what virtual reality (VR) is and why it is worth your time to become a VR pioneer as well as some of the areas within which it is being used. You will also learn about three essential concepts in VR: the place illusion, the plausibility illusion, and the embodiment illusion, which are essential for creating genuine immersion in VR. Additionally, you will find out about the popular headsets currently on the market that you will need to follow along with this book and be introduced to the term *degrees of freedom*.

## What Is Virtual Reality?

There is much excitement around the topic of virtual reality, also known as VR. The definition of *virtual reality* can be extensive, encompassing everything that happens in the digital world, like social networking, online marketing, and so forth. However, more often, the term is used to refer to a medium that immerses users in a computer-generated, simulated representation of a natural or fantasy world, allowing them to see, feel, hear, and interact with the simulated environment and the objects within it. As users are completely immersed in and engaged with this interactive experience, they can look around, move about, and interact with objects without ever having to break the illusion of being in a virtual world. VR is made possible by using a headset, input controllers, gloves, or even full bodysuits.

© Christopher Coutinho 2022
C. Coutinho, *Unity® Virtual Reality Development with VRTK4*, https://doi.org/10.1007/978-1-4842-7933-5_2

# Become a VR pioneer now, and create the future!

Since the VR market is still very young, a lot of room remains for breakthroughs. Creating something completely new is a unique opportunity that VR provides you.

It took approximately 27 years for PCs to grow from representing 2% to representing 70% of the type of computer most used in the United States, approximately 13 years for the Internet to reach that level, and approximately eight years for smartphones to get there. Many analysts have predicted that VR will reach this point within the next five to seven years. This leaves you two to three years to get trained in VR development and three to four years to create something that will significantly impact the VR ecosystem.

Creating features for a new product is complex, involving testing, failing, and then testing again. Given that the whole VR industry is currently in the test-and-fail mode, rapid prototyping in VR is what will gain you maximum leverage, and that is what this book is all about.

# What Can You Do with VR?

You may believe that VR is only suitable for entertainment or gaming, but the fact is, other industries have started to take note of its potential and popularity as well. VR is still in infancy, and we are currently only in the first generation of consumer VR hardware. Having not even come close to discovering everything we could do with VR, you could be the one to discover something new and become a VR pioneer.

# Medical and Mental Health

The use of 3D visualization is not new to the medical industry. X-rays, CT scans, and MRIs have helped doctors immensely in diagnosis and treatment for years. Likewise, VR has the potential to have profound effects in medicine, neuroscience, psychology, and pain management. VR has already been extremely effective with helping treat fears, phobias, stress-related disorders, bipolar disorders, cognitive rehabilitation, and other psychological conditions. It has benefitted health care professionals and patients across a multitude of disciplines.

# Automotive Engineering and Design

VR has also been an effective tool for engineering and design applications. VR design eliminates the need for building physical prototypes. The automotive industry uses VR to help visualize products within virtual environments before physical prototypes are made, allowing designers to see how parts fit together. VR is also being used in this industry to help customers get a sense of how their car would look and feel before ordering it.

# Training and Education

Training and education is another field in which VR has been a potent tool. While many other types of media communicate verbally via ideas, VR communicates via direct, hands-on experience. This is possible due to VR's combination of interaction and true immersion. Aircraft pilots, firefighters, oil field workers, and others are some professions where training is done by VR. It is also used in education, helping students to learn new languages by using VR environments with applications like Linguisticator.

# Architecture, Construction, and Real Estate

VR provides an immersive experience that allows a user to explore space on a real-world scale in a way that is not possible via other mediums. In the world of construction, traditional designs have made use of flat technical drawings and 3D models. However, VR has changed what is possible by creating a realistic representation of spaces. Architects and engineers can now explore every inch of a construction project and identify any issues before construction begins, potentially avoiding delays and unnecessary costs. VR has also been tremendously helpful in real estate, wherein the environment can either be fully modeled in 3D or photographed as a 360-degree panorama, which provides an immersive sense of the space and its surroundings that the user would not be able to experience without visiting the actual physical location.

# Entertainment and Journalism

The ability of VR to create the simulated experience of being present through immersion makes it a compelling medium with which to narrate a story with a deep sense of empathy, something that is harder to achieve on a flat screen. The entertainment industry, gaming in particular, is where VR is making the most waves. However, there are other areas of entertainment, such as music and cinema, where VR is making an impact as well. Music concerts put on by famous artists have been released as VR events that allow viewers to recreate the experience of front-row seating. Oculus and Netflix have also released their version of a cinematic experience, allowing viewers to watch films in a different way. Virtual tourism and documentaries are other exciting aspects of VR cinema.

VR is also being used in what is known as immersive journalism, where news is produced in a form where people can gain first-person experiences of the events or situations described in news stories. By having viewers wear a VR headset, they enter virtual worlds and scenarios where they can experience the news events firsthand.

## Advertising and Retail

VR offers a range of ways for customers to experience products. A person wanting to purchase a car can experience the car in virtual reality, make color choices, select the car's interior features, and more, all from within the comforts of their home. It enables retailers to reach customers who cannot visit their showrooms, increasing the likelihood of making a sale. It also allows the customer the opportunity to try out the product before buying it. VR is also used in advertising to build an emotional connection with a brand by immersing a customer in a virtual experience that creates a deep sense of connection with the product.

## Gaming in VR

It is no secret that VR has changed the overall gaming experience. VR does not just show you the game as you play it; it immerses you directly in the game, allowing you to become the protagonist and have experiences and interactions with actors and objects within the game world as if you were really in it. There are also input controllers with haptic feedback to simulate tactile sensations that allow for complex interactions, immersion, and presence, which wouldn't be possible using traditional game controllers. The ability provided to the player to interact with actors and objects all around them, along with the ability to move about in the virtual world, is what makes gaming in VR truly incredible.

# Immersion and Presence in VR

Now that we've gotten a good idea of what VR is and the many things you can do with it, it is time to delve further into what makes VR work.

Let us begin by talking about immersion in VR. Immersion is often used to describe the perceived experience of being physically present in a virtual world . For an experience to be genuinely immersive, certain illusions need to be created.

## Place Illusion

The place illusion creates the feeling of being in a physical place even though you realize you're not there. Your brain decides that you are in the virtual world rather than the real world. Place illusion can occur even if nothing is happening in the virtual world at the time. Because you are in a virtual world and you can look around, your brain decides that this is where you are. The place illusion is the first of the three illusions that lead to true immersion, where your brain believes that events occurring around you are genuinely taking place.

## Plausibility Illusion

The plausibility illusion creates the feeling that the events you are engaged with are really happening. Your brain decides that these events feel genuine. It is different from the place illusion, as you can feel like you are in a place but at the same time not believe that anything is actually happening there. The plausibility illusion is the second of the three illusions that leads to true immersion.

## Embodiment Illusion

The embodiment illusion is unique to virtual reality in that it has to do with your own body. Where in the real world you can look down and you see your own body, VR can be programmed to recreate that experience by allowing you to see a virtual body in place of your own body when you look down. The embodiment illusion gives rise to the third illusion, which is the illusion of body ownership or embodiment—that is, the belief that the virtual body is actually your body.

True immersion in virtual reality stems from the three illusions occurring at the same time:

1.  Believing that you are in a place even though your physical self knows you are not actually there (the place illusion)

2.  Events occurring in a place and you responding to them even though your physical self knows they are not actually happening (the plausibility illusion)

3.  Looking down and seeing your virtual body and believing and acting like it is your own body even though your physical self knows it is not (the embodiment illusion)

# VR Hardware and Technology

The most common way of immersing a user into a virtual world is by using a head-mounted display (HMD). Even though there are other ways of creating VR, the method we will use in this book requires a HMD, also commonly known as a VR headset.

A VR headset can take you to levels of immersion where you believe you are walking on the moon or trying to survive on a battlefield even though you are just in your living room.

You may be wondering how this all works. The concepts for displaying VR content across different types of available HMD devices are similar. Two streams of content are sent to the headset, whether to one display or two. A set of lenses inside the headset focuses and reshapes the content each eye sees, creating a stereoscopic 3D image. This is done by adjusting the 2D images to mimic how your eyes view the world in real life.

VR headsets can be either tethered or untethered. A tethered device like the Oculus Rift, HTC Vive, or Sony's PSVR requires wires that attach the VR headset to a desktop, laptop, or console to deliver VR content. A headset such as the Oculus Quest or Vive Focus, on the other hand, is an untethered headset that does not need to be connected to a desktop or a laptop.

Some VR headsets only track the user's direction, while others track changes to the user's position. The term *degrees of freedom* (DoF) is used to distinguish between headsets that only track direction and those that track both direction and position.

# Input Controllers

Although the VR headset is the main component of a VR system, most VR headsets also come with input controllers that allow users to interact within the VR world.

3DOF devices have input controllers that are essentially pointers, allowing users to take aim but not to reach out and grab something.

6DOF high-end devices have special controllers that function like virtual hands and are tracked by the same sensors that track the HMDs. These controllers allow you to use your hands in various ways within VR through a combination of buttons, triggers, and thumb sticks.

# 3DOF

A VR device that only tracks rotation but does not track position is referred to as a 3DOF device, as it only tracks three DOF in terms of rotation: the degree to which the device is rotating around its upward-pointing y-axis (*yaw*), or rotating sideways, the degree to which it is rotating around its forward-pointing z-axis (*roll*), and the degree to which it is tilting forward or backward on its horizontal x-axis (*pitch*).

3DOF devices track rotation only, so users can look around and point but cannot move from side to side.

The Oculus Go and Samsung Gear headsets are examples of 3DOF devices.

# 6DOF

A VR device that tracks both position and rotation is referred to as a 6DOF device. This device tracks all six degrees of freedom: yaw, roll, pitch, up-down movement, side-to-side movement, and forward-backward movement.

6DOF devices track both positions and rotation, so that users can look and move around.

Most first-generation 6DOF devices like the original HTC Vive and the Oculus Rift required base stations to provide positional tracking on desktop systems. However, untethered headsets like the Oculus Quest and the Vive Focus use camera arrays to track the headset's position within the room, so they do not require base stations. This technology is referred to as inside-out tracking.

The HTC Vive, Oculus Rift, HTC Vive Focus, and Oculus Quest headsets are 6DOF devices. You will need to have one of these to follow along with this book.

# Summary

In this chapter, we went over virtual reality and why now is the best time to get into VR development. We also looked at the areas where VR is currently being used. You learned about the importance of immersion in VR and the three illusions of place, plausibility, and embodiment that create true immersion in VR. You also learned about the various types of VR headsets available, both tethered and untethered, and the degrees of freedom they support, as well as the benefits of input controller peripherals that accompany VR systems.

# CHAPTER 3

# Setting Up Your Project for VR Development

The goal of this chapter is to set up a Unity3D project for virtual reality development. I will discuss the VR hardware requirements and the versions of Windows and Unity that you will be using. I will walk you through setting up the required SDKs, Unity's XR plugin management, choosing the various Player settings within Unity, and finally, switching your platform for Android development. You will also import your first Unity package, which will serve as the environment in which you will build your VR framework.

## VR Hardware Prerequisites

To follow along with the content in this book, you'll need to have either an Oculus Rift, Oculus Rift S, Oculus Quest, or an HTC Vive headset, which are all 6DOF. As we proceed, I'll assume that you have already set up your headset and ensured it is working, indicating that your computer is VR ready. If you haven't, now is a good time to do this. Both Oculus and Steam VR provide system tools that allow you to check whether your computer meets the minimum requirements to be VR ready. Head to `www.vive.com/eu/setup/` or `www.oculus.com/setup/`, and run through the guided installation and setup process listed there. Lastly, ensure that you have your VR headset set to developer mode . Be sure to test out your headset and ensure that it is working before setting up your development environment.

If the VR system you're using is Oculus Quest, it would be good to connect your Oculus Quest to your PC or laptop with a link cable and playtest using link mode. Doing this would be more convenient than having to deploy a complete build to the Oculus Quest each time you need to do a test run. You do not need to get the Oculus-approved link cable. There are several cheaper options available online from Anchor, Belkin, and Amazon. I use a six-foot Anchor USB C to USB 3 cable.

© Christopher Coutinho 2022
C. Coutinho, *Unity® Virtual Reality Development with VRTK4*, https://doi.org/10.1007/978-1-4842-7933-5_3

# Unity Prerequisites and Oddities

The only requirement for following along with the content in this book is that you use Windows 10 and Unity version 2020.3.15f2. The project we will build throughout this book uses Unity's LTS, version 2020.3.15f2, which is the latest LTS version at the time of this writing. I have experienced with different versions of Unity 2020, and even though LTS has a lot of oddities, I suggest you stick with LTS version 2020.3.15f2 throughout the exercises in this book. Other LTS versions do not provide any new features anyway. One thing you should not do is upgrade midway throughout your project to a newer version of LTS. Doing so will cause your project to malfunction.

When installing Unity, ensure that you set up the Android Build Support by checking the boxes for Android SDK, NDK Tools, and OpenJDK . Also, ensure that you check the box for the module, Windows Build Support (IL2CPP).

# Setting Up Your VR project

As part of this book, you have been provided with Unity package files that you will download and import into your Unity project, as explained in this chapter.

To proceed, you'll need to download the provided Unity package file, "VRTK_ Playground," to an easily accessible location, such as your desktop or any other folder on your computer.

Then, launch the Unity hub, click the New button in the upper right-hand corner, and ensure that you select the latest version of Unity, LTS 2020.3.x, that you downloaded. Note that I am using Unity Hub, version 2.4.5.

As shown in the dialog box in Figure 3-1, select VR in the Templates section . Then, choose an appropriate location in which to save your project. Give your project a proper name; I have named mine "VR_Playground." Finally, click the Create button to set up the project, and Unity's editor will be open on your desktop. You will be greeted with a VR Project Template dialog asking you to select an appropriate platform. Click the Close button on this dialog, allowing the Unity editor to display its default sample scene. On the far-right side of the editor, you will notice the Tutorial tab. Click the vertical ellipsis button on this tab and select Close, as you won't need it. In the "Assets" folder on the Project tab, you will notice that three folders have already been set up by default. Using the VR template that is listed, you have avoided the need to manually set up XR Plugin Management, which you would otherwise need to do, should you have chosen the 3D template.

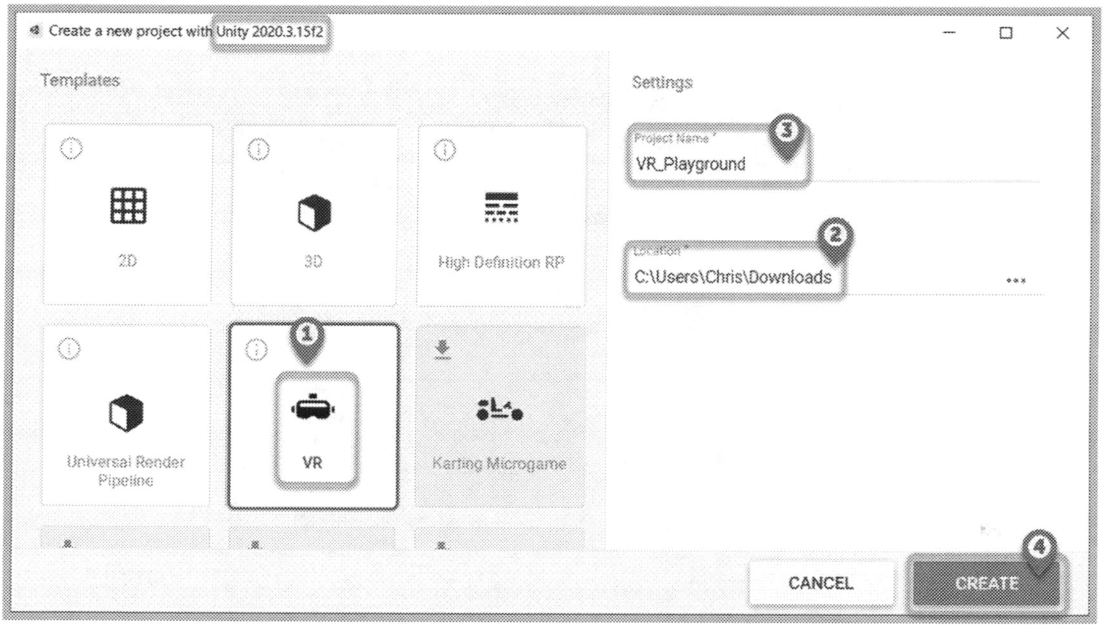

*Figure 3-1.*  *Creating a new Unity3D project*

Within the Unity editor console tab, you may see a message stating that a new Visual Studio Editor package version is available and asking you to update to this latest version for better visual studio integration. To do so, open the Package Manager in Unity, select the Visual Studio Editor item from the pane on the left, and click the Update to 2.x.x button.

# Importing the Unity Package File

Now that you have downloaded the provided Unity package file, "VRTK_Playground," it's time to import it into your project.

From the main menu, select Assets ➤ Import Package ➤ Custom Package. Navigate to the folder where you saved the downloaded Unity package file, select it, and click the Open button within the Import Package window. An Import Unity Package window will pop up, as shown in Figure 3-2. Click the All button, then the Import button. Unity will then begin its importing process, importing all the objects in the Unity package into your project.

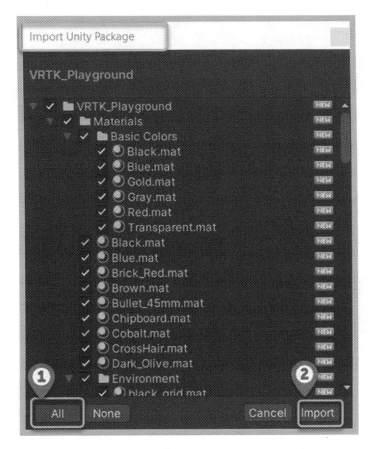

*Figure 3-2.  Importing the Unity package file*

Your Unity console will now display three error messages, as shown in Figure 3-3. You can ignore these messages for now. They indicate that a couple of namespaces are missing. The messages will disappear once you install version 4 of the VRTK in the next chapter.

*Figure 3-3.  Error messages indicating that namespaces are missing*

Now that you have imported the provided VRTK_Playground unity package, go to the "Assets" folder in your Project tab and delete the "Scenes" folder, as it is no longer required. Note that a new "VRTK_Playground" folder is now available in your "Assets" folder. Expand the "VRTK_Playground" folder and then expand the "Scenes" folder, and you will find a Demo scene. Double-click this scene to launch it in the Unity editor. You will be asked whether you'd like to save the Sample Scene that is currently open. Click the Don't Save button, as you do not need the Sample Scene anymore. Select the Scene tab within the Unity editor to view your VR framework environment. Select the Game tab within the Unity editor, and you will note that it displays a message stating that there are no cameras rendering. This is because there is no camera set up within your Demo scene yet.

Let's start by exploring the Demo scene and the game objects that comprise it. First, we'll select the Scene tab to switch back to the scene view. Figure 3-4 displays your Demo scene. Within the hierarchy, the parent Environment game object has been expanded and some of its child objects have been expanded, too. You will begin exploring your Demo scene by examining the game objects within the Environment object and noting their Tag and Layer settings within the inspector.

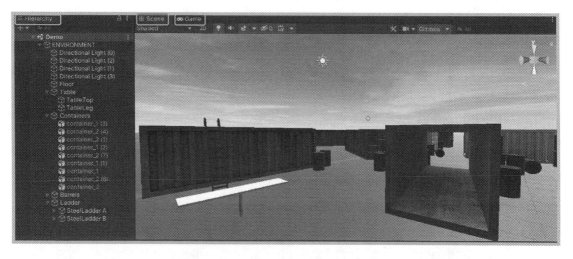

***Figure 3-4.*** *Demo scene with objects within the hierarchy expanded*

First, expand the Environment game object within the hierarchy, then expand all the child objects; namely, Table, Containers, Barrel, and Ladder. The Ladder game object contains two child game objects: Steel Ladder A and Steel Ladder B. Expand these objects.

Let's now look at each game object within the hierarchy and note the collider components they have been set up with and their Layer and Tag settings .

Begin by selecting the Floor game object in the hierarchy . Note that the inspector has been set up with a mesh collider, its Layer has been set to Water, and it has been left Untagged.

Now, select the Table game object in the hierarchy, and note that it is made up of Table Top and Table Leg game objects, both of which have box colliders on them. Also note that their Layer and Tag properties have been left at their default values.

With the Containers game object expanded in the hierarchy, select any Container game object within it. All Container child game objects within the Containers parent game object have similar components. Note that all the Container child game objects have been fitted with a box collider. Also note that their Layer and Tag properties have been left at their default values.

With the Barrels game object expanded in the hierarchy, select any Barrel game object in it. All Barrel child game objects within the Barrels parent game object have similar components. Note that all the Barrel child game objects have been fitted with a box collider. Also note that their Layer and Tag properties have been left at their default values.

With the Ladder game object expanded, as well as both Steel Ladder A and Steel Ladder B child game objects, you will see that both of the child game objects contain several numbered Collision game objects. With the Move Tool on Unity's toolbar toggled on, select several of the numbered Collision game objects in the hierarchy to see them highlighted within the scene view. Note that each of these numbered Collision game objects denotes either a side portion or a rung of the ladder. All the numbered game objects have been fitted with capsule colliders. As we will see in later chapters, this kind of collider setup allows you to grab onto either side of the ladder's rungs and climb up.

---

**Note**   Should you shut down Unity and then relaunch it for whatever reason, you may be prompted with a message asking if you would like to enter safe mode, as shown in Figure 3-5. Click the Ignore button. The compilation errors that this message refers to are the three errors listed earlier in this chapter, which will disappear once you have installed version 4 of the VRTK.

---

*Figure 3-5.* *Dialog box prompting you to enter safe mode*

# Exploring the XR Plugin Management for Unity

Let's begin by exploring the XR Plugin Management that Unity set up for you by default when you used the VR template provided. To do so, navigate to the main menu and select Edit ➤ Project Settings to open the Project Settings dialog box. From the pane on the left, select and expand the XR Plugin Management item, and you will notice that it has two child items—namely, Oculus and Windows Mixed Reality—set up by default. You won't be developing for a Windows Mixed Reality device in this book, so select the Oculus item from beneath XR Plugin Management. On the pane on the right, you will see the PC, Mac & Linux Standalone settings tab, as well as the Android tab. On both these tabs, the Stereo Rendering mode has been set up by default. Also, for the Android tab, target devices have been set to Quest and Quest 2 by default.

Now, select the XR Plugin Management item from the pane on the left, and you will see the PC, Mac & Linux Standalone settings tab as well as the Android tab visible in the right pane. Both these tabs provide you with check boxes listing plug-ins from providers that you can use. However, as shown in Figure 3-6, there is no Steam VR plug-in listed here. However, this will not be a cause for concern if you're using an HTC Vive device, as you will circumvent this by using the VRTK-provided Camera Rigs and Unity XR plugin management framework prefab.

**Figure 3-6.** *XR Plugin Management, with no Steam VR Plug-in included in the list*

The Oculus plug-in has already been installed by default, so you may now close the Project Settings dialog.

If you're building for the HTC Vive, even though the XR Plugin Management does not support a plug-in for Steam VR, you won't need to download the Steam VR Plugin from the Unity Asset store to have your framework work with your HTC Vive devices. However, you will need to have the Steam VR client installed on your PC to build to the HTC Vive.

# Importing the Oculus Integration SDK

You, however, need to download and import the Oculus Integration SDK, as the VRTKs Camera Rigs, Oculus Integration wrapper will require it. This will become clearer once you install version 4 of the VRTK in the next chapter.

I'm using the latest version of the Oculus Integration SDK currently available, version 29, and I advise you to do the same. You can download the Oculus Integration SDK from the Unity asset store or the Oculus Developer site; the latter is a repository for all earlier versions.

Log in to the Unity asset store and search for Oculus Integration, and download and import it into your project. The Package Manager dialog should then open. If not, you can launch it by selecting Window ➤ Package Manager from the main menu. On the left-hand pane, ensure that the Item Oculus Integration is selected and then click the Import button located in the bottom right corner of the right-hand pane. The Import Unity Package dialog will be displayed. Click the Import button to begin importing the Oculus

Integration SDK into your project. Once you're done, close the Package Manager. Then, navigate to the "Assets" folder in the Project tab, where you will notice an Oculus folder, which is essentially the Oculus Integration SDK.

---

**Note**   Upon restarting Unity, you may be prompted with an Update Oculus Utilities Plugin dialog box stating that a new OVR Plugin is available and recommending that you use it. Click the Yes button to proceed. You will then most likely be prompted with another dialog asking you to restart Unity. Click the Restart button. You may also be asked to upgrade spatializer plug-ins. Go ahead and click Upgrade, then click Restart. Unity will restart with your Demo scene launched.

---

# Choosing Player Settings within Unity

Now, navigate to the main menu and select Edit ➤ Project Settings to open the Project Settings dialog box. On the left-hand pane, select the Player item. On the right-hand pane, select the PC, Mac & Linux Standalone settings tab. Expand the Other Settings section and scroll down to the Configuration section. If you didn't install Windows Build Support (IL2CPP) when setting up Unity, set the Scripting Backend property to Mono . Set the API Compatibility Level property to .NET 4.x. In the Configuration section , ensure that the Active Input Handling property has been set to Input Manager (Old), as shown in Figure 3-7.

*Figure 3-7.*   *Other Settings section configuration properties in the PC, Mac & Linux Standalone settings tab*

With the Other Settings section still open, click the Android Settings tab. Scroll down until you see the Lightmap Encoding property, and set its value to Normal Quality .

Then scroll further down until you see the Identification section. Ensure that the Minimum API level property has been set to Android 6.0 "Marshmallow" (API level 23).

Scroll further down to the Configuration section and set the API Compatibility Level to .NET 4.x. Next, locate the Target Architectures section that follows, and ensure that the box for ARMv7 is unchecked and the box for ARM64 is checked.

Scroll further down to the bottom of the Configuration section and ensure that the Active Input Handling property has been set to Input Manager (Old), as shown in Figure 3-8.

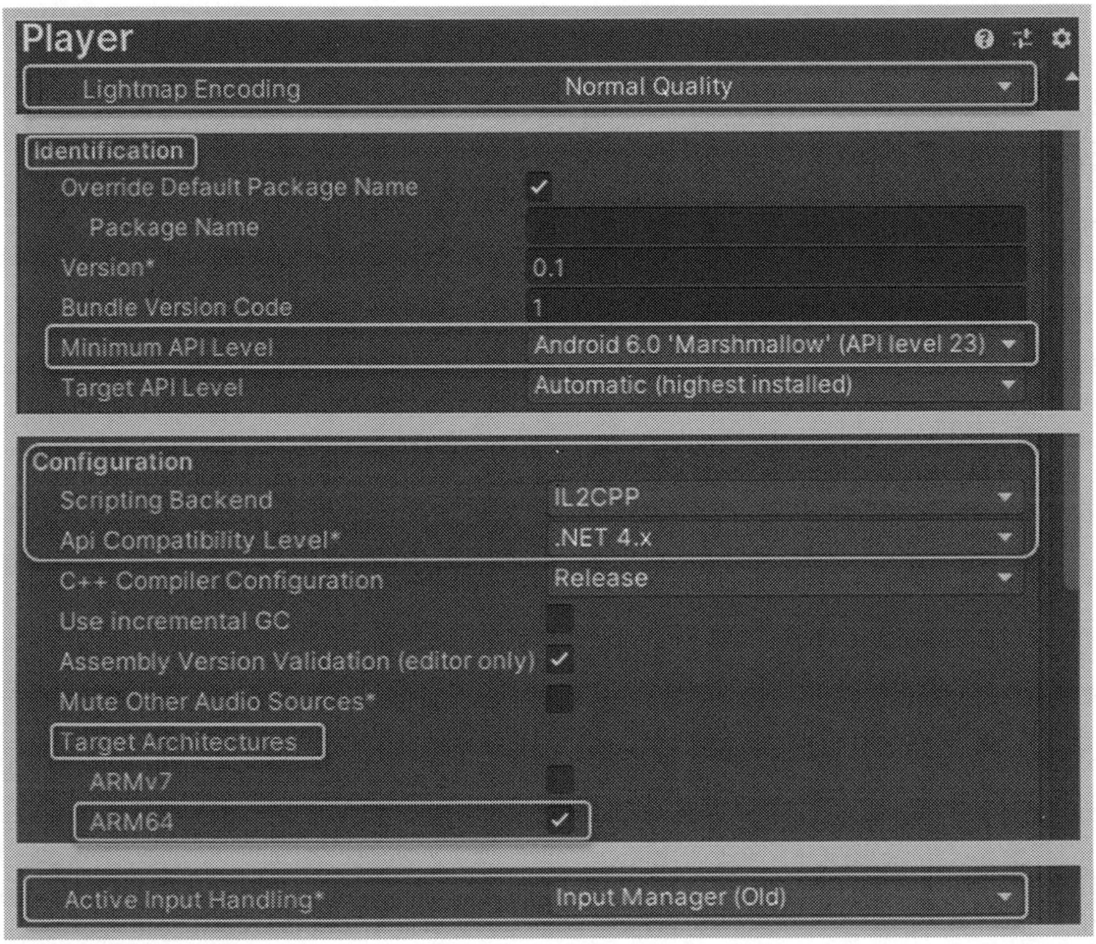

**Figure 3-8.** *Android settings tab in the Other Settings section: Lightmap Encoding, Identification, and Configuration properties*

Next, scroll up to the top, where you'll see the Rendering section. Ensure that the Color Space property has been set to Linear, as shown in Figure 3-9.

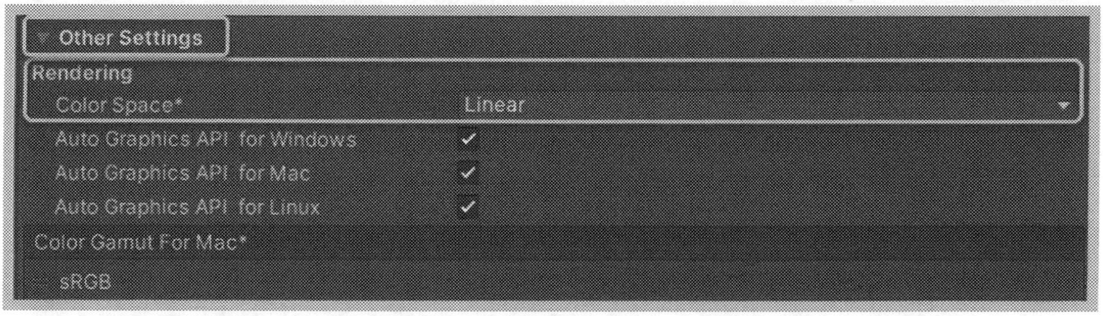

***Figure 3-9.*** *Android settings tab in Other Settings: Rendering the Color Space property*

Finally, collapse the Other Settings section and close the Project Settings dialog.

On the main menu, select File ➤ Build Settings to open the Build Settings dialog box. Then, click the Add Open Scenes button to add your Demo scene to the Scenes in Build list box. By default, you'll notice that the Platform has been set to PC, Mac & Linux Standalone. These default platform settings are sufficient if you're building for the HTC Vive or the Oculus Rift. However, if you're deploying to the Oculus Quest, you'll need to select Android as your platform. After this is done, change the Texture Compression property to ASTC and set the Compression Method property to LZ4. If you have your Oculus Quest connected to your PC, you can click the Refresh button beside the Run Device property and select your Oculus device from the drop-down. Finally, click the Switch Platform button. Unity will begin its importing process, which can take a while, see Figure 3-10.

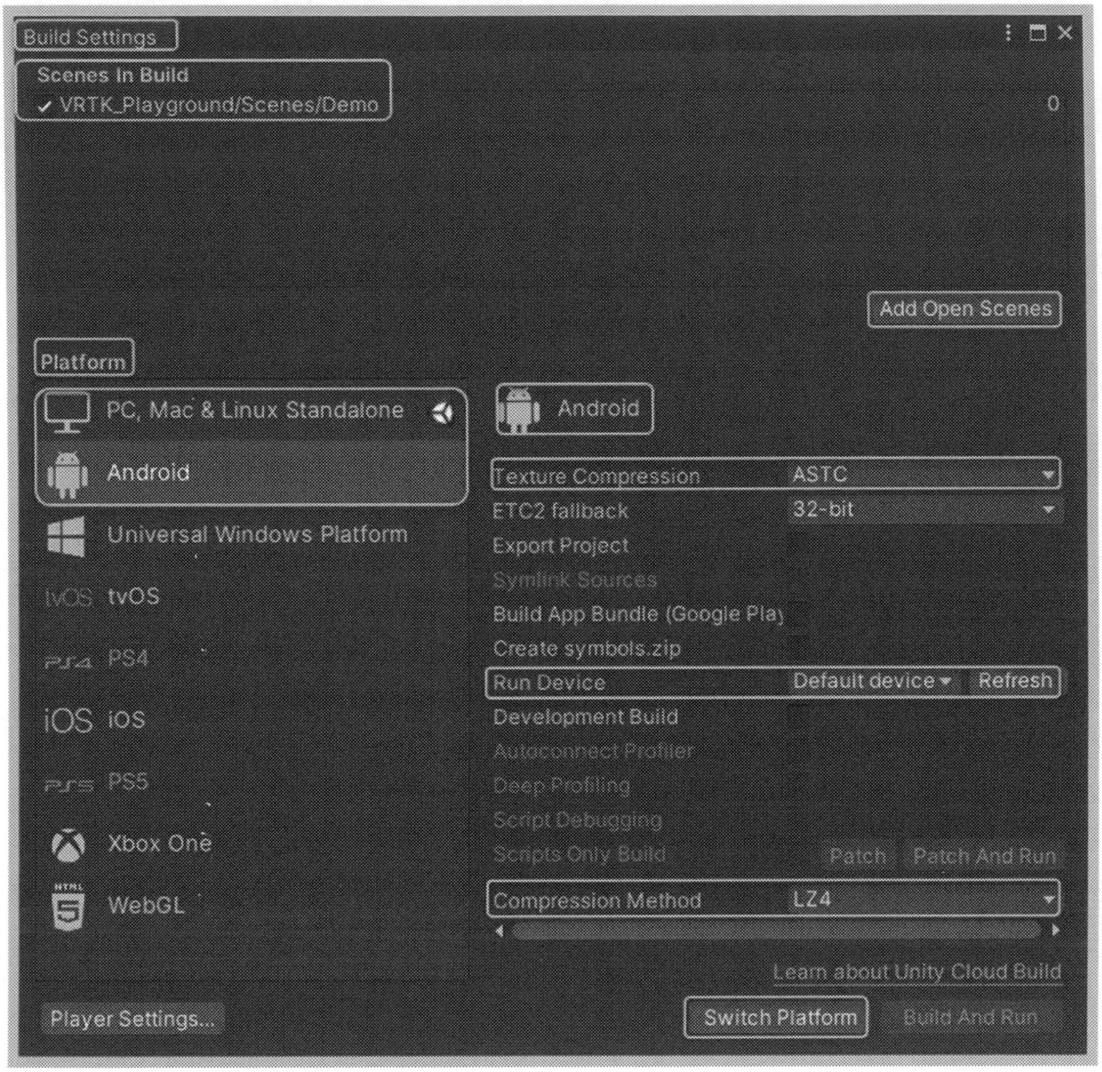

*Figure 3-10.*  *Build Settings dialog box for deploying a project to a Oculus Quest headset*

# Summary

In this chapter, we went over the various VR hardware prerequisites and the hardware you'll need to follow along with this book. We explored prerequisites for the Windows version of Unity. You created a new empty VR project and then downloaded and imported the Unity package file provided to you in the new VR_Playground project. The assets you imported via the Unity package file set the environment in which you will build your VR framework. You explored each game object within the environment provided. Next, you delved into the XR Plugin Management for Unity and saw the default plug-ins installed. You then downloaded and imported the Oculus Integration SDK, which we will use once we have installed version 4 of the VRTK packages in a later chapter. Lastly, you set up several Player settings within Unity and looked at the Build Settings dialog box and saw how you could switch your development platform to work with an Android-based device like the Oculus Quest. In the next chapter, we'll take a look at version 4 of the VRTK.

# CHAPTER 4

# Importing VRTK 4 Tilia Packages

In this chapter, we will go over how to import VRTK 4 Tilia packages into a project using the manifest.json file. You will learn how to add manifest lines for several Tilia packages in your project's manifest.json file. You will then see how these packages are reflected in the Package Manager and how they can be updated. We'll also look at the Tilia input axis definitions that get added to Unity's Input Manager. Finally, we'll look at the "Packages" folder in the project tab to see how the Tilia packages have been structured.

## Importing Version 4 of VRTK

Now that you have set up your project for VR development, it's time to bring version 4 of the VRTK Tilia packages into your project. VRTK 4 comprises a repository of several Tilia packages that provide valuable features for developing spatial solutions. These Tilia packages are like the packages you have probably seen available within Unity's Package Manager and can be found within the Package Manager once imported.

All Tilia packages can be accessed by visiting the following site: `www.vrtk.io/tilia.html`. The beauty of version 4 of the VRTK is that you can install only the packages that are required for your project.

Note that packages are categorized under several headings on the site—namely, Camera Rigs, Developer Tools, Indicators, Input, Interactions, Locomotors, Mutators, Output, SDK, Trackers, Utilities, and Visuals—as shown in Figure 4-1.

© Christopher Coutinho 2022
C. Coutinho, *Unity® Virtual Reality Development with VRTK4*, https://doi.org/10.1007/978-1-4842-7933-5_4

*Figure 4-1.* Screen where VRTK 4 Tilia packages are available on the VRTK website

For our purposes, we will install all the packages that will be helpful for working with projects in this book. You can always add a new package by adding its manifest line to your project's manifest.json file. You are not compelled to install every package listed here, even though you can.

You can look at the packages available in CameraRigs by clicking on the chevron beside the heading. Note that the package lists its current release version, beneath which is a short package description and, following that, a manifest line for each type of camera rig available. You can copy this line using the Copy button to the right of it and paste it into your project's manifest.json file for all the packages you may require for your project. Below the manifest line are links to the package documentation and GitHub, as shown in Figure 4-2.

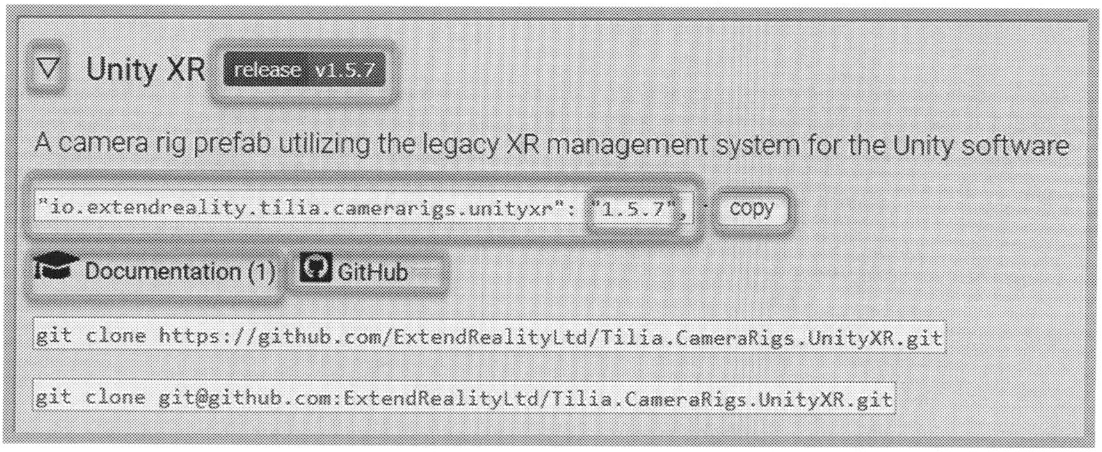

▽ **Unity XR** `release  v1.5.7`

A camera rig prefab utilizing the legacy XR management system for the Unity software

`"io.extendreality.tilia.camerarigs.unityxr": "1.5.7",`   copy

🎓 Documentation (1)   💠 GitHub

`git clone https://github.com/ExtendRealityLtd/Tilia.CameraRigs.UnityXR.git`

`git clone git@github.com:ExtendRealityLtd/Tilia.CameraRigs.UnityXR.git`

***Figure 4-2.*** *Tilia package manifest line*

To bring Tilia packages into your project, you need to modify your projects manifest. json file, which is available within your project's "Packages" folder, so that it contains all the manifest lines of the VRTK Tilia packages you need for your project.

As part of this book, you've been provided with a modified manifest.json file to download, which will overwrite the manifest.json file that currently exists. Note that you cannot access the manifest.json file directly from the Unity editor; you need to get it using Windows file explorer.

This modified manifest.json file contains all the manifest lines from the Tilia page located at www.vrtk.io/tilia.html, as required for this book's projects.

Start by downloading the modified version of the manifest.json file to an easily accessible location on your PC. With Unity open, and its Demo scene showing, select the Project tab and then the "Packages" folder. Once you've done that, right-click the folder on the shortcut menu that shows up, and then select Show in Explorer, as shown in Figure 4-3.

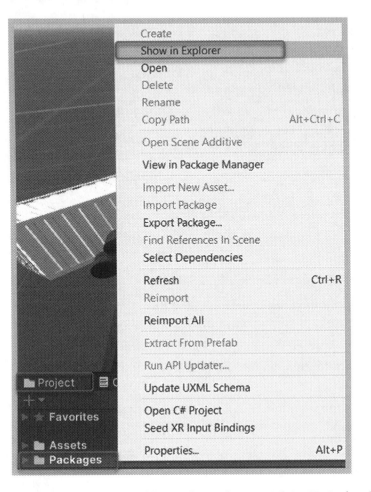

***Figure 4-3.*** *Opening the Windows file explorer from within Unity's editor*

Doing this will open Windows file explorer externally for you, with the "Packages" folder selected. Now, shut down Unity, ensuring that you have quit the Unity application entirely and only have the Windows file explorer open, with the "Packages" folder highlighted. Then, double-click the "Packages" folder to open it, and you should see the manifest.json file that you need to download to replace the old manifest.json file. In the "Packages" folder, select the existing manifest.json file and delete it. Now copy the modified manifest.json file you downloaded as part of this book and paste it into the "Packages" folder.

Next, open the manifest.json file using a text editor such as Notepad. Scroll through this file, and you'll notice that several of the manifest lines in Tilia packages that you need are included. Note the entries for the scopedRegistries and dependencies.

For any Tilia package you'd like to include in your project, you must copy its manifest line from the Tilia page and paste it somewhere within the dependencies section. Ensure that you don't duplicate manifest lines in your manifest.json file. A screenshot of the modified manifest.json file is shown in Figure 4-4. Each manifest line shows the version number of its specific Tilia package toward the end of the line. As updates are made to the various Tilia packages, you can update to the latest version using Unity's Package Manager, as discussed later in this chapter.

***Figure 4-4.*** *Contents of the manifest.json file*

Finally, close the manifest.json file. Now, using the Unity hub, launch your VR_ Playground project. The Unity Package Manager will immediately begin resolving and importing the various Tilia packages listed within your manifest.json file.

Before Unity's editor loads, you may be prompted with a warning message, as displayed in Figure 4-5, which says that native platform back ends for the new input system haven't been enabled in player settings and asks whether you'd like to enable them. This new input system is not relevant to VR development using VRTK 4. The VRTK provides you with a plethora of prefabs for obtaining input from various VR controllers, and you need to click No to proceed.

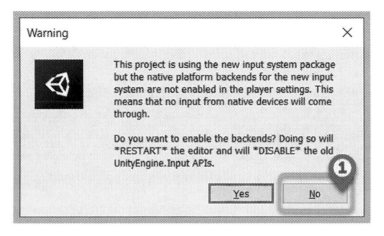

***Figure 4-5.*** *Warning message asking whether you want to enable back ends for the new input system, for which you should click No*

---

**Note**    The warning message shown in Figure 4-5 will pop up each time you launch Unity. Make sure you always click No, as the new input system is not relevant to VR development using version 4 of the VRTK.

---

Unity will now continue the importing process, which may take a while. Once it's complete, you may get a message requesting that you upgrade spatializer plug-ins. Click to upgrade. You will then be asked to restart Unity. Click to restart. You will be immediately prompted with another dialog box stating that a new scoped registry is now available within Unity's Package Manager and telling you that VRTK's Tilia packages are now a part of Unity's Package Manager. You can close this dialog box now. Unity will now restart, and you will see the warning message shown in Figure 4-5. Click No.

Once Unity's editor launches, you'll notice that another dialog box has popped up, which is the Manage Unity Input Manager Axis Definitions dialog. This box states that Tilia would like to add its own input axis definitions to Unity's Input Manager. All you need to do is click the Add Input Definitions button at the bottom of the dialog to add twenty Tilia input axis definitions to Unity's Input Manager. Also, within the project settings dialog that is open in Unity's editor, note that a `scopedRegistries npmjs` has been added, which has two scopes within it, as shown in the manifest.json file in Figure 4-4. Now close this project settings dialog.

Next, select the console tab and note that the three runtime errors you got in the last chapter have disappeared, as version 4 of the VRTK has been imported into your project. Clear the console of any warning message that may have shown up.

Congratulations! you have now successfully set up VRTK 4 within your project.

You now need to verify that the twenty Tilia input axis definitions have been added to Unity's Input Manager. To do so, select Edit ➤ Project Settings on the main menu, and from within the pane on the left, select the item Input Manager . From the pane on the right, expand the Axes section and scroll down to the bottom, where you will see that the twenty Tilia input axis definitions have been added. Finally, close the project settings dialog.

# Unity's Package Manager and VRTK 4 Tilia Packages

The advantage of having VRTK 4 Tilia packages as part of the Package Manager is that now, at any time, you can open the Package Manager and select any Tilia package. You can then check if any new update is available for a specific package and update the package by simply clicking the Update button. Let's see how this can be achieved.

On the main menu, select Window ➤ Package Manager and allow it to load. From the Packages drop-down within the Package Manager dialog box, select the In Project item. All the packages available in your current project will be listed, showing you all the Tilia packages that were imported. Select any Tilia package from the left pane that has an arrow next to its version number, which indicates that a newer version of this Tilia package is available. The pane on the right lists the date that the package was published and gives a brief description of the package. If the package has an update, you will note an Update to x.x.x version button at the bottom of the right pane. Click this button to update to the newer version of the selected package. Once the package has been updated, its item on the left will reflect the latest version number with a checkmark displayed beside it. Figure 4-6 shows the Package Manager with the Tilia packages that were added to it. Finally, close the Package Manager dialog box.

***Figure 4-6.*** *Package Manager with the imported Tilia packages listed*

# Exploring the "Packages" Folder

Let's now proceed to look at the "Packages" folder available in the Project tab. To do so, select the Project tab and expand the "Packages" folder within it. Scroll down about halfway, and you will notice all the Tilia packages listed. Select and expand any Tilia package from within the left pane of your project tab. You will notice that every package comprises the same folder structure, as shown in Figure 4-7. Now, expand the "Runtime" folder and select the "Prefabs" folder, your primary area of focus within all Tilia packages. You will see that the right pane contains prefabs of interest, enabling you to create the awesome VR mechanics in later chapters of this book.

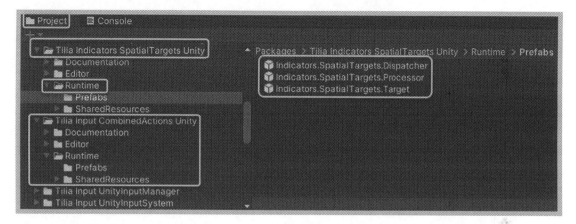

***Figure 4-7.*** *Tilia Package prefabs are located in the "Packages" folder of the Project tab*

# Summary

In this chapter, we imported version 4 of the VRTK Tilia packages into our project. We looked at the various Tilia packages that are available for VR development. We used the provided manifest.json file to import several Tilia packages into our project. We then saw how these Tilia packages are reflected within Unity's Package Manager and how to update them. Lastly, we explored the "Packages" folder, noting how the Tilia packages have been structured, and looked at its "Prefabs" folder that contains prefabs that provide you with the awesome VR mechanics you seek.

# CHAPTER 5

# Setting Up VRTK's Camera Rigs

You might have noticed that the demo scene provided has no camera in it. In this chapter, we will begin setting up our VRTK Camera Rig with several camera prefabs. We will first set up a Unity XR Camera Rig, which can be thought of as a universal camera that will work with HTC Vive and Oculus headsets. Next, we will implement the Oculus Camera Rig, which explicitly uses the Oculus Integration SDK you downloaded. This Oculus Camera Rig will work exclusively with the Oculus headset. We will then put in place a specialized Spatial Simulator rig, which VRTK provides to enable you to run your VR projects within Unity's editor. Next, we will set up the Tracked Alias prefab, which can represent any XR hardware. All of this is made available via Tilia packages within the "Packages" folder. Finally, we will go on to test your VR scene using the Spatial Simulator as well as your VR headset.

## Setting Up Individual Camera Rigs

Let's first set up the individual Camera Rigs within the Demo scene. We'll begin by creating a new empty game object at the root of your Demo scene. Name this game object "[VRTK_SETUP]" and reset its transform. Then, add another empty game object as this object's child. Name this child game object "[VRTK_CAMERA_RIGS_SETUP]." All the Camera Rig prefabs you add to your Demo scene will reside as children within this child game object.

Change the Transform Position values for this [VRTK_CAMERA_RIGS_SETUP] game object to: $X$ = -12.75; $Y$ = 0; and $Z$ = -6. Then, change the Transform Rotation values for this game object to: $X$ = 0; $Y$ = 0; and $Z$ = 0.

These values will ensure that you are facing forward within your VR world.

© Christopher Coutinho 2022
C. Coutinho, *Unity® Virtual Reality Development with VRTK4*, https://doi.org/10.1007/978-1-4842-7933-5_5

# Setting Up the Unity XR Camera Rig

With your [VRTK_CAMERA_RIGS_SETUP] game object selected in the hierarchy, navigate to the Project tab and expand the "Packages" folder. Then, navigate to the "Tilia Camera Rigs, Unity XR" package folder and expand it until you reach its "Prefabs" folder. In the right pane, you will see the Camera Rigs, Unity XR prefab. Drag and drop this prefab onto the [VRTK_CAMERA_RIGS_SETUP] game object in the hierarchy, making it a child, as shown in Figure 5-1. Your Demo scene now finally has its first camera in it.

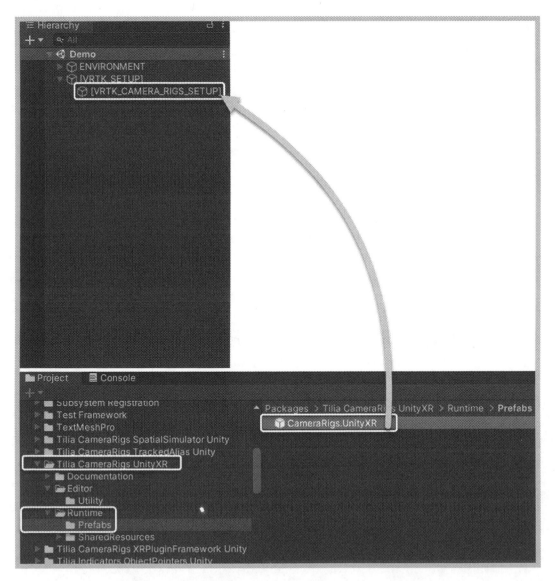

***Figure 5-1.*** *Setting up Camera Rigs in Unity XR*

# Setting Up the Oculus Camera Rig

With your [VRTK_CAMERA_RIGS_SETUP] game object selected in the hierarchy, navigate to the Project tab and expand the "Packages" folder. Then, navigate to the "Tilia SDK, Oculus Integration, Unity" package folder and expand it until you reach its prefabs folder. In the right pane, you'll notice the Camera Rigs, Oculus Integration prefab. Drag and drop this prefab onto the [VRTK_CAMERA_RIGS_SETUP] game object selected in the hierarchy, making it a child, as shown in Figure 5-2. To accommodate this Camera Rig, Oculus Integration prefab, we downloaded version 29 of the Oculus Integration SDK from the Unity asset store.

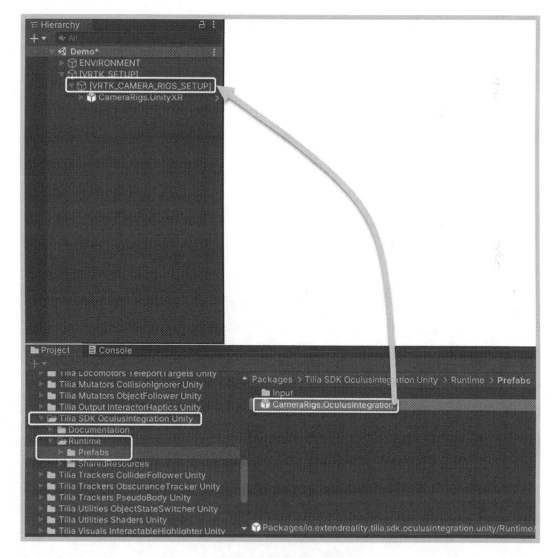

***Figure 5-2.*** *Setting up Camera Rigs Oculus integration*

# Setting Up the Spatial Simulator

The Spatial Simulator allows you to run your VR project within Unity's editor itself without the need to mount your headset each time you want to perform a test run. It uses the standard keyboard and mouse input to function. An exciting aspect of the Spatial Simulator is that it even works with an Xbox controller. By connecting an Xbox controller to your computer, you can have all the basic VR controller functionality available to you for testing within Unity's editor. This makes debugging your VR project a whole lot easier.

With your [VRTK_CAMERA_RIGS_SETUP] game object still selected in the hierarchy and with the "Packages" folder expanded, navigate to the "Tilia Camera Rigs, Spatial Simulator, Unity" package folder and expand it until you reach its "Prefabs" folder. In the right pane, you'll notice the Camera Rigs, Spatial Simulator prefab. Drag and drop this prefab onto the [VRTK_CAMERA_RIGS_SETUP] game object in the hierarchy, making it a child, as shown in Figure 5-3.

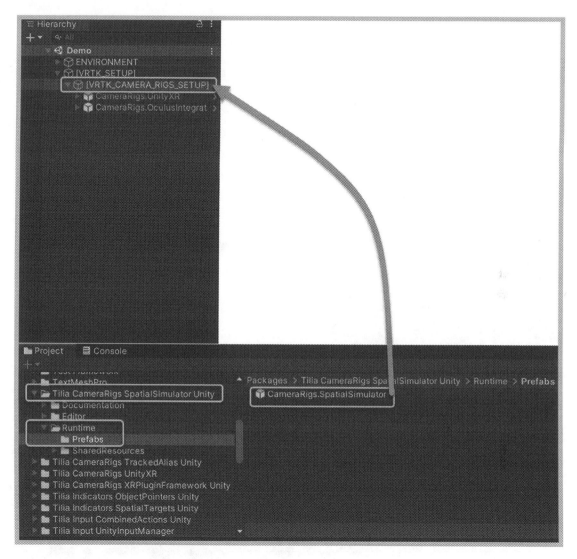

***Figure 5-3.*** *Setting up Camera Rigs Spatial Simulator*

# Setting Up the Tracked Alias

As discussed later in this chapter, the Tracked Alias is a generic Camera Rig representing XR hardware. It is also the last Camera Rig prefab you need to attach to your [VRTK_CAMERA_RIGS_SETUP] game object as its child. With this game object still selected in the hierarchy and the "Packages" folder expanded, locate the "Tilia Camera Rigs, Tracked Alias, Unity" package folder and expand it until you reach its "Prefabs" folder. In the right pane, you'll notice the Camera Rigs, Tracked Alias prefab.

Drag and drop this prefab onto the [VRTK_CAMERA_RIGS_SETUP] game object in the hierarchy, making it a child, as shown in Figure 5-4.

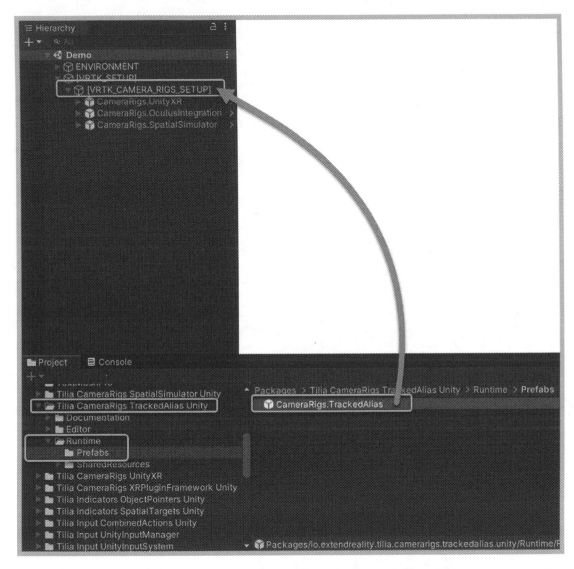

***Figure 5-4.*** *Setting up the Camera Rigs, Tracked Alias prefab*

The Camera Rigs prefabs previously discussed can also be accessed via Unity's main menu by going to Game Object ➤ Tilia ➤ Prefabs ➤ Camera Rigs. There, you'll find all the prefabs that you just set up, and you could have set them up using this menu option, too.

> **Note**    For the Camera Rigs, in the Tracked Alias Facade component of the Tracked Alias game object in the hierarchy, you may find that the Tracked Alias Settings, Elements property isn't visible in the Inspector. If this is the case, you need to shut down Unity entirely and restart it, and this property will then become visible. This uncanny behavior doesn't happen when using version 2019.4.x of Unity LTS. It seems to only be an oddity with version 2020.3. x of Unity LTS. Any time you find VRTK component properties missing, you'll need to restart Unity.

# Configuring the VRTK's Tracked Alias

The Tracked Alias is a sort of generic Camera Rig that can represent any type of hardware. An Oculus Camera Rig, Steam VR Camera Rig, Unity XR Camera Rig, or a Spatial Simulator Camera Rig can all be hooked up to a Tracked Alias. If you activate the Camera Rig you want to use, you can leave the rest to the Tracked Alias. From then on, whatever you need to do, you can do it against this Tracked Alias. This way, you don't need to worry about the different Camera Rigs you have in your scene and how you should handle them. The Tracked Alias allows you to track any active valid SDK Camera Rig that has been included within the Elements list of the Tracked Alias settings, which is essentially a list of Camera Rigs within your scene. Thus, you can track any active Camera Rig in your scene that has been hooked up to the Tracked Alias without being explicitly tied to it.

# Hooking Camera Rigs to the Tracked Alias

In the [VRTK_CAMERA_RIGS_SETUP] game object in the hierarchy, select its child game object, Camera Rigs, Tracked Alias. Within the Inspector, ensure that its Tracked Alias Facade component has been expanded. Locate the Tracked Alias, Elements, Size property (zero by default) within this component. This property is shown in Figure 5-5. Note that this is the property I was referring to in the Note as potentially not being visible, explaining that if you restart Unity, it will resurface.

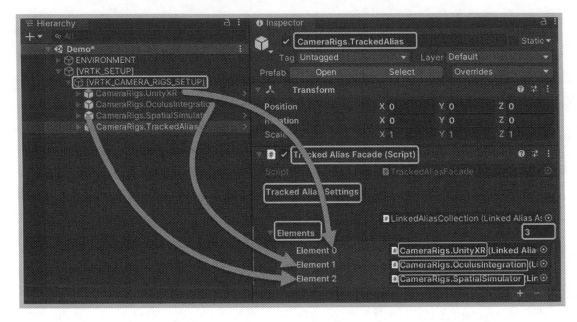

*Figure 5-5.* *Camera Rigs hooked up to the Tracked Alias*

Change the value of this Size property to 3, as you have three Camera Rigs available for your use in the form of element slots. Drag and drop the Camera Rigs, Unity XR game object from the hierarchy into the newly created Element 0 slot of the Tracked Alias Settings property. Next, drag and drop the Camera Rigs, Oculus Integration game object into the Element 2 slot of the Tracked Alias Settings property. Then, drag and drop the Camera Rigs, Spatial Simulator game object into the Element 3 slot of the Tracked Alias Settings property. Now your Tracked Alias Settings will have three cameras listed, any of which your Tracked Alias can now utilize. However, you need to ensure that you keep just one Camera Rig active from within the [VRTK_CAMERA_RIGS_SETUP] game object in the hierarchy. The active Camera Rig is the one that the Tracked Alias will use. Figure 5-5 shows the Tracked Alias Facade component, with its Tracked Alias Settings property values.

# Test using the Spatial Simulator

Now that your Tracked Alias has been set up, it's time for you to test your scene within Unity's editor using the Camera Rigs, Spatial Simulator. As mentioned earlier, you first need to ensure that you have just one Camera Rig active in the hierarchy. The Camera Rigs, Spatial Simulator should be the active Camera Rig, as you'll be testing using Unity's editor.

From within the [VRTK_CAMERA_RIGS_SETUP] game object in the hierarchy, select the Camera Rigs located above the Spatial Simulator, Camera Rigs, Unity XR, and Camera Rigs, Oculus Integration. Within the Inspector, uncheck the box to deactivate both of these Camera Rigs. Ensure that the only active Camera Rigs are the CameraRigs. SpatialSimulator and the Camera Rigs.Tracked Alias, as shown in Figure 5-6.

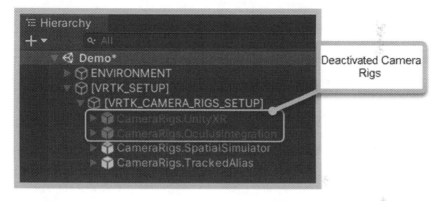

*Figure 5-6.* *Camera Rigs deactivated in the hierarchy to playtest scene in Unity's editor*

Now hit the Play button within Unity's editor toolbar and wait a couple of seconds for your playable scene to load within Unity's editor. Once your playable scene is up and running, you can use your mouse to rotate yourself about as well as look up and down. The yellow and red pins represent your simulated left and right controllers. Pressing number two on the keyboard will activate the movement and rotation of your left controller pin. Pressing number three will activate the movement and rotation of your right controller pin. Pressing number one will deactivate the movement and rotation of both the simulated left and right controllers. It will instead activate the movement and rotation of the simulated play area. To enable yourself to move within your VR world, you need to ensure that you have first exited the left or right controller movement and rotation mode by pressing number one on the keyboard. Now you can use the *W, A, S,* and *D* keys on your keyboard to move about within your VR world.

# Universal Camera Rig

You can think of the Unity XR Camera Rig as a universal Camera Rig that you can use with your HTC Vive and Oculus headsets. If you're developing for Steam VR devices, such as the HTC Vive, you can only use the Camera Rigs, Unity XR setup. On the other hand, if you're developing solely for Oculus devices, such as the Oculus Rift or the Oculus Quest, you would be better off using the Camera Rigs, Oculus Integration setup. Note that you can use your Oculus headset with the Camera Rigs, Unity XR setup, too. However, you can't use your HTC Vive headset with the Camera Rigs, Oculus Integration setup.

# Configuring the Oculus OVR Camera Rig

The child game object, OVR Camera Rig, within the Camera Rigs, Oculus Integration game object, requires one of its property values to be changed. To do so, select and expand the Camera Rigs, Oculus Integration game object in the hierarchy from within the [VRTK_CAMERA_RIGS_SETUP] game object. Now select its OVR Camera Rig child object, and in the Inspector, ensure that its OVR Manager component is expanded. Locate the Tracking Section, within which you'll find the property Tracking Origin Type. By default, this property has been set to Eye Level. Change the property to Floor Level using the drop-down beside the property.

# Testing Spatial Movement Using a VR Headset

Now it's time to test out spatial movement within your VR world using your VR headset. If you're using an Oculus headset, you can deactivate Camera Rigs, Unity XR in the hierarchy and instead activate Camera Rigs, Oculus Integration. On the other hand, if you're using an HTC Vive headset, you need to ensure that Camera Rigs, Oculus Integration has been deactivated and Camera Rigs, Unity XR has been activated. Always ensure that only one Camera Rig is active in the hierarchy. As you'll be testing with your VR headset, only one Camera Rig can be active in the hierarchy, so you'll need to deactivate the Camera Rigs, Spatial Simulator. As discussed earlier, this simulator is only used when you want to playtest within Unity's editor.

Hit the Play button and mount your VR headset. You'll now be able to look around your VR world and you'll also be able to physically move within it, constrained to the limits of your Chaperone or Guardian boundary setup. You don't have your controllers set up yet, so there isn't much to do other than walk around.

# Summary

In this chapter, we went over how to set up the VRTK's Camera Rigs. We looked at about the different types of Camera Rigs that the VRTK provides you with that are accessible via its Tilia packages. We then went about setting up each of these individual Camera Rigs. You learned about the Tracked Alias into which all your Camera Rigs are hooked up. You also learned about the Spatial Simulator and how it can be used for playtesting within Unity's editor. We went on to playtest the VR scene within Unity's editor using the Spatial Simulator. You learned about the universal Camera Rig that the VRTK has made available to you. We then configured the Oculus OVR Camera Rig, and finally tested spatial movement within our VR world using the VR headset.

# CHAPTER 6

# Setting Up Interactors and Virtual Hands

With your Camera Rig setup complete, you now need to set up your Left and Right controller game objects, which will mimic your real-life hand movements and map to the transform of your VR controllers. In this chapter, we will first go over what an Interactor and an Interactable are. We will then set up the default controller models provided by the VRTK, which are two cuboid objects representing your hands. However, to increase immersion in Virtual Reality, we will replace these cuboid hands with virtual animated hands. After reviewing how to set up the Oculus-provided hands, you'll go on to set up your very own custom hands that can be used with the Spatial Simulator and the Camera Rigs, Unity XR setup.

## Interactors versus Interactables

To get the hands working in VR, you need to understand the concept of an Interactor and an Interactable. An Interactor is something that knows when it is touching another object with which it can interact. If you close your eyes and grab onto a small exercise ball with your hand, your hand will immediately know it has grabbed onto something. In the program, your hand is referred to as an Interactor, and the exercise ball you grab is the Interactable.

Interactors allow users to interact with the virtual world, offering them a way to select and grab objects. On the other hand, an Interactable is a game object within the virtual world with which the user can interact. In the previous example, the Interactable is the exercise ball. The VRTK provides you with two standard ways to interact with an Interactable. Direct Interaction allows the user to directly interact with objects in the VR world, such as by virtually grabbing a cup with your hand. Other examples of Direct Interaction would be flipping a switch and pressing a button.

49

The VRTK also provides another form of Interaction in the form of a distance grabber. The distance grabber gives you an invisible beam with a visible reticle to identify Interactable objects in your VR world. It allows such Interactable objects to be grabbed from a distance by simply pressing the Grab button set up on the Interactor. In the previous example, the cup could also be grabbed via a distance grab. However, you wouldn't want to distance grab a switch or a button. We will look at Interactable objects and how to go about grabbing them in a later chapter.

# Setting up Interactors on Controllers

Let's begin by having your VR controllers work as Interactors, using cuboid avatars to represent your controllers, which are your virtual hands. With your Demo scene loaded, navigate to its Project tab and expand the "Packages" folder. Locate the Tilia Interactions, Interactables Unity package and expand it until you reach its runtime folder. Then, expand its "Interactors" folder and select its "Prefabs" folder.

In the right pane, you'll notice the Interactions Interactor prefab. This prefab needs to be added as a child to both the Left and Right controller aliases within the Camera Rigs, Tracked Alias game object in the hierarchy.

From within the [VRTK_CAMERA_RIGS_SETUP] game object in the hierarchy, expand its Camera Rigs, Tracked Alias child game object. Then, expand its Aliases game object until you see its Left and Right Controller Alias game objects and expand both of them.

From within the right pane of your Project tab, drag and drop the Interactions Interactor prefab onto the Left Controller Alias game object in the hierarchy, making a child of it. Select this Interactions Interactor game object in the hierarchy and rename it "Interactions Interactor Left" to represent your left hand (controller).

Next, from within the right pane of your Project tab, drag and drop the Interactions Interactor prefab onto the Right Controller Alias game object in the hierarchy, making it a child. Select this Interactions Interactor game object in the hierarchy and rename it "Interactions Interactor Right" to represent your Right Hand (controller). Figure 6-1 shows these Interactors after they have been set up.

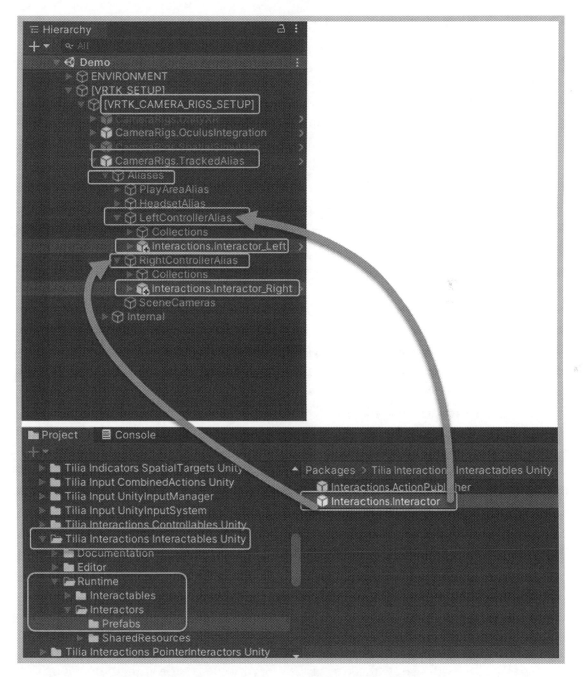

***Figure 6-1.*** *Interactors set up on the Left and Right controllers*

## Testing Out Your New Cuboid Avatar Interactors

You can now test your scene within Unity's editor using the Spatial Simulator to see what your new virtual hands look like. But before playing your scene, ensure that within the [VRTK_CAMERA_RIGS_SETUP] game object in the hierarchy, the Camera Rigs, Spatial Simulator has been activated and the Camera Rigs, Unity XR and Camera Rigs, Oculus Integration have both been deactivated.

With your scene now playing within Unity's editor, note how your hands look. You'll see that there are two cubes, yellow and red pins, stuck within your controller. These are your new cuboid virtual hands. You can move them about by moving your mouse around. You can also use the number keys two and three to use either your left or right hand only, as discussed in the last chapter. Now your new cuboid virtual hands have been fitted with the VRTK's Interactors, which means that they are now set up to enable you to grab any Interactable object.

## Setting Up Realistic Animated Virtual Hands

In this section, you'll learn how to set up realistic animated virtual hands to replace your cuboid hands. The VRTK doesn't provide you with any animated hands; however, the Oculus Integration SDK does provide you with its version of animated virtual hands, which you will set up for your Camera Rigs, Oculus Integration. Camera Rigs, Unity XR and Camera Rigs, Spatial Simulator don't provide animated virtual hands. The animated virtual hands provided by Oculus will only work with the Camera Rigs, Oculus Integration setup; they won't work with either your Camera Rigs, Unity XR or your Camera Rigs, Spatial Simulator setup. You could get the Oculus-provided hands to work with your Camera Rigs, Unity XR or Camera Rigs, Spatial Simulator setup. Still, it would involve writing some code, wherein you would need a script that maps button states to different hand animations to get this working. As this book is all about using a no-coding approach, we'll take a different route here, for which I've provided you a Unity package—namely, Unity VR Hands—that you need to download and import into your project. This Unity package provides you with a Custom Hand, with some basic animations set up that you'll use with your Camera Rigs, Unity XR and Camera Rigs, Spatial Simulator setups.

# Animated Hands for Camera Rigs Oculus Integration

This section will teach you how to enable the hands provided by Oculus to work with the Camera Rigs, Oculus Integration setup. If you're building for the HTC Vive exclusively, you can skip this part.

From within the Unity editor, select the Project tab, expand the "Assets" folder and select the "Oculus" folder. In the search box in the right pane of the Project tab, type in "Custom Hand." You'll notice that the prefabs, Custom Hand Left, and Custom Hand Right show up. These prefabs are located in the Assets ➤ Oculus ➤ Sample Framework ➤ Core ➤ Custom Hands folder. Ensure that you use them only to set up your Oculus hands, not any other Oculus hand prefab.

Now, select the Custom Hand Left prefab within the Project tab. In the Unity hierarchy, expand the Camera Rigs, Tracked Alias game object, and further expand its Aliases game object. Then, expand its Left Controller Alias game object, expand the Interactions Interactor Left game object, and select and expand the Avatar Container game object. Next, drag and drop the Custom Hand Left prefab from the Project pane onto the Avatar Container game object, making it a child. Figure 6-2 shows the Custom Hand Left prefab nested as a child of your Left Controller Alias's Avatar Container game object.

Within Unity's hierarchy, expand the Camera Rigs, Tracked Alias, and Aliases game objects. Then, expand the Right Controller Alias game object, expand its Interactions Interactor Right game object, and, finally, select and expand its Avatar Container game object. Now, drag and drop the Custom Hand Right prefab from the Project pane onto the Avatar Container game object. Figure 6-2 shows the Custom Hand Right prefab nested as a child of your Right Controller Alias's Avatar Container game object. Take a minute to ensure that you have dropped the correct prefabs into the proper locations within the hierarchy.

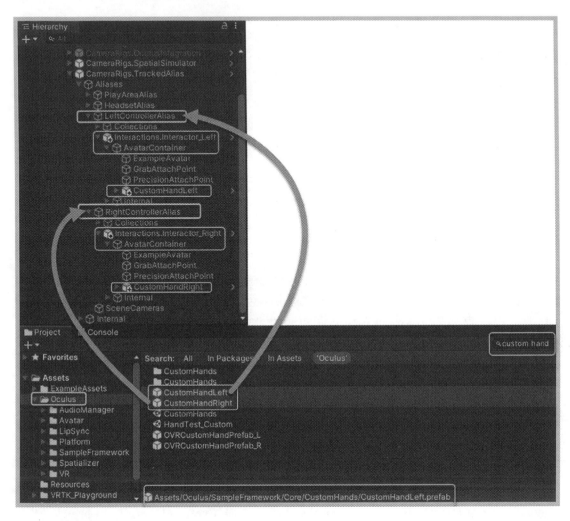

***Figure 6-2.*** *Oculus custom hands set up on the Left and Right controllers*

Select both Custom Hand Left and Custom Hand Right game objects within the hierarchy, and look at the Inspector. You will see that it contains an OVR Grabber component for both hands. Disable this component for both by unchecking its checkbox within the Inspector. You'll be using VRTKs grab interaction system instead. All you need from the Oculus Hands are its models and animations.

# Playtesting Your Scene Using Your Oculus Headset

From within the [VRTK_CAMERA_RIGS_SETUP] game object in the hierarchy, you activate Camera Rigs, Oculus Integration and deactivate both Camera Rigs Unity XR and Camera Rigs, Spatial Simulator. Your Camera Rigs, Tracked Alias must always be active.

Now you are all set to test your new Oculus-provided hands with your Oculus headset. To do so, hit the Play button within Unity's editor and mount your Oculus headset. Press your Grab or Trigger button on your Oculus controller to activate your hands within the scene. Now, press the Grab button on your Oculus controller, and you should see your middle, ring, and pinky fingers animate. Then, press the Trigger buttons on your Oculus controller, and you should see your index finger animate. Last, press down on your Thumbstick with your thumb to see your thumbs animate. Notice that your cuboid hands are part of your Oculus hands. You'll learn how to turn off these cuboid hands in a later section of this chapter.

Now it's time to test out your Oculus Hands using the Camera Rig, Unity XR setup. Do this by hitting the Play button again in Unity's editor to stop your scene from playing. From within the [VRTK_CAMERA_RIGS_SETUP] game object in the hierarchy, deactivate Camera Rigs, Oculus Integration and activate Camera Rigs, Unity XR instead. Tap the Play button within Unity's editor and mount your Oculus headset. Try pressing the various buttons on your Oculus controller. You'll notice that your Oculus hands will no longer animate if the Camera Rigs, Unity XR or Camera Rigs, Spatial Simulator setup are enabled. Your Oculus-provided hands will work exclusively with the Camera Rigs, Oculus Integration setup.

# Animated Hands for Unity XR and Spatial Simulator Camera Rigs

As we saw in the previous section, your Oculus hand and finger animations won't work with the Camera Rigs, Unity XR or the Camera Rigs, Spatial Simulator setups. This doesn't mean that they won't ever work with these setups. Some code would be required to get them working, wherein you would need a script that maps button states to different hand animations. However, as this is a no-coding course, we will take a different approach here, for which I have provided you a Unity package—namely, Unity

VR Hands—that you'll need to download and import into your project. This Unity package provides you with a Hand Proto custom hand prefab with some basic animation setup, which you'll use with your Camera Rigs, Unity XR and Camera Rigs, Spatial Simulator setups.

First, download the Unity VR Hands unity package, provided as part of this book's downloads, onto your desktop or any other easily accessible folder. Drag and drop this "Unity VR Hands" unity package file into your open projects "Assets" folder. An import Unity package dialog box will pop up. Import the entire package by clicking the Import button. This may take a few seconds. Within your Assets folder, you'll notice that a new "VR Hands" folder has been created. Your Hand Proto custom hand prefab is now available within the "Prefabs/Tutorial" folder.

Let's begin by setting up this Hand prototype. Navigate to the Assets ➤ VR Hands ➤ Prefabs ➤ Tutorial folder, which you'll notice contains your Hand Proto prefab. You'll use this prefab to create both Left and Right custom hands for use with the Camera Rigs, Unity XR and Camera Rigs, Spatial Simulator setups.

Select the Hand Proto prefab available in the right pane of your Project tab, and look at the Inspector. It contains an Animator component, whose Controller property has been set to Hand Controller. Examine the Hand Controller by double-clicking the Controller property value in the Inspector, which will thereby launch the Animator window. You'll see that the window comprises four animations: Open, Grab, Release, and Teleporting. These are the basic animations made available to you. You can always create additional animations for each finger if you want to.

Now navigate back to the "Assets ➤ VR Hands ➤ Prefabs ➤ Tutorial" folder. Your Hand proto prefab will be available in the right pane of your Project tab. Within the hierarchy, ensure that both the Left and Right Controller Alias game objects are expanded to the point where you can see their Avatar Container game object. They should already be expanded for you, as shown in Figure 6-2.

Now drag and drop the Hand Proto prefab, available within the right pane of your Project tab, onto the Avatar Container game object of the Left Controller Alias. Select this Hand Proto game object in the hierarchy and rename it "Hand Proto Left" to represent your left hand. Adjust the Inspector's Transform, Position values so that they appear as follows: $X = 0.003$; $Y = -0.005$; and $Z = 0$. Then adjust the Inspector's Transform, Scale values so that they are as follows: $X = -0.85$; $Y = 0.85$; and $Z = 0.85$. You may want to tweak these values further so that your left hand is positioned and scaled well for you.

By default, the provided Hand Proto prefab represents a right hand, but you haven't been provided with a separate Left-Hand prefab. A common trick used is to mirror the right hand to look like a left hand. To enable this mirroring, you need to set the $X$ scale value of your Hand Proto prefab to a negative value. You'll notice that for the Hand Proto prefab that you previously set up against your Left controller Alias, you explicitly set its Transform X Scale value to -0.85, which essentially mirrored the Right-Hand Proto prefab to look and function like a left hand.

Now let's begin setting up your Right Hand. Drag and drop the Hand Proto prefab, available within the right pane of your Project tab, onto the Avatar Container game object of the Right Controller Alias. Select this Hand Proto game object in the hierarchy and reassign the Inspector's Transform, Position values as follows: $X = -0.003$; $Y = -0.005$; and $Z = 0$. Then adjust its Transform, Scale values as follows: $X = 0.85$; $Y = 0.85$; and $Z = 0.85$. You may want to tweak these values further so that your right hand is positioned and scaled well for you. Note that the X Scale value for your Right Hand is positive and does not need to be mirrored.

## Playtesting the Scene Using Your VR Headset

From within the [VRTK_CAMERA_RIGS_SETUP] game object in the hierarchy, deactivate Camera Rigs, Oculus Integration and Camera Rigs, Spatial Simulator and activate Camera Rigs, Unity XR. Your Camera Rigs, Tracked Alias must always be active. As mentioned earlier, you can even use your Oculus headset with the Camera Rigs, Unity XR setup.

In the hierarchy within each of the Avatar Container game objects, deactivate the provided Oculus hands; namely, Custom Hand Left and Custom Hand Right. Ensure that your Hand Proto Left and Hand Proto Right are both active.

Now you are all set to test your custom hand prototypes with your VR headset. To do so, hit the Play button in Unity's editor and mount your VR headset. Try pressing the various buttons on your VR controller, and you'll notice that your VR custom hand prototypes do not animate. This is because you still need to capture your controller's input, based on which you can decide which animation you want to be played. You didn't face this problem with the provided Oculus hands because capturing controller input using these hands was taken care of by the Oculus components that accompany the Oculus hand prefabs.

You're provided four animations for your custom hand prototype, Open, Grab, Release, and Teleporting. You'll capture controller input to function as follows:

- When you press the Grip button on any of your controllers, the Grab animation will play.

- When you press the Thumbstick (Trackpad) on any of your controllers, the Teleporting animation will play.

- When you release the Thumbstick (Trackpad) or Grab button, the Release animation will play.

# Animating Custom Prototype Hands

To animate your custom prototype hands so that they can be used with the Camera Rigs, Unity XR and Camera Rigs, Spatial Simulator setups, you first need to find a way to capture input from your controllers. You may capture input from your VR controllers and other devices such as an Xbox controller, keyboard, and mouse. The Xbox controller, keyboard, and mouse would ideally be used when playtesting your scene using the Spatial Simulator. As input can come from different input devices, you need to consolidate such varied input into a single object, which other objects can later poll.

## Capturing the Grip, Mouse, or Bumper Button Input

Now, let's look at an example of a Grab action that can be initiated via either VR controllers Grip buttons or an Xbox controllers Left or Right, Bumper buttons. Also, using the mouse, a Grab action may be initiated against the Left Hand by pressing the left mouse button and against the Right Hand by pressing the Right mouse button. For your Demo scene, you'll be capturing Grab input using the mouse, Oculus controllers, HTC Vive controllers, and Xbox controllers that are input from four separate devices for each hand. Whenever you decide to introduce a new device, you need to wire its Grab signal to every object in your game that wants to listen for a Grab action, which could get messy.

The solution is to wire the Grab signals from all devices into an intermediary object and then have other objects poll this intermediary object. To achieve this level of indirection, the VRTK provides you with two fundamental simplistic action components—namely, the Boolean action and the Float action—that you will utilize to capture controller device input.

In the example previously cited, you want to know if your VR controller's Grip button was pressed, initiating a Grab action. The Grip button on your VR controller emits a Boolean value of either True or False. When the Grip button is pressed, the value True is emitted, and when the Grip button is released, the value False is emitted.

Likewise, if the left or right mouse button is pressed, initiating a Grab action, the True value is emitted and when the button is released, the value False is emitted. If either of the Bumper buttons on the Xbox controller were pressed, initiating a Grab action, the value True would be emitted and when the buttons are released, the value False would be emitted. You need to listen only for Boolean values for when a Grab action occurs via a Grip, Mouse, or Bumper button is pressed, and you will utilize the Boolean action component to capture such input.

The VRTK provides you with its Tilia Input, Unity Input Manager package, which contains controller mappings for buttons across several devices. These mappings allow you to listen for input from any button associated with its supported controller devices. The VRTK provides controller mappings for Oculus, Open VR, Xbox, and Windows Mixed Reality devices.

Let's set this up by listening for a Grab action from the Oculus, HTC Vive, and Xbox controllers, as well as the mouse. You'll recollect that a Grab action occurs when your VR Controllers Grip button is pressed, your Xbox controllers' Bumper buttons are pressed, or either your left or right mouse buttons are pressed.

Start by selecting the [VRTK_SETUP] game object in the hierarchy, right-click it, and then select Create Empty from the context menu that pops up to create a new empty game object. Rename this new game object "[VRTK_Input_Controllers]." You need to capture input from four devices: the Oculus, the HTC Vive, the Xbox, and the Mouse.

Then, select the Project tab and expand its "Packages" folder. Locate its Tilia Input, Unity Input Manager package. Expand its "Runtime and Prefabs" folder, and select its "Controller Mappings" folder. Within the right pane, you'll notice many device names for which controller mappings are available; namely, the Oculus, Open VR, Windows Mixed Reality, and Xbox controller. The controller mappings you're interested in are the Xbox controller, the Oculus Touch Left and Right controllers, and the Open VR Left and Right controllers. Your HTC Vive will use the Open VR Left and Right controller mappings. Note that nothing has been provided explicitly for mapping the Mouse or Keyboard buttons.

From within the right pane of the Project tab, select the prefabs, Xbox Controller, Oculus Touch Left Controller, Oculus Touch Right Controller, Open VR Left Controller, and Open VR Right Controller. Now drag and drop these prefabs onto the [VRTK_Input_Controllers] game object in the hierarchy, making them children. Figure 6-3 shows this setup with the Left Thumbstick and Left Grip game objects expanded.

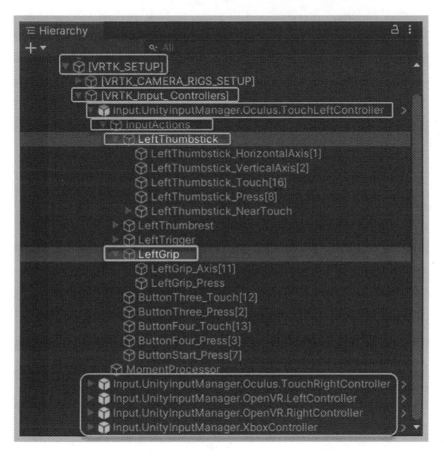

***Figure 6-3.*** *Input Controller mappings for various input controllers*

Before hooking up the various controller buttons, let's briefly explore the Input, Unity Input Manager, and Oculus Touch Left Controller game objects to see how the controller input buttons have been organized. A similar organizational structure applies to both the Open VR and Xbox controllers, with the button names differing slightly.

From within the [VRTK_Input_Controllers] game object in the hierarchy, expand the Input, Unity Input Manager, Oculus Touch Left Controller game object. Then, expand its "Input Actions" folder. You'll immediately notice that all the buttons available on the physical Oculus controller have been mapped here, along with different inputs you can capture for each button. Now expand the Left Thumbstick game object. You will see that for this Left Thumbstick, you can capture input for the following actions that can be performed against it: moving the Thumbstick horizontally or vertically, touching the Thumbstick, pressing down on it, and making a near touch against it. Similarly, you can capture input from other buttons on your controller to have a list of actions that can be performed against them.

Let's look at one more button on your Oculus Touch Left Controller game object. Expand the Left Grip game object and you'll notice that for this grip, you can capture input for your left controller's Grip button being pressed and the extent to which it has been pushed in. You could thus ensure that only if the Grip button is pushed in over 50% of the way would you allow a Grab action to occur and play the Grab animation. Figure 6-3 shows this setup with the Left Thumbstick and Left Grip game objects expanded. Similar buttons and actions exist for the Input, Unity Input Manager, Oculus Touch, Right Controller, Input, Unity Input Manager, Open VR, Left, and Right controllers and Input, Unity Input Manager Xbox controller.

As discussed earlier, the input can come from different input devices, so you need to consolidate such varied input into a single object that other objects can later poll. For a Grab action, you can obtain input from three separate devices for each hand; that is, six unique Grip input signals and mouse input via the left and right mouse buttons, for a total of eight *Grab* signals.

To deal with the six Grip input signals that can be raised by your controllers and the two input signals produced by clicking your left and right mouse button, first create two intermediary game objects. One game object will listen for a left-hand Grip or left mouse press, and the other will listen for a right-hand Grip or Right mouse press. Six of these Grip presses originate from either your Oculus, HTC Vive, or Xbox controllers. The left and right mouse button clicks account for the other two Grab actions. The two intermediary game objects you'll create will be named, "Left-Hand Grab" and "Right-Hand Grab." All button action input associated with your Left-Hand controller device will be channeled into the Left-Hand Grab game object and all button action input associated with the right-hand device will be directed into the Right-Hand Grab game object. A left mouse button click will be channeled into the Left-Hand Grab game object, and a right mouse button click will be directed into the Right-Hand Grab game object. As all these input values are purely Boolean values, both your Left-Hand Grab and Right-Hand Grab game objects will need to contain a Boolean action component that can receive Boolean (True/False) values only.

Let's set this up now. In the hierarchy, select the Demo scene game object and right-click it. From the context menu that pops up, select Game Object ➤ Create Empty. Reset the Transform of this newly created empty game object and rename it "Button Input Actions." Note that this game object is a child of your Demo (scene) game object.

You now need to configure your Button Input Actions game object. Select this game object in the hierarchy and create two new empty child objects in it. Rename the objects "Left-Hand Grab" and "Right-Hand Grab." Select both game objects in the hierarchy, and within the Inspector, click the Add Component button. In the search box that shows up below the button, search for "Boolean Action" and add this component to both objects. Within this Boolean Action component, locate and expand its Sources property and set its size to 4, according to which four-element slots will be made available. Each of these slots will reference the concerned controller buttons input action you want to listen for. Figure 6-4 shows what this setup looks like so far.

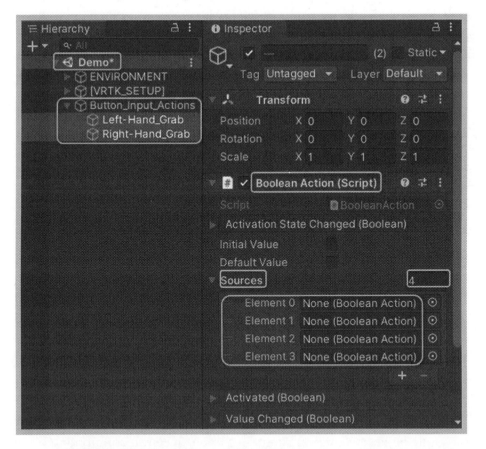

***Figure 6-4.*** *Left-Hand Grab and Right-Hand Grab intermediary game objects with their Boolean Action component set up*

Earlier in this section, we noted that controller mappings hadn't been provided for the Mouse or Keyboard buttons. You'll need to set up these mappings yourself. Let's deviate a bit by first setting up controller mappings for your left and right mouse buttons, as these will be the required input to pass into your sources Element property slots for both the Left-Hand Grab and Right-Hand Grab game objects. Setting up controller mappings for keyboard buttons will be discussed later, as we are currently concerned with capturing input for when a Grip, Mouse, or Bumper button is pressed.

From within the hierarchy, select the [VRTK_Input_Controllers] game object and right-click it. Create a new empty child game object and rename it "Mouse Input." In the Project tab, with the Tilia input, Unity Input Manager package folder still expanded, select the "Actions" folder in the "Prefabs" folder. In the right pane, you'll notice three action prefabs. Select the Input, Unity Input manager, Button action prefab, and drag and drop it onto the Mouse Input game object in the hierarchy. Rename it "Input, Unity Input Manager, Button action Mouse Right." Duplicate this game object so that the copy is a child of Mouse Input and rename it, "Input, Unity Input Manager, Button action Mouse Left." Select the Input, Unity Input Manager, Button Action Mouse Right game object in the hierarchy, and within the Inspector, ensure that the Unity Input Manager, Button Action component is expanded. Locate the KeyCode property. Scroll through its drop-down list and select the item Mouse 1. This captures the action of a Right mouse button click, in which case a Boolean value of True will be emitted.

Next, select the Unity Input Manager, Button Action Mouse Left game object from within the hierarchy. In the Inspector, ensure that the Unity Input Manager, Button Action component has been expanded. Locate the KeyCode property. Scroll through its drop-down list and select the item Mouse 0. This captures the action of a left mouse button click, in which case a Boolean value of True will be emitted. These controller mappings now enable you to listen for button input action that happens against any of your listed devices.

Now, let's return to hooking up all eight Grab signals among your Left-Hand Grab and Right-Hand Grab game objects. The left-hand Grip, press action input raised by your left-handed controller for either an Oculus, Xbox, or HTC Vive device, or a left mouse button click, will be hooked up to the Left-Hand Grab game object. Thus, your Left-Hand Grab intermediary game object receives four Grab input signals that need to be plugged into the four element slots shown in Figure 6-4. The same analogy applies to hooking up inputs produced by your right-hand controller and right mouse button, wherein these inputs need to be hooked up to your Right-Hand Grab intermediary game object.

Let's set up these connections for your Left-Hand Grab intermediary game object first. From within the hierarchy, select and expand the [VRTK_Input_Controllers] game object. Expand the Input, Unity Input Manager, Oculus Touch Left Controller game object. Then expand its Input Actions game object and Left Grip game object.

Next, from within the [VRTK_Input_Controllers] game object, expand the Input, Unity Input Manager, Open VR Left Controller game object. Then expand its Input Actions game object and its Left Grip game object.

Next, from within the [VRTK_Input_Controllers] game object, expand the Input, Unity Input Manager, Xbox Controller game object. Then, expand its Input Actions game object.

Finally, expand the Mouse Input game object from within the [VRTK_Input_Controllers] game object. With these input sources expanded, let's capture input when a left-hand Grip press or a left mouse button click occurs.

From within the hierarchy, select the Left-Hand Grab game object. Note that your Boolean Action Sources property has four element slots in the Inspector, as shown in Figure 6-4.

From within the expanded Input, Unity Input Manager, Oculus Touch Left Controller game object, drag and drop the Left Grip Press game object into the Sources property Element 0 slot, as shown in Figure 6-5. Now, from within the expanded Input, Unity Input Manager, Open VR Left Controller game object, drag and drop the Left Grip Press game object into the Element 1 slot of the Sources property, as shown in Figure 6-5. Next, from within the expanded Input, Unity Input Manager, Controller game object, drag and drop the Left Bumper Press [4] game object into the Sources property Element 2 slot, as shown in Figure 6-5. Last, from within the expanded Mouse Input game object, drag and drop the Input, Unity Input manager, Button action Mouse Left, game object into the Element 3 slot of the Sources property, as shown in Figure 6-5.

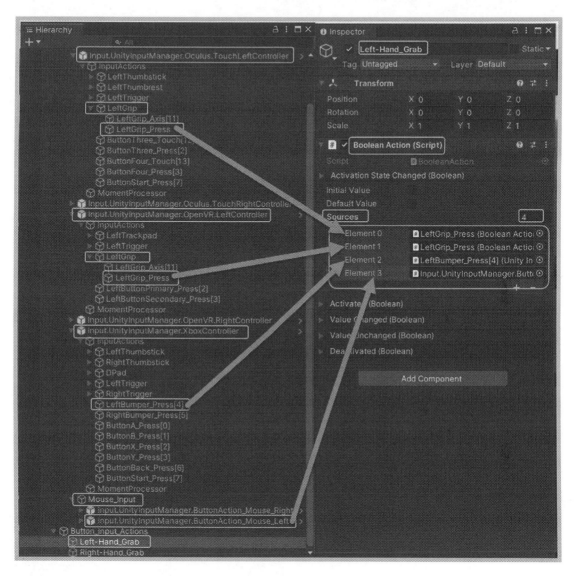

***Figure 6-5.*** *Hooking up the Left Grip, Bumper, and Mouse (press) inputs to the Left-Hand Grab intermediary game object*

Now that we're done capturing input for a Left-Hand Grab, let's set ourselves up to capture input for a Right-Hand Grab. With the [VRTK_Input_Controllers] game object expanded, collapse the game objects Input Unity Input Manager Oculus Touch Left Controller; Input Unity Input Manager Open VR Left Controller; and Input Unity Input Manager X-Box Controller. Let the Mouse Input game object remain expanded, as you will be referring to its Input, Unity Input Manager, Button action Mouse Right child game object.

From within the hierarchy, with the [VRTK_Input_Controllers] game object still expanded, expand the Input, Unity Input Manager, Oculus Touch Right Controller game object. Then expand its Input Actions game object, followed by expanding its Right Grip game object.

Next, expand the Input, Unity Input Manager, Open VR Right Controller game object. Then expand its Input Actions game object, followed by expanding its Right Grip game object.

After that, expand the Input, Unity Input Manager, X-Box Controller game object. Then, expand its Input Actions game object. Finally, ensure that the Mouse Input game object has been expanded, too.

Now that these input sources are all expanded, let's capture input when a right-hand Grip press or a right mouse button click occurs. From within the hierarchy, select the Right-Hand Grab game object. Note that your Boolean Action Sources property has four element slots in the Inspector, as shown in Figure 6-4.

From within the expanded Input, Unity Input Manager, Oculus Touch Right Controller game object, drag and drop the Right Grip Press game object into the Sources property Element 0 slot, as shown in Figure 6-6. Now, from within the expanded Input, Unity Input Manager, Open VR Right Controller game object, drag and drop the Right Grip Press game object into the Element 1 slot of the Sources property, as shown in Figure 6-6. Next, from within the expanded Input, Unity Input Manager, X-Box Controller game object, drag and drop the Right Bumper Press [5] game object into the Sources property Element 2 slot, as shown in Figure 6-6. Last, from within the expanded Mouse Input game object, drag and drop the Input, Unity Input manager, Button Action Mouse Right game object into the Element 3 slot of the Sources property, as shown in Figure 6-6.

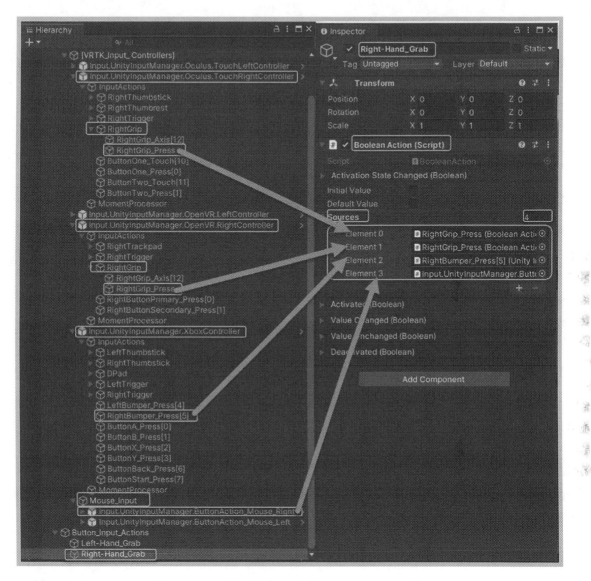

***Figure 6-6.*** *Hooking up Right Grip, Bumper, and Mouse (press) inputs to the Right-Hand Grab intermediary game object*

You finally have your controller mappings set up to capture input from four devices against two hands for a Grab Action. Now you need something to happen when a Grab action takes place. Animate your custom prototype hands with the Grab animation available. You'll need to set up this Grab animation on each of your hands.

In the hierarchy, with your Button Input Actions game object expanded, select the Left-Hand Grab game object. In the Inspector, you'll notice its Activated Boolean and Deactivated Boolean events. The Activated Boolean event will be triggered as soon as a left-hand grab takes place. When this happens, you'll need to play the Grab animation for your left hand. Expand this Activated Boolean event within the Inspector and click the plus symbol located in its bottom right corner to add an event listener box for this Activated event.

Your left hand is represented by the Hand Proto Left game object. It can be located within the hierarchy by navigating to [VRTK_CAMERA_RIGS_SETUP] ➤ Camera Rigs, Tracked Alias ➤ Aliases ➤ Left Controller Alias ➤ Interactions Interactor Left ➤ Avatar Container.

With the Avatar Container for the Left Controller, Alias expanded, drag and drop its Hand Proto Left game object into the box located below the Runtime Only drop-down property of the Activated event, as shown in Figure 6-7. From the drop-down located at the right of the Runtime Only drop-down property, select the option Animator and then Play (string). Essentially, this is telling the Animator component on the Hand Proto Left game object to play a specific animation. In the box available below the Animator Play drop-down, type in the name of the animation you'd like played when the Activated event is triggered after a Grab action has occurred. In this case, the name to type in is "Grab."

Now, let's set up the Deactivated Boolean event on your Left-Hand Grab game object. This Deactivated Boolean event will be triggered when an "un-Grab" occurs— that is, when you release the Grip button on your left controller. When this happens, you need to play the Release animation for your left hand. Expand this Deactivated Boolean event within the Inspector and click the plus symbol located in its bottom right corner to add an event listener box for this Deactivated event.

With the Avatar Container for the Left Controller, Alias expanded, drag and drop its Hand Proto Left game object into the box located below the Runtime Only drop-down property of the Deactivated event, as shown in Figure 6-7. In the drop-down located at the right of the Runtime Only drop-down property, select the option Animator and choose the option Play (string). Essentially, this tells the Animator component on the Hand Proto Left game object to play a specific animation. In the box available below the Animator, Play drop-down, type in the name of the animation you'd like played when the Deactivated event is triggered after an un-Grab has occurred. Here, the name to type in is "Release."

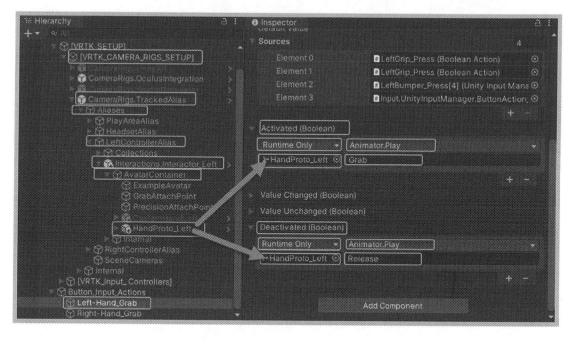

***Figure 6-7.*** *Setting up the Grab animation to play after a Grab action and the Release animation to play after an un-Grab action(Left-Hand Grab game object)*

Now that you're done setting up animations against your left hand, you need to set up the same animations against your right hand. You can achieve this by setting up the Activated and Deactivated events for when a right-hand Grab occurs. Let's set this up now.

Start by selecting the Right-Hand Grab game object in the hierarchy, with your Button Input Actions game object still expanded. In the Inspector, you'll notice its Activated Boolean and Deactivated Boolean events. The Activated Boolean event will be triggered as soon as a right-hand Grab takes place. When this happens, you need to play the Grab animation for your right hand. Expand this Activated Boolean event within the Inspector and click the plus symbol located at its bottom right corner to add an event listener box for this Activated event.

Your right hand is represented by the Hand Proto right game object. It can be located within the hierarchy by navigating to [VRTK_CAMERA_RIGS_SETUP] ➤ Camera Rigs, Tracked Alias ➤ Aliases ➤ Right Controller Alias ➤ Interactions Interactor Right ➤ Avatar Container.

With the Avatar Container for the Right Controller, Alias expanded, drag and drop its Hand Proto Right game object into the box located below the Runtime Only drop-down property of the Activated event, as shown in Figure 6-8. From the list you get when you click the right of the Runtime Only drop-down property, select the option Animator and then Play (string). Essentially, this tells the Animator component on the Hand Proto Right game object to play a specific animation. In the box available below the Animator.Play drop-down, type in the name of the animation you'd like played when the *Activated* event is triggered after a Grab action has occurred. In this case, the name of the animation to type in is "Grab."

Now let's set up the Deactivated Boolean event on your Right-Hand Grab game object. This event will be triggered when an un-Grab occurs—that is, when you release the Grip button on your Right controller. When this happens, the Release animation should be played for your right hand. Expand this Deactivated Boolean event within the Inspector and click the plus symbol located in its bottom right corner to add an event listener box for this Deactivated event.

With the Avatar Container for the Right Controller, Alias expanded, drag and drop its Hand Proto Right game object into the box located below the Runtime Only drop-down property of the Deactivated event, as shown in Figure 6-8. From the drop-down located at the right of the Runtime Only drop-down property, select the option Animator and then, Play (string). Essentially, this tells the Animator component on the Hand Proto Right game object to play a specific animation. In the box available below the Animator. Play drop-down, type in the name of the animation you'd like played after the *Deactivated* event has been triggered for an un-Grab. The name to type in here is "Release."

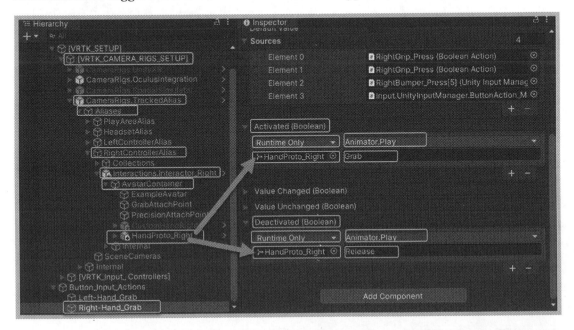

***Figure 6-8.*** *Setting up the Grab animation to play after a Grab action and the Release animation to play after an un-Grab action (Right-Hand Grab game object)*

## Playtesting the Grab and Release Hand Animations

To playtest the Grab and Release animations, expand the [VRTK_CAMERA_RIGS_ SETUP] game object in the hierarchy and activate Camera Rigs, Spatial Simulator and deactivate Camera Rigs, Unity XR and Camera Rigs, Oculus Integration. Also, make sure that Camera Rigs, Tracked Alias is permanently active.

Now, hit the Play button within Unity's editor and wait for your scene to load. When your Demo scene is playing, click your left and right mouse buttons to see your left and right hands respectively animate. If you have an Xbox controller connected to your computer, you can press its Left and Right controller buttons to see your Left and Right Hand animate. You'll only need to use the Camera Rigs, Spatial Simulator with your Xbox controller. Finally, hit the Play button again to stop your scene from playing.

Next, test your scene using your VR Headset. From within the [VRTK_CAMERA_ RIGS_SETUP] game object, activate Camera Rigs, Unity XR and deactivate Camera Rigs, Spatial Simulator and Camera Rigs, Oculus Integration. Hit the Play button within Unity's editor and wait for your scene to load. When your Demo scene is playing, mount your VR headset and grab your VR controllers. Press the Grip buttons on your left and right controllers to see your hands and grab animation working.

## Capturing Thumbstick and Keyboard Input

Now that you have your Grab animation working with your VR controllers' Grip buttons, your Xbox controllers, Bumper buttons, and your left and right mouse buttons, it's time to learn how to capture your controller's Thumbstick and keyboard input. In this section, upon receiving input from your controller Thumbsticks or pressing the *Q* or *P* keys on your keyboard, we'll make the Teleporting animation play. Pressing the *Q* key will simulate a left-hand Thumbstick press, while pressing the *P* key will simulate a right-hand Thumbstick press. The procedure is like what you underwent to set up your Grab animation. The only difference is that you won't need to set up the Deactivated Boolean event here. When the Teleporting animation ends, you'll be reverted to an open hand by default.

From within the hierarchy, select the [VRTK_Input_Controllers] game object. Right-click it and create a new child empty game object. Rename this object "Keyboard Input." In the Project tab, with the "Tilia input, Unity Input Manager" package folder still expanded, select the "Actions" folder in the "Prefabs" folder. In the right pane, you'll notice three action prefabs. Select the Input, Unity Input manager, Button Action prefab, and drag and drop it onto the Keyboard Input game object in the hierarchy. Rename it "Input, Unity Input Manager, Button Action Q." You'll use the *Q* key on the keyboard to represent a left-hand Thumbstick press. Duplicate this game object so that the copy is a child of Keyboard Input. Rename this duplicated object "Input, Unity Input Manager, Button Action P." You'll use the *P* key on the keyboard to represent a right-hand Thumbstick press. Select the Input, Unity Input Manager, Button Action Q game object in the hierarchy, and within the Inspector, ensure that the Unity Input Manager, Button Action component has been expanded. Locate the KeyCode property. Scroll through its drop-down list and select the letter *Q*. This captures a Q key press, resulting in a Boolean value of True being emitted.

Next, select the Unity Input manager, Button Action P game object from within the hierarchy. In the Inspector, ensure that the Unity Input Manager, Button Action component has been expanded. Locate the KeyCode property. Scroll through its drop-down list and select the letter *P*. This captures a *P* key press, resulting in a Boolean value of True being emitted. These Keyboard input mappings now enable you to listen for either a *Q* or *P* key being pressed. You can capture several keypad key presses using this procedure.

Select the Button Input Actions game object in the hierarchy and create two new empty child objects within it. Rename these objects "Left-Hand Thumbstick Press" and "Right-Hand Thumbstick Press." Select both of these game objects in the hierarchy, and within the Inspector, click the Add Component button. In the search box that shows up below this button, search for Boolean Action and add this component to both objects. Within this Boolean Action component, locate and expand its Sources property and set its size to 4, according to which four-element slots will be made available. Each of these element slots will reference a controller Thumbsticks button input action that you want to listen for. Figure 6-9 shows what this setup looks like so far.

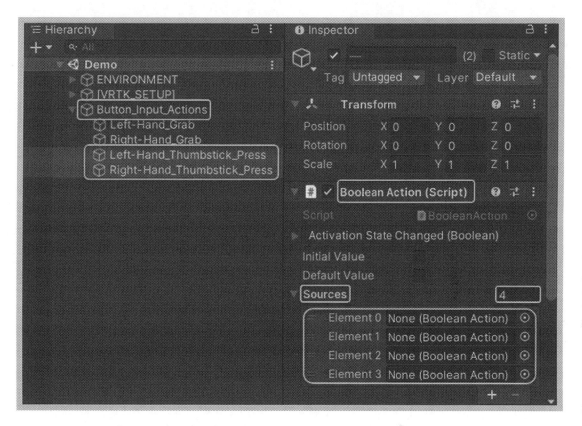

***Figure 6-9.*** *Left-Hand Thumbstick press and Right-Hand Thumbstick press intermediary game objects with their Boolean action component set up*

Now, let's connect all eight Thumbstick press signals among your Left-Hand Thumbstick Press and Right-Hand Thumbstick press game objects. The Left-Hand Thumbstick input, raised by your left-handed controller for either the Oculus, Xbox, or HTC Vive devices, or the *Q* key press, will be hooked up to the Left-Hand Thumbstick Press game object. Thus, your Left-Hand Thumbstick Press intermediary game object will receive four input signals that need to be plugged into the four element slots shown in Figure 6-9. The same analogy applies to hooking up inputs produced by your right-handed controller and *P* key press, according to which these inputs need to be hooked up to your Right-Hand Thumbstick Press intermediary game object.

Let's set up these connections for your Left-Hand Thumbstick Press intermediary game object first. From within the hierarchy, select and expand the [VRTK_Input_Controllers] game object. Expand the Input, Unity Input Manager, Oculus Touch Left Controller game object. Then expand its Input Actions game object, followed by expanding its Left Thumbstick game object.

Next, from within the same game object, expand the Input, Unity Input Manager, Open VR Left Controller game object. Then expand its Input Actions game object, followed by expanding its Left Trackpad game object.

After that, from within the same game object, expand the Input, Unity Input Manager, Xbox Controller game object. Then expand its Input Actions game object, followed by expanding its Left Thumbstick game object.

Finally, from within this game object, expand the Keyboard Input game object.

With these input sources expanded, let's capture input for when a left-hand Thumbstick or the Q key is pressed.

From within the hierarchy, select the Left-Hand Thumbstick Press game object. Note that your Boolean Action Sources property has four element slots in the Inspector, as shown in Figure 6-9.

From within the expanded Input, Unity Input Manager, Oculus Touch Left Controller game object, drag and drop the Left Thumbstick Press [8] game object into the Sources property Element 0 slot, as shown in Figure 6-10. Now, from within the expanded Input, Unity Input Manager, Open VR Left Controller game object, drag and drop the Left Trackpad Press [8] game object into the Element 1 slot of the Sources property, as shown in Figure 6-10.

Next, from within the expanded Input, Unity Input Manager, X-Box Controller game object, drag and drop the Left Thumbstick Press [8] game object into the Element 2 slot of the Sources property, as shown in Figure 6-10.

Last, from within the expanded Keyboard Input game object, drag and drop the Input, Unity Input Manager, Button Action Q game object into the Element 3 slot of the Sources property, as shown in Figure 6-10.

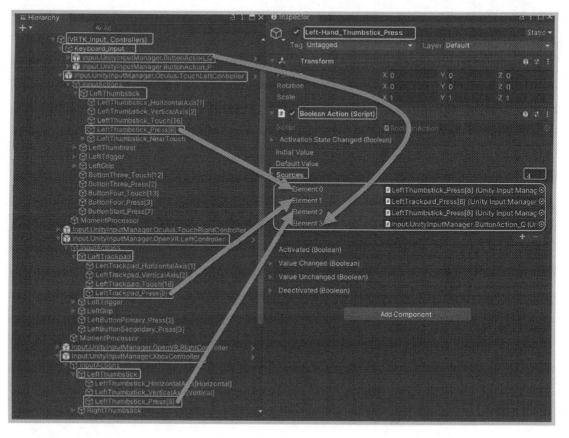

**Figure 6-10.** *Hooking up Left Thumbstick and Keyboard (press) inputs to the Left-Hand Thumbstick Press intermediary game object*

Now that we're done capturing input for a Left-Hand Thumbstick Press, let's set ourselves up to capture input for a Right-Hand Thumbstick Press. With the [VRTK_Input_Controllers] expanded, collapse the Input Unity Input Manager Oculus Touch Left Controller; Input Unity Input Manager Open VR Left Controller and Input Unity Input Manager Xbox Controller Left Thumbstick game objects. Keep the Keyboard Input game object expanded as you refer to its Input, Unity Input manager, Button Action P child game object.

From within the [VRTK_Input_Controllers] game object, expand the Input, Unity Input Manager, Oculus Touch Right Controller game object. Then expand its Input Actions game object, followed by expanding its Right Thumbstick game object.

Next, expand the Input, Unity Input Manager, Open VR Right Controller game object. Then expand its Input Actions game object, followed by expanding its Right Trackpad game object.

After that, with the Input, Unity Input Manager, Xbox Controller, Input Actions game object expanded, increase the size of its Right Thumbstick game object. Your Keyboard Input game object should already be expanded.

With these input sources expanded, let's capture input when a right-hand Thumbstick or the *P* key on the keyboard is pressed. From within the hierarchy, select the Right-Hand Thumbstick Press game object. Note that your Boolean Action Sources property has four element slots in the Inspector, as shown in Figure 6-9.

From within the expanded Input, Unity Input Manager, Oculus Touch Right Controller game object, drag and drop the Right Thumbstick Press [9] game object into the Element 0 slot of the Sources property, as shown in Figure 6-11.

Now, from within the expanded Input, Unity Input Manager, Open VR Right Controller game object, drag and drop the Right Trackpad Press [9] game object into the Element 1 slot of the Sources property, as shown in Figure 6-11.

Next, from within the expanded Input, Unity Input Manager, X-Box Controller game object, drag and drop the Right Thumbstick Press [9] game object into the Element 2 slot of the Sources property, as shown in Figure 6-11. Last, from within the expanded Keyboard Input game object, drag and drop the Input, Unity Input manager, Button Action P game object into the Element 3 slot of the Sources property, as shown in Figure 6-11.

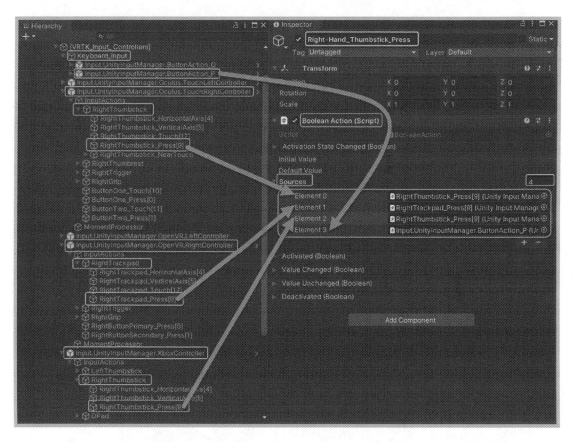

***Figure 6-11.*** *Hooking up the Right Thumbstick and Keyboard (press) inputs to the Right-Hand Thumbstick Press intermediary game object*

You now have your controller mappings set up to capture input from four devices against two hands when the Thumbstick, *Q*, or *P* keys are pressed. Now you need something to happen when any of these actions takes place; what should happen is that your custom prototype hands animate with the Teleporting animation available. You will need to set up this Teleporting animation on each of your hands.

In the hierarchy, with your Button Input Actions game object expanded, select the Left-Hand Thumbstick Press game object. In the Inspector, you'll notice its Activated Boolean event. This event will be triggered as soon as a Left-Hand Thumbstick Press takes place. When this happens, you need to play the Teleporting animation for your left hand. Expand this Activated Boolean event within the Inspector and click the plus symbol located at its bottom right corner to add an event listener box for this Activated event.

Your left hand is represented by the Hand Proto Left game object within the hierarchy. It can be located by navigating to [VRTK_CAMERA_RIGS_SETUP] ➤ Camera Rigs, Tracked Alias ➤ Aliases ➤ Left Controller Alias ➤ Interactions Interactor Left ➤ Avatar Container.

Now, with the Avatar Container of the Left Controller, Alias expanded, drag and drop its Hand Proto Left game object into the box located below the Runtime Only drop-down property of the Activated event, as shown in Figure 6-12. From the drop-down located at the right of the Runtime Only property, select the option Animator and choose Play (string). Essentially, this tells the Animator component on the Hand Proto Left game object to play a specific animation. In the box available below the Animator Play drop-down, type in the name of the animation you'd like played when the Activated event is triggered after the Thumbstick or *Q* key has been pressed. Type "Teleporting" into this box.

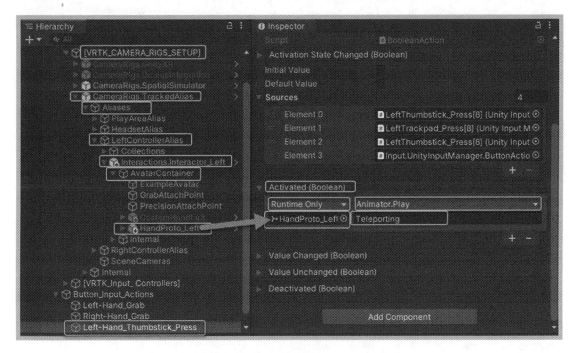

***Figure 6-12.*** *Setting up the Teleporting animation to play after the Left Thumbstick or Q key has been pressed(Left-Hand Thumbstick Press)*

Now that you're done setting up the Teleporting animation against your left hand, you need to set up the same animation against your right hand. This is achieved by setting up its Activated event for when the Right-Hand Thumbstick or *P* key is pressed.

In the hierarchy, with your Button Input Actions game object still expanded, select the Right-Hand Thumbstick Press game object. In the Inspector, you'll notice its Activated Boolean event. The event will be triggered as soon as the right-hand Thumbstick or *P* key is pressed. When this happens, you need to play the Teleporting animation for your right hand. Expand the Activated Boolean event within the Inspector and click the plus symbol located at its bottom right corner to add an event listener box for this Activated event.

Your right hand is represented by the Hand Proto Right game object within the hierarchy. It can be located by navigating to [VRTK_CAMERA_RIGS_SETUP] ➤ Camera Rigs, Tracked Alias ➤ Aliases ➤ Right Controller Alias ➤ Interactions Interactor Right ➤ Avatar Container.

With the Avatar Container for the Right Controller, Alias expanded, drag and drop its Hand Proto Right game object into the box located below the Runtime Only drop-down property of the Activated event, as shown in Figure 6-13. From the drop-down located at the right of the Runtime Only property, select the option Animator and then choose Play (string). Essentially, this tells the Animator component on the Hand Proto Right game object to play a specific animation. In the box available below the Animator Play drop-down, type in the name of the animation you'd like played when the Activated event is triggered after the Thumbstick or *P* key has been pressed. Type "Teleporting" into this box. You might have noticed that a Deactivated Boolean event wasn't set up for your Thumbstick press, as when the Teleporting animation ends, you will revert to an open hand by default.

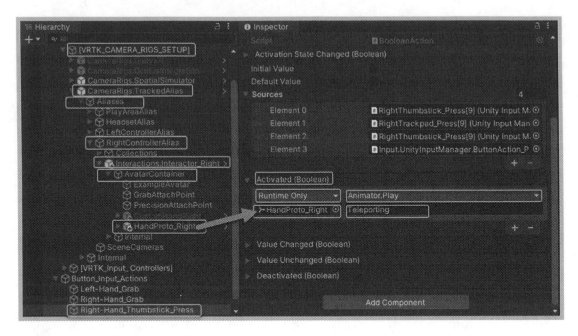

*Figure 6-13.* *Setting up the Teleporting animation to play after the Right Thumbstick or P key has been pressed (Right-Hand Thumbstick Press)*

## Playtesting Teleporting Hand Animation

Expand the [VRTK_CAMERA_RIGS_SETUP] game object in the hierarchy and activate Camera Rigs, Spatial Simulator and deactivate Camera Rigs, Unity XR and Camera Rigs, Oculus Integration. Also, ensure that Camera Rigs, Tracked Alias is permanently active.

Hit the Play button within Unity's editor and wait for your scene to load. With your Demo scene playing, press the *Q* key on your keyboard to see your left thumb animate and press the *P* key to see your right thumb animate. If you have an Xbox controller connected to your computer, you can press its Left and Right Thumbsticks to see your Left and Right thumbs animate. You'll need to use the Camera Rigs, Spatial Simulator only with your Xbox controller. Finally, hit the Play button again to stop your scene from playing.

Now test your scene using your VR Headset. From within the [VRTK_CAMERA_RIGS_SETUP] game object, activate Camera Rigs, Unity X, and deactivate Camera Rigs, Spatial Simulator and Camera Rigs, Oculus Integration. Hit the Play button within Unity's editor and wait for your scene to load. When your Demo scene is playing, mount your VR headset and grab your VR controllers. Press the Thumbsticks (Trackpads) on your Left and Right controllers to see your thumbs animate using the Teleporting animation.

# Summary

In this chapter, we started by learning what an Interactor and an Interactable are. We then set up Interactors on both our Left and Right controllers and tested out the cuboid avatar hands provided by the VRTK. We then put in place realistic animated hands for our Camera Rigs, Oculus Integration setup and playtested our Demo scene with our new Oculus-provided hands.

Next, we began a long journey toward setting up custom hands for our Spatial Simulator and Camera Rigs, Unity XR. You learned why the Oculus-provided hands wouldn't work out of the box with the Camera Rigs, Spatial Simulator, and Camera Rigs, Unity XR.

We imported the custom prototype hands provided with the Unity package for the project. We went on to set up our Hand Proto prefab and learned how to mirror it, and repositioned and resized it to our liking. We also looked at the animations provided to us, along with the Hand Proto prefab.

Next, we took a deep dive, learning how to animate our prototype hands based on controller input. We began by setting up a Grab animation to obtain input from four devices across two hands for eight input signals to be captured. We used the Boolean action component to capture this input and learned how to set it up.

You learned to capture input from your Oculus, HTC Vive, and Xbox controllers, and input from the mouse when a Grab action occurred by pressing the Grip button on the controllers. You then learned about the Activated and Deactivated events and set them up to play an appropriate animation.

You learned how to use an intermediary game object to obtain a level of indirection by channeling several inputs into one game object and then having interested objects poll this intermediary game object. You also learned how to capture input from your Oculus, HTC Vive, and Xbox controller Thumbsticks, as well as keyboard input, and you used this input to play a Teleporting animation. Finally, we tested your Demo scene to ensure that the controllers, mouse, and keyboard input we captured worked correctly.

# CHAPTER 7

# Configuring Interactor Functionality and Setting Up Velocity Trackers

We're still not done connecting all the dots in setting up fully functional VR hands. We still need to configure the Interactors for both of our hands to provide the all-important ability to grab an Interactable object. Currently, we have our hands set up and the grab animation enabled to respond to a grip press. However, we haven't yet told the Interactor components on both hands to engage their grab mechanism. In this chapter, you'll learn how to engage the grabbing mechanism for both Interactors. You'll also learn about the example avatar cuboid objects and their importance in helping your grab interactions work. We'll set up a very basic cube Interactable to test whether our Interactor's grabbing mechanism is working. Finally, we'll set up velocity trackers on our Left and Right controllers.

## Setting Up the Grab Action Property on Interactors to Enable Grabbing

Within the hierarchy, navigate to [VRTK_CAMERA_RIGS_SETUP] ➤ Camera Rigs, Tracked Alias ➤ Aliases ➤ Left Controller Alias ➤ Interactions Interactor Left. In the Inspector, ensure that the Interactor Facade component has been expanded. Within the Interactor Settings section, you'll notice a Grab Action property that hasn't been populated. You'll also notice that this Grab Action property can only accept a Boolean

© Christopher Coutinho 2022
C. Coutinho, *Unity® Virtual Reality Development with VRTK4*, https://doi.org/10.1007/978-1-4842-7933-5_7

Action component. Suppose this component of the Grab Action property happens to emit a True value. In that case, your Left-hand Interactors grab mechanism will be initiated, allowing you to grab an Interactable.

In the previous chapter, you directed all your Left devices, the Grip, Bumper, and Left mouse button inputs, into an intermediary game object: the Left-Hand Grab. This object contained a Boolean Action component. Now, this is precisely what the Grab Action property on your Left-hand Interactor desires. By connecting the Left-Hand Grab game object to the Grab Action property, you direct all left-hand device, grip (grab) inputs into this Grab Action property. The property can now listen for the Grip button press action of any left controller device. As soon as it receives this input, which if True—that is, if the Grip, Bumper, or Left Mouse button are pressed—will engage its grabbing mechanism for its Left Interactor. The same analogy applies for activating the grabbing mechanism against your Right Interactor, where you connect the Right-Hand Grab game object to its Grab Action property.

If you are building just for Oculus, you can drag and drop only the Oculus Touch Left Controllers, Left Grip Press button action object into the Grab Action property and be done with it. However, if you are building for other devices like the HTC Vive, Windows Mixed Reality devices, and the Spatial Simulator, you will need to keep changing the input for this Grab Action property depending on which device you want to use. Setting up an intermediary game object such as the Left-Hand Grab game object has provided you with a level of indirection where you can channel all possible ways a Left-Hand Grip press can occur into the intermediary game object, Left-Hand Grab. It has enabled you to decouple the grabbing action from other actions, allowing you to provide it to the Grab Action property.

Let's set this up against your Interactions Interactor Left game object first. With the Interactions Interactor Left game object selected in the hierarchy, expand the Button Input Actions game object. Drag and drop its Left-Hand Grab game object into the Grab Action property of the Interactions Interactor Left game object, as shown in Figure 7-1.

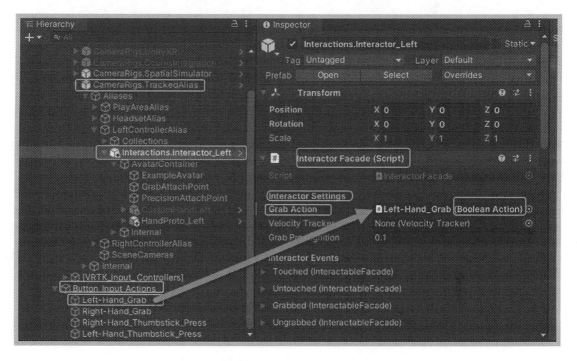

*Figure 7-1.* *Setting up the Grab Action property for the Left Interactor*

Now, let's set up the Grab Action property for the Interactions Interactor Right game object. To do so, collapse the Left Controller Alias game object in the hierarchy. Expand the Right Controller Alias game object and select its Interactions Interactor Right game object. With the Button Input Actions game object expanded, drag and drop its Right-Hand Grab game object into the Grab Action property of the Interactions Interactor Right game object, as shown in Figure 7-2.

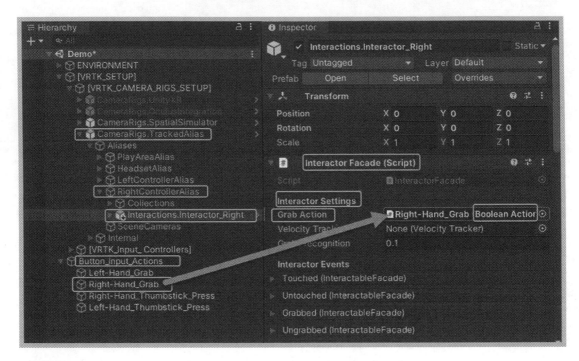

*Figure 7-2.* *Setting up the Grab Action property for the Right Interactor*

The grab mechanism for both of your controllers is now functional.

# Setting Up an Interactable Object

To test that our Interactors work, we need to set up a basic Interactable object so that our Interactors have something to work with. The Interactable object will be discussed in greater detail later in the book. For now, we'll set up a very simple cube interactable game object, which will be placed on the table within our scene.

Start by selecting the Environment game object from within the hierarchy. Then, from within the main menu of the Unity Editor, select Game Object ➤ Tilia ➤ Prefabs ➤ Interactions ➤ Interactables ➤ Interactions Interactable. An Interactions Interactable (white cube) game object will be paced within your scene. Expand the Environment game object in the hierarchy and select its Interactions Interactable child game object. Double-click it to have it obtain the focus. You will notice that it got embedded within one of the containers in your scene and is halfway into the floor. Let's reset its position and scale it so that we have it sitting on the table scaled down in size. Within the

Inspector, set its Transform, position property values as follows: $X$ = -12.831; $Y$ = 0.785; and $Z$ = -4.312. Set its Transform, scale property values for $X$, $Y$, and $Z$ to 0.1. Now, you'll see a much smaller-sized white Interactable cube sitting perfectly on your table.

With your Interactions Interactable (white cube) game object still selected in the hierarchy, rename it "White Cube." Within the Inspector, ensure that its Interactable Facade component has been expanded. Scroll down a bit until you see its Grab Action Settings section. Ensure that its Grab Type property has been set to "Hold Till Release." This setting indicates that you must continually press your Grip button on your controller to hold onto your white cube Interactable object. When you release the Grip button on your controller, an "ungrab" will occur and the Interactable object (white cube) will fall out of your hand. Set the Primary Action property value to Interactable Grab Action Follow in the Primary Actions settings section. In the Follow Settings section, ensure that the Follow Tracking property has been set to Follow Transform. Last, set the Secondary Action property within the Secondary Actions Settings section to Interactable Grab Action Swap. These properties will be explained in Chapter 8 - Interactable Game Objects, that deals with Interactable objects. Figure 7-3 shows the Interactable Facade component with these property values set up.

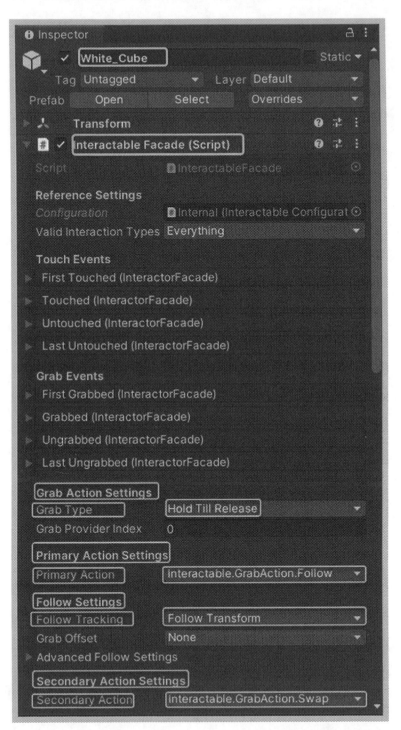

***Figure 7-3.*** *Setting up properties for your Interactable game object (white cube)*

# Exploring the Example Avatar Cuboid Object

Within the hierarchy, navigate to [VRTK_CAMERA_RIGS_SETUP] ➤ Camera Rigs, Tracked Alias ➤ Aliases ➤ Left Controller Alias ➤ Interactions Interactor Left ➤ Avatar Container ➤ Example Avatar. In the Inspector, you'll notice that your Example Avatar game object mesh has been set to a cube, and you could even set up a sphere mesh here. Most important, it has a Box collider on it that has been set up as a trigger, according to which its Is Trigger property has been checked. The Box collider on this cube is what enables your Grab interactions to work.

# Testing Your Hand Proto Left and Hand Proto Right Game Objects

Let's now test the grabbing mechanism using your Hand Proto Left and Hand Proto Right game objects. Ensure that within the hierarchy, both these objects are active. Also, make sure your Oculus-provided hands, Custom Hand Left and Custom Hand Right, have been deactivated, as shown in Figure 7-4.

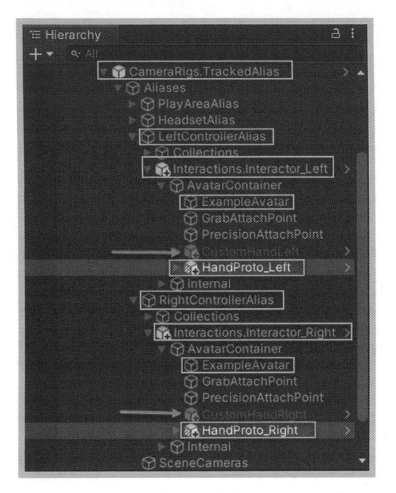

**Figure 7-4.** *Setup for testing the grabbing mechanism on Hand Proto Left and Hand Proto Right*

Ensure that within the [VRTK_CAMERA_RIGS_SETUP] game object, you have only the Camera Rigs, Spatial Simulator, and Camera Rigs, Tracked Alias game objects active. Then, hit the Play button and wait for your scene to load in Unity's editor.

Maneuver yourself to move closer to the table by using the *W*, *A*, *S*, and *D* keys on your keyboard. Position yourself so that your Right hand slightly penetrates the white cube on the table. Now click the right mouse button. You'll notice that you have grabbed the cube. Upon releasing the right mouse button, the cube will fall from your hand. Now try grabbing the cube with your Left hand by positioning yourself such that your Left hand is penetrating the white cube on the table slightly. Now click the left mouse button.

You'll notice that you have grabbed the cube. Upon releasing the left mouse button, the cube will fall from your hand. You can now grab the white cube using your custom-provided prototype hands.

While still in Playtest mode, select both Example Avatar game objects in the hierarchy and deactivate the Box Collider component within the Inspector. Now return to your Game window and try to grab the white cube with either your Left or Right hand. Whatever you do, you will no longer be able to grab the white cube. This indicates that the Box collider on your cuboid hands is working in conjunction with the Rigidbody on your Interactors to allow your grab mechanism to function. Essentially, you need some collider set up as a Trigger on your custom prototype hands, currently available to you via the Example Avatar game object. Finally, exit Play mode.

# The Grab Mechanism with Oculus-Provided Hands

The Example Avatar game object is not only an integral part of your custom-provided prototype hands; it is also required by your Oculus-provided hands to have their grabbing mechanism function.

As shown in Figure 7-3, select one of the Oculus-provided hands, either the Custom Hand Left or Custom Hand Right, from within the hierarchy. Expand the hand until you see its child game objects Grab Volume Big and Grab Volume Small. Upon examining these game objects in the Inspector, you'll see that both have been fitted with capsule colliders with their Is Trigger property checked. Logically this entails that you won't require the Example Avatar with its Box collider to be set up as a Trigger to enable the grabbing mechanism when using the Oculus-provided hands, as they already have the required trigger colliders on them. However, it would be interesting to understand at a deeper level exactly how this grab mechanism is being triggered to enable it to function with your Oculus-provided hands.

To engage (trigger) the Interactors Grab mechanism, the collision Trigger event on the Box collider of the Example Avatar game object must reach the Rigidbody on the Interactions Interactor game object. For its grab action mechanism to function, the VRTK requires that a touching collider event be received at its Interactor game object level, where it has a Rigidbody component present. In Unity, Collision Trigger events are propagated only up to the closest Rigidbody available. In the setup where you're using your Proto hands, you won't face any issues. There is just one intermediate Trigger Collider in the hierarchy (on the Example Avatar) between your Hand Proto game object and its Interactions Interactor game object. However, this isn't the case with your Oculus-provided hands, where trigger colliders exist on the game objects, Grab Volume Big, Grab Volume Small, and Example Avatar, thereby not allowing a touching collider event to be received at the Interactor game object level. Here, a Rigidbody component is present, thus not allowing the grabbing mechanism to trigger.

Looking at the Oculus-provided hand, Custom Hand Right, you'll see that it has capsule colliders set up as a trigger within its child game objects Grab Volume Big and Grab Volume Small. Now, when a collision trigger event occurs, it will only reach as far as the Rigidbody on the Custom Hand Right game object. Its collision trigger event will never get to the Rigidbody on the Interactions Interactor game object. As stated in the previous paragraph, the VRTK requires that, for its grab action mechanism to be engaged, a touching collider event be received at its Interactor game object level, where it has a Rigidbody component present. As this is not the case with your Custom Hand Right game object, the Interactors grab mechanism will never be triggered. Unity's rule specifying that Collision Trigger events are propagated only up to the closest Rigidbody available ensures that the touching collider event reaches only as far as the Rigidbody on the Custom Hand Right game object.

To work around this setback, you could remove the Rigidbody component on the Custom Hand Right game object. The Collision Trigger events would then propagate up to the Rigidbody on the Interactions Interactor game object. However, the moment you attempt to remove the Rigidbody component on the Custom Hand Right game object, you will be notified that the OVR Grabber component depends on it. Well, you have disabled the OVR Grabber component, so you may as well remove it. Attempting to remove the OVR Grabber component notifies you that the Hand component depends on it. You can't remove the Hand component as required, and as all these components are dependent on one another, you have no choice but to live with the Rigidbody component on the Custom Hand Right game object.

Ideally, you don't want to mess around with changing code in the OVR Grabber and Hand components, as you don't want to break anything in the Oculus-provided hand prefab.

The simplest way is to ignore the capsule colliders and the Rigidbody in the Custom Hand Right game object. You have the Example Avatar game object with its Trigger Box collider available, so all you need is to allow it to be a part of your Oculus-provided hands. This way, you may use its trigger collider to communicate collision trigger events to the Rigidbody on the Interactions Interactor game object.

# Setting Up the Example Avatar Object

As you will need to share the Example Avatar game object between the custom prototype hands and the Oculus-provided hands for each of your controllers, you should position this Example Avatar cuboid object appropriately to work well with both types of hands. To ensure this happens, you'll first align your Hand Proto Left as closely as possible to your Oculus-provided Custom Hand Left. Once they are well aligned and overlapping, you'll go about aligning the Example Avatar game object appropriately so that the grabbing functionality works well regardless of whether you're using the custom prototype hands or the Oculus-provided hands. Getting these alignments right requires that you adjust the values and then test to see how it looks. You may want to tweak the provided values to suit your liking. These values have been obtained by physically moving the Hand Proto game object in the scene view and getting it to best align with its Oculus Custom Hand counterpart. This exercise needs to be performed for both Left and Right hands.

Within the hierarchy, ensure that you expand the Camera Rigs, Tracked Alias to replicate what's shown in Figure 7-3. First, activate both of the Oculus-provided hands: Custom Hand Left and Custom Hand Right. Double-click on either of these hands to enable it to obtain focus. Using the Axis gizmo available in the right top corner within scene view, orient your hands to face forward and preferably with a top view. You'll notice that your custom prototype hands and Oculus-provided hands are entwined. If you select your Oculus-provided hands, Custom Hand Left and Custom Hand Right, you'll notice that their Transform Position values across $X$, $Y$, and $Z$ are all zero.

Next, from within the hierarchy, select the Hand Proto Left game object. Set the Transform Position values in the Inspector as follows: $X$ = -0.0312; $Y$ = -0.0207; and $Z$ = -0.022. Your left hands have now been aligned. You may want to further fine-tune these values to your liking.

Now let's align your right hands. From within the hierarchy, select the Hand Proto Right game object. Set the Transform Position values in the Inspector as follows: $X$ = 0.038; $Y$ = -0.02; and $Z$ = -0.015. Your right hands have now been aligned. You may want to further fine-tune these values to your liking.

Last, you need to align the Example Avatar game objects available within your left and right Interactions Interactor game objects. You should align these Example Avatar cuboid game objects to be positioned within the middle of your hands. When these game objects make contact with an Interactable object, and upon pressing the Grip button on your controller, its grabbing mechanism will be triggered. The Example Avatar cuboid game object controls the triggering of the grabbing mechanism, not the hands. The hands only play the appropriate animation to make the grab look realistic.

Select the Example Avatar game object nested in the Interactions Interactor Left game object from within the hierarchy. Set its Transform Position values as follows: $X$ = -0.0076; $Y$ = -0.0298; and $Z$ = -0.0253. You may want to further fine-tune these values to your liking. With the Example Avatar game object still selected, deactivate its Mesh Renderer component within the Inspector. This ensures that you will no longer see the left cuboid hand.

Next, select the Example Avatar game object nested in the Interactions Interactor Right game object from within the hierarchy. Set its Transform Position values as follows: $X$ = 0.0156; $Y$ = -0.024; and $Z$ = 0.008. You may want to further fine-tune these values to your liking. With the Example Avatar game object still selected, deactivate its Mesh Renderer component within the Inspector. This ensures that you will no longer see the right cuboid hand.

Lastly, ensure that you keep either the custom prototype hands or the Oculus-provided hands active. You don't want both types of hands to be active in the hierarchy. The one you choose to keep active depends on which VR device you're using.

If you have an Oculus headset, it would be good to test that your grabbing mechanism works with the Oculus-provided hands. Ensure that you activate your Oculus-provided hands and deactivate the custom prototype hands. Also, make sure that Camera Rigs, Oculus Integration is activated and Camera Rigs, Unity XR, Camera Rigs, Spatial Simulator are deactivated.

If you have an Xbox controller hooked to your computer, you can test the grabbing mechanism using the Bumper buttons. You'll need to ensure that you have the Camera Rigs, Spatial Simulator active.

As locomotion hasn't yet been set up against your controllers, you'll still need to move using the $W$, $A$, $S$, and $D$ keys on your keyboard. Locomotion will be dealt with in an upcoming chapter.

Congratulations! You now have your VR hands working and can grab objects, too.

# Setting Up Velocity Trackers

When an Interactor grabs an Interactable object, you may require that the Interactor's velocity be applied to the Interactable object. For example, if you pick up a ball and throw it, you may want the speed you're moving your controller at to be applied to the ball so that you can control the power of your throw. In VR, it's mostly your Headset, Left Controller and Right Controller that can move freely in the virtual world, so ideally, it would be one of these objects whose velocity you would track. Your VRTK Camera Rigs, Tracked Alias prefab, already has the relevant Velocity Tracker components on the appropriate aliases.

Within the hierarchy, navigate to [VRTK_CAMERA_RIGS_SETUP] ➤ Camera Rigs, Tracked Alias ➤ Aliases. Select the three game objects in the hierarchy: Headset Alias, Left Controller Alias, and Right Controller Alias. Within the Inspector, you'll notice that these objects all contain the Velocity Tracker Processor component responsible for tracking the concerned device velocity, see Figure 7-5.

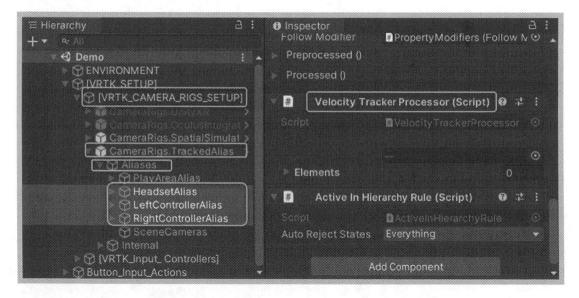

***Figure 7-5.*** *Velocity Tracker Processor component available on the Headset Alias, Left Controller Alias, and Right Controller Alias*

Let's set up the velocity tracker against your left and right Interactors. In the hierarchy, select and expand the Left and Right Controller Alias game objects. Select the Interactions Interactor Left game object. In the Inspector, ensure that the Interactor Facade component has been expanded. You'll see that a Velocity Tracker property is available within the Interactor Settings section. Drag and drop the Left Controller Alias from the hierarchy into this Velocity Tracker property, as shown in Figure 7-6.

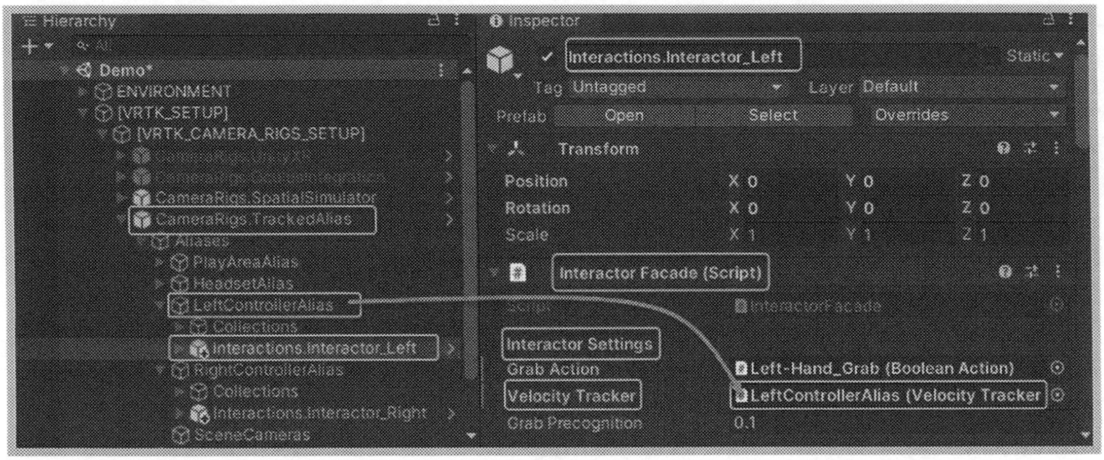

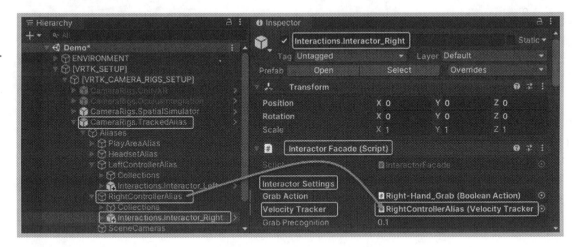

***Figure 7-6.*** *Setting up the Velocity Tracker against the Left Interactor*

Next, select the Interactions Interactor Right game object within the hierarchy. In the Inspector, ensure that the Interactor Facade component has been expanded. You'll see that a Velocity Tracker property is available in the Interactor Settings section. Drag and drop the Right Controller Alias from the hierarchy into this Velocity Tracker property, as shown in Figure 7-7.

***Figure 7-7.*** *Setting up the Velocity Tracker against the Right Interactor*

# Summary

In this chapter, we went over how to get your Interactor grab mechanism to work against your custom prototype hands and the Oculus-provided hands. Setting up the grab mechanism to work with your custom prototype hands was very straightforward, but setting it up for the Oculus-provided hands was not as clear. We had to delve deeper into understanding how collision trigger events are propagated in Unity, up to its closest Rigidbody. We saw how the Rigidbody and colliders provided as part of the Oculus hands are a sort of roadblock in getting your grab mechanism working. You learned how to circumvent this roadblock without the use of code. You then learned how to set up your Example Avatar game object to be shared between your custom prototype hands and the Oculus-provided hands. Finally, you learned how to set up velocity trackers against your VR controllers.

# CHAPTER 8

# Interactable Game Objects

As discussed previously, an Interactable is a game object in the virtual world that a user can interact with. Now that you have your Interactors and your grabbing mechanism working, it's time to set up Interactions with real-life objects. In the last chapter, you learned how to interact with a cube game object. In this chapter, you'll learn how to pick up Interactable objects using precision pickup points, as well as how to set up custom orientation handles on Interactable objects. You'll also learn about the various secondary actions that you can set up on your Interactable objects. These secondary actions allow you to swap an object between your hands, perform a two-handed grab against an object, and guide the object using your secondary grabbing hand, as well as to scale an object.

## Picking Up Objects

With the VRTK, as with all VR tool kits, you can't just pick up any object. For an object to be grabbable, it must be set up as an Interactable object. In the last chapter, we created an Interactable cube game object that could be picked up. In this chapter, we'll set up a couple of Interactable objects that you can pick up using either of your controllers (hands).

An Interactable game object can be notified about Interactor actions, such as an Interactor touch. It can also react to input actions, such as a Grip press. Interactable game objects can perform two actions depending upon which Interactor is acting upon it. In the case of the Interactable white cube we set up in the last chapter, either our left or right Interactor could grab it depending on which Interactor grabbed it first.

The first grab attempt from an Interactor is called the Primary Grab action. While this is occurring, any Secondary grab attempt from a different Interactor is called the Secondary Grab action. For example, if you had a long weapon such as a sniper rifle, you would ideally need both hands to manage it. If you were to grab the trigger hold

© Christopher Coutinho 2022
C. Coutinho, *Unity® Virtual Reality Development with VRTK4*, https://doi.org/10.1007/978-1-4842-7933-5_8

of this sniper rifle with your right hand, then a Primary Grab action would have been performed by your right hand, or right Interactor. To ensure that you can aim well using the scope on the sniper rifle, you will need to support it with your left hand, which means your left hand needs to grab the rifle somewhere on the front to stabilize it. This left-hand grab, in addition to the ongoing right-hand grab, is referred to as the Secondary Grab action. It occurs via a different Interactor; namely, your left Interactor. You may or may not want a secondary grab to occur, the choice of which can be configured on the Interactable via its Interactable Facade component.

As you'll be testing out most of the properties of your Interactable objects via the Spatial Simulator, ensure that you have deactivated the Oculus-provided hands— namely, the Custom Hand Left and Custom Hand Right—within the hierarchy. Also, ensure that your Hand Proto Left and Hand Proto Right hands have been activated to represent the hands that the Camera Rigs, Spatial Simulator and Camera Rigs, Unity XR can use. Last, make sure that Camera Rigs, Spatial Simulator has been activated and Camera Rigs, Unity XR and Camera Rigs, Oculus Integration have been deactivated.

Select the white cube Interactable object in your Demo scene, available in the Environment game object in the hierarchy. Double-click it to enable it to obtain focus. Scroll down to the Interactable Facade component in the Inspector. You'll notice that there are two actions an Interactable object can perform: the Primary Action, which is visible within the Primary Action Settings section, and the Secondary Action, which is visible within the Secondary Action Settings section.

First, let's examine the Primary Action property, which allows you the functionality to pick up (grab). Locate the Primary Action property within the Interactable Facade component in the Inspector. Note that its drop-down value has been set to Interactable Grab Action Follow. This indicates that it should follow its grabbing Interactor (hand) once the Interactable is grabbed. We tested the ability to grab an Interactable object in the last chapter, and it worked well. However, if you want an object to be un-grabbable, probably at a certain point during gameplay, you can change this property's setting to Interactable Grab Action None. This will ensure that your Interactors can no longer grab the white cube, see Figure 8-1.

Let's test this out now. Set the drop-down value for the white cubes' Primary Action property to Interactable Grab Action None. Now playtest the Demo scene using the Spatial Simulator and pick up the white cube sitting on the table with your left or right hand. You won't be able to, as its Primary Action property has been set to Interactable Grab Action None. Reset the Primary Action property to Interactable Grab Action Follow.

The drop-down action, Custom, available to both the Primary and Secondary Action, is utilized if you intend to code the Grab action yourself. In this case, the Interactable custom editor won't override any custom changes.

Now, look at the Grab Action Settings section located above the Primary Action Settings. Here, the Grab Type property has been set to Hold Till Release. This indicates that you must have the Grip button on your controller pressed continually to hold onto an Interactable object. The moment you release the Grip button, an ungrab will occur and the object will fall out of your hand. You've already tested this out in the last chapter and know that it works.

Next, set the Grab Type property to Toggle and let's test it out. We can playtest your Demo scene using the Spatial Simulator. Pick up the white cube using your right hand by clicking the right mouse button. But don't keep the right mouse button pressed down continually; release it once you have grabbed onto the cube. Note that the cube stays attached to your hand. To ungrab the white cube, simply click the right mouse button again. You'll notice that the cube falls from your hand. That's how the Toggle option works. A single mouse button click or Grip button press grabs the Interactable object, while a subsequent mouse button click or Grip button press ungrabs it, see Figure 8-1.

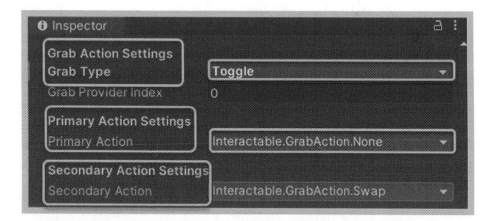

*Figure 8-1.* *Some properties of an Interactable Object available within its Interactable Facade component: Grab Type, Primary Action, and Secondary Action*

# The Follow Tracking Property

With the white cube selected in the hierarchy and its Interactable Facade component expanded in the Inspector, locate the Follow Settings section and then the Follow Tracking property that has been set to Follow Transform. The option Follow Transform will allow your cube Interactable object to pass through other objects with colliders on them. Let's try it out.

Hit the Play button to playtest your Demo scene using Unity's editor. Grab the white cube on the table and walk forward using the *W* key on your keyboard to approach the container in front of you. If you try pushing the white cube through the container, you'll notice that it passes through easily. Using the *W*, *A*, *S*, and *D* keys, maneuver yourself close to the ladder. Now try pushing the white cube through the sides of the ladder or any of its rungs. You'll find that it passes through easily. Both the ladder and container have been fitted with colliders. However, your white cube doesn't collide with them; instead, it passes through. This may be the effect you desire or possibly not. Now, hit the Play button to stop your Demo scene from playing.

Suppose you don't want your Interactable objects passing through other objects that have colliders on them. In that case, you'll need to set the Follow Tracking property on your Interactable object to Follow Rigidbody. Let's try it out now. After setting the Follow Tracking property to Follow Rigidbody, hit the Play button to playtest your Demo scene using Unity's editor. Grab the white cube on the table and walk forward by pressing the *W* key on your keyboard to approach the container in front of you. Try pushing the white cube through the container and you'll see that it won't pass through. Using the *W*, *A*, *S*, and *D* keys, maneuver yourself so that you're close to the ladder. Now try pushing the white cube through the sides of the ladder or any of its rungs. You'll see that it won't pass through. Instead, it collides and rolls about as if being dragged around by your hand. This may be the outcome you desire. Figure 8-2 shows the Follow Tracking property set to the value Follow Rigidbody. The other options available in the Follow Tracking property are used with the Angular drives provided by the VRTK that we'll explore in a later chapter. Now, set the Follow Tracking property to Follow Transform.

***Figure 8-2.*** *The Follow Tracking Property set to Follow Rigidbody*

# Picking Up an Interactable Object Using Precise Grab Points

A precision grab gives you the ability to grab an Interactable object at the point your Interactor collides with it. To set this up, all you need to do is set the Grab Offset property to Precision Point. To demonstrate a precision grab, we'll use a lifelike object, which you'll need to download from the Unity Asset store at https://assetstore.unity.com/packages/3d/props/industrial/workplace-tools-86242. Log in to the Unity Asset store and search for the freely available asset "Workplace Tools." Download and import these tools into your project. After that's complete, you'll see that a new "Workplace Tools" folder has been added to your "Assets" folder.

Before looking at the *Grab Offset* property, let's explore the white cube Interactable game object available in the Environment game object of the hierarchy. Select and expand your white cube game object and then expand its Mesh Container game object, and you'll notice the cube game object you've been interacting with so far. Select this object in the hierarchy and look at the Inspector. You'll see that it comprises a cube mesh with a default material and a Box Collider. To make any object Interactable, you must change the Mesh property here and use an appropriate collider that correctly encompasses the new object's mesh shape. Another way to make an object Interactable is to drag a prefab of the object (that contains a mesh) onto the Mesh Container game object nested within the white cube object, making a child of the game object. Then, you need to disable the cube game object nested within the Mesh Container game object. Let's set this up now so that you can replace your white cube mesh with the Drill Machine prefab available in your "Workplace Tools" folder.

Within the "Assets" folder in your Project tab, navigate to the "Workplace Tools" folder and select the "Prefabs" folder. You'll see that the right pane contains a Drill prefab. Ensure that the Mesh Container game object, nested within the white cube game object, has been selected. Drag and drop the Drill prefab onto the Mesh Container game object selected in the hierarchy, making it a child. Finally, disable the cube object nested within the Mesh Container game object. Now, you've replaced your default dull-white cube mesh with a more realistic Drill machine. In the hierarchy, select the parent white cube game object and rename it "Drill Machine."

Let's now scale, position, and set up appropriate colliders for your Drill machine. Select and expand the Drill game object nested within the Mesh Container game object. With the Drill game object selected, right-click it, and from the context menu that pops up, select Prefab ➤ Unpack Completely. Then, select the Drill Machine game object in the hierarchy and set the Transform Scale property for $X$, $Y$, and $Z$ to 0.25. Next, set its Transform Position values as follows: $X$ = -12.831; $Y$ = 0.8436; and $Z$ = -4.213. This ensures that your Drill machine will sit well on the table. Double-click the Drill Machine game object in the hierarchy to enable it to obtain focus so that you can ensure that it is sitting well on the table. You may want to fine-tune these values to your liking.

Now ensure that the Drill game object nested within the Drill Machine has been expanded in the hierarchy. Select its Body, Top Front, and Trigger Main child game objects in the hierarchy. From within the Inspector, remove the Mesh Collider component from all of these child game objects. (Mesh colliders are expensive.) Now select the Body child game object in the hierarchy and add a Box collider component to it. Use the Edit Collider property within the Box collider component to ensure that the Box collider encompasses the Drill Machine well. The default Box collider settings worked well for me. You don't need to set up any collider for the Top Front and Trigger Main child game objects, even though you can if you want to. Figure 8-3 displays the setup for your Drill machine.

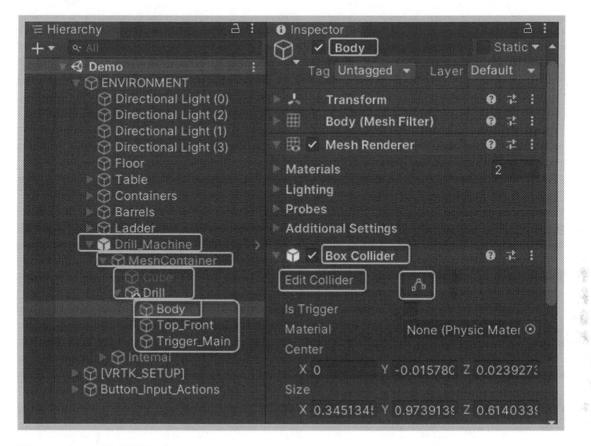

*Figure 8-3. Drill Machine setup*

Let's now proceed to set up the Grab Offset property so that you can grab your Drill Machine at a precise point. With the Grab Offset property value set to None, grabbing an Interactable object will result in the Interactable's origin point snapping to the Interactor's origin point. If you were to playtest your Demo scene now, this is how grabbing the Drill Machine would work. Go ahead and give it a try.

You'll see that this works well for basic grabs, like grabbing your cube. However, you may want to grab an Interactable object from a precise predefined position. You may even want to orient it to your Interactor in a particular position and rotation. You can achieve a precision point grab using the Grab Offset property available in the Interactable Facade component. Now that we have a Drill machine that has a distinct shape, let's set up its Grab Offset property so that it can be grabbed at a predefined precise point. Currently, with its Grab Offset property set to *None*, you can grab it on its handle, which is its origin point.

Precision Point allows you to grab your Drill Machine Interactable object at the precise point at which your hand's Interactor collides with it. Select the Drill Machine game object in the hierarchy. In Interactable Facade component of the Inspector, locate the Grab Offset property and set its value to Precision Point, as shown in Figure 8-4.

**Figure 8-4.** *The Grab Offset Property set to Precision Point*

You can playtest your scene in Unity's editor by hitting the Play button. Once your Demo scene loads, approach your Drill Machine and try grabbing it at its Base using either your left or right hand. Note how you can grab the machine at a precise point. Now try grabbing the Drill Machine from the top, somewhere up-front, and note again how you can grab it precisely at the point you choose. Finally, hit the Play button to stop your Demo scene from playing.

# Custom Pickup Placements

To make it easier to interact with your Interactable item and make it feel more realistic, you may want the grabbing Interactor to position and rotate the Interactable item in a specific way when you pick the Interactable item up. This is an effective technique to use when you want your grabbed Interactable items to be oriented differently when grabbed.

To achieve the specific orientation you desire, you'll need to set the Grab Offset property value on your Drill Machine to Orientation Handle. Go ahead and set this property value and you'll see that a Show Orientation Container button immediately shows up below the Grab Offset property setting. Click this button and within the hierarchy window, your Drill Machine game object will automatically expand to display its Orientation Handles child game object, as shown in Figure 8-5.

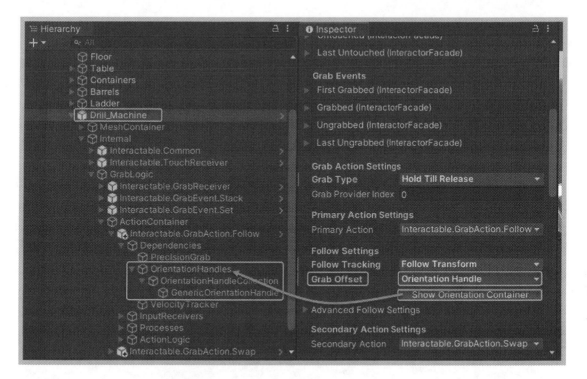

**Figure 8-5.** *Expanded Orientation Handles game object revealed upon clicking the Show Orientation Container button*

Now, expand the Orientation Handles game object in the hierarchy until you see the Generic Orientation Handle game object, as shown in Figure 8-6. Select this game object, and set the Transform Position values in the Inspector as follows: $X = 0$; $Y = 0.5$; and $Z = -0.5$. Set the Transform Rotation value for the $X$-axis to -90.

Test your scene in Unity's editor by hitting the Play button. Approach your Drill Machine, and grab it with either your left or right hand. You'll see that you have grabbed it by its rear top end.

You can fine-tune the grab position to your liking by adjusting the Generic Orientation Handle game object's position in the scene editor. This way, you can ensure that your hand grab looks more realistic, without being embedded within the Drill machine when grabbed.

With the Generic Orientation Handle game object still selected in the hierarchy, rename it "Generic Orientation Handle Right." This will be the grab orientation of your Drill machine when you grab it with your right hand. For your left hand, we'll set up a different grab orientation by duplicating the Generic Orientation Handle Right game object, renaming it "Generic Orientation Handle Left," and selecting it. It will remain a child of the Orientation Handle Collection game object. Set the Transform Rotation value for its $X$-axis to 90.

You now need to provide your orientation handles logic for using the Generic Orientation Handle Left and Right game objects whenever you grab the Drill machine with either hand.

In the hierarchy, select the Orientation Handles game object. Ensure that the Game Object Relations component has been expanded in the Inspector. Then, expand its Elements property, and you'll see that its size value is set to 1 by default. Change the size value to 2, and you'll see that two element slots, Element 0 and Element 1, are made available. Expand both slots. You'll see that the Value property for both slots has been populated with the Generic Orientation Handle Right game object. The Value property for Element 0 is fine. Now, drag and drop the Generic Orientation Handle Left game object from the hierarchy into the Element 1 slot Value property.

You now have two different orientation handles that you can choose from when grabbing your Drill Machine, see Figure 8-6.

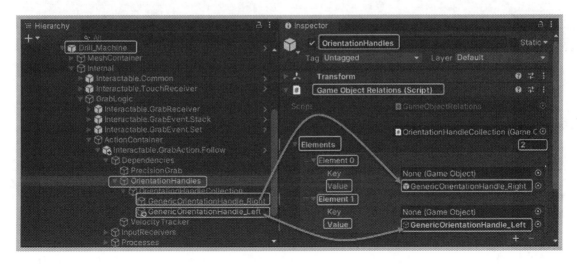

***Figure 8-6.*** *Setting up the left and right orientation handles*

You now need to instruct the Game Object Relations component, shown in Figure 8-6, about which Interactor needs to be paired up with which orientation handle. You've set up the Generic Orientation Handle Right to work with your right hand and the Generic Orientation Handle Left to work with your left hand. To let your Interactors know which orientation handle they should be paired up with, you need to associate your Interactions Interactor Right, available in your Right Controller Alias, with the Key property of the Element 0 slot.

Likewise, you need to associate your Interactions Interactor Left, available in your Left Controller Alias, with the Key property of the Element 1 slot.

Expand the Camera Rigs, Tracked Alias game object in the hierarchy until you locate its Interactions Interactor Left game object nested within the Left Controller Alias. Next, with the Camera Rigs, Tracked Alias game object still expanded, locate the Interactions Interactor Right game object nested within the Right Controller Alias.

Within the hierarchy, you should have your Orientation Handles game object for the Drill Machine still expanded. Select this Orientation Handles game object. In the Inspector, you need to populate the Key properties for the Element 0 and Element 1 slots. Scroll down within the hierarchy so that you can see the Camera Rigs, Tracked Alias game object. Drag and drop the Interactions Interactor Right game object from the hierarchy into the Key property of the Element 0 slot of the Game Object Relations component. Then, drag and drop the Interactions Interactor Left game object into the Key property of the Element 1 slot in the Game Object Relations component.

Now, look at the Game Object Relations component in the Inspector. It clarifies things to know that the Interactions Interactor Right game object has been paired with the Generic Orientation Handle Right game object, as well as that the Interactions Interactor Left game object has been paired with the Generic Orientation Handle Left game object. This can be seen in Figure 8-7.

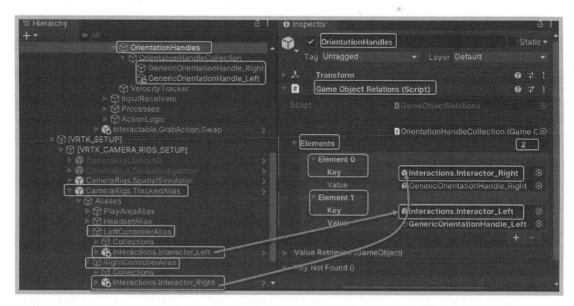

***Figure 8-7.*** *Pairing up your Interactors with the correct orientation handles*

Using this simple setup, you can create many more orientation handles and then associate them with the Value property of the Game Object Relations component to grab an object so that it may be oriented differently.

Now, playtest your scene within Unity's editor by hitting the Play button. Once your Demo scene loads, approach your Drill Machine and grab it using your right hand, noticing the way it is oriented (facing downward). Drop the Drill Machine from your right hand onto the table and then grab it using your left hand. You will notice that it oriented itself differently (facing upward) than when you right hand grabbed it. The orientation for each hand changes based upon the way your generic orientation handles are set up.

# Adding Secondary Grab Actions to Interactable Objects

So far, you have set up a Primary Grab action on your Interactable object. The first grab attempt from an Interactor against an Interactable object is called a Primary Grab action. A secondary grab attempt from a different Interactor against the same interactable object that takes place while the primary grab is occurring is called a Secondary Grab action. The next section will show you to set up some commonly used Secondary Grab actions against your Interactable object.

## Swapping Objects between Hands with a Secondary Grab Action

The most common Secondary Grab action that you can use is the Interactable Grab Action Swap. This Secondary Grab action allows you to swap an Interactable object back and forth between your hands.

For testing out these Secondary Grab actions, you need to use your VR headset. I would advise that your switch to the Camera Rigs, Unity XR setup, as you can test both Oculus and HTC Vive devices using this setup. Ensure that you deactivate Camera Rigs, Oculus Integration and Camera Rigs, Spatial Simulator. The Camera Rigs, Tracked Alias should always be active.

Select the Drill Machine located within the Environment game object in the hierarchy. Ensure that its Interactable Facade component has been expanded. Locate the Secondary Action property, which can be found within the Secondary Action Settings section. Select the Interactable Grab Action Swap option from its drop-down, as shown in Figure 8-8.

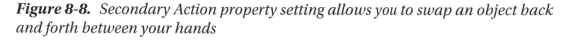

*Figure 8-8.* *Secondary Action property setting allows you to swap an object back and forth between your hands*

Now, hit the Play button in the Unity editor to playtest your Demo scene using your VR headset. As soon as it starts playing, mount your VR headset. Grab the Drill Machine with your right hand, and then, using your left hand, grab the Drill Machine out of your right hand. You will notice that it snaps to your left hand. Thus the Interactable object is now being swapped between your hands. Swap the Drill Machine back and forth between your hands to get a feel of the Swap Secondary Grab action working. Once satisfied, exit the Play mode.

Now set the Secondary Action property to Interactable Grab Action None. Hit the Play button within the Unity editor to playtest your Demo scene, again using your VR headset. Mount your VR headset as soon as your the scene starts playing. Grab the Drill Machine with your right hand, and then, using your left hand, try grabbing the Drill Machine out of your right hand. You will notice that you won't be able to. This is because you have set the Secondary Action property to Interactable Grab Action None.

## Performing a Two-Handed Grab with a Secondary Grab Action

A two-handed grab is handy to use on longer objects, like a rifle, that need to be supported by a secondary hand. It provides secondary hand support and allows you to guide the direction of the object using your secondary hand.

Before setting up this two-handed Secondary Grab action, ensure that the Grab Type property for your Drill Machine has been set to Hold Till Release. Also, set the Grab Offset property to Precision Point.

With the Drill Machine game object still selected in the hierarchy, set its Secondary Action property to Interactable Grab Action Control Direction, as shown in Figure 8-9. This Interactable Grab Action Control Direction setting allows you to perform this two-handed grab.

*Figure 8-9.* *Secondary Action property setting that allows you to set up a two-handed grab*

Hit the Play button within the Unity editor to playtest your Demo scene using your VR headset. As soon as the scene starts playing, mount your VR headset. Grab the Drill Machine with your right hand, which is now your primary grabbing hand, and then grab the Drill Machine somewhere at the front with your left hand. After that, move your left hand up, down, left, and right. Notice how you can control the direction your Drill Machine faces by simply maneuvering your left hand. This Secondary Grab action would be beneficial if you created a First Person Shooter (FPS) game that used long weapons that require a two-handed grab.

# Scaling an Interactable Object with a Secondary Grab Action

You may find the need to scale the size of an object. For example, if you have a virtual tablet device within your app, you may want to provide the user the flexibility to scale this virtual tablet to make it either larger or smaller. This is easily achievable by setting the virtual tablet game objects' Secondary Action property to Interactable Grab action Scale. In this section, you'll set up the Secondary Action property on your Drill Machine to allow it to be scaled either up or down in size.

With the Drill Machine game object still selected in the hierarchy, set its Secondary Action property to Interactable Grab Action Scale, as shown in Figure 8-10. This Interactable Grab Action Scale setting is what allows you to scale your Drill machine in size.

***Figure 8-10.*** *Secondary Action property setting that allows you to scale an object*

Hit the Play button in the Unity editor to playtest your Demo scene using your VR headset. As soon as the scene starts playing, mount your VR headset. Grab the Drill Machine somewhere at the top with your right hand. Then, perform a secondary grab somewhere at the bottom of the Drill Machine with your left hand. After that, move both hands (controllers) away from each other to see your Drill Machine scale up in size. Now, move both hands (controllers) toward each other to see your Drill Machine scale down in size.

# Creating a Unity Layer for Interactable Objects

Finally, let's set up a Unity layer to which all Interactable objects within your scene will be assigned. We'll call this layer "Interactable." All interactable objects in your project must be assigned to this Layer.

From within the hierarchy, select the Drill Machine game object. Within the Inspector, click the Layer drop-down and select Add Layer. Ensure that the Layers drop-down is expanded in the Tags and Layers dialog box in the Inspector pane. In the Text Box for the first-available vacant User Layer, type in "Interactable" as the layer name. In the hierarchy, select the Drill Machine game object again. Note that within the Inspector, the Layer still shows "Default," as you have only created the Layer so far and not yet assigned it to your Drill Machine game object. Now, from the Layer drop-down in the Inspector, select the Interactable layer. You will be asked whether you want to set the layer to Interactable for all child objects. Click No, This Object Only.

For this newly created Interactable layer, you need to set up its Collision Matrix, which determines whether game objects assigned to different layers and to the same layer can collide.

From within Unity Editors main menu, select Edit ➤ Project Settings to bring up the Project Settings dialog. From the pane on the left, select Physics. You'll see your Layer Collision Matrix on the right with your newly added Interactable layer showing. Ensure that you uncheck the boxes Interactable and Ignore Ray Cast at the intersection of layers.

You don't want the objects in these two layers colliding with each other, which you'll learn the reasons for when you add a Pseudo body in a later chapter. Also, uncheck the boxes Interactable and Interactable at the intersection between layers. You may keep these checked if you want your Interactables to interact with each other. For now, though, leave them unchecked, as shown in Figure 8-11.

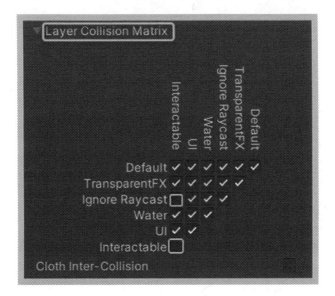

***Figure 8-11.***  *Layer Collision Matrix setup*

Note that you can access the Tags and Layer dialog to create new Tags or Layers from within Project Settings.

Last, navigate to the Example Avatar game objects, nested within the Avatar Container of your Interactions Interactor Left and Interactions Interactor Right game objects. Select these Example Avatar game objects, and note that they have been assigned to the Ignore Ray Cast Layer by default. The layer setting for these Example Avatar game objects will be recalled again in a later chapter.

# Summary

In this chapter, we took a deep dive into setting up interactable objects within the VRTK. We began by looking at how a Primary Grab action differs from a Secondary Grab action. We went on to set up and test different property values for the Primary Grab action. We tested out the two settings available to the Grab Type property. We then examined the Follow Tracking property and learned how to set it up to disallow an Interactable object from passing through other objects in our scene. We then imported a free asset from the Unity Asset Store in order to set up an Interactable object that is more realistic than the white cube in the scene. We learned how to set up the new Drill Machine game object to become an Interactable object. We then explored the Grab Offset property and learned how to pick up a Drill Machine using a precise point. We went over how to set up orientation handles against an interactable object, which allowed us to grab an object and orient it differently for each of our hands. We learned how to add Secondary Grab actions, including swapping an object back and forth between our hands, performing a two-handed grab against an object, and scaling an object in size, to our Interactable object. Last, we set up a Unity layer that we could assign all interactable objects in our scene too.

# CHAPTER 9

# Moving Around the Virtual World: Teleportation

The ability to move within the virtual world is an essential part of any VR experience. In this chapter, you'll learn how to get yourself moving in the virtual world. We'll begin by implementing a commonly employed movement scheme referred to as teleportation. Teleportation is not the only way to move around in your virtual world, though; the VRTK provides you with quite a few alternatives for movement, which we'll look at in upcoming chapters. VR movement, or locomotion, as it's commonly referred to, can assume many forms, and the VRTK provides you with a surfeit of mechanics when it comes to locomotion. Some of the different options available include teleportation, free movement, arm-swinging locomotion, and hulk style movement, as well as being allowed to walk to where you want to go in the virtual world, while being physically constrained to the boundaries of your Guardian or Chaperone. Some forms of locomotion, primarily free movement and rotation, may cause nausea if you aren't used to performing them in a VR setting. If you start to feel any discomfort, take a break and get some fresh air.

In this chapter, you'll learn to implement the three forms of teleportation that the VRTK provides: Instant Teleport, Dash Teleport, and Teleport Targets, which all cover long distances. You'll learn how to set up an arrow pointer on your controllers that you can use to rotate yourself in the virtual world. You'll finally learn how to set up a Unity NavMesh for Teleportation.

## Teleport Locomotion

The main reason why teleportation is so prevalent in VR is that it helps avoid motion sickness. Motion sickness occurs when there's a mismatch between what you see and what you feel. Teleportation allows you to move the user from place to place rather

© Christopher Coutinho 2022
C. Coutinho, *Unity® Virtual Reality Development with VRTK4*, https://doi.org/10.1007/978-1-4842-7933-5_9

than having them move smoothly within the virtual world. Teleportation may break the illusion of immersion, but at the same time, it entirely avoids motion sickness, as it doesn't create a sense of motion at all. If the illusion of immersive movement is not a priority, then the teleport form of locomotion is ideal. For example, it could be used in a VR history museum setting to allow users to teleport from artifact to artifact.

Before we begin setting up teleportation using the VRTK, let's look at how it works. When you press the designated teleport button on your VR controller, a ray-cast is fired from your head or hand until it either collides with an object that you can teleport against or reaches its desired distance. If the layer for your teleport area (Floor) has been set up for teleportation, the VRTK's teleport pointer turns green, indicating that a teleporting movement is possible. However, if no valid area for teleportation can be found, the VRTK's teleport pointer will stay red, indicating that a teleporting movement can't happen. When you release the designated teleport button, depending on when you want the teleportation to occur, you'll be repositioned at the point where the ray-cast collided if a valid teleport area is found.

## Capturing Inputs to Trigger Teleportation

In Chapter 6, we went over how to set up several intermediary game objects—namely, the Left-Hand Grab and Right-Hand Grab—-into which varied device inputs involved with a left- or right-hand grab action could be channeled. We also consolidated input for either a Right or Left Thumbstick press into two intermediary game objects: Right-Hand Thumbstick Press and Left-Hand Thumbstick Press. All the above intermediary game objects reside in the Button Input Actions game object. Any game object interested in listening for these button actions could then poll these intermediary game objects. This section will use this same approach to channel input actions that trigger a teleport into an intermediary game object.

A teleport can be triggered in one of four ways: by pressing the *T* key on the keyboard, by pressing the Left Thumbstick button on the Oculus controller, by pressing the Left Trackpad button on the HTC Vive controller, and by pressing the Left Thumbstick button on the Xbox controller. Each of these four input actions need to be channeled into an intermediary game object.

Let's begin by setting up an intermediary game object into which to channel these input actions. In the hierarchy, select and expand the Button Input Actions game object. Create a new empty game object within it and rename it "Curved Teleport Ray Pointer."

With this game object selected in the hierarchy, click the Add Component button in the Inspector. Add a Boolean Action component to this game object. With the Boolean Action component expanded, locate the Sources property and set its size to 4. Four element slots will be made available and you will have four input actions that you need to listen for.

As you probably noted in Chapter 6, the VRTK doesn't provide you with an out-of-the-box prefab to capture keyboard input for every key on your keyboard. You need to set this up, just as you did for capturing input for the *Q* and *P* keys in Chapter 6. Here you will capture input when the *T* key is pressed.

Select the VRTK Input Controllers game object from within the hierarchy and expand its Keyboard Input child game object. Select the Input Unity Input Manager Button Action P game object in the hierarchy and duplicate it. Rename the copied game object "Input Unity Input Manager Button Action *T*." With this game object selected in the hierarchy, locate its Key Code property in the Inspector, and in the drop-down, select the letter *T*. The input mapping for the *T* key will now allow you to listen for a *T* key press on the keyboard. You could capture several key presses using this procedure.

Now, let's begin hooking up all input actions to trigger a teleport into the Curved Teleport Ray Pointer intermediary game object by following these steps:

1. From within the hierarchy, with the VRTK Input Controllers game object expanded, ensure that the Keyboard Input game object has been expanded.

2. Expand the Input, Unity Input Manager, Oculus Touch Left Controller game object. Then expand its Input Actions game object, followed by expanding its Left Thumbstick game object.

3. Expand the Input, Unity Input Manager, Open VR Left Controller game object. Then expand its Input Actions game object, followed by expanding its Left Trackpad game object.

4. Finally, expand the Input, Unity Input Manager, X-Box Controller game object. Then expand its Input Actions game object, followed by expanding its Left Thumbstick game object.

With these input sources expanded, let's now capture input for when the left-hand Thumbstick or the *T* key is pressed. Select the Curved Teleport Ray Pointer game object from within the hierarchy, a child of the Button Input Actions game object. Note that your Boolean Action Sources property has four element slots in the Inspector, as shown in Figure 9-1. Now follow these steps:

1.  From within the expanded Input, Unity Input Manager, Oculus Touch Left Controller game object, drag and drop the Left Thumbstick Press [8] game object into the Element 0 slot of the Sources property, as shown in Figure 9-1.

2.  From within the expanded Input, Unity Input Manager, Open VR Left Controller game object, drag and drop the Left Trackpad Press [8] game object into the Element 1 slot of the Sources property, as shown in Figure 9-1.

3.  From within the expanded Input, Unity Input Manager, X-Box Controller game object, drag and drop the Left Thumbstick Press [8] game object into the Element 2 slot of the Sources property, as shown in Figure 9-1.

4.  From within the expanded Keyboard Input game object, drag and drop the Input, Unity Input manager, Button action T game object into the Element 3 slot of the Sources property, as shown in Figure 9-1.

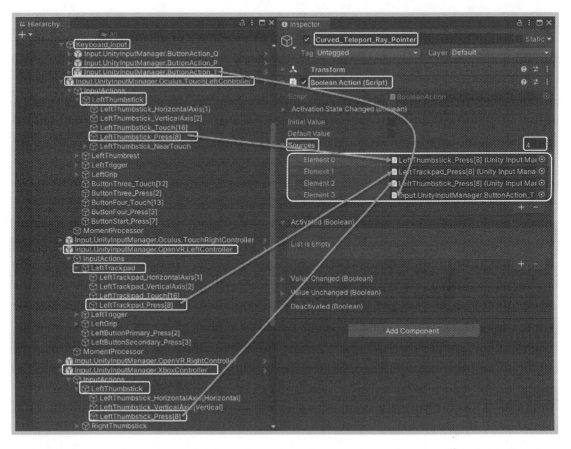

***Figure 9-1.*** *Hooking up Left Thumbstick and* T *Key (press) inputs to the Curved Teleport Ray Pointer intermediary game object*

## Setting Up a Curved Teleport Pointer

One of the prerequisites for implementing teleportation is having a pointer in the scene. The Curved Pointer, also known as a Bezier Pointer, casts a curved beam from an origin point a certain distance into the world and then down, until it collides with a collider. As this curved beam almost always collides with the Floor, the Curved Pointer has become a popular choice when implementing teleport locomotion.

First, let's set up this Curved Pointer. In the hierarchy, select the VRTK SETUP game object and create an empty child game object within it. Rename this child game object "VRTK RAY POINTERS." All your pointers, curved or straight, will reside here. This will allow you to locate them quickly.

Select the Project tab and expand the "Packages" folder. Locate the "Tilia Indicators, Object Pointers, Unity folder" and expand it until you reach its "Prefabs" folder. Select the "Prefabs" folder, and from the pane on the right, drag and drop the Indicators, Object Pointers, Curved prefab onto the VRTK RAY POINTERS game object in the hierarchy. You have now set up your first curved pointer as a child of the VRTK RAY POINTERS game object. Select this curved pointer and rename it "Layer Teleport Curved Pointer" to indicate that it will allow teleportation anywhere within a valid Teleport Layer in your virtual world.

There are two ways you can teleport about in your virtual world: first, by teleporting onto any object that has been assigned a valid Teleport Layer, and second, by using explicitly defined Teleport Targets, as will be seen in a later section (Teleporting using Teleport Targets) of this chapter.

With the Layer Teleport Curved Pointer game object selected in the hierarchy, look at the Inspector and ensure that its Pointer Facade component has been expanded. Locate the Follow Source property in the Pointer Settings section of the Pointer Facade component. It's this property that determines which game object the teleport ray should originate from. If you want your Layer Teleport Curved Pointer to originate from your Left Controller, then drag and drop the Left Controller Alias game object into this Follow Source property. If you want your Layer Teleport Curved Pointer to originate from your Right Controller, then drag and drop the Right Controller Alias game object into this Follow Source property.

Throughout this book, you'll have all your curved teleport pointers originate from your Headset. In many scenarios, it is preferable to allow players to select the area to which to teleport using their head rather than their hands. For example, in a VR FPS (First Person Shooter), when you're dual-wielding guns, you wouldn't want to aim the gun at the Floor just so that you can teleport.

In the hierarchy, expand the VRTK CAMERA RIGS SETUP game object. Then expand its Camera Rigs, Tracked Alias game object and drag and drop the Headset Alias game object into the Follow Source property. Your Layer Teleport Curved Pointer will be deactivated by default.

The Activation Action Property in the Pointer Settings section accepts a Boolean action. It will be responsible for activating and deactivating your Layer Teleport Curved Pointer. When the Activation Action property emits a True value, your Layer Teleport Curved Pointer will be activated, and when it emits a False value, the pointer will be deactivated.

The Curved Teleport Ray Pointer intermediary game object you set up in the previous section has been fitted with a Boolean Action component. All button actions that need to display the Layer Teleport Curved Pointer have been channeled into this game object. It is a perfect fit for your Activation Action property, as it contains the Boolean Action component that your Activation Action property desires. As soon as one of the button actions being listened for is triggered in the intermediary Curved Teleport Ray Pointer game object, its value will be passed to the Activation Action property, and if True, the Layer Teleport Curved Pointer will be displayed.

Now, drag and drop the Curved Teleport Ray Pointer intermediary game object into this Activation Action Property. Figure 9-2 displays this setup so far.

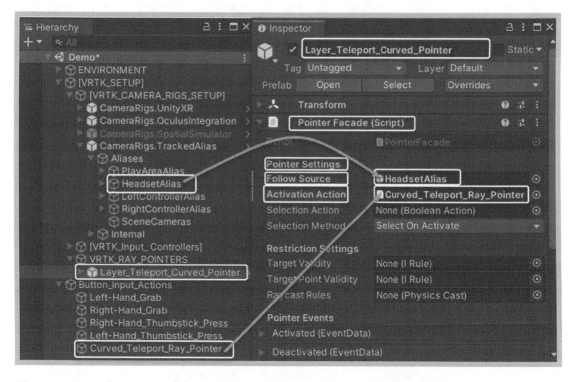

***Figure 9-2.*** *The Layer Teleport Curved Pointer game object setup so far*

The Activation Action property you hooked up is only responsible for enabling the Layer Teleport Curved Pointer. It won't physically teleport the player to a new location. The Selection Action property, in conjunction with the Selection Method property, ensures that the player is teleported to the new location once a True value is emitted.

The Selection Action property needs to be provided with a well-defined set of button actions. When any of these button actions are triggered, the player will be physically teleported to the new location. You already have a well-defined set of button actions in the Curved Teleport Ray Pointer intermediary game object. You'll assign this intermediary game object to the Selection Action property. The moment a button action being listened for in the Curved Teleport Ray Pointer intermediary game object is triggered, your Selection Action property will emit a True value, resulting in the player being teleported to the new location.

You may have noticed that the Curved Teleport Ray Pointer intermediary game object serves two purposes. First, it enables the Layer Teleport Curved Pointer when the Activation Action property emits a True value. Second, it physically teleports the player to the new location when the Selection Action property is True. Both of these properties can be seen in Figure 9-2.

So far, you've displayed your Layer Teleport Curved Pointer and ensured that the player is physically teleported to the new location. Now, you need to decide when the actual teleport should take place. You'll use the Selection Method property to make this decision.

You could have the physical teleport occur as soon as your controller's Left Thumbstick button is pressed. In this case, your Layer Teleport Curved Pointer would be enabled and you'd be immediately teleported to whichever point the Layer Teleport Curved Pointer is pointing at when the Left Thumb Stick button is pressed. This wouldn't allow you even a split second to decide where you want to teleport to, so this setup won't work.

To set up a working teleport, you'll need to ensure that the physical teleport occurs not when pressing down on your Left Thumbstick button or the *T* key, but rather when you release either of these components. The moment you press down on either of them, your Layer Teleport Curved Pointer will be displayed. So long as you don't release the Thumbstick button or the *T* key, the pointer emitting from your headset will be continually displayed, allowing you to move your head about and point to a precise location where you want to teleport. The moment you release either of these features, you'll be immediately teleported to the location your Layer Teleport Curved Pointer is pointing. This is a very subtle change that you need to comprehend.

Let's begin setting this up now on the Layer Teleport Curved Pointer. Ensure that you've selected the Layer Teleport Curved Pointer game object in the hierarchy. Drag and drop the Curved Teleport Ray Pointer intermediary game object into the text box of the Selection Action property. Then, set the Value for the Selection Method property to Select on Deactivate to indicate that you want the physical teleport to occur only when the Left Thumbstick or *T* key is released. Figure 9-3 displays the setup for your Layer Teleport Curved Pointer game object so far.

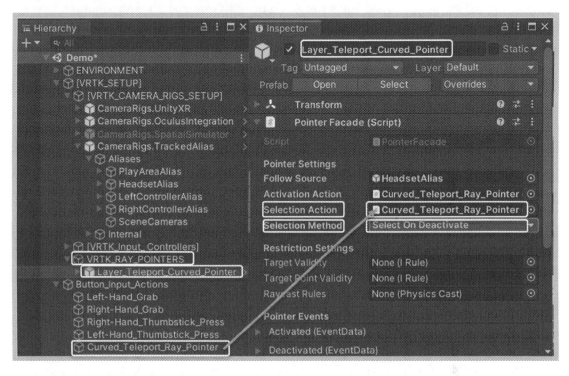

***Figure 9-3.** The Layer Teleport Curved Pointer game object setup so far*

You can test your scene using the Camera Rigs, Spatial Simulator and the Camera Rigs, Unity XR setups. Note that you won't be able to teleport about within your VR world yet. However, you'll be able to display your Layer Teleport Curved Pointer, which originates from your Headset, upon pressing your controller Left Thumbstick or the *T* key(spatial simulator mode).

Let's now set up a valid Teleport area using layers. Your goal is to allow the player to teleport only to anywhere on the Floor, and not to any other game objects in the scene. Select the Floor game object in the hierarchy, and note that its layer has been set to Water. You need to allow the player to teleport onto any game object whose layer has been set to Water. Thus, if you were to assign the Table game object the layer of Water, the player should teleport onto the table.

In the hierarchy, select the Layer Teleport Curved Pointer game object and look at the Inspector. In the Pointer Facade component, there is a Target Validity property that will only accept a Rule game object in its Restriction Settings section. This property determines what the Layer Teleport Curved Pointer considers a valid Teleport target. As this property will accept a Rule object only, you need to set up a Rule for what the Layer Teleport Curved Pointer considers a valid target and then assign this Rule to the Target Validity property.

Select the Demo scene in the hierarchy. Create an empty game object as its child and reset its transform. Rename this game object "Rules." All rules you create in this book will be stored as children of this Rules game object. Select the newly created game object in the hierarchy, and create an empty game object as its child and rename it "Teleport Layer." With the Teleport Layer game object selected in the hierarchy, click the Add component button in the Inspector and add the Any Layer Rule component. Set its Layer Mask property to Water.

You have just created your first Teleport Layer rule. When attached to the Target Validity property of the Layer Teleport Curved Pointer game object, you can teleport anywhere in your Floor game object, as your Floor has been assigned the layer Water. Essentially, you have told your Layer Teleport Curved Pointer that any game object whose layer has been set to Water is considered a Valid (teleport) Target. The Layer Teleport Curved Pointer should display its default valid green color, allowing a teleport to occur. When the Layer Teleport Curved Pointer encounters a game object whose layer is not set to Water, the Layer Teleport Curved Pointer will be red, indicating an invalid teleport area.

Let's set this up now. From within the hierarchy, drag and drop the Teleport Layer game object into the text box of the Target Validity property, as shown in Figure 9-4.

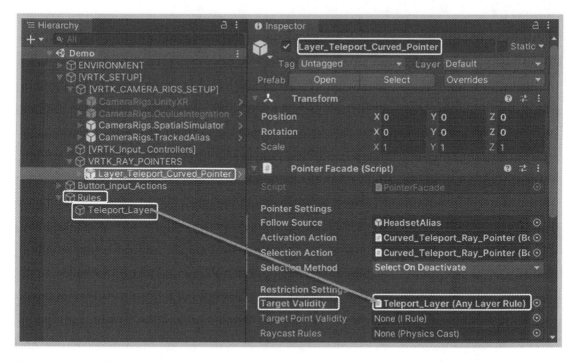

***Figure 9-4.*** *The Layer Teleport Curved Pointer game object setup so far*

Playtest your scene using the Camera Rigs, Spatial Simulator and the Camera Rigs, Unity XR setups. You will notice that you still can't teleport about within your VR World. However, when you press down on your controller's Left Thumbstick or press the *T* key on the keyboard (in the Spatial Simulator mode) and direct the Layer Teleport Curved Pointer emitting from your headset to anywhere on the Floor, it will display in its valid green teleport state. However, if you direct the pointer at the table, ladder, or barrel, it will display its invalid red teleport state.

# Setting up a Teleporter for Instant Teleportation

Instant Teleportation happens when a valid teleport area is found; at this point, the user is instantly repositioned, usually with a camera fade to eliminate motion sickness. In the last section, you set up your curved teleport pointer to facilitate teleportation. In this section, you'll set up an Instant Teleporter game object that will enable you to teleport within your virtual world.

The Layer Teleport Curved Pointer is responsible for recognizing a valid teleport and initiating it. The Teleporter game object is responsible for moving the Play Area to a new location, which essentially moves your Virtual Player to this new location. You need to hook up the Teleporter to your Layer Teleport Curved Pointer so that the moment a valid Selection Action occurs and the Selected event on the Layer Teleport Curved Pointer is triggered, the Teleporter will execute its teleport functionality.

Let's now set up this Teleporter game object. We can do this by selecting the VRTK SETUP game object in the hierarchy and creating a new empty child game object that we'll rename "VRTK TELEPORTERS." All Teleporters you create will be stored as children of this game object. Now, select the Project tab and expand the "Packages" folder. Locate the "Tilia Locomotors Teleporter Unity" folder and expand it until you reach its "Prefabs" folder. Select the folder, and from the pane on the right, drag and drop the Locomotors Teleporter Instant prefab onto the VRTK TELEPORTERS game object in the hierarchy.

From within the hierarchy, expand the Camera Rigs Tracked Alias game object. Then, expand its Aliases game object.

Select the Locomotors Teleporter Instant game object in the hierarchy, and ensure that its Teleporter Facade component has been expanded. You need to set up several properties here so that this Instant Teleporter knows what object should move when a teleport occurs and how it should be moved. In the Teleporter Settings section of the Teleporter Facade component, several properties need to be set.

The Target property indicates which game object should move when the Teleport method is called from the Layer Teleport Curved Pointer. The game object that needs to be moved here is the Play Area Alias. Doing this tells the Teleporter that when you teleport, Play Area Alias needs to be moved to the new location, which essentially moves your virtual player to its new location. Drag and drop the Play Area Alias game object from the hierarchy into the Target property text box, as shown in Figure 9-5.

For the Offset property, drag and drop the Headset Alias game object from the hierarchy into the Offset property text box, as shown in Figure 9-5. For the Offset Usage property, select Offset always with Destination Rotation, as shown in the figure. Now, upon being teleported to the destination, you will be rotated. This may be the effect you desire.

Check the box for the Apply Destination Rotation property, as shown in Figure 9-5. Then, drag and drop the Scene Cameras game object from the hierarchy into the Camera Validity property text box, as shown in the figure. This lets your Teleporter know about the cameras in the scene against which it can apply a camera blink. Last, set the Target Validity property to the Teleport Layer rule you created in the last section.

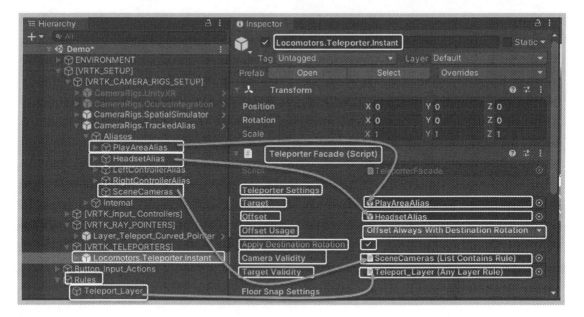

***Figure 9-5.*** *Setting up the Instant Teleporter*

Last, you need to hook up this Locomotors Teleporter Instant game object to your Layer Teleport Curved Pointer. Do this by selecting the Layer Teleport Curved Pointer game object in the hierarchy. Expand its Selected event in the Inspector and click the plus symbol located in the bottom right-hand corner to add an event listener box. Now, drag and drop the Locomotors Teleporter Instant game object from the hierarchy into the event listener text box. For the function to execute when this event is invoked, select Teleporter Facade Teleport, available in the "Dynamic Event Data" section of the context menu that pops up, see Figure 9-6.

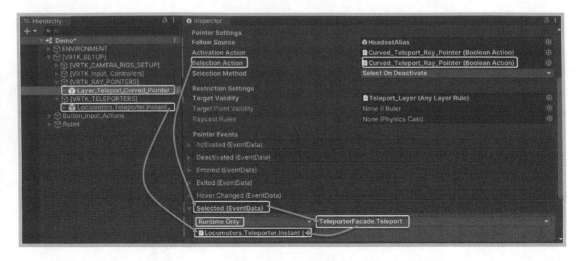

**Figure 9-6.** *Hooking up the Instant Teleporter to the Layer Teleport Curved Pointer*

Now, when the Left Thumbstick button or *T* key is pressed, your Layer Teleport Curved Pointer will be displayed, allowing you to select a point where you want to teleport to. At the same time, the Selection Action property emits a True value triggering the Selected event. This event executes its Teleporter Facade teleport method resulting in the player being teleported to the new location.

Playtest your scene using the Camera Rigs, Spatial Simulator and the Camera Rigs, Unity XR setups. You will see that you can now teleport about within your virtual world.

## Setting Up a Teleporter for Dash Teleportation

Dash Teleportation can be thought of as a slight twist on Instant Teleportation. Dash Teleportation happens when a valid teleport area is found and the player gradually moves over time in a linear motion until the specific teleport point is reached. With Instant Teleportation, you probably noticed that you experience a fade effect. With Dash Teleportation, you're jolted forward upon confirming your teleport destination.

Let's get Dash Teleportation set up now. Within the hierarchy, select and expand the VRTK TELEPORTERS game object. Then, select the Project tab and expand the "Packages" folder. Locate the "Tilia Locomotors Teleporter Unity" folder and expand it until you reach its "Prefabs" folder. Select this folder, and from the pane on the right, drag and drop the Locomotors Teleporter Dash prefab onto the VRTK TELEPORTERS game object in the hierarchy.

From within the hierarchy, expand the Camera Rigs, Tracked Alias game object as well as its Aliases game object. Select the Locomotors Teleporter Dash game object in the hierarchy, and ensure that its Teleporter Facade component has been expanded. You now need to set up the same properties you did while setting up the Locomotors Teleporter Instant game object.

Drag and drop the Play Area Alias game object from the hierarchy into the Target property parameter, as shown in Figure 9-7. This tells the Teleporter that when you teleport, the Play Area Alias needs to be moved to the new location, which essentially moves your virtual player to its new location. For the Offset property, drag and drop the Headset Alias game object from the hierarchy into the Offset property parameter, as shown in the figure.

For the Offset Usage property, you'll use a different value from the one you used for the Locomotors Teleporter Instant game object. We do this so that you can see how the rotation changes when you use a different setting. From the drop-down for this property, select Offset Always Ignore Destination Rotation, as shown in Figure 9-7. Now, upon being teleported to the destination, you won't be rotated. This may be the effect you desire. Uncheck the box for the *A*pply Destination Rotation property, as shown in the figure. For the Camera Validity property, drag and drop the Scene Cameras game object from the hierarchy into the Camera Validity property parameter, as shown in the figure. Last, drag and drop the Teleport Layer game object from within the Rules game object to the Target Validity property parameter, as shown in Figure 9-7.

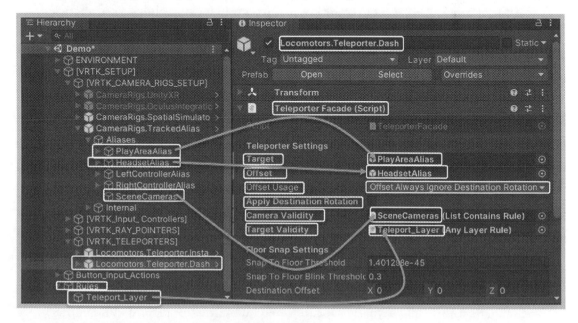

***Figure 9-7.*** *Setting up the Dash Teleporter*

Finally, you need to hook up this Locomotors Teleporter Dash game object to your Layer Teleport Curved Pointer. In the hierarchy, select the Layer Teleport Curved Pointer game object. Expand its Selected event within the Inspector and click the plus symbol located in its bottom right-hand corner to add an event listener box. Now, drag and drop the Locomotors Teleporter Dash game object from the hierarchy into the event listener text box. For the function to execute when this event is invoked, select Teleporter Facade Teleport, available in the "Dynamic Event Data" section of the context menu that pops up. This setup is like what you see in Figure 9-6 except for the fact that the event listener text box has now been populated with the Locomotors Teleporter Dash game object.

Now, playtest your scene using the Camera Rigs, Spatial Simulator and the Camera Rigs, Unity XR setups. You'll see that you can Dash teleport about within your virtual world and you won't automatically be rotated upon reaching your destination. You might have noticed the subtle difference between an Instant and Dash teleport.

Well, now you can Instant and Dash teleport yourself about within your virtual world. However, it would be good if you could also rotate yourself around by pushing your Thumbstick to the left or right. In the next section, we'll see how to set this up.

# Rotating Around Within the Virtual World

Currently, if you want to rotate around within your virtual world, you need to use the mouse. In this section, we'll set up rotation using your Left Controller's Thumbstick so that you can both teleport and rotate using a single device. It's not essential that you only set up rotation against your Left Controller's Thumbstick; you can also set it up against your Right Thumbstick.

Let's begin by setting up two intermediary game objects that we'll use to capture Horizontal and Vertical Axis movement against your Left Controller's Thumbstick. One intermediary game object will be responsible for capturing any Horizontal input movement emitted by all of the controllers' Left Thumbsticks. The other intermediary game object will capture any Vertical input movement emitted by all of the controllers' Left Thumbsticks. You'll be capturing input against three devices, the Oculus, HTC Vive, and Xbox controllers. Your mouse has already been set up to allow you to rotate.

Select and expand the Button Input Actions game object in the hierarchy, and create two new empty child game objects within it. Rename the first child game object "Thumbstick Horizontal Axis Left." When you move your controller's Left Thumbstick horizontally, its input values will be captured here. Rename the second child game object "Thumbstick Vertical Axis Left." When you move your controller's Left Thumbstick vertically, this is where its input values will be captured. Select both of these game objects in the hierarchy and within the Inspector, click the Add Component button and add a Float Action component to both game objects. It's important to note that your Thumbsticks' horizontal and vertical movement yields a floating-point value that you need to capture. Therefore, you have to set up Float Action components on both intermediary game objects.

With the Thumbstick, Horizontal Axis Left and Thumbstick Vertical Axis Left game objects still selected in the hierarchy, expand the Sources property and change its size value to 3. Three Element slots will be made available to you. You'll be capturing axis input against your Left Controllers' Thumbsticks only against three devices—namely, the Oculus, HTC Vive, and Xbox Left Controllers.

Within the hierarchy, expand the VRTK INPUT CONTROLLERS game object.

Now, expand the Input Unity Input Manager Oculus Touch Left Controller until you locate the Left Thumbstick Horizontal Axis [1] game object. Then, expand the Input Unity Input Manager Open VR Left Controller until you locate the Left Trackpad Horizontal Axis [1] game object. Last, expand the Input Unity Input Manager, X-Box Controller until you locate the Left Thumbstick Horizontal Axis [Horizontal] game object.

Within the hierarchy, select the Thumbstick Horizontal Axis Left intermediary game object. You will consolidate the Left Thumbstick Horizontal Axis movement input from the Oculus, HTC Vive, and Xbox Left Controllers into this intermediary game object.

Drag and drop the Left Thumbstick Horizontal Axis [1] game object from the hierarchy into the Element 0 slot of the Float action component. Then, drag and drop the Left Trackpad Horizontal Axis [1] game object from the hierarchy into the Element 1 slot. Finally, drag and drop the Left Thumbstick Horizontal Axis [Horizontal] game object from the hierarchy into the Element 2 slot. You have now captured Horizontal Axis movement input against the Left Controller of three devices, as shown in Figure 9-8.

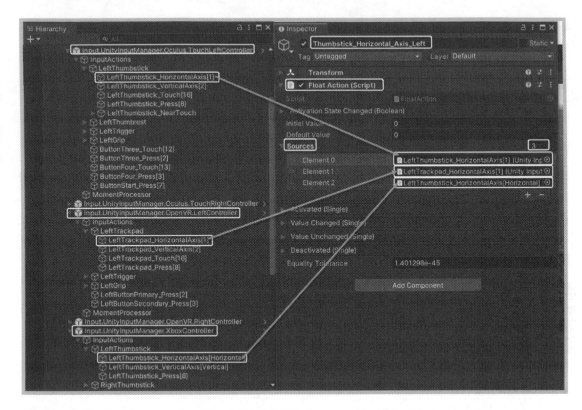

**Figure 9-8.** *Setting up the Thumbstick Horizontal Axis Left intermediary game object*

Within the hierarchy, select the Thumbstick Vertical Axis Left intermediary game object. You'll consolidate the Left Thumbstick Vertical Axis movement input from the Oculus, HTC Vive, and Xbox Left Controllers into this intermediary game object.

Drag and drop the Left Thumbstick Vertical Axis [2] game object from the hierarchy into the Element 0 slot of the Float action component. Next, drag and drop the Left Trackpad Vertical Axis [2] game object from the hierarchy into the Element 1 slot of the Float action component. Finally, drag and drop the Left Thumbstick Vertical Axis [Vertical] game object from the hierarchy into the Element 2 slot of the Float Action component.

You have now captured Vertical Axis movement input against the Left Controller of three devices, as shown in Figure 9-9. This gives you a way to listen for Horizontal and Vertical Axis input against the Left Controller Thumbstick for all three devices.

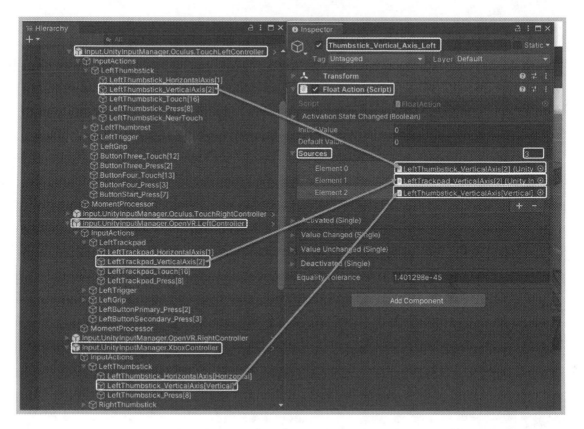

***Figure 9-9.*** *Setting up the Thumbstick Vertical Axis Left intermediary game object*

## Playing Animation When the Left Thumbstick Is Flicked

When using the Camera Rigs, Spatial Simulator and X-Box Controller or Camera Rigs, Unity XR along with your custom prototype hands, you would ideally want to get some visual feedback against your custom virtual hands whenever you flick the Left Thumbstick on your controller horizontally or vertically. This visual feedback can be provided by playing the same Teleporting animation you play when you press down on the Left Thumbstick to teleport within the virtual world. You'll play this Teleporting animation whenever you receive input after either a Horizontal or Vertical Left Thumbstick Axis flick has happened.

Let's set up this animation for when a Horizontal or Vertical Axis Thumbstick movement occurs against your Left Controllers. Expand the Camera Rigs Tracked Alias game object in the hierarchy and then expand its Aliases game object. After that, expand the Left Controller Alias game object until you reach its Hand Proto Left game object.

Now, select the Thumbstick Vertical Axis Left intermediary game object in the hierarchy. Expand the Activated event In the Inspector and click the plus symbol located in its bottom right corner to add an event listener box to this Activated event. From the hierarchy, drag and drop the Hand Proto Left game object into the event listener box of the Activated event. For the function, select Animator Play (string) and in the text box below it, type in the name of the animation that should play (e.g., "Teleporting"), as shown in Figure 9-10.

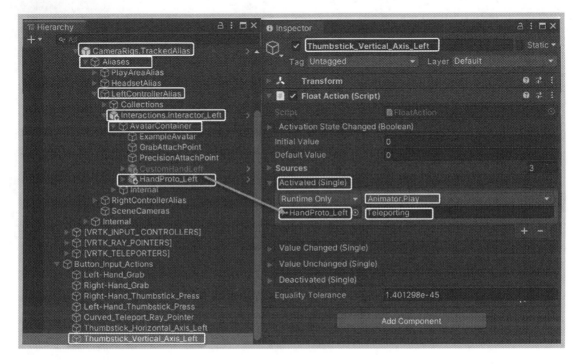

***Figure 9-10.*** *Setting up the Teleporting animation to play when the Left Controller's Thumbstick is flicked vertically*

You have now set up the Teleporting animation to play whenever your Left Thumbstick is flicked vertically.

Now, from within the hierarchy, select the Thumbstick Horizontal Axis Left intermediary game object. Expand the Activated event in the Inspector and click the plus symbol located in the bottom right corner to add an event listener box to this Activated event. From the hierarchy, drag and drop the Hand Proto Left game object into the event listener box of the Activated event. For the function, select Animator Play (string), and in the text box below it, type in the name of the animation that should play (e.g., "Teleporting"), as shown in Figure 9-11.

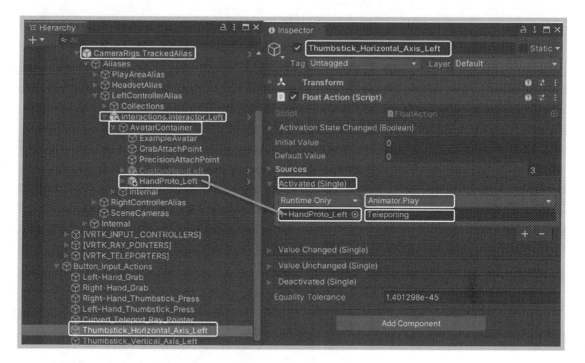

***Figure 9-11.*** *Setting up the Teleporting animation to play when the Left Controller's Thumbstick is flicked horizontally*

You have now set up the Teleporting animation to play whenever your Left Thumbstick is flicked horizontally.

## Rotating Using an Arrow Pointer

To enable yourself to rotate in the virtual world, you'll need to set up an arrow pointer that you can rotate around using your Left Controller's Thumbstick. This arrow pointer will be positioned at the very end of your curved teleport pointer. By rotating this arrow pointer around using the Thumbstick, you can have it face the direction you'd like to end up facing after being teleported.

Along with this book, you were provided an "Arrow_Pointer" unity package file that you need to import into your project now. Once imported, you'll have the "Arrow Pointer" folder in your "Assets" folder. This folder contains an arrow pointer prefab that you will rotate around.

In the hierarchy, select the VRTK SETUP game object and create a new empty child game object within it. Rename this child game object "VRTK TELEPORT ROTATE." You'll set up the rotation mechanism here. It can only be used in conjunction with teleportation.

Select the Project tab and expand the "Packages" folder. Locate the "Tilia Input, Combined Actions, Unity" folder and expand it until you reach its "Prefabs" folder. Select the this folder, and from the pane on the right, drag and drop the Input Combined Actions Axes to Angle prefab onto the VRTK TELEPORT ROTATE game object in the hierarchy.

The Combined Actions prefabs allow you to create more complex input types like movement and rotation data. Here, you'll use the Input Combined Actions Axes to Angle to convert the floating-point Thumbstick Axis data into rotation information, allowing you to rotate the arrow pointer.

Ensure that the VRTK TELEPORT ROTATE game object is selected in the hierarchy and create a new empty child game object within it. Rename this child game object "Pointer Rotator." With this game object selected in the hierarchy, click the Add Component button in the Inspector and add a Float to Vector 3 component. This component will emit a rotation angle as a Euler angle that rotates the arrow pointer.

With the Pointer Rotator game object still selected in the hierarchy, click the Add Component button in the Inspector and add the Transform Euler Rotation Mutator component to this game object. The Float to Vector 3 component will emit a Euler rotation angle to the Transform Euler Rotation Mutator component, rotating the arrow pointer.

Now, select the Layer Teleport Curved Pointer in the hierarchy. It is a child of the VRTK RAY POINTERS game object. Expand the pointer until your reach its Valid Container child game object and select it. This game object can be found by navigating to Layer Teleport Curved Pointer ➤ Object Pointer Internal ➤ Elements ➤ Destination ➤ Elements Cylinder ➤ Valid Container.

The Arrow prefab is located within your Assets ➤ Arrow Pointer ➤ Prefabs folder. Drag and drop this Arrow prefab onto the Valid Container game object in the hierarchy, making the game object a child.

Now, select the Arrow game object in the hierarchy and adjust its Transform properties as follows: Set the Transform, Position to: $X = 0$; $Y = 0.2$; and $Z = -0.136$. Set its Transform, Rotation Z value to 90.

Then, select the Pointer Rotator game object in the hierarchy. It is available as a child of the VRTK TELEPORT ROTATE game object you created in this section. Next, drag and drop the Valid Container game object into the Target property parameter of the Transform Euler Rotation Mutator component, as shown in Figure 9-12.

Within the Mutate on Axis property of the Transform Euler Rotation Mutator component, uncheck the *X* and *Z* boxes, as shown in Figure 9-12. You want only the box for the *Y*-axis to be checked, as your arrow pointer just needs to rotate around this axis to face a new direction in the scene.

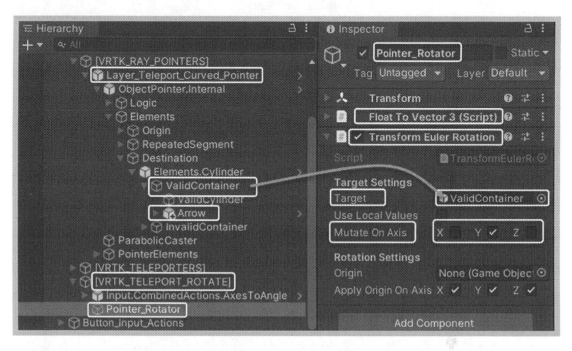

***Figure 9-12.*** *Setting up the Transform Euler Rotation component on the Pointer Rotator game object*

With the Pointer Rotator game object still selected in the hierarchy, expand its Float to Vector 3 component as well as its Transformed (Vector 3) property. Click the plus button in the bottom right corner of the property to add an event listener box, as shown in Figure 9-13.

Now, drag and drop the Transform Euler Rotation Mutator component of the Pointer Rotator game object into the event listener text box of the Transformed (Vector 3) property. For the function to perform, first select Transform Euler Rotation Mutator from the drop-down and then the Do Set Property item in the Dynamic Vector 3 section, as shown in Figure 9-13.

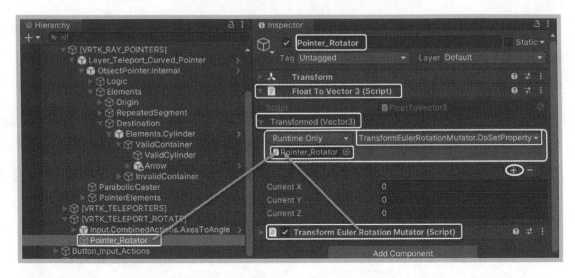

***Figure 9-13.*** *Setting up the Float to Vector 3 component on the Pointer Rotator game object*

Now, select the Input Combined Actions Axes to Angle game object in the hierarchy. It is available as a child of the VRTK TELEPORT ROTATE game object you created in this section. Next, expand the Button Input Actions game object in the hierarchy. Drag and drop the Thumbstick Horizontal Axis Left game object into the Horizontal Axis property parameter of the Axes to Angle Action component. Then, drag and drop the Thumbstick Vertical Axis Left game object into the Vertical Axis property parameter of the Axis to Angle Action component. Next, drag and drop the Headset Alias game object into the Direction Offset property parameter of the Axes to Angle Action component. Figure 9-14 shows the Input Combined Actions Axes to Angle game object setup so far.

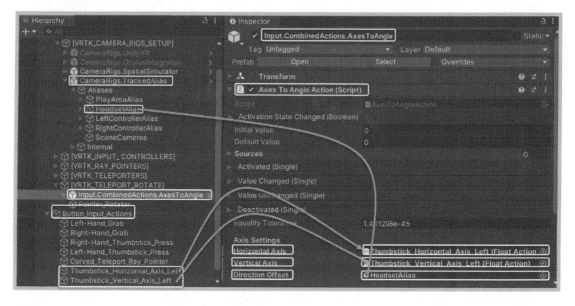

**Figure 9-14.** *Setting up the Input Combined Actions Axes to Angle game object*

Expand the Value Changed event and click the plus button located in its bottom right corner to add an event listener text box. Drag and drop the Pointer Rotator game object into the text box of the Value Changed event. For the function to execute when the Value Changed event is triggered, select Float to Vector 3 from the drop-down and then select Current Y, available within the Dynamic Float section of the context menu that pops up, see Figure 9-15.

Now, add another event listener text box to the Value Changed event. Drag and drop the Pointer Rotator game object into this text box. For the function to execute when the Value Changed event is triggered, select Float to Vector 3 from the drop-down and then select the Do Transform item in the Static Parameters section of the context menu that pops up, see Figure 9-15.

Next, set the Horizontal and Vertical Deadzone bounds to -0.55 and 0.55, as shown in Figure 9-15. These Deadzone values indicate that you need to push your Thumbsticks over these set threshold values to trigger a button input action. You may want to further tweak these values to your liking.

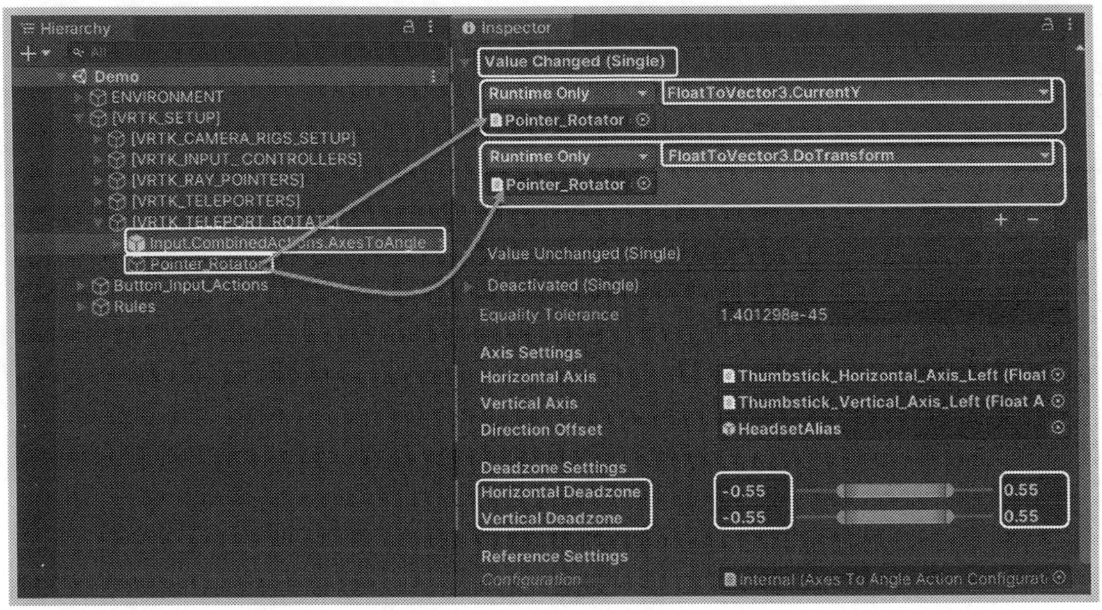

***Figure 9-15.*** *Setting up the Value Changed event and Deadzone settings for the Input Combined Actions Axes to Angle game object*

Finally, note that you're still in Dash Teleport mode. To enable yourself to teleport and face your arrow pointer's direction, you need to change two settings on your Locomotors Teleporter Dash game object, which you'll find nested within the VRTK TELEPORTERS game object in the hierarchy. Select the Locomotors Teleporter Dash game object in the hierarchy. In the Inspector, set the value of the Offset Usage property to Offset Always with Destination Rotation. Also, check the box for the Apply Destination Rotation property. This will enable you to face the direction your arrow pointer was pointing upon being teleported.

Note that when teleporting, you must rotate your arrow pointer to face a new direction while keeping your Left Thumbstick pressed down. This may require some finger dexterity on your part. Once you have your arrow pointer pointing in the direction you want to end up facing, release your hold against your Left Thumbstick.

You'll be teleported to the new location facing the direction your arrow pointer was rotated.

You can playtest your scene using the Camera Rigs, Spatial Simulator and the Camera Rigs, Unity XR setups. Note that you can rotate the arrow pointer at the end of your Curved Teleport Ray by pressing down on your Left Thumbstick button and moving your Left Thumbstick either forward, backward, left, or right. This allows you to change the direction of your arrow pointer in 90-degree increments. With your Left Thumbstick button still pressed down, roll the Left Thumbstick so that the arrow pointer moves around in smaller increments. You'll be teleported to the new location upon releasing your hold on the Left Thumbstick. You'll notice that you've been rotated to face the direction your arrow pointer was facing. You can now rotate and teleport onto any location of the Floor using your controllers.

# Unity's NavMesh-Based Teleportation

In this section, we'll use Unity's NavMesh to map out a valid teleport area within your scene. This will allow you to teleport anywhere within this valid NavMesh area. Setting up NavMesh is hugely beneficial, as you can create AI enemy bots that can navigate it.

To set up NavMesh, you need some static geometry in your scene that can be baked into Unity NavMesh. Ensure that the Gizmos button on your Scene tab has been toggled on, as shown in Figure 9-16.

You'll use the Containers, Barrels, Table, Ladder, and Floor game objects available in the Demo scene for static geometry. In the hierarchy, expand the Environment game object and select the Floor game object. Check the Static box, located in the upper right-hand corner of the Inspector. Next, expand the Containers game object in the hierarchy, and select all the container game objects in it. In the Inspector, check the Static box. Next, expand the Barrels game object in the hierarchy, and select all the barrel game objects within it. In the Inspector, check the Static box to ensure every barrel is marked static. Now, select the Table game object in the hierarchy. Check its Static box, located in the upper right-hand corner of the Inspector. When prompted to enable the static flags for all the child objects, select the button Yes, Change Children. Finally, select the Ladder game object in the hierarchy. Check its Static box, located in the upper right-hand corner of the Inspector. When prompted to enable the static flags for all the child objects, select the button Yes, Change Children.

Now, you need to bake a Unity NavMesh into your scene. From the main menu within the Unity Editor, select Window ➤ AI ➤ Navigation. This opens a new Navigation tab beside the Inspector tab. Select the Navigation tab, and click on the Bake tab located at the top. Set the Agent Radius property to 0.5. Ensure the Agent height property is set to 2, the Max Slope property is set to 45, and the Step Height property is set to 0.4. The other property values on the Bake tab can stay at their defaults. Now, click the Bake button to have Unity bake a NavMesh. You should see a fleeting progress bar baking the NavMesh for your scene in the bottom right-hand corner of the Unity Editor window. Upon completion, you'll see the baked NavMesh in your scene, as shown in Figure 9-16.

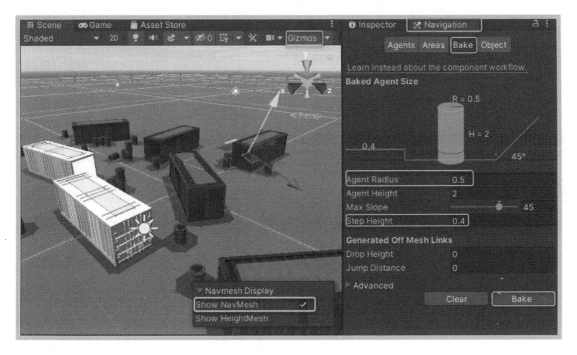

**Figure 9-16.**  *Setting up the baked NavMesh in Unity*

If you don't see the baked NavMesh as displayed above, ensure that your Gizmos button has been toggled on and the Show NavMesh button box has been checked. Once you have baked your Unity NavMesh, you need to set up a rule telling your Layer Teleport Curved Pointer to only consider your Unity NavMesh area as a valid Teleport Target.

Expand the VRTK RAY POINTERS game object in the hierarchy and select the Layer Teleport Curved Pointer game object. This curved pointer allows you to teleport anywhere within your Floor or onto any object whose layer has been set to Water. Currently, only the layer of your Floor game object has been set as such. Now, let's create a new NavMesh rule that will tell your Layer Teleport Curved Pointer that it can teleport the player only within the limits of the NavMesh setup.

Select and expand the Rules game object in the hierarchy, and create a new empty game object and rename it "Teleport NavMesh." Select this game object in the hierarchy and within the Inspector, click the Add Component button to add a new NavMesh Rule component.

Now, select the Layer Teleport Curved Pointer game object in the hierarchy, and within the Inspector, locate its Target Point Validity property within the Restriction Settings section. Drag and drop the Teleport NavMesh rule game object you just created into this Target Point Validity property parameter.

Note that you now have two rules in place, one that you just set up against the Target Point Validity property and another that already existed for the Target Validity property. Remove the Target Validity property rule by right-clicking the Target Validity property label and selecting Revert from the context menu that pops up. This ensures that your Layer Teleport Curved Pointer has just the one rule it needs to comply with now, which is the Teleport NavMesh rule.

In the Pointer Facade component of your Layer Teleport Curved Pointer game object, scroll down to the bottom, locate its Selected event, and expand it. Click the object within its event listener box to have the Locomotors Teleporters Dash game object highlight within the hierarchy. Select this game object and locate its Target Validity property in the Inspector. Note that this property has been set to the Teleport Layer rule. Remove this rule by right-clicking the Target Validity property label and selecting Revert from the context menu that pops up. Next, select the Locomotors Teleporter Instant game object in the hierarchy and locate its Target Validity property within the Inspector. Remove this Teleport Layer rule as well. Now you can be assured that your Layer Teleport Curved Pointer will only use the Teleport NavMesh rule to teleport the player.

Playtest your scene using the Camera Rigs, Spatial Simulator and the Camera Rigs, Unity XR setups. Note that you can teleport about as before. As long as you aim your Layer Teleport Curved Pointer within the bounds of the NavMesh area, your teleport pointer will display in its valid green state and you'll be able to teleport. The moment your Layer Teleport Curved Pointer aims at a spot outside the bounds of the NavMesh, like somewhere very close to a Container or Barrel edge, its invalid red state will be activated.

# Teleporting Using Teleport Targets

In this chapter's final section, you'll set up Teleport Targets, which are ideally used when the player needs to cover large distances, like when traversing massive terrains. Some VR experiences won't allow you to teleport everywhere. Instead, they rely on fixed hotspots, or Teleport Targets, to limit the player's movement about the virtual world to using these Teleport Targets. These targets are the VRTK's prefabs for earmarking certain specific points or areas that you can teleport to. They are ideal for creating immersive experiences and puzzle games like Mist and Riven. Also, if your VR experience requires you to traverse large terrains, strategically positioned Teleport Targets will help create a great VR experience.

The VRTK allows you to achieve this targeted teleportation by providing two prefabs, a *Teleport Targets Point* and a *Teleport Targets Area*. In this section, you'll learn to set up both types of Teleport Targets.

Start by selecting the Demo scene game object within the hierarchy and creating a new empty game object in it. Rename it "Teleport Targets." All your Teleport Targets, be they Point or Area Teleport Targets, will reside as children within this Teleport Targets game object.

Let's now set up a couple of Teleport Target points. Expand the "Packages" folder within the Project tab; locate the Tilia Locomotors, Teleport Targets Unity package; and expand it until you reach its "Prefabs" folder. In this folder, drag and drop the Locomotors Teleport Targets Point prefab onto the Teleport Targets game object in the hierarchy. Rename the game object "Locomotors Teleport Targets Point Zero," and set its Transform Position values as follows: $X = -18$; $Y = 0$; and $Z = -2$. Then, duplicate this game object twice, so that you have, in total, three Teleport Target Points in the scene. Rename these new points "Locomotors Teleport Targets Point One" and "Locomotors Teleport Targets Point Two." Select the former point in the hierarchy and set its Transform Position values to $X = -9$; $Y = 0$; and $Z = -2$. Then, select the latter and set the following values: $X = -13.5$; $Y = 0$; and $Z = -8$.

For Teleport Targets to work, you need a Spatial Target Dispatcher in your scene. I made this prefab available to you in the VRTK. Let's set this up first, and then I will explain how it works. In the hierarchy, select the VRTK SETUP game object and create a new empty child game object within it. Rename the child game object "VRTK SPATIAL TARGET DISPATCHER."

Expand the "Packages" folder within the Project tab and locate the Tilia Indicators, Spatial Targets, Unity package. Expand it until you reach its "Prefabs" folder. In this folder, drag and drop the Indicators Spatial Targets Dispatcher prefab onto the VRTK SPATIAL TARGET DISPATCHER game object in the hierarchy.

Now, expand the VRTK RAY POINTERS game object in the hierarchy. Duplicate its Layer Teleport Curved Pointer child game object, and rename the copied game object "Spatial Target Teleport Curved Pointer." This descriptive name emphasizes that this pointer is exclusively dedicated to teleporting to spatial target points and areas. You need this new dedicated Spatial Target Teleport Curved Pointer, as its setup is different from that of the Layer Teleport Curved Pointer, which can only be used with the standard and NavMesh-based teleportation you set up in earlier sections, not when you want to teleport about using spatial target points or areas.

With the Spatial Target Teleport, Curved Pointer selected in the hierarchy, locate its Selected event within the Pointer Face component of the Inspector and delete the Locomotors Teleporter Dash item from within the event listener text box. You won't be calling the Dash Teleporter directly when a Selection Action occurs. Instead, you need to call the Indicators Spatial Targets Dispatcher.

Ensure that the Spatial Target Teleport Curved Pointer game object is selected within the hierarchy, and then locate and expand the VRTK SPATIAL TARGET DISPATCHER game object in the hierarchy. Drag and drop the Indicators Spatial Targets Dispatcher into the Selected event text box within the Pointer Facade component of the Spatial Target Teleport Curved Pointer game object. For the function, select Spatial Target Dispatcher, Do Dispatch Select from within the Dynamic Event Data section, as shown in Figure 9-17.

Next, you need to set up the Entered event on the Pointer Facade component of the Spatial Target Teleport Curved Pointer game object. Expand the Entered event and click the plus symbol located in the bottom right corner to add a new event listener. Drag and drop the Indicators Spatial Targets Dispatcher into the Entered event text box within the Pointer Facade component of the game object. For the function, select Spatial Target Dispatcher, Do Dispatch Enter from within the Dynamic Event Data section, as shown in Figure 9-17.

Last, you need to set up the Exited event on the Pointer Facade component of the Spatial Target Teleport Curved Pointer game object. Expand the Exited event and click the plus symbol located in the bottom right corner to add a new event listener. Drag and drop the Indicators Spatial Targets Dispatcher into the Exited event text box within the Pointer Facade component of the Spatial Target Teleport Curved Pointer game object. For the function, select Spatial Target Dispatcher, Do Dispatch Exit from within the Dynamic Event Data section, as shown in Figure 9-17.

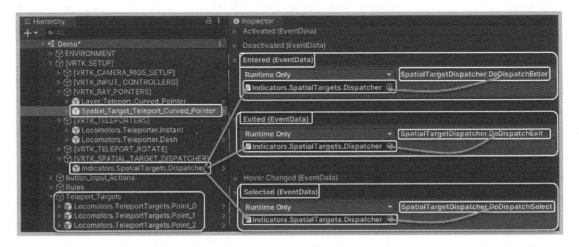

***Figure 9-17.*** *Setting up the Spatial Target Teleport Curved Pointer to call on the Indicators Spatial Targets Dispatcher when the Selected, Entered, and Exited events are triggered*

Note that as the three Teleport Target Points in the Demo scene are Spatial Targets, they can receive the three events you have set up above: Do Dispatch Select, Do Dispatch Enter, and Do Dispatch Exit. These events get called when any of the three Teleport Target Points are selected, entered, or exited.

The three Teleport Targets you've set up are spatial targets that need to receive a Dispatch event from a Spatial Targets, Dispatcher. Your Spatial Target Teleport Curved Pointer will now no longer directly call on the Instant or Dash Teleporter within its Selected event; instead, it will call on the Indicators Spatial Targets Dispatcher set up for its Selected, Entered, and Exited events.

Each Teleport Target Point is a spatial target that can receive any Dispatch event emitted by the Spatial Targets Dispatcher. Whenever the Selection Action is activated on the Spatial Target Teleport Curved Pointer, its Selected event is triggered, which in turn calls on the Do Dispatch Select method of the Indicators Spatial Targets Dispatcher.

As your Teleport Target Points are spatial targets, they can receive a Dispatch event emitted by the Indicators Spatial Targets Dispatcher directed at the selected Teleport Target Point. When they receive this Dispatch event, their Activated event gets triggered, wherein the Teleport method then calls on either the Instant or Dash Teleporter. We'll set up this Activated event on all three Teleport Target Points in the Demo scene shortly.

Before proceeding further, let's select the Layer Teleport Curved Pointer game object in the hierarchy and deactivate it, as two Teleport Pointers can't be active at the same time. As we'll be working with Spatial Teleport Point and Area Targets that require the Spatial Target Teleport Curved Pointer game object, we need to ensure that only this game object is active in the hierarchy.

Select the Spatial Target Teleport Curved Pointer game object in the hierarchy. Then, choose the Target Point Validity property label in the Pointer Facade component of the Inspector, right-click it, and select Revert to remove the Rule set up against this property.

You'll need to set up a new rule for the Target Validity property. The very first Teleport Layer rule you created that was assigned to this property enabled you to teleport onto any object that had its layer set to Water, which was your Floor game object.

When using Teleport Target Points, or areas, your goal is to not allow the player the freedom to teleport anywhere within the level except these predefined points. To achieve this, you need to negate the Teleport Layer rule and assign it to the Target Validity property. The Teleport Layer rule encompasses the entire Floor object. When you negate this rule, it results in the player being unable to teleport anywhere on the Floor object, which will work well because the player will then be forced to teleport only onto the Teleport Target Points, or areas that have been set up.

Let's begin by setting up a new rule that negates your Teleport Layer rule. Then, we'll use this negated rule as the value for the Target Validity property of the Spatial Target Teleport Curved Pointer game object.

From within the hierarchy, select and expand the Rules game object and create a new child game object in it. Rename the child game object "! Teleport Layer" to represent a Negated Teleport Layer rule. With the ! Teleport Layer game object selected in the Inspector, add a new Negation Rule component to it. Drag and drop your Teleport Layer rule from the hierarchy into the Rule text box of this Negation Rule component. Thus, you can quickly negate an existing rule by simply using the Negation Rule component, as shown in Figure 9-18.

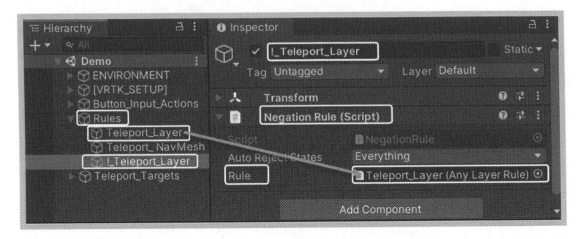

**Figure 9-18.** *Setting up the Negated Teleport Layer rule*

Now, select the Spatial Target Teleport Curved Pointer game object in the hierarchy. Then, drag and drop the ! Teleport Layer rule game object from the hierarchy into the Target Validity property parameter in the Pointer Facade component of the Spatial Target Teleport Curved Pointer game object, as shown in Figure 9-19.

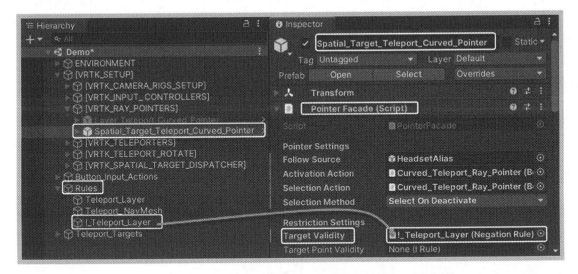

**Figure 9-19.** *Hooking up the Negated Teleport Layer rule to the Target Validity property of the Spatial Target Teleport Curved Pointer game object*

As you'll want to retain the ability to rotate the arrow pointer when teleporting using the Teleport Target Points, or areas, you'll need to change the Target property of your Pointer Rotator game object. Currently, this property points to the Valid Container game object in the Layer Teleport Curved Pointer game object that you deactivated. You need to have the property point to the Valid Container in the Spatial Target Teleport Curved Pointer game object. This is the pointer you'll be using with the Teleport Target Points, or areas.

Let's set this up now. In the hierarchy, select and expand the VRTK TELEPORT ROTATE game object and then select its child Pointer Rotator game object. In the Inspector in the Transform Euler Rotation Mutator component, select the Target property and delete the Valid Container game object. Now, expand the Spatial Target Teleport Curved Pointer game object until you locate the Valid Container game object that contains your arrow pointer. This game object can be found by navigating as follows: Spatial Target Teleport Curved Pointer ➤ Object Pointer Internal ➤ Elements ➤ Destination ➤ Elements Cylinder ➤ Valid Container.

Drag and drop the Valid Container game object from the hierarchy into the Target property of the Transform Euler Rotation Mutator component of the Pointer Rotator game object, as shown in Figure 9-20. You have now completed the setup of your Spatial Target Teleport Curved Pointer.

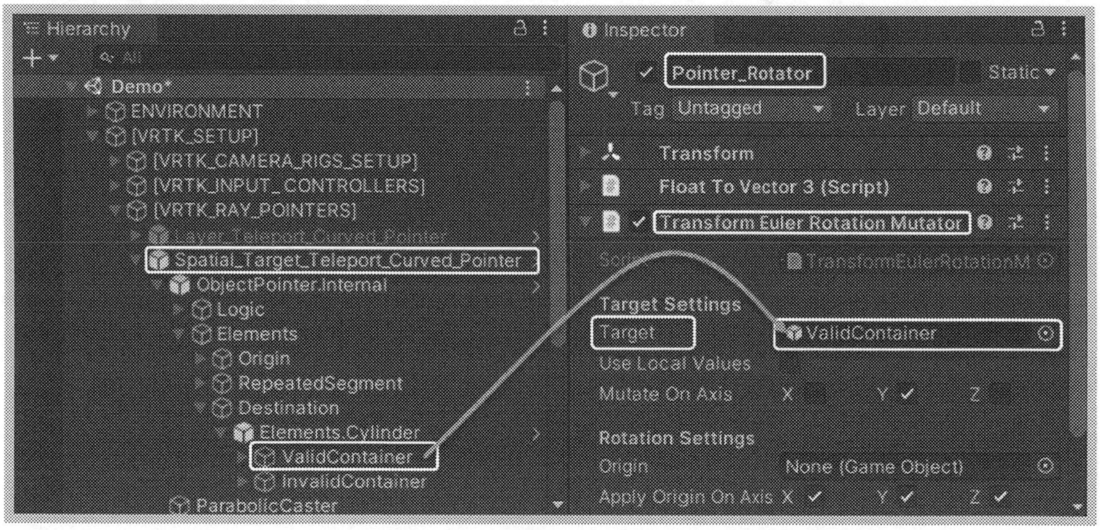

**Figure 9-20.** *Setting up the Valid Container game object on the Pointer Rotator*

Let's now configure the Activated events for the three Teleport Target Points in your Demo scene. Select and expand the Teleport Targets game object in the hierarchy, and then select all three Teleport Target Points in that object. Within the Inspector, ensure that the Spatial Target Facade component has been expanded. Within the Target Events section, locate and expand the Activated event. Click the plus symbol located in the bottom right corner of this Activated event to add an event listener box, see Figure 9-21.

Now, from within the VRTK TELEPORTERS game object, drag and drop either the Instant or Dash Teleporter game object into the event listener box of the Activated event within the Spatial Target Facade component of the Teleport Target Point game objects. For the function, select Teleporter Facade, and from the context menu that pops up, select the Teleport item in the "Dynamic Data Surface" section, as shown in Figure 9-21.

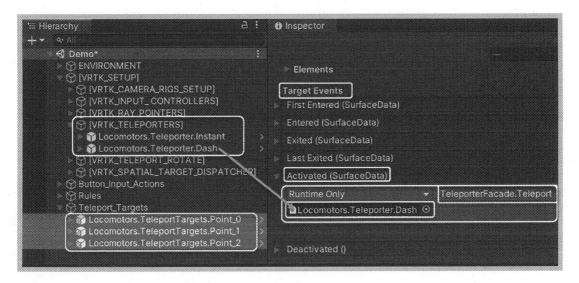

**Figure 9-21.** *Setting up Teleport Targets Points to use a Dash teleport for teleportation from one Target Point to another*

Playtest your Demo scene using the Camera Rigs, Spatial Simulator and the Camera Rigs, Unity XR setups. First, try teleporting anywhere in the confines of the Floor. Note that you won't be able to do so. Now, point toward any of the Teleport Target Points until you see your green teleport ray dipping into it. Upon releasing your Left Thumbstick, you'll be teleported to that point. Play around by teleporting to either of the other two visible Teleport Target Points available. Note that once you teleport yourself onto a Teleport Target Point, it is turned off. Rotate your arrow pointer to ensure that you are oriented in the direction your arrow pointer was rotated upon being teleported to your Target Point.

Now, let's set up a Teleport Target Area, which works similarly to a Teleport Target Point. The benefit of a target Area is that it allows you to define a much larger area or zone that you can teleport to.

From within the hierarchy, select and expand the TELEPORT TARGETS game object. With the Project tab, select and expand the "Packages" folder. Locate the Tilia Locomotors Teleport Targets Unity package. Expand it until you reach its "Prefabs" folder. From within this folder, drag and drop the Locomotors Teleport Targets Area prefab onto the TELEPORT TARGETS game object in the hierarchy. Set its Transform Position values to $X = -12.82$; $Y = 0$; and $Z = -4.24$. Set its Transform Scale values to $X = 3$; $Y = 1$; and $Z = 3$. This provides you with a square Teleport Target Area. Note that you can change the size of your target area by simply changing the $X$ and $Z$ values of its Transform Scale property.

Select the Locomotors Teleport Targets Area game object in the hierarchy, and within the Inspector, ensure that its Spatial Target Facade component has been expanded. Within the "Target, Events" section, locate and expand the Activated event. Click the plus symbol located in the bottom right corner of this Activated event to add an event listener box.

Now, from within the VRTK TELEPORTERS game object, drag and drop either the Instant or Dash Teleporter game object into the event listener box of the Activated event, within the Spatial Target Facade component of the Locomotors Teleport Targets Area game object. For the function, select Teleporter Facade, and from the context menu that pops up, select the Teleport item available in the Dynamic Data Surface section, as shown in Figure 9-22.

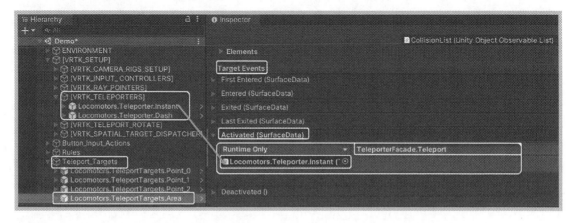

**Figure 9-22.** *Setting up Teleport Targets Area to use an Instant teleport for teleportation*

Playtest your Demo scene using the Camera Rigs, Spatial Simulator and the Camera Rigs, Unity XR setups by teleporting yourself into the Teleport Targets area you've set up. Then, teleport to the other Teleport Target Points. You'll find that you can only teleport between your newly set-up Teleport Targets area and the three Teleport Target points. You can't teleport anywhere else within the Demo scene.

# Summary

This chapter has taught you all you need to know about teleportation using the VRTK. We started by reviewing what teleportation is and why it is considered one of the better forms of locomotion in the VR world. We went on to capture input for pressing the Left Thumbstick against your controllers and the *T* key against the keyboard.

We consolidated all these inputs into an intermediary game object. We then set up a curved teleport pointer and learned how to hook it up to this intermediary game object. We created our first Teleport Layer rule that allowed us to teleport onto any object whose layer had been set to Water.

You learned about the two types of teleporter prefabs provided by the VRTK and went on to set up Instant and Dash teleportation mechanics. You also learned the subtle differences between these teleport methods. We went on to set up rotation to enable ourselves to rotate around in the virtual world using our controllers.

We set up an arrow pointer to provide a visual cue of the direction we'd like the player rotated upon being teleported. You learned how to use the Transform Euler Rotation Mutator component to rotate the arrow pointer and player within the virtual world.

We then turned our attention to using Unity's NavMesh and created a new Teleport NavMesh rule to enable teleportation to a Unity NavMesh. You learned about Teleport Targets as the other method available for teleporting around in the virtual world. You learned that you could either create Teleport Target Points or a Teleport Target area.

We first created three Teleport Target Points, or areas, in our Demo scene and saw that these target points require a particular VRTK prefab, the Indicators Spatial Target Dispatcher, to function. We set up an Indicators Spatial Target Dispatcher to dispatch events to Teleport Target Points and areas. We then created a negated Teleport Layer rule that assisted us with teleportation using Teleport Target Points or areas.

We created a new Spatial Target Teleport Curved Pointer to use when teleporting using spatial target points or areas. You learned that only one curved teleport pointer could be active in the scene at any time. We hooked up the Activated event on our Teleport Target Points, which was responsible for ensuring that teleportation occurred flawlessly. We ended the chapter by setting up a Teleport Target area and playtested our Demo scene to ensure that all our Teleport Targets were working.

# CHAPTER 10

# Seamless Locomotion

In this chapter, we'll look at an immersive movement mechanism that allows players to move smoothly in the VR world. If your game or experience is immersive, it's more convincing if the illusion of immersion isn't constantly being broken in the teleport movements. Seamless locomotion is also commonly referred to as slide movement and rotation. It's worth noting that this form of locomotion isn't for everyone. Players who are new to VR or just sensitive to it may not find this sliding movement and rotation comfortable, and it can cause nausea. Using seamless locomotion, the player can move around the virtual world by simply gliding along the floor surface, moving forward, back, or strafing left and right. The VRTK provides you with four ways to achieve this seamless locomotion, with each form involving a very subtle change. We'll learn to implement all four forms of seamless locomotion provided in the VRTK.

## Capturing Horizontal and Vertical Axis Input

In the last chapter, you used a Float Action component to capture your Left Thumbstick's vertical and horizontal movement input. You created the Thumbstick Horizontal and Vertical Axis Left game objects to capture this input from three devices: the Oculus, HTC Vive, and Xbox left controllers. These game objects are available as children of the Button Input Actions game object. We'll now look at another method for capturing vertical and horizontal movement input against your Thumbsticks.

An alternative to using a Float Action component to capture a controller's horizontal or vertical movement input is to use the VRTK-provided 1D Axis Action. Both methods will provide you with the same result; however, it's good to understand all the options you have available.

Let's begin implementing this new 1D Axis Action. From within the hierarchy, select and expand the Button Input Actions game object, and expand the "Packages" folder in the Project tab and locate the Tilia Input Unity Input Manager package. Expand it until you reach its "Actions" folder in the "Prefabs" folder. In the right pane of the "Actions" folder, you'll see the Input Unity Input Manager 1D Axis Action prefab. Drag and drop this prefab onto the Button Input Actions game object in the hierarchy. Rename this Input Unity Input Manager 1D Axis Action game object "Thumbstick Horizontal Axis Input."

With the Thumbstick, Horizontal Axis Input game object selected in the hierarchy, ensure that its Unity Input Manager Axis 1D Action component has been expanded in the Inspector. Locate the Axis Name property and type in the value "Horizontal." This sets up your Unity Input Manager Axis 1D Action to listen to the Unity Input Manager setting for any changes against the horizontal axis, which correlates to the left-right movement of the Thumbstick on your Xbox, Oculus, or HTC Vive controller, see Figure 10-1.

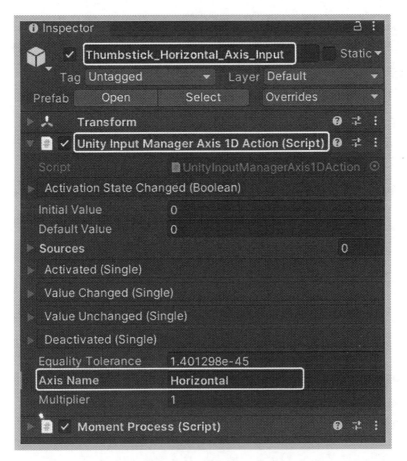

***Figure 10-1.*** *Setting the Axis Name property to Horizontal*

Duplicate the Thumbstick Horizontal Axis Input game object, and rename it "Thumbstick Vertical Axis Input." With the Thumbstick Vertical Axis Input game object selected in the hierarchy, ensure that its Unity Input Manager Axis 1D Action component has been expanded in the Inspector. Locate the Axis Name property and type in the value "Vertical." This sets up your Unity Input Manager Axis 1D Action to listen to the Unity Input Manager setting for any changes against the axis named Vertical, which correlate to the up-down movement of the Thumbstick on your Xbox, Oculus, or HTC Vive controller, see Figure 10-2.

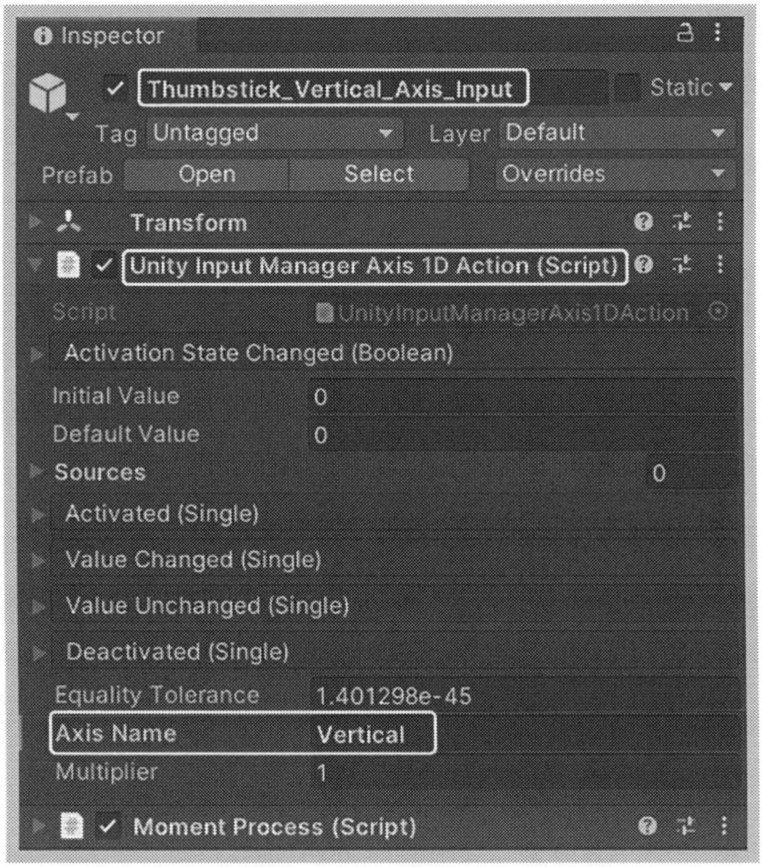

***Figure 10-2.*** *Setting the Axis Name property to Vertical*

# Strafing Movement

Strafing is the simplest form of seamless locomotion provided by the VRTK. With this form of locomotion, you can move forward, backward, left, and right. Let's set this up now.

Select the VRTK SETUP game object in the hierarchy and create a new empty child game object in it. This game object will contain all possible seamless locomotion mechanics provided by the VRTK. Rename this new empty child game object "VRTK PLAYER SLIDE ROTATE."

Expand the "Packages" folder in the Project tab, locate the Tilia Locomotors Axis Move Unity package, and expand it until you reach its "Prefab" folder. In the right pane of this folder, you'll see four prefabs provided by the VRTK that allow for seamless movement and rotation. Each of these prefabs offers a subtle variant of the slide movement and rotation.

Drag and drop the Locomotors Axis Move Vertical-Slide Horizontal-Slide prefab onto the VRTK PLAYER SLIDE ROTATE game object in the hierarchy. With the Locomotors Axis Move Vertical-Slide Horizontal-Slide game object selected in the hierarchy, rename it "Locomotors Axis Move Vertical-Slide Horizontal-Slide STRAFING."

Ensure that the Axis Move Façade component for this game object has been expanded in the Inspector. Located under the Axis Settings heading are the Horizontal and Vertical Axis properties. Drag and drop the Thumbstick Horizontal Axis Input game object from the hierarchy into the Horizontal Axis property. Then, drag the Thumbsticks Vertical Axis Input game object from the hierarchy into the Vertical Axis property parameter, see Figure 10-3. Expand the Camera Rigs, Tracked Alias game object in the hierarchy and then expand its Aliases game object.

Now, we need to set up the properties in the "Target Settings" section. The Target property determines which object will slide around the scene. As you want to move within the scene, you'll need to move your Play Area Alias around. Drag and drop the Play Area Alias game object from the hierarchy into this Target property parameter, see Figure 10-3.

The Forward Offset property is used to determine which game object should be used to determine your forward direction. As you always walk forward in the direction you're facing, you need to set this property to your Headset Alias game object. Drag and drop this game object from the hierarchy into the Forward Offset property parameter, as shown in Figure 10-3.

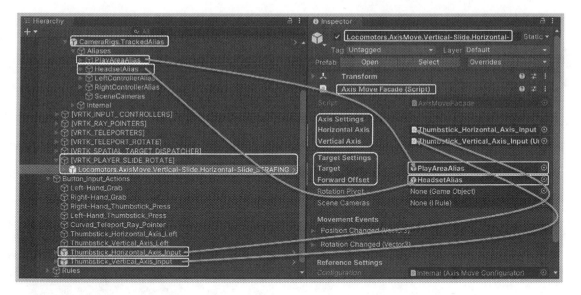

**Figure 10-3.** *Setting up the Locomotors Axis Move Vertical-Slide Horizontal-Slide STRAFING game object*

Ideally, we'd have some animation play as we flick our Thumbstick forward, back, left, or right. We'll use the same Teleporting animation we did when we implemented the Thumbstick Horizontal Axis Left and Thumbstick Vertical Axis Left game objects.

Select the Thumbsticks Horizontal Axis Input and Thumbsticks Vertical Axis Input game objects in the hierarchy. In the Inspector, locate and expand their Activated event, and click the plus symbol located in the bottom right corner to add an event listener box, see Figure 10-4.

Now, from within the Avatar container for the Left Controller Alias, drag and drop the Hand Proto Left game object into the event listener box of the Activated event. For this function, select the Animator Play string. For the name of the animation to play, type "Teleporting" into the text box below, as shown in Figure 10-4.

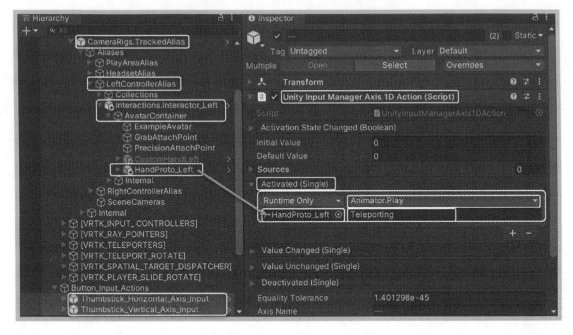

***Figure 10-4.*** *Setting up the Thumbstick Horizontal and Vertical Axis Input game objects to play the Teleporting animation when the Left Thumbstick is pushed either forward, back, left, or right*

Playtest your Demo scene using your VR headset with the Camera Rigs, Unity XR setup and your Xbox controller with the Camera Rigs, Spatial Simulator setup. Notice that you can now slide yourself forward and back by pushing your left controller Thumbstick up and down. You'll also notice your left hand playing the Teleporting animation. Strafing has also been enabled, wherein pushing your Thumbstick toward the left causes you to move left and pushing it to the right causes you to move right. This is an elegant and simplistic behavior provided by the Locomotors Axis Move Vertical-Slide Horizontal-Slide prefab.

# Free Movement Smooth Rotation

As the name suggests, the Free Movement Smooth Rotation prefab allows you not only to slide smoothly and freely but also to rotate smoothly and freely. However, in my opinion, this smooth rotation is inclined to induce motion sickness for all forms of seamless locomotion discussed in this chapter.

Your "Tilia Locomotors Axis Move Unity Package Prefabs" folder should still be expanded. From it, drag and drop all three remaining prefabs, the Locomotors Axis Move Vertical-Slide Horizontal-Smooth Rotate, Locomotors Axis Move Vertical-Slide Horizontal Snap Rotate, and Locomotors Axis Move Vertical Warp Horizontal Snap Rotate, onto the VRTK PLAYER SLIDE ROTATE game object in the hierarchy.

Deactivate all three newly added Locomotor game objects in the hierarchy, as just one can be active at any point in time. Select the Locomotors Axis Move Vertical-Slide Horizontal-Smooth Rotate game object in the hierarchy, and rename it "Locomotors Axis Move Vertical-Slide Horizontal-Smooth Rotate FREELY."

Ensure that the Axis Move Facade component for this game object has been expanded in the Inspector. Located under the Axis Settings heading are the Horizontal and Vertical Axis properties. Drag and drop the Thumbstick Horizontal Axis Input game object from the hierarchy into the Horizontal Axis property. Then, drag the Thumbsticks Vertical Axis Input game object from the hierarchy into the Vertical Axis property parameter, as shown in Figure 10-5.

The Camera Rigs, Tracked Alias game object and its Aliases game object should already be expanded in the hierarchy. Drag and drop the Play Area Alias game object from the hierarchy into the Target property parameter, see Figure 10-5.

Next, drag and drop the Headset Alias game object from the hierarchy into the Forward Offset property parameter, as shown in Figure 10-5.

To enable rotation, we need to set up the Rotation Pivot property. The Rotation Pivot is a designated pivot point around which your Target will rotate. You have set your Target property to the Play Area Alias, so your Play Area Alias needs to rotate around this designated pivot point. Also, this pivot point needs to be a child game object of your Play Area Alias. Expand the Play Area Alias game object in the hierarchy and you'll see that nested within it is its child, the Headset Origin game object, which you can use as the Rotation Pivot.

Drag and drop the Headset Origin game object from the hierarchy into the Rotation Pivot property parameter, as shown in Figure 10-5. Then, drag and drop the Scene Cameras game object from the hierarchy into the Scene Cameras property parameter, as also shown in the figure.

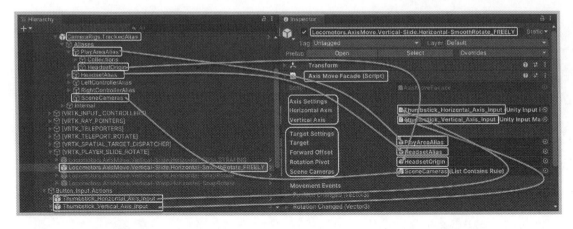

***Figure 10-5.*** *Setting up the Locomotors Axis Move Vertical-Slide Horizontal-Smooth Rotate FREELY game object*

Last, activate the Locomotors Axis Move Vertical-Slide Horizontal-Smooth Rotate FREELY game object in the hierarchy and deactivate the Locomotors Axis Move Vertical-Slide Horizontal-Slide STRAFING game object, as you can't have more than one of these game objects active at one time.

Playtest your Demo scene using your VR headset with the Camera Rigs, Unity XR setup and your Xbox controller with the Camera Rigs, Spatial Simulator setup. Notice that you can now slide yourself about by pushing your left controller's Thumbstick forward and backward. You can also rotate yourself around by pushing your left controller's Thumbstick left or right. Play around with this free-flowing sliding movement and rotation you've set up. It's also important to note that if you keep your Left Thumbstick continually pressed either to the left or to the right you'll keep rotating, which can cause motion sickness.

# Free Movement Snap Rotation

As the name suggests, the Free Movement Snap Rotation prefab provides you a smooth sliding movement with a snap rotation, allowing you to snap rotate to face a new direction in predefined degree increments. It also provides you with an optional fade-in or fade-out with each snapped rotation. This will dramatically reduce the motion sickness you may have encountered with the smooth rotation set up in the earlier section (Free Movement Smooth Rotation).

164

Let's start setting it up by activating the Locomotors Axis Move Vertical-Slide Horizontal-Snap Rotate game object in the hierarchy and deactivating the Locomotors Axis Move Vertical-Slide Horizontal-Smooth Rotate FREELY game object. Note that you can't have more than one of these Locomotors game objects active at one time.

Ensure that the Axis Move Facade component for this game object has been expanded in the Inspector. Located under the Axis Settings heading are the Horizontal and Vertical Axis properties. Drag and drop the Thumbstick Horizontal Axis Input game object from the hierarchy into the Horizontal Axis property. Then, drag the Thumbsticks Vertical Axis Input game object from the hierarchy into the Vertical Axis property parameter, see Figure 10-6.

The Camera Rigs, Tracked Alias game object and its Aliases game object should already be expanded in the hierarchy. Drag and drop the Play Area Alias game object from the hierarchy into the Target property parameter, as shown in Figure 10-6.

Next, drag and drop the Headset Alias game object from the hierarchy into the Forward Offset property parameter, as shown in Figure 10-6. With the Play Area Alias game object expanded in the hierarchy, drag and drop the Headset Origin game object into the Rotation Pivot property parameter, also shown in the figure.

Ideally, you want your camera view to fade in and fade out each time you snap rotate, as this would reduce any potential motion sickness caused by an instant snap rotation. The Locomotors Axis Move Vertical-Slide Horizontal-Snap Rotate prefab has already been set up to fade. However, you need to tell it which cameras to fade.

Drag and drop the Scene Cameras game object from the hierarchy into the Scene Cameras property parameter. This lets your Locomotors Axis Move Vertical-Slide Horizontal-Snap Rotate game object know that it needs to fade out these scene cameras each time a snap rotation occurs, see Figure 10-6.

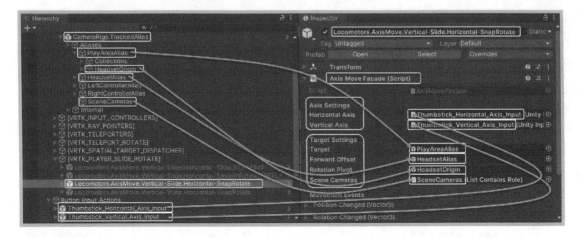

**Figure 10-6.** *Setting up the Locomotors Axis Move Vertical-Slide Horizontal-Snap Rotate game object*

You may want to change the amount of rotation that is applied per snap. By default, whenever a snap rotation occurs, you are rotated 45 degrees. A 45-degree snap rotation works well and there is no need to change it. However, just so you know where and how this change can be made, let's change the snap rotation to 35 degrees. To do this, we'll need to drill down into the Locomotors Axis Move Vertical-Slide Horizontal-Snap Rotate game object.

Select this game object in the hierarchy and expand it until you reach its Input Axis game object. You can do this by navigating as follows: Locomotors Axis Move Vertical-Slide Horizontal-Snap Rotate ➤ Internal ➤ Rotation Mutator ➤ Input Axis.

With the Input Axis game object selected in the hierarchy, ensure that its Axes to Vector 3 Action component has been expanded in the Inspector. Locate the Multiplier property within the Axis Settings section and set its *Y* value to 35. This changes the rotational multiplier on the *Y*-Axis to 35 degrees, allowing you to rotate by 35 degrees on every snap, see Figure 10-7.

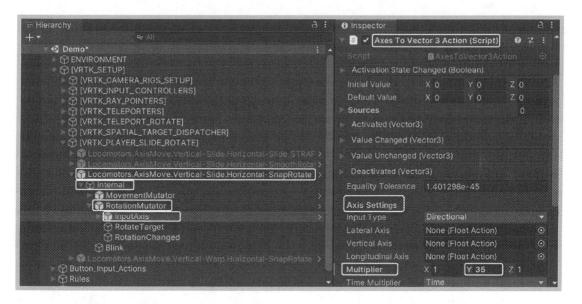

***Figure 10-7.*** *Setting up the snap rotation to rotate in 35-degree increments*

Let's playtest the *Demo* scene using our VR headset with the Camera Rigs, Unity XR setup and our Xbox controller with the Camera Rigs, Spatial Simulator setup. Note that you can now slide yourself about by pushing your left controller's Thumbstick forward and backward. You can also rotate yourself around by pushing your left controller's Thumbstick left or right. Also note that you can't keep your left controller Thumbstick continually pushed left or right, which was possible with the Free Movement Smooth Rotation, so expect to keep snap rotating. However, you'll notice that you can now snap rotate in 35-degree increments and fade in and fade out with each rotation, which essentially eliminates motion sickness.

# Free Movement Warp Snap Rotation

The difference between the Snap Rotation and the Warp Snap Rotation is that Warp Snap Rotation provides you with a vignette effect when moving forward, backward, and rotating. In the case of the Snap Rotation, you can keep your Left Thumbstick continually pressed either forward or backward and you will continue to move in the world, which isn't possible with Warp Snap Rotation. With the latter, for every forward and backward movement, you need to push or pull against your Left Thumbstick.

Activate the Locomotors Axis Move Vertical Warp Horizontal Snap Rotate game object in the hierarchy and deactivate the Locomotors Axis Move Vertical-Slide Horizontal-Snap Rotate game object, as you can't have more than one of these Locomotors game objects active at one time.

Ensure that the Axis Move Facade component for this game object has been expanded in the Inspector. Located under the Axis Settings heading are the Horizontal and Vertical Axis properties. Drag and drop the Thumbstick Horizontal Axis Input game object from the hierarchy into the Horizontal Axis property. Then, drag the Thumbsticks Vertical Axis Input game object from the hierarchy into the Vertical Axis property parameter, see Figure 10-8.

The Camera Rigs, Tracked Alias game object and its Aliases game object should already be expanded in the hierarchy. Drag and drop the Play Area Alias game object from the hierarchy into the Target property parameter, as also shown in Figure 10-8.

Next, drag and drop the Headset Alias game object from the hierarchy into the Forward Offset property parameter, as again shown in Figure 10-8. Then, with the Play Area Alias game object expanded in the hierarchy, drag and drop the Headset Origin game object into the Rotation Pivot property parameter, as shown in the figure.

Drag and drop the Scene Cameras game object from the hierarchy into the Scene Cameras property parameter, see Figure 10-8. By default, the rotational snap setting has been set to rotate the player in 45-degree increments with every snap. Leave it at this 45-degree rotation.

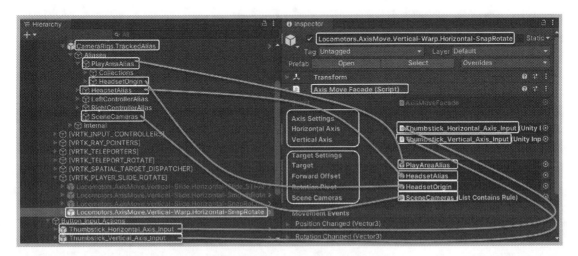

**Figure 10-8.** *Setting up the Locomotors Axis Move Vertical Warp Horizontal Snap Rotate game object*

Now, playtest your Demo scene using your VR headset with the Camera Rigs, Unity XR setup and your Xbox controller with the Camera Rigs, Spatial Simulator setup. Note that you can slide yourself about by pushing your left controller's Thumbstick forward and backward. However, with the Free Movement Snap Rotation, you can't keep your Left Thumbstick continually pushed forward or back, so expect to move it constantly when using it. Next, push your left controller's Thumbstick to the left or right, and you'll see that you can snap rotate in 45-degree increments and fade in and fade out with each rotation. You'll also notice that as you move forward or back, you experience the vignette's fade-in and fade-out effect.

## Summary

In this chapter, we reviewed what seamless locomotion is and how it provides you with immersive movement. We explored the four different ways the VRTK allows you to achieve such movement. We started by learning about VRTKs 1D Axis Action, which provided us with a new way of capturing Horizontal and Vertical Axis input against our Thumbstick. We then went over the Strafing movement mechanism and how to set it up. We also set up the Teleporting animation against the Thumbsticks Horizontal Axis Input and Vertical Axis Input game objects. You learned how to set up Free Movement Smooth Rotation, which you found out causes the most significant motion sickness of all types of movement and rotation. We set up the Free Movement Snap Rotation mechanism, and learned to change the snap rotation value from its default, eliminating the motion sickness encountered with Free Movement Smooth Rotation as a result of its optional fade-in, fade-out effect. We set up the final form of seamless locomotion, which is probably the best method for implementing Free Movement Warp Snap Rotation. Here, in addition to the fade-in, fade-out effect being applied upon every snap rotation, a vignetted fade-in, fade-out effect was also applied upon each forward or backward movement, thereby essentially eliminating motion sickness. You finally learned about the subtle differences between the Free Movement Snap Rotation and the Free Movement Warp Snap Rotation.

# CHAPTER 11

# Arm-Swinging Movement

Teleporting and seamless locomotion are excellent. However, in certain situations, allowing players to swing their arms as they move can increase immersion, as in the real world doing this is as natural as walking. It allows the player to decide how fast they want to move and allows for small, accurate movements. If you were creating an endless runner game in VR, arm swinging would create a truly immersive and natural experience of moving. In this chapter, we'll see how to set up an arm-swinging locomotion technique that we can use as we get moving in the VR world. Note that this aspect of locomotion isn't provided in most VR frameworks that you purchase from the Unity Asset store.

## Move in Place Locomotion

Arm-swinging movement is more commonly referred to as Move in Place locomotion. To get this arm-swinging movement working, you've been provided with a prefab that you need to set up. However, note that it was a member of the VRTK community who provided this prefab. As such, it exists as a different scope within the npmjs scoped registry. You can view this scoped registry by navigating to Edit ➤ Project Settings ➤ Package Manager.

## Capturing Thumbstick Touch Input

Before configuring the Move in Place game object, we need to set up two intermediary game objects, one for each hand, that can be used to determine when an arm swing occurs. We'll enable the Move in Place movement to happen only when the Left or Right Thumbstick is being touched. The two intermediary game objects you'll create will need to explicitly test for a Thumbstick touch action occurring on either the Left or Right Thumbstick of your VR controllers. We'll test for this Thumbstick touch occurring only against your HTC Vive and Oculus devices only, not against the XBox controller.

© Christopher Coutinho 2022
C. Coutinho, *Unity* Virtual Reality Development with VRTK4*, https://doi.org/10.1007/978-1-4842-7933-5_11

To set this up, select and expand the Button Input Actions game object in the hierarchy, and create two new empty child game objects within it. Select the first newly created empty child game object and rename it "Left Hand Thumbstick Touch." Then, select the second newly created empty child game object and rename it "Right Hand Thumbstick Touch."

Select both the Left Hand Thumbstick Touch and Right Hand Thumbstick Touch game objects in the hierarchy. Click the Add Component button and add a Boolean Action component to both of these game objects in the Inspector. Ensure that the Boolean Action component is expanded. Expand Sources, and set its size to 2. You now have two element slots available.

Now, select just the Left Hand Thumbstick Touch game object in the hierarchy. Then, drag and drop the Oculus Left Thumbstick Touch 16 game object from the hierarchy into the Element 0 slot. Next, drag and drop the Open VR Left Trackpad Touch 16 game object from the hierarchy into the Element 1 slot.

Your Left Thumbstick Touch button action for your Oculus and HTC Vive controllers has now been set up, see Figure 11-1.

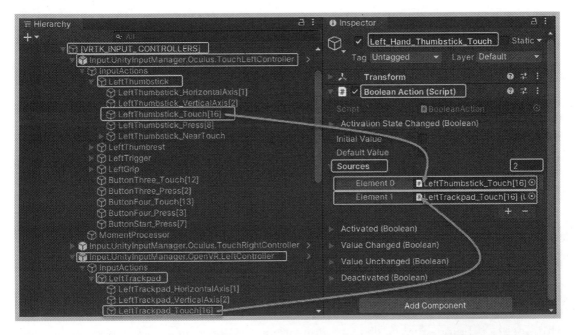

***Figure 11-1.***  *Setting up the Left Hand Thumbstick Touch intermediary game object to capture the HTC Vive and Oculus VR controllers Left Thumbstick touch input*

Now, select just the Right Hand Thumbstick Touch game object in the hierarchy. Drag and drop the Oculus Right Thumbstick Touch 17 game object from the hierarchy into the Element 0 slot. Next, drag and drop the Open VR Right Trackpad Touch 17 game object from the hierarchy into the Element 1 slot. This sets up the Right Thumbstick Touch button action for your Oculus and HTC Vive controllers, see Figure 11-2.

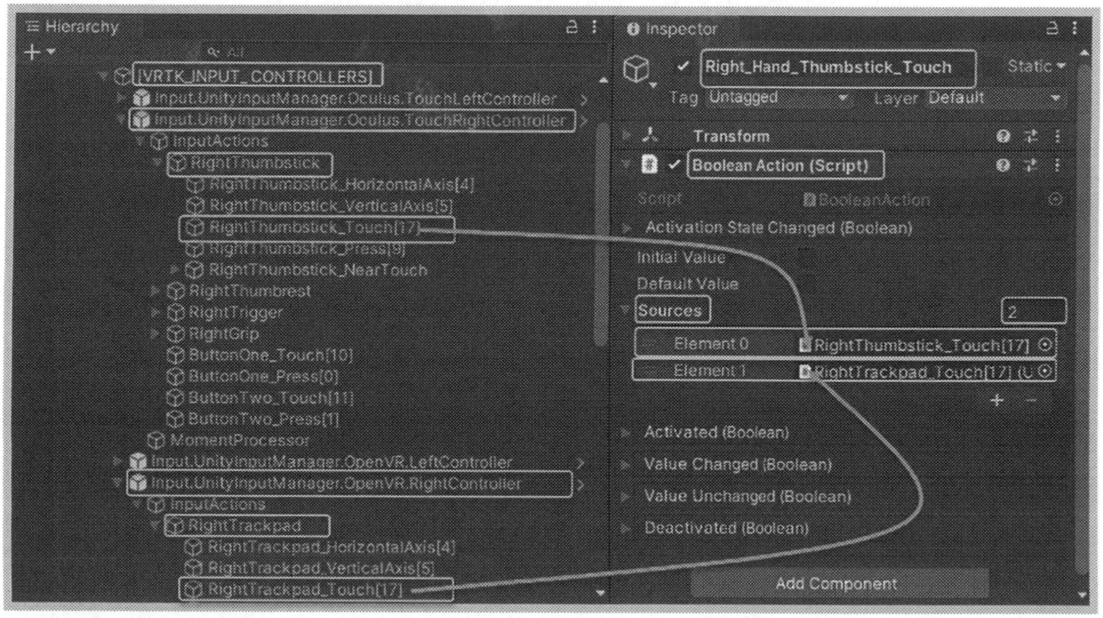

**Figure 11-2.** *Setting up the Right Hand Thumbstick Touch intermediary game object to capture the HTC Vive and Oculus VR controllers Right Thumbstick touch input*

## Setting Up the Move in Place Locomotion

Let's now set up the Move in Place locomotion mechanic within our Demo scene. We'll set up this Arm-Swinging Locomotion to work with our VR controllers only, not with the XBox controller, as it doesn't make sense to swing the XBox controller.

With your Demo scene open, select the VRTK SETUP game object in the hierarchy, and create a new empty child game object within it and rename it "VRTK MOVE IN PLACE." Next, select the Project tab, and expand the "Packages" folder until you locate the Fight 4 Dream Locomotors Move in Place, Unity package. Expand this folder until you reach its "Prefabs" folder, in the right pane of which you'll notice the Move in Place prefab. Drag and drop this prefab onto the VRTK MOVE IN PLACE game object in the hierarchy.

Select the Move in Place game object in the hierarchy and ensure that the Move in Place component has been expanded within the Inspector .

You now need to set up several properties within this Move in Place component. Drag and drop the Left Hand Thumbstick Touch game object from the hierarchy into the Left Controller Action property parameter of the Move in Place component. Then, drag and drop the Right Hand Thumbstick Touch game object from the hierarchy into the Right Controller Action property parameter of the same component.

These settings enable the Move in Place component to listen for a Thumbstick touch occurring on either the right or left controller, see Figure 11-3.

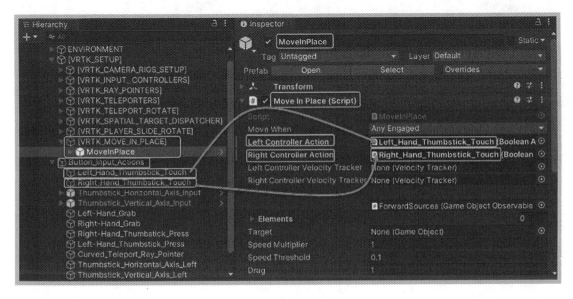

***Figure 11-3.*** *Setting up the Move in Place game object to listen for a Thumbstick touch occurring against either the right or left controller*

As discussed in Chapter 7, your Left and Right Controller Aliases are fitted with Velocity Tracker Processor components. The Move in Place game object previously displayed requires its Left and Right Controller Velocity Tracker properties to be populated. You'll populate these properties with the Left and Right controller Alias game objects located within the Camera Rigs, Tracked Alias game object.

Expand the Camera Rigs, Tracked Alias, and then expand its Aliases game object. Drag and drop the Left Controller Alias from the hierarchy into the Left Controller Velocity Tracker property parameter. Next, drag and drop the Right Controller Alias from within the hierarchy into the Right Controller Velocity Tracker property parameter, as shown in Figure 11-4.

Next, expand the "Elements" section, available beneath Forward Sources, and set its size to 1 to have an Element 0 slot made available. Here, you need to specify which game object should be used to determine your forward direction. As you always walk forward in the direction you're facing, you need to set this property to your Headset Alias game object. Drag and drop this game object from the hierarchy into this Element 0 slot, as shown in Figure 11-4.

The Target property determines which object will slide around in the Demo scene. As you want to move within the Demo scene, you need to set this property to the Play Area Alias. Drag and drop the Play Area Alias game object from the hierarchy into the Target property parameter, as shown in Figure 11-4.

Now, set the Speed Multiplier property value to 1.5. You can tweak this value depending upon the speed at which you want to move. Also, set the Speed Threshold value to 0.1. Last, set the Drag value to 1. You may want to tweak this value as well so that your player comes to a halt quicker, see Figure 11-4.

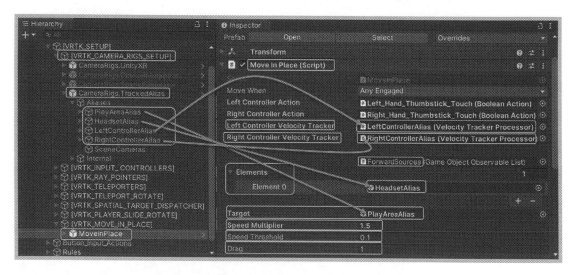

***Figure 11-4.*** *Setting up the remaining properties for the Move in Place game object*

You have now completed your Arm-Swinging Locomotion setup, and it's time to test it out. Playtest your scene using your VR headset along with the Camera Rigs, Unity XR setup to give the Move in Place locomotion a try.

Touch your left or right controller to swing your arms back and forth, like you do when walking. The faster you move your arms, the faster you'll move forward in the VR world. Note that you only need to touch your Thumbsticks; you don't need to press them in.

While swinging your arms back and forth, look in the direction you want to go and the direction of your movement will change accordingly. Touch the Thumbstick of only one controller to move only that arm back and forth. You can try this out against your right controller. You'll see that you can move even by swinging just one arm.

You have now created a fantastic form of real-life movement.

# Summary

In this chapter, we learned what Move in Place locomotion is and how it provides you with immersive true-to-life movement. We set up two intermediary game objects to capture Thumbstick touch input against our left and right controllers. We then set up the Move in Place locomotion prefab that enabled our arm-swinging locomotion to work. You saw that by just swinging one arm, you were able to move within your VR world. Finally, you tested out this new locomotion mechanism using your VR headset.

**CHAPTER 12**

# Setting Up a Pseudo-Body

In the last two chapters on seamless locomotion and arm-swinging movement, you probably noticed that you could easily pass through the solid containers, barrels, ladder, and table available in the Demo scene. In most cases, you wouldn't want such behavior to happen though. Ideally, you want yourself to be stopped the moment you collide with a solid object. All barrels, containers, ladder, and tables have been fitted with colliders that aren't Triggers. However, you can still pass through these objects. To ensure that this doesn't happen, you will need to set up a pseudo-body. This chapter is dedicated to setting up this pseudo-body to enforce the Plausibility Illusion, wherein you cannot pass through solid objects. We will also review a commonly used technique wherein the player's headset fades to black upon their head colliding with a solid object.

## Advantages of Having a Pseudo-Body

A pseudo-body allows you to provide a virtual presence for the position of your real-world body in a spatial scene. You can also apply in-game physics to your pseudo-body, which will enable you to climb a ladder and walk up steps as well as fall from heights.

The pseudo-body creates a Rigidbody that tracks your real-world head position and translates it into your spatial environment. Your pseudo-body needs to be set up in such a way that it provides you the ability to prevent yourself from passing through solid objects and ensures that your prototype hands and Oculus-provided hands as well as interactors don't collide with it. If a collision does occur between your pseudo-body and these objects, it will result in weird movement behavior. Let's begin setting up this pseudo-body and configure it in a manner that lives up to the requirements just discussed.

© Christopher Coutinho 2022
C. Coutinho, *Unity® Virtual Reality Development with VRTK4*, https://doi.org/10.1007/978-1-4842-7933-5_12

# Pseudo-Body Setup

In the hierarchy, select the VRTK SETUP game object and create an empty child game object within it and rename it to "VRTK PSEUDOBODY."

Then, select the Project tab and expand the "Packages" folder. Locate the Tilia Trackers Pseudo-Body Unity package and expand it until you reach its "Prefabs" folder. From the pane on the right, drag and drop the Trackers Pseudo-Body prefab onto the VRTK PSEUDOBODY game object in the hierarchy and select it. Set the Layer for this Trackers Pseudo-Body game object to Ignore Ray Cast. When prompted to set the Layer to ignore ray cast for all child objects, click Yes, Change Children.

This ensures that your pseudo-body will not collide with the Interactable objects you grab. You'll recall that all Interactable objects in your Demo scene need their Layer set to Interactable.

Also, if you look at your Layer Collision Matrix, as shown in Figure 12-1, you'll notice that you've disabled collisions between Layers, Interactable, and Ignore Ray Cast. This ensures that a collision will never occur between your pseudo-body and the grabbed object in your hand as long as this grabbed object layer has been set to Interactable.

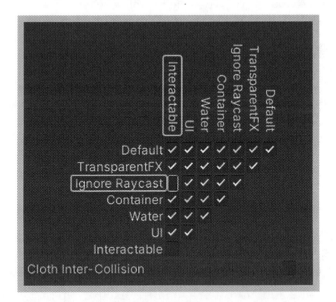

*Figure 12-1.* *Layer Collision Matrix setup thus far*

It's important to note that you should avoid all external collisions with your pseudo-body. The pseudo-body follows your headset, and any external collision that take place while it's in motion will result in weird movement behavior.

Let's now set up the Source and Offset properties for your pseudo-body. These are available in the Pseudo-Body Facade component of the "Tracking Settings" section in the Inspector.

The Source property determines which game object your pseudo-body should follow. Your headset and controllers are the objects that are tracked and move about in the real world, so it's appropriate that you have your pseudo-body follow your headset.

Drag and drop the Headset Alias game object from the hierarchy into the Source property parameter of the Pseudo-Body Facade component. Now, whenever your headset moves in the real world, your pseudo-body will follow it.

The Offset property is an optional positional offset that can be used by the Source when it is not centered, such as when the headset is not centered within the Play Area. Thus, if you as the player are not standing in the center of the Play Area, this Offset will be used in computing your optimal location.

Drag and drop the Play Area Alias game object from the hierarchy into the Offset property parameter.

Now, let's turn our attention to the "Interaction Settings" section. Here, you need to specify the Interactors that the pseudo-body should ignore. You have two Interactors in your Demo scene. Expand Elements located beneath Ignored Game Object and set its size to 2. You'll see that two element slots are made available.

From the hierarchy, drag and drop the Interactions Interactor Left game object into the Element 0 slot. Then, drag and drop the Interactions Interactor Right game object into the Element 1 slot. Figure 12-2 displays these settings against the pseudo-body component.

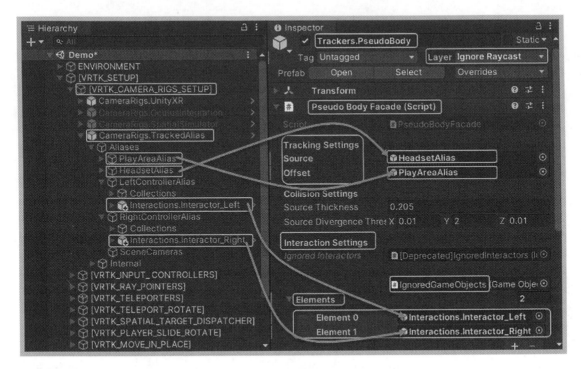

*Figure 12-2.  Setting up the Trackers Pseudo-Body*

Playtest your scene using the Camera Rigs, Spatial Simulator along with the keyboard. Using the *W* key, walk forward toward the container in front of you. You'll see that you can still pass through this solid container fitted with a box collider. Finally, stop your Demo scene from playing.

# Implementing a Rollback Mechanic

There are two ways that you can prevent yourself from passing through solid objects. The preferred method is to force your position to be rolled back to where the pseudo-body's collider is located whenever a divergence occurs between your headset and the pseudo-body's collider. We'll look at setting up this method first. The other, more straightforward solution is to fade your headset view to black whenever your head collides with a solid object within the VR world.

Ensure that the Gizmos button within Unity's editor has been toggled on. Playtest your scene using the Camera Rigs, Spatial Simulator again. Then, using the *W* key, walk forward toward the container in front of you. Ensure that you push your hands through the container.

Now, switch to the Scene tab in Unity's editor. Double-click the Trackers Pseudo-Body game object in the hierarchy to allow it to obtain focus. As shown in Figure 12-3, your headset (camera) and hands have diverged from your pseudo-body. The green capsule outline you see in the figure represents your pseudo-body's collider that has been stopped from colliding with the container while you are in it. Your headset (represented by the camera gizmo icon) along with your hands have passed through the container. You can walk into the container; however, your pseudo-body won't follow you into the container. Here is a situation where a divergence has occurred between your headset and your pseudo-body. When this happens, all that needs to be done is that your position needs to be rolled back to the location of the pseudo-body's collider. It's essential to see what this divergence looks like visually, as depicted in Figure 12-3, so that you can understand how to go about using the pseudo-body to prevent yourself from penetrating through the container.

***Figure 12-3.*** *A divergence between your pseudo-body and your headset and hands*

In the event you don't see the pseudo-body collider, you can enable it as follows: From within the hierarchy, select and expand the Trackers Pseudo-Body game object. Next, expand the Collidable Volume game object and select the Child Collider game object within it. Then, in the Capsule Collider component of the Inspector, click the Edit Collider button to turn on the Capsule Collider.

To set up this *Rollback* mechanic, you first need to set up some Body Events, which are crucial to ensuring that you can't pass through solid objects. They also ensure that no weird collision behavior arises when attempting to climb any object in your virtual world.

With the Trackers Pseudo-Body game object selected in the hierarchy, and its pseudo-body component expanded, locate and expand the Still Diverged event in the "Body Events" section. This event will be used to solve the divergence issue wherein the headset remains diverged from the pseudo-body.

Whenever your headset has diverged from your pseudo-body, the Still Diverged event will be triggered, essentially letting you know that the divergence has occurred. When this event fires, you need to ensure that you roll back your position to where the pseudo-body collider is located, thereby forcing yourself out of the container. Whenever this event is fired, it is easily achievable by calling upon the Solve Body Collisions method, available against the pseudo-body via its Pseudo-Body Facade component.

Let's set up this event now. With the Still Diverged event expanded in the Inspector, click the plus symbol in the bottom right corner to add an event listener. Drag and drop the Trackers Pseudo-Body game object from the hierarchy into the event listener box of the Still Diverged event. For the function, select Pseudo-Body Facade, Solve Body Collisions.

This ensures that the moment your headset and pseudo-body have diverged, the Still Diverged event will be triggered, which in turn calls the Solve Body Collisions method, resulting in your position being rolled back to the location of the pseudo-body collider. By doing this, you no longer can enter a solid object. Figure 12-4 shows the Still Diverged event set up against your Trackers Pseudo-Body game object.

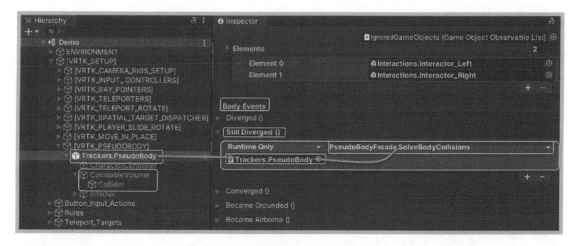

**Figure 12-4.** *Setting up the Still Diverged( ) event to solve for body collisions (effecting a rollback) when a divergence occurs*

Before we begin testing our Demo scene, we need to ensure that our prototype hands and Oculus-provided hands don't collide with our pseudo-body. We've already made sure that the pseudo-body will ignore both of our Interactors by setting them up as part of the Ignored Game Objects Elements in the Pseudo-Body Facade component.

Now, let's increase this Ignored Game Objects element's size to 6. We'll next add our Hand Proto Left and Hand Proto Right and Oculus-provided Custom Hand Left and Custom Hand Right as game objects that need to be ignored by the pseudo-body.

Drag and drop the Hand Proto Left and Hand Proto Right as well as the Oculus-provided Left and Right Custom Hands into the four new element slots you created as follows:

1. Drag and drop Custom Hand Left into the Element 2 slot.

2. Drag and drop Hand Proto Left into the Element 3 slot.

3. Drag and drop Custom Hand Right into the Element 4 slot.

4. Drag and drop Hand Proto Right into the Element 5 slot.

Any object you don't want colliding with the pseudo-body can be added to this Ignored Game Objects list, see Figure 12-5.

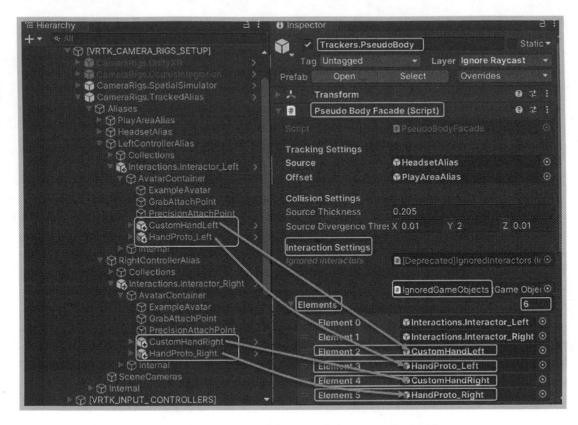

**Figure 12-5.** *Completing the setup of the Trackers Pseudo-Body*

Now, playtest your Demo scene using your VR headset with the Camera Rigs, Unity XR setup. Note that you won't be able to pass through the containers or barrels. As you attempt to pass through any of these solid objects, you'll find yourself being pushed back. Divergence is being resolved here via the Solve Body Collisions method.

Using a form of slide locomotion, approach the ladder and push your Thumbstick forward. You'll see that you can ascend the ladder and climb to the top of the container. Now, approach the edge of the container, and if you're wearing your VR headset, take that leap of faith and jump, or if using your Xbox controller, push forward on the Thumbstick, and you'll find that you can jump off the container using the controller as well.

Last, try having your hands interact with your pseudo-body. You should find no weird behavior. Grab the Drill machine on the table and push it toward your pseudo-body. You won't find any weird behavior here either. Note that the Layer for the Drill machine had been set to Interactable.

# Fading the Headset View to Black on Collision

VRTK provides you with a Collision Fader prefab that detects when the player's VR headset collides with another game object, fading the screen to a solid color when that happens. This solves the issue wherein players can push their head through a game object and see the inside clipping area, which is an undesired effect. The reasoning behind this is that if the player pushes their head through an object where it shouldn't be, then fading to a color (e.g., black) will make the player realize they've done something wrong and they'll probably step backward naturally. However, one disadvantage of fading to black is that the player can continue to push forward through the solid object. Hence, this Collision Fader prefab is best used in conjunction with the pseudo-body's rollback mechanic. Again, this depends on what you want to achieve in your game.

Before setting up this headset collision fade mechanic, select the VRTK PSEUDOBODY game object in the hierarchy and deactivate it. You'll first test the headset collision fade mechanic without having the rollback mechanic set up against the pseudo-body. Later, you'll activate the VRTK PSEUDOBODY game object to see how you can have both mechanics function together, which could be the effect you desire.

Let's now begin setting up this headset collision fade mechanic. In the hierarchy, select the VRTK SETUP game object and create a new empty game object within it. Rename the child game object "VRTK HEADSET COLLISION FADE."

Select the Project tab and expand the "Packages" folder. Locate the Tilia Visuals Collision Fader Unity package and expand it until you reach its "Prefabs" folder. Drag and drop the Visuals Collision Fader prefab you see in the right-hand pane onto the VRTK HEADSET COLLISION FADE game object in the hierarchy.

With the Visuals, Collision Fader game object selected in the hierarchy, ensure that its Collision Fader Facade component has been expanded in the Inspector. You need to set up several properties in the "Tracking Settings" section to get the Collision Fader working. For the Source property, drag and drop the Headset Alias game object from within the Camera Rigs, Tracked Alias game object into the Source property parameter, as shown in Figure 12-6. The Source property needs to be set to your Headset Alias, as you want your screen to fade to black when the player pushes their head through a solid object like one of the containers you have in the Demo scene.

For the Camera Validity property, drag and drop the Scene Cameras game object into this property parameter. This lets the Collision Fader know which cameras the fade should be applied against.

Last, the Collision Validity property requires you to set up a rule to determine which objects in the scene will activate a fade to black. You'll have your headset fade to black only when you attempt to push your head through any of the containers within the Demo scene.

Let's first create a new layer that will be applied to all containers within the Demo scene. We'll call this layer "WorldStaticMeshes." From the Unity Editor's main menu, navigate to Edit ➤ Project Settings ➤ Tags and Layers. From within the Tags and Layers pane available on the right, expand the Layers drop-down and locate the first-available empty User Layer. Type "WorldStaticMeshes" into the text box on the right. Finally, close the Project Settings dialog box.

Now, select the Environment game object in the hierarchy, and then select and expand its Containers child game object. You'll see that each of the containers has its Layer set to Default. Select all nine Container game objects that are children of the main Containers game object. In the Inspector, expand the Layer drop-down and select the layer WorldStaticMeshes. This ensures that each Container game object within the Demo scene will be assigned this layer.

You can now create a Collision Fader rule using the Any Layer Rule component that has its Layer Mask set to WorldStaticMeshes and apply this rule to the Collision Validity property. By doing this, when your headset collides with any Container game object in the scene, the Collision Validity property emits a True value, kicking the fade into a black effect.

In the hierarchy, select and expand the Rules game object. Create a new empty child game object within it and rename it "Headset Collision Fader." With this game object selected in the hierarchy, click the Add Component button in the Inspector and add the Any Layer Rule component. With this expanded, set its Layer Mask property to WorldStaticMeshes.

Select the Visuals Collision Fader game object in the hierarchy. Drag and drop the Headset Collision Fader rule game object into its Collision Validity property parameter.

You have now completed the setup for the Visuals Collision Fader game object, see Figure 12-6.

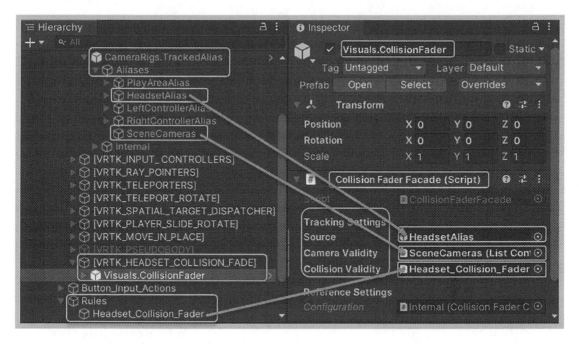

***Figure 12-6.*** *Setting up the Visuals Collision Fader game object*

Test your Demo scene using your VR headset with the Camera Rigs, Unity XR setup or the Camera Rigs, Oculus Integration setup. The one you choose to use will depend upon which headset you're using. Approach any container in your VR world and try pushing your head through it. You'll see that your headset screen immediately fades to black.

With one of the seamless forms of locomotion active, push forward against your VR controller's Left Thumbstick for a few seconds and you'll see that you pass through the container and exit on the opposite side. Even though your headset view fades to black when your head is pushed through the container, nothing is stopping the player from pushing themselves forward. This may be the effect you desire, but probably not. You may not want your player to be able to enter a solid object like a container. The pseudo-body you set up in the last section (Pseudo-Body Setup) can help out here.

Select the VRTK PSEUDOBODY game object in the hierarchy and activate it. Now, playtest your Demo scene again. Approach any container in your VR world and try pushing your head through it. You'll find that your headset screen immediately fades to black. While your headset is faded to black, push forward against the Left Thumbstick of your VR controller, attempting to pass right through the container and exit on the opposite side. Notice that it is not possible to pass through the container. This is because the pseudo-body rollback mechanic you set up is now in play. The moment a divergence occurs, you are rolled back. Also, having set up the Collision Fader component, your headset view fades to black, a visual cue that the object is impenetrable. Most paid VR frameworks available in the Unity Asset store don't provide you with this sort of a rollback mechanic, which helps with plausibility illusion in your VR worlds.

# Summary

In this chapter, we reviewed a fundamental concept, the pseudo-body. Almost any experience or game you create will definitely require this pseudo-body to enhance the Plausibility Illusion. Before setting up this pseudo-body, you saw that it was possible to pass through solid objects in your Demo scene, which is not what you want to happen in your VR world. Setting up a pseudo-body helped eliminate this strange behavior.

We first went over the advantages associated with having a pseudo-body. We then set up a pseudo-body. You learned to configure the properties available against your Pseudo-Body Facade component. We then took a deep dive into understanding how the rollback mechanic works with the pseudo-body, preventing the player from passing through solid objects.

You learned about the concept of divergence and how to set up the Still Diverged event to facilitate the rollback mechanic. Finally, you learned about the headset collision fade mechanic, which is commonly used to create the illusion of solid objects being impenetrable. You also learned about the downside of this approach. You then learned how to use the Collision Fader in conjunction with the pseudo-body to achieve the best of both worlds.

# CHAPTER 13

# Climbing in VR

The ability to climb up objects, Tomb Raider style, to get to your destination is one of the most enthralling things you can do in VR. The VRTK makes climbing a breeze, allowing you to make almost any surface climbable. Need to climb a fence, a ladder, or perhaps a wall, no worries. This climbing mechanic can be easily created using a customized Interactable prefab that handles the climbing action in conjunction with the pseudo-body to handle the physics of the player's body. In this chapter, we'll make all Containers and the Ladder in our Demo scene climbable.

## Climbing Mechanic Requirements

The VRTK provides you with two prefabs that are necessary to set up a climbing mechanic. To set up this climbing mechanic against game objects within your Demo scene, you'll first require a Climbing Controller, whose responsibility is to communicate with the pseudo-body you already set up. You'll also need a unique Climbable Interactable object that an Interactor can grab, which will serve as the foundation for your climbable object. Let's begin by setting up the Climbing Controller.

## Setting Up the Climbing Controller

To start, select the VRTK SETUP game object from within the hierarchy, and create an empty child game object and rename it "VRTK CLIMBING."

Then, select and expand the "Packages" folder from within the Project tab. Locate the Tilia Locomotors Climbing Unity package and expand it until you reach its "Prefabs" folder. Drag and drop the Locomotors Climbing prefab available in the right-hand pane onto the VRTK CLIMBING game object in the hierarchy.

© Christopher Coutinho 2022
C. Coutinho, *Unity® Virtual Reality Development with VRTK4*, https://doi.org/10.1007/978-1-4842-7933-5_13

You now need to tell this Locomotors Climbing controller about the pseudo-body available in your Demo scene. This pseudo-body allows your Locomotors Climbing controller to apply world physics to your pseudo-body. With the Locomotors Climbing controller game object selected in the hierarchy, ensure that its Climbing Facade and Pseudo-Body Climb Target components have been expanded in the Inspector. Drag and drop the Trackers Pseudo-Body game object from the hierarchy into the Pseudo-Body Facade property parameter of the Pseudo-Body Climb Target component, as shown in Figure 13-1.

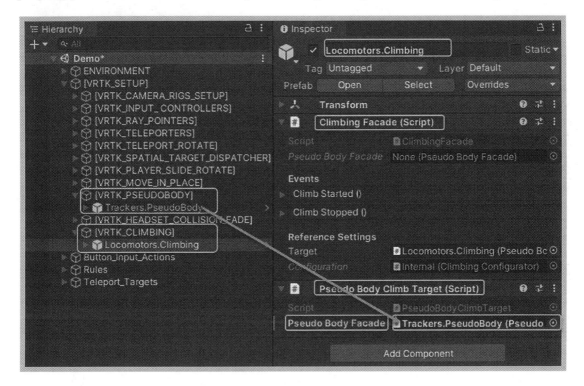

***Figure 13-1.*** *Setting up the Locomotors Climbing controller*

Within the Demo scene, you'll convert all Containers and the Ladder into climbable objects. To achieve this, the VRTK provides you with an Interactions Climbable prefab that an Interactor can grab. To make these objects climbable, you'll need to add this Interactions Climbable prefab to each Container and the Ladder within the Demo scene.

# Making the Containers Climbable

You'll notice that the Demo scene has nine Containers in it, each of which has an appropriate Mesh and is fitted with a Box Collider. You'll also notice that all these Containers have already been placed at strategic locations in the scene. You don't want to change the position of these Container game objects when setting them up as climbable objects.

Let's begin setting up the Containers to be climbable now. With the Tilia Locomotors Climbing Unity package "Prefabs" folder still selected within the Project tab, drag and drop the Interactions Climbable prefab into the hierarchy so that it is a child of your Demo scene. In the Scene tab, you'll see that this Interactions Climbable prefab is simply a cube object with a box collider. You can verify this by selecting the Interactions Climbable game object in the hierarchy and navigating as follows: Interactions Climbable ➤ Internal ➤ Interactions Interactable ➤ Mesh Container ➤ Cube. This is depicted in Figure 13-2.

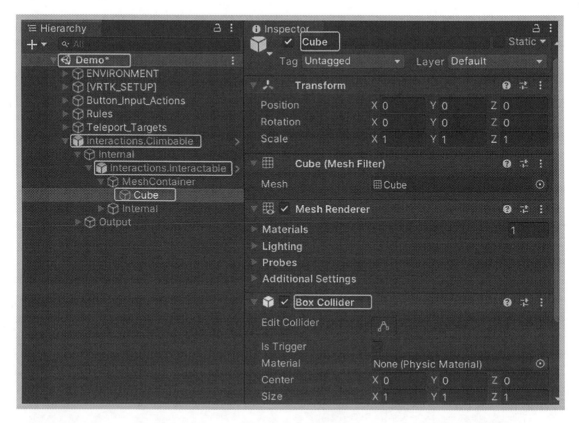

***Figure 13-2.*** *Navigating to the Cube child game object in the Interactions Climbable game object*

To make a Container climbable, all you need to do is swap out the Cube game object shown in Figure 13-2 with your Container game object, which already contains a Mesh and box collider. For each Container you want to make climbable, you need to have a corresponding Interactions Climbable game object in the scene, so that its Cube game object can be swapped out with the concerned Container game object. For the Demo scene, this would mean you require nine Interactions Climbable game objects.

The procedure applied here is similar to the one you used when you swapped out your Interactable Cube for the Drill machine. Looking at Figure 13-2, you'll see that the Interactions Climbable game object has an Interactions Interactable nested in it. This is the same Interactable that allowed you to grab the Drill machine.

You first need to set up a total of nine Interactions Climbable game objects in your scene, as you have nine Containers that need to make climbable. Select the Interactions Climbable game object in the hierarchy and duplicate it so that you have in total nine . From within the hierarchy, expand the Environment game object and then expand its Containers child game object, see Figure 13-3.

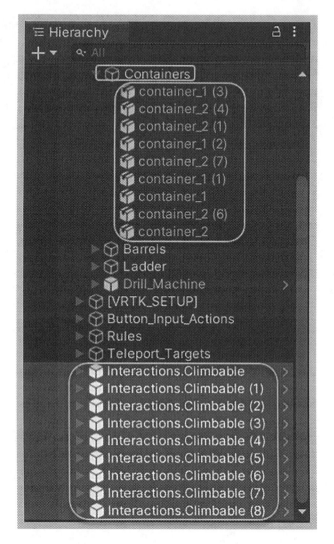

***Figure 13-3.*** *Hierarchy showing a total of nine created Interactions Climbable game objects*

Next, select the first Container available in the Containers game object and ensure that the Transform component in the Inspector has been expanded. Copy these Transform settings by clicking the three vertical dots to the right of the Transform Component heading and then selecting the Copy Component menu item, as shown in Figure 13-4.

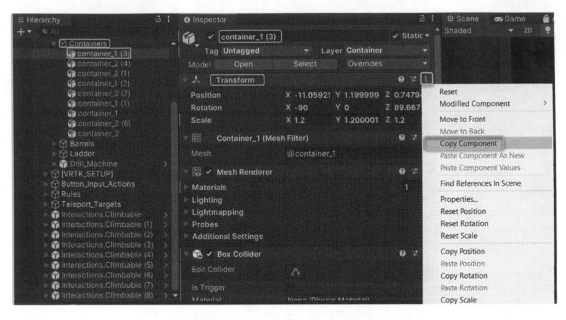

***Figure 13-4.*** *Copying the Transform settings for the first Container game object*

Now, select the first Interactions Climbable game object in the hierarchy. Ensure that the Transform component in the Inspector has been expanded, and then expand the context menu for its Transform component by clicking the three vertical dots to the right of its Transform component heading. Then, select the Paste Component Values menu item, as shown in Figure 13-5.

This orients your Interactions Climbable white cube to the position of the Container whose transform values you copied. You'll notice the white cube sitting in the Container.

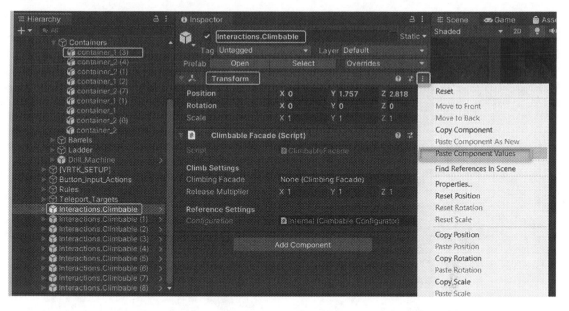

***Figure 13-5.*** *Pasting the copied Transform setting values of the first Container game object into the first Interactions Climbable game object Transform*

Now, expand this Interactions Climbable game object in the hierarchy until you reach its Cube game object, which is nested within the Mesh Container game object. This is depicted in Figure 13-2. Deactivate this Cube game object, as you want your Container game object to become the actual Mesh.

Next, drag the Container whose Transform values you copied from the "Containers" folder in the hierarchy and drop it onto the Mesh Container game object that is nested in the Interactions Climbable game object. This game object is currently expanded in the hierarchy, see Figure 13-6. Select this Container game object, which is now a child of the Mesh Container of the Interactions Climbable game object, and reset its Transform. Last, select this Interactions Climbable game object and rename it "Container 1." You now need to set up the remaining eight Containers in the Demo scene using the same procedure as previously explained.

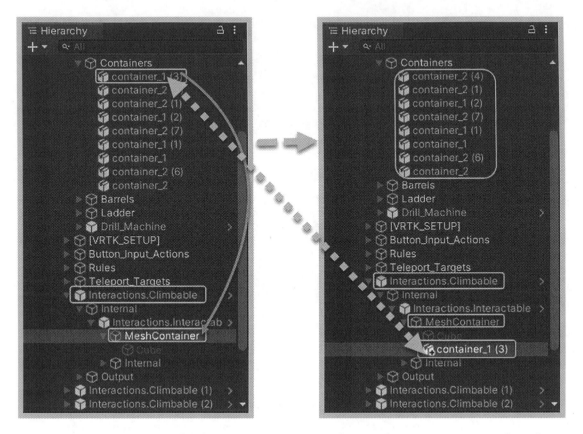

***Figure 13-6.*** *Dragging the first Container onto the Mesh Container nested in the Interactions Climbable game object and thereby making it a child replacing the original Cube game object*

Once you've set up all nine Container objects to be climbable, select all of them in the hierarchy. Then, drag and drop them onto the Containers game object in the Environment game object. With all nine Containers still selected in the hierarchy, ensure that their Climbable Facade component has been expanded in the Inspector. Now, drag and drop the Locomotors Climbing game object from the hierarchy into the Climbing Facade property parameter. This connects each of your nine climbable Container game objects to the Locomotors Climbing controller, see Figure 13-7.

Now, you have all nine Containers grouped in the Containers game object, and they are all climbable.

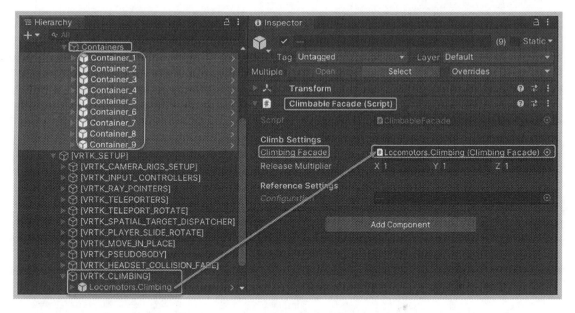

***Figure 13-7.*** *Connecting the Locomotors Climbing controller to each of the climbable Containers*

# Making the Ladder Climbable

Let's now set up your Ladder to be climbable. The procedure is similar to the one you used for making your Containers climbable. You'll notice that your Ladder comprises two objects: Steel Ladder A and Steel Ladder B, each of them having its own Mesh and colliders. The Ladder game object is located in the hierarchy in the Environment game object. To set up this Ladder, you'll need two Interactions Climbable prefabs, one for setting up *Steel Ladder A* to be climbable and the other for setting up *Steel Ladder B* similarly.

You should still have the "Prefabs" folder selected in your Tilia Locomotors Climbing Unity package. Drag and drop the Interactions Climbable prefab in the right-hand pane onto the Ladder game object in the hierarchy, and rename it "Interactions Climbable Steel Ladder A." Then, duplicate this steel ladder and rename it "Interactions Climbable Steel Ladder B."

Select both Interactions Climbable Steel Ladders in the hierarchy, and within the Inspector, ensure that their Climbable Facade components have been expanded. Drag and drop the Locomotors Climbing Controller game object from the hierarchy into the Climbing Facade property parameter.

Your Interactions Climbable Steel Ladder A and B game objects have now been made aware of the Locomotors Climbing controller, see Figure 13-8.

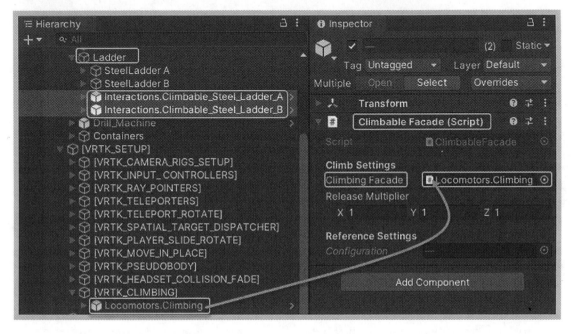

***Figure 13-8.*** *Connecting the Locomotors Climbing controller to the Interactions Climbable of Steel Ladder A and Steel Ladder B*

Next, select the Steel Ladder A game object in the hierarchy. Copy its Transform settings by clicking the three vertical dots to the right of its Transform component heading and then selecting the Copy component menu item, as shown in Figure 13-9.

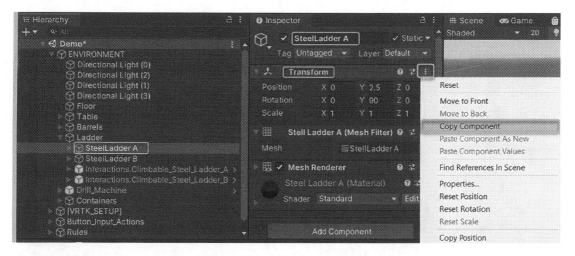

***Figure 13-9.*** *Copying the Transform settings for the Steel Ladder A game object*

Now, select the Interactions Climbable Steel Ladder A game object in the hierarchy, and expand the context menu for its Transform component by clicking the three vertical dots to the right of its Transform Component heading. Then, select the Paste Component Values menu item, as shown in Figure 13-10.

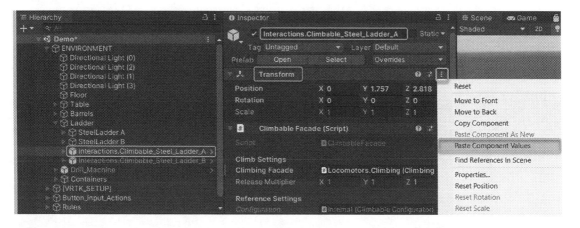

***Figure 13-10.*** *Pasting the copied Transform setting values of the Steel Ladder A game object into the Interactions Climbable Steel Ladder A game object Transform*

You have now embedded your Interactions Climbable Steel Ladder A, represented by a large white cube, in the Steel Ladder A game object whose transform values you copied. This is depicted in Figure 13-11.

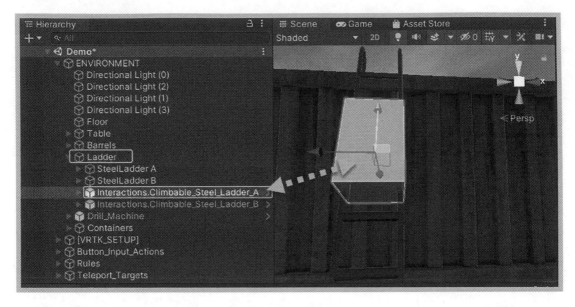

***Figure 13-11.*** *The large white cube embedded in Steel Ladder A represents your Interactions Climbable Steel Ladder A game object*

Now, from within the hierarchy, expand the Interactions Climbable Steel Ladder A game object until you reach its Cube object nested within the Mesh Container. Deactivate this Cube game object, as you want your Steel Ladder A game object to become the actual Mesh. Next, drag and drop the Steel Ladder A game object in the "Ladder" folder onto the Mesh Container game object nested within Interactions Climbable Steel Ladder A that is currently expanded in the hierarchy, see Figure 13-12.

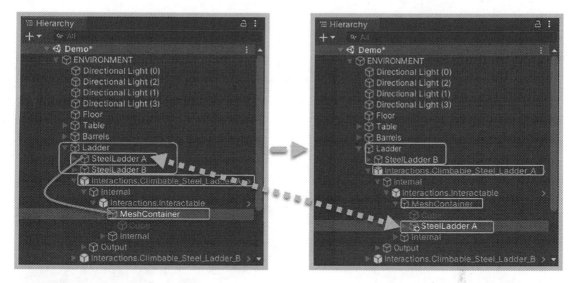

*Figure 13-12.*  *Dragging Steel Ladder A onto the Mesh Container nested within the Interactions Climbable Steel Ladder A game object and thereby making it a child replacing the original Cube game object*

Last, select the Steel Ladder A game object that is now a child of the Mesh Container and reset its Transform. We now need to set up Steel Ladder B using the same procedure we used for Steel Ladder A.

## Deactivating Untouched Events on Climbable Game Objects

While climbing up any climbable object, you may find yourself falling for no apparent reason. This behavior may happen when you have your pseudo-body solving for body collisions during a climb. When pulling yourself up a Container, your pseudo-body will attempt to solve the body collision with the Container upon colliding with it. If you happen to let go of your grab at the same time, the Ungrab on Untouch Process attached to the Untouched event will be activated, as discussed later in the chapter, causing you to fall unexpectedly. There are a couple of ways to solve this issue. Let's adopt the most straightforward approach.

Select and expand the Interactions Climbable Steel Ladder A game object in the hierarchy and locate its Interactions Interactable child game object and select it. In the Inspector, with the Interactable Facade component expanded, locate and expand the Untouched event in the "Touch Events" section. Set the drop-down value for this event, which currently is set to Runtime Only, to Off. This turns off the Untouched event, thereby not allowing it to execute whenever an Ungrab (Untouch) occurs while climbing. This ensures that the function attached to the Ungrab on Untouch Process in the event listener box is never called, guaranteeing that the unexpected falling behavior never occurs, see Figure 13-13.

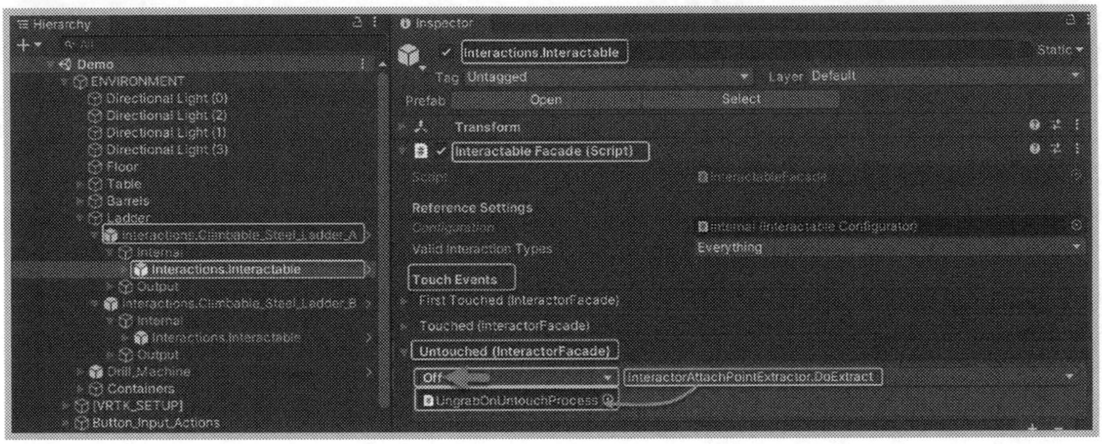

***Figure 13-13.*** *Turning off the Untouched event, nested in the Interactions Interactable game object, for Interactions Climbable Steel Ladder A*

Finally, you need to turn off this Untouched event for the Interactions Climbable Steel Ladder B game object, as well as for all nine climbable Container game objects in the Demo scene.

Now, playtest the climbable mechanic you've set up in the Demo scene. Climb up a couple of Containers as well as the Ladder, and you'll notice that while climbing, you may encounter some jittering. Go ahead and try this out now.

To do away with this unwarranted jittering, you need to assign your Ladder and all the Containers to the Ignore Raycast layer. In the hierarchy, ensure that you have collapsed your Ladder and Containers game objects. Then, select these game objects in the hierarchy, and when prompted to set the Ignore Raycast layer for all child objects, select the button Yes, change children, as shown in Figure 13-14.

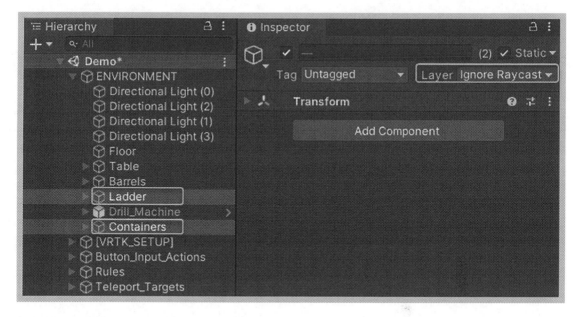

*Figure 13-14. Setting the Layer for the Ladder and all Container game objects to Ignore Raycast*

Go ahead and try out your climbing mechanic now to ensure you don't experience any unexpected falling behavior or jittering while climbing.

You have now created an extremely sophisticated climbing mechanic and can easily climb any climbable object Tomb Raider style.

## Summary

In this chapter, we learned how to set up climbing in VR using the VRTK's provided prefabs. We started by setting up a Locomotors Climbing controller game object responsible for communicating with our pseudo-body during a climb. We then explored the Interactions Climbable prefab and learned how to set it up against each of the nine available Containers in the Demo scene. We next hooked up our Locomotors Climbing controller to each of our climbable Containers using the Climbing Facade property in the Climbable Facade component of our Climbable Container game objects. We used the same procedure to enable the Ladder to be climbable.

Finally, we went over a particular unexpected falling behavior that could occur while climbing on account of our pseudo-body attempting to solve for body collisions. To eliminate this possible falling behavior, we deactivated the Untouched event located within each climbable object's Interactions Interactable game object. We also learned that by assigning our Ladder and Containers to the Ignore Raycast layer, we could eliminate any jittering that occurs while climbing.

# CHAPTER 14

# Movement Amplifier

You've experienced several locomotion mechanics so far. In this chapter, we'll set up a final locomotion mechanic provided by the VRTK, aptly called the Movement Amplifier. When setting up your Oculus Guardian or your HTC Vive Chaperone, you're restricted by the room space you have available. Your movement within your VR World is limited by the room space you have in the real world. Every step you take forward in your available real-world room space is a step forward in your virtual world. Unless you have palatial room space, your physical movements in the real world will soon have you encountering your Guardian or Chaperone without having moved any significant distance in your VR world. The Movement Amplifier prefab provided by the VRTK helps overcome this setback. Using this prefab, you can amplify your movements within the virtual world, making it easier for you to cover further virtual distances despite having limited real-world room space. Thus, each step you take in the real world can be amplified to cover a much larger distance in your virtual world.

## Movement Amplifier Setup

In the hierarchy, select the VRTK SETUP game object, and create a new empty child game object within it and rename it "VRTK MOVEMENT AMPLIFIER." Then, select the Project tab and expand the "Packages" folder and locate the Tilia Locomotors Movement Amplifier Unity package. Expand the package until you locate its "Prefabs" folder.

With the "Prefabs" folder selected, drag and drop the Locomotors Movement Amplifier prefab in the right-hand pane onto the VRTK MOVEMENT AMPLIFIER game object in the hierarchy, making it a child. With the Locomotors Movement Amplifier game object selected in the hierarchy, ensure that its Movement Amplifier Facade component has been expanded in the Inspector.

© Christopher Coutinho 2022
C. Coutinho, *Unity® Virtual Reality Development with VRTK4*, https://doi.org/10.1007/978-1-4842-7933-5_14

Next, let's set up its Source and Target properties in the "Tracking Settings" section. The Source property represents the source object whose movement needs to be observed. Expand the Camera Rigs, Tracked Alias game object in the hierarchy. Drag and drop the Headset Alias game object into the Source property parameter, as shown in Figure 14-1. The real-world movement of the source game object is amplified by the value of the Multiplier property and applied to your Play Area Alias (Target), thereby amplifying the Player's movement in the virtual world.

The Target property represents the game object against which the computed amplified movement is to be applied. As the Player's movement in the VR World needs to be amplified, you'll set this Target property value to the Play Area Alias. Drag and drop the Play Area Alias game object into the Target property parameter, as shown in Figure 14-1.

You now need to set up values for the properties in the "Movement Settings" section. You could leave the Ignored Radius property at its default value. Any source object movement occurring within the limits of the radius value specified here won't be amplified. It's important to note that you shouldn't set this value to a very small number, as this could lead to amplification occurring while crouching, which is something you most likely wouldn't want to have happen. At the same time, feel free to play around with this value and see what works best for you. For now, though, leave the Ignored Radius property value at its default of 0.25.

The final property that you need to set is the value for the Multiplier property. I found the default value of 2 to be too small to obtain any noticeable amplified movement. Set the value for the Multiplier property to 10. At this level, one step forward in the real world will amplify your movement tenfold in the VR World. This is all that's required to get the Movement Amplifier working, see Figure 14-1.

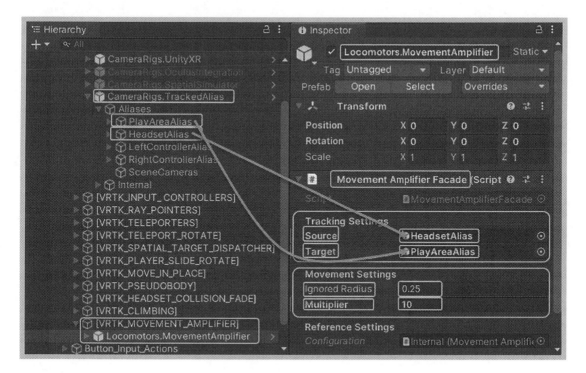

***Figure 14-1.*** *Setting up the Locomotors Movement Amplifier game object*

# Testing Amplified Movement

It's now time to test out this amplified movement mechanic. This mechanic only amplifies your actual physical movement in the real world. For amplified movement to work, you need to physically walk about in the confines of your Guardian or Chaperone. Amplified movement should not be used with other forms of locomotion like teleportation, arm swinging, or seamless locomotion, as a clash will occur. Ideally, each locomotion method should be used independently. You should toggle off all other forms of locomotion when using a specific locomotion mechanic to prevent different forms of locomotion from clashing with one another.

To test out this amplified movement locomotion method using your VR headset, hit the Play button in Unity's editor to playtest your Demo scene. Take a couple of steps forward in your real-world room space, and you'll see that you've moved a lot further in the virtual world than you have in the real world. Now walk backward a couple of steps, and you'll find that you cover a lot more ground in the virtual world. Turn yourself around and move forward in the direction you're facing, and you'll see that you can cover a lot more distance in the virtual world. This is a great locomotion mechanic that you can use in several situations. It's something you wouldn't find readily available in other VR tool kits.

## Summary

In this relatively short chapter, we looked at the final locomotion mechanic provided by the VRTK, which is something rarely found in other VR tool kits. You learned how to amplify player movement in the virtual world based on actual physical movement in a limited real-world room space. You learned about the various properties available as part of the Movement Amplifier Facade component and how you can tweak values for the Ignored Radius and Multiplier properties to fine-tune your amplified movement. Finally, we tested out this Amplified Movement mechanic.

# CHAPTER 15

# Distance Grabbing

In Chapter 6, I mentioned that the VRTK provides you with two standard ways to interact with an Interactable game object. Direct Interaction is the most common form of Interaction. The other form of Interaction is the ability to grab an object from a distance.

The Distance Grab mechanic allows you to grab an object from a distance without physically approaching the object. It provides you with an invisible beam with a visible reticle to identify Interactable objects in the VR world and allows such Interactable objects to be grabbed from a distance by simply pressing the Grab button on the Interactor.

In VR, you have the projective ability to influence a physical object without physically interacting with it. If you as the player drop your weapon in a VR FPS (First Person Shooter) game, you ideally don't want to physically bend down to pick it up. You can avoid doing this by turning on the Distance Grab mechanic, which will allow the weapon move into your hand.

In this chapter, we'll revisit the grabbing mechanic by setting up a Distance Grabber. The VRTK provides you a distance grab pointer in the form of a blue pulsating reticle that shows up when you point toward an Interactable game object. This is the standard out-of-the-box approach provided to you by the VRTK.

If you're some distance away from the Interactable game object you want to grab, and if the object is not large enough, it becomes difficult to point precisely at that game object and have the blue pulsating reticle show up. To overcome this drawback, you'll learn to set up a straight pointer that aids in precisely pointing at the Interactable game object and performing the distance grab a lot more easily.

You'll also learn to limit the grab distance so that you can't grab an object from, say, 100 meters away, though if your game requires that, you could set that up as well. Along the way, you'll learn how to set up a Toggle Action.

© Christopher Coutinho 2022
C. Coutinho, *Unity® Virtual Reality Development with VRTK4*, https://doi.org/10.1007/978-1-4842-7933-5_15

# Prerequisites for Distance Grabbing

Before setting up the Distance Grabber, we need to ensure that on the Oculus-provided Custom Hand Right, we deactivate the Capsule Colliders in its Grab Volume Big and Grab Volume Small child game objects. This is essential for having the distance grab pointer and its reticle emit from your hand.

To do this, select the Oculus-provided Custom Hand Right game object in the hierarchy and expand it until you see its Grab Volume Big and Grab Volume Small child game objects. In the Inspector, deactivate their Capsule Colliders, see Figure 15-1. If you are left-handed and would like your distance grab pointer and its reticle to emit from your left hand, then ensure that you deactivate the same Capsule Colliders on the Oculus-provided Custom Hand Left.

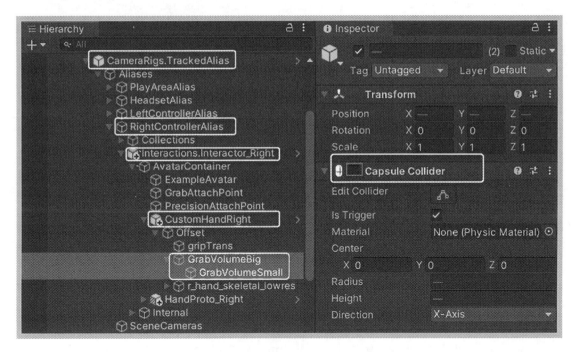

***Figure 15-1.*** *Deactivating both Capsule Colliders on the Oculus-provided Custom Hand Right*

# Setting Up the Distance Grabber

Select and expand the VRTK SETUP game object in the hierarchy and create a new empty child game object and rename it "VRTK DISTANCE GRAB." Select the Project tab and expand the "Packages" folder. Locate the Tilia Interactions Pointer Interactors Unity package, and expand it until you reach its "Prefabs" folder.

With the "Prefabs" folder selected, drag and drop the Interactions Pointer Interactors Distance Grabber prefab in the right pane onto the hierarchy's VRTK DISTANCE GRAB game object. Rename this prefab "Interactions Pointer Interactors Distance Grabber Right," as it's set up against your right hand.

Ensure that the Distance Grabber Facade component in the Inspector has been expanded. In the "Interaction Settings" section, the Interactor property determines which Interactor the Distance Grabber is associated with. In this case, you will associate it with the right-hand Interactor. However, you can also associate it with the left-hand Interactor if you're left handed. The procedure is the same. If you would like both of your hands to perform a distance grab, you need to add another Distance Grabber prefab for your left hand and associate it with your left-hand Interactor.

To set up the Distance Grabber against your right-hand Interactor, expand the Camera Rigs, Tracked Alias game object in the hierarchy, then expand its Aliases game object, and then expand its Right Controller Alias game object. Drag and drop the Interactions Interactor Right game object from the hierarchy into the Interactor property parameter in the Distance Grabber Facade component.

Test the Demo scene using either the Spatial Simulator or your VR headset. Point your right hand at the Drill machine on the table. You should notice a light-bluish pulsating reticle appear over the Drill machine. This cue serves as an indicator that you may now distance grab the Drill machine. When the reticle appears over the Drill machine, the moment you press the right mouse button or the Grab button on your right controller, the Drill machine will instantly snap to your hand.

Now, move further away from the table and try pointing your hand at the Drill machine to get the bluish pulsating reticle to appear. You'll find it difficult to precisely point your hand at the Drill machine. To solve this problem, you will create a straight ray pointer that will emit from your hand, allowing you to easily point at Interactable objects at a distance and grab them.

If you don't want the Drill machine to snap to your hand instantly, you can configure a telekinesis movement, where y the Drill machine will slowly levitate toward your hand. We'll set up both these functionalities next.

# Setting Up a Telekinesis Grab

Note that you weren't required to populate the Follow Source property in the Interaction Settings section, as doing this is optional. If you don't populate this Follow Source property, the current Interactor is used by default.

Now, let's set up the telekinesis movement and have a grabbed Interactable object levitate toward your hand over half a second. In the Distance Grabber Facade component, set the Transition Duration property value to 0.5. With this setting, the Drill machine or any other selected Interactable game object will take half a second to reach your hand from the moment you press the Grab button. The higher the Transition Duration property value, the longer the selected Interactable game object will take to reach your hand.

Playtest the Demo scene now and try out your new levitating behavior. You'll see that the Drill machine no longer instantly snaps to your hand. It instead moves slowly toward your hand over half a second.

# Setting Up a straight pointer to Grab Interactable Objects

Next, let's set up a straight pointer to show up, which will be easier to point at an Interactable object. Select the Interactions Pointer Interactors Distance Grabber Right game object in the hierarchy, and expand it until you reach its Pointer Elements game object.

You'll need to navigate as follows: Interactions Pointer Interactors Distance Grabber Right ➤ Internal ➤ Pointer ➤ Indicators Object Pointers Straight ➤ Pointer Elements, see Figure 15-2.

Now expand this Pointer Elements game object in the hierarchy and you'll see that it contains three child game objects: Origin, Repeated Segment, and Destination. Select all three. In the Inspector, ensure that the Pointer Element component has been expanded.

Locate the "Visibility Settings" section in the Pointer Element component. You'll see that the Element Visibility property is currently set to Always Off. To ensure that your straight pointer is displayed, with all three child objects still selected in the hierarchy, change the value of their Element Visibility property to On When Pointer Activated, as shown in Figure 15-2.

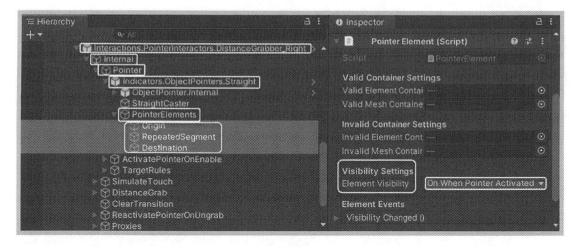

*Figure 15-2.* *Configuring the Distance Grabber's straight pointer to display when active*

Playtest your Demo scene using the Spatial Simulator or your VR headset. You'll notice a red straight pointer emanating from your right hand. Aim the red pointer at the Drill machine, and you'll see it turns green and the bluish pulsating reticle is visible at the end of this green-ray pointer. Press the right mouse button or the Grab button on your right controller, and your Drill machine will levitate toward your hand.

Now, place the Drill machine back on the table. Move back so that you're positioned near the Container behind the table. You're now quite a distance away from the Drill machine. Point your Distance Grabber's straight pointer toward the Drill machine so that it turns green. Press the right mouse button or the Grab button on your right controller and grab the Drill machine again. You'll find that it's now a lot easier to grab the Drill machine with the assistance of the straight pointer.

## Changing the Straight Pointer's Grabbing Distance

Let's now learn how to change the grab distance for the straight pointer. We'll reduce this distance so that we can only grab Interactable game objects that are within a ten-meter radius.

With the Pointer Elements game object expanded in the hierarchy, select the Straight Caster game object directly above it. In the Inspector, ensure that the Straight Line Cast component is expanded. Locate the Maximum Length property, which is set to the value 100 by default, and change the value to 10, see Figure 15-3.

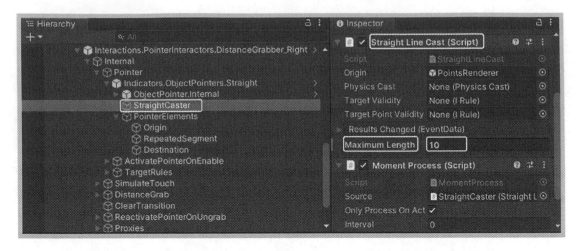

***Figure 15-3.*** *Reducing the grabbing distance of your Distance Grabber*

Playtest your *Demo* scene again using the Spatial Simulator or your VR headset. You'll see that if you're within a ten-meter distance from the Drill machine, you'll be able to grab it, but if you move beyond this distance, you won't any longer be able to do so.

You may have noticed that currently your Distance Grabber's straight pointer is always on regardless of whether you intend to do a distance grab. In the next section, we'll learn how to activate and deactivate the straight pointer as we deem fit.

# Activating and Deactivating the Distance Grabber

In the previous section, our Distance Grabber was set to always be on, with the straight pointer displayed. In this section, we'll learn to set up the *A* button on the Oculus controller, the *X* button on the Xbox controller, and the Spacebar key on the keyboard to enable the Distance Grabber to be toggled on and off. Since the HTC Vive doesn't provide the *A*, *B*, *X*, or *Y* buttons as does the Oculus controller, you'll use the Right Trackpad Touch 17 button action to toggle the Distance Grabber on and off.

To achieve this, we'll utilize a new Toggle Action component provided by the VRTK that allows you to have your buttons and key presses function like a toggle. When you press the Spacebar key or the appropriate button on your controllers once, you'll activate the Distance Grabber along with its pointer. Pressing either of them again will deactivate these items.

Let's first set up a simple Toggle game object with a Toggle Action component on it. Select the Button Input Actions game object in the hierarchy and create a new empty child game object and rename it "Toggle." Then, click the Add component button in the Inspector and add a Toggle Action component to this game object.

You now need to set up the Activated and Deactivated events against the Toggle Action component of the Toggle game object. To do so, expand the Activated and Deactivated events. Click the plus symbol located in the bottom right corner of each of these events to add an event listener to each of them. Then, drag and drop the Interactions Pointer Interactors Distance Grabber Right game object from the hierarchy into the event listener box of the Activated event. For the function, select Game Object, Set Active in the "Static Parameters" section, and ensure you check the box below, which is equivalent to setting a True value, see Figure 15-4.

Essentially, what you're doing is activating the Interactions Pointer Interactors Distance Grabber Right game object when the Activated event is fired. This occurs when you press either the appropriate controller button or the spacebar key the first time, which results in the Toggle being activated.

Next, drag and drop the Interactions Pointer Interactors Distance Grabber Right game object from the hierarchy into the event listener box of the Deactivated event. For the function, select Game Object, Set Active in the "Static Parameters" section and ensure you uncheck the box below, which is equivalent to setting a False value, see Figure 15-4.

In this case, what you're doing is deactivating the Interactions Pointer Interactors Distance Grabber Right game object when the Deactivated event is fired. When you subsequently press either the appropriate controller button or the Spacebar key, it will result in the Toggle being deactivated.

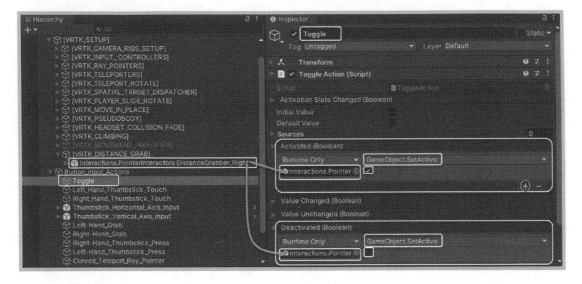

**Figure 15-4.** *Setting up the Toggle game object to activate and deactivate the Distance Grabber*

Now it's time to capture the various inputs discussed at the beginning of this section, which, when triggered, will result in toggling your Distance Grabber on and off. Let's begin by capturing the Spacebar key press against the keyboard.

In the hierarchy in the VRTK SETUP game object, locate and expand the VRTK INPUT CONTROLLERS game object. Then, expand its Keyboard Input game object. Duplicate the Input Unity Input Manager Button Action T game object and rename the copied game object "Input Unity Input Manager Button Action Spacebar." This will be used to capture a spacebar key press. In the hierarchy, with the Input Unity Input Manager Button Action Spacebar game object selected, locate the Key Code property in the Unity Input Manager Button Action component in the Inspector. From its dropdown, select the Space key menu item. You can now be assured that a spacebar key press will be captured.

With the Input Unity Input Manager Button Action Spacebar game object still selected in the hierarchy, locate and expand its Activated event. Click the plus symbol in the bottom right corner of the Activated event to add an event listener. Now, drag and drop the Toggle game object from the hierarchy into the event listener box of this Activated event. For the function, select Toggle Action, Receive in the "Dynamic Bool" section, see Figure 15-5.

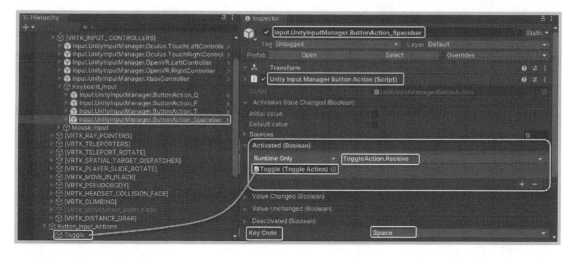

***Figure 15-5.*** *The Spacebar key press calling on the Toggle game object asking it to receive a Boolean value*

Let me now explain how this works. The moment you press the Spacebar key on the keyboard, the Unity Input Manager, Button Action Spacebar game object fires its Activated event. This event calls on your Toggle game object that has been fitted with a Toggle Action component, asking it to receive a Boolean value. This sets the Toggle Action to On—that is, a True state—causing the *Activated* event in the Toggle Action component to trigger, which results in your Distance Grabber game object being activated.

Note your Toggle Action is now set to On—that is, a True state. The next Spacebar key press received by the Toggle Action will toggle it off. When you press the Spacebar key another time, your Input, Unity Input Manager, Button Action Spacebar game object will fire its Activated event again. This event calls on your Toggle game object that has been fitted with a Toggle Action component, asking it to receive a Boolean value, which will set this Toggle Action to Off—that is, a False state—causing the Deactivated event in the Toggle Action to trigger, which results in your Distance Grabber game object being deactivated.

You are thus toggling the Distance Grabber and its straight pointer on and off via the Toggle Action component on your Toggle game object. At this point, you can run the Demo scene in Spatial Simulator mode and hit the Spacebar key on the keyboard to see the straight pointer of your Distance Grabber toggle off and on. In the hierarchy, you'll also notice that the Interactions Pointer Interactors Distance Grabber Right game object is enabled and disabled upon pressing the Spacebar key.

As discussed at the beginning of this section, let's set up the *A* button on the Oculus controller, the *X* button on the Xbox controller, and the Right Trackpad Touch 17 button on the HTC Vive to enable the Distance Grabber to toggle on and off. In the hierarchy, with the VRTK INPUT CONTROLLERS game object expanded, also expand the Oculus Touch Right controller game object and Input Actions and select the Button One Press [0] game object. In the Inspector, ensure that the Unity Input Manager Button Action component has also been expanded. Then, locate and expand the Activated event. Click the plus symbol located in the bottom right corner to add an event listener. Drag and drop the Toggle game object from the hierarchy into the event listener box of this Activated event. For the function, select Toggle Action Receive from within the "Dynamic Bool" section.

You have now set up your right Oculus controller's *A* button to function as a toggle that will switch your Distance Grabber on and off. Note that the Key Code property has been set to a default value of Joystick Button 0, as shown in Figure 15-6.

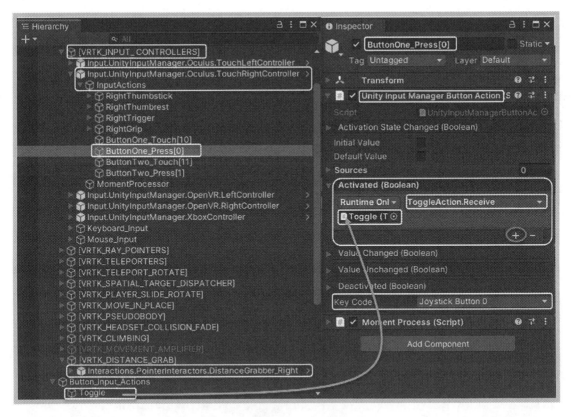

***Figure 15-6.*** *The Oculus right controller's* A *button press calls on the Toggle game object, asking it to receive a Boolean value*

With the *VRTK INPUT CONTROLLERS* game object expanded, collapse the Oculus Touch Right Controller game object. Expand the X-Box Controller game object, then expand Input Actions, and select the Button X Press [2] game object. In the Inspector, ensure that the Unity Input Manager Button Action component has been expanded. Locate and expand the Activated event. Click the plus symbol located in the bottom right corner to add an event listener. Drag and drop the Toggle game object from the hierarchy into the event listener box of this Activated event. For the function, select Toggle Action Receive from within the "Dynamic Bool" section.

You have now set up your Xbox controller's *X* button to function as a toggle that will switch your Distance Grabber on and off. Note that the Key Code property shown in Figure 15-7 has been set to a default value of Joystick Button 2—a Key Code value that differs from that set for your right Oculus controller's *A* button. You'll notice that your physical Oculus and Xbox controllers feature the buttons *A*, *Y*, *X*, and *B*. If you select the Button A Press [0] game object in the X-Box controller game object in the hierarchy and look at its Key Code property in the Inspector, you'll see that it has been set to the Joystick Button 0 value by default. This is the same Key Code value used by your right Oculus controller's *A* button. If you attempt to set up toggling your Distance Grabber via the X-Box controller to work with its *A* button, there will be a clash between the similar Key Code values. This is the reason I have chosen to use the *X* button on the Xbox controller to toggle the Distance Grabber on and off.

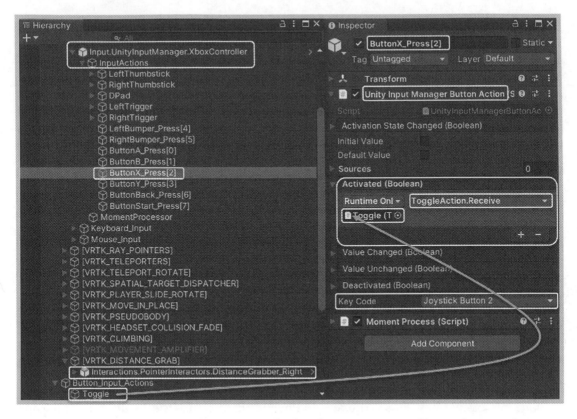

***Figure 15-7.*** *Pressing the Xbox controller's* X *button press calls on the Toggle game object, asking it to receive a Boolean value*

Finally, let's set up the Right Trackpad Touch 17 button on the HTC Vive to toggle the Distance Grabber on and off. In the hierarchy, with the VRTK INPUT CONTROLLERS game object expanded, collapse the X-Box Controller game object. Expand the Open VR Right Controller game object, then expand Input Actions and the Right Trackpad game object, and select the Right Trackpad Touch 17 game object. In the Inspector, ensure that the Unity Input Manager Button Action component has been expanded. Locate and expand the Activated event. Click the plus symbol located in the bottom right corner to add an event listener. Drag and drop the Toggle game object from the hierarchy into the event listener box of this Activated event. For the function, select Toggle Action Receive from within the "Dynamic Bool" section.

You have now set up your HTC Vive Right Controllers Trackpad to function as a toggle. Upon executing subsequent touches against the HTC Vive Right Controllers Trackpad, your Distance Grabber will be toggled on and off. Note that the *Key Code* property shown in Figure 15-8 has been set to a default value of *Joystick Button 17*—a Key Code value that differs from that set for the right Oculus controller's *A* button and the X-Box controller's *X* button.

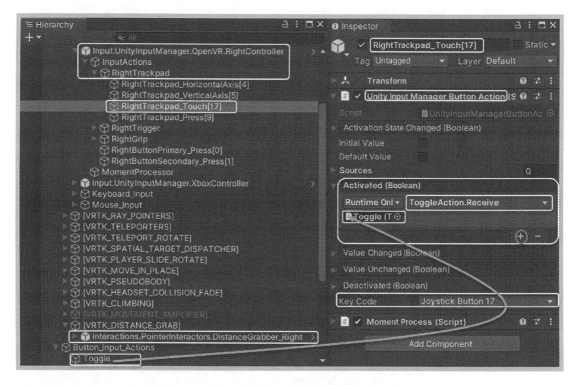

***Figure 15-8.*** *Pressing the HTC Vive right controller's Trackpad Touch [17] button calls on the Toggle game object, asking it to receive a Boolean value*

Before proceeding to test your Demo scene, ensure that you deactivate the Interactions Pointer Interactors, Distance Grabber Right game object, as outlined in Figure 15-8. You don't want your Demo scene to start with the Distance Grabber showing. Select the Interactions Pointer Interactors, Distance Grabber Right game object in the hierarchy and uncheck its box in the Inspector to deactivate it.

Now, playtest your Demo scene using the Camera Rigs, Spatial Simulator via the keyboard and the Xbox controller. Also, ensure that you test using your VR headset using either the Camera Rigs, Unity XR or Camera Rigs, Oculus Integration setup.

Once your Demo scene loads, you'll see that your Distance Grabber's straight pointer isn't initially visible. Press the *A* button on your Oculus right controller or the *X* button on your Xbox controller, tap the Right Controllers trackpad of your HTC Vive, or press the Spacebar key on the keyboard to activate the straight pointer on the Distance Grabber.

Now perform a distance grab against the Drill machine. Also, try turning off your Distance Grabber's straight pointer by pressing the button you used to toggle it on a subsequent time. Note that pressing the defined toggle button once toggles the straight pointer on and pressing it again toggles it off. Play around with your newly created Toggle and distance grab mechanic.

# Automatically Deactivating the Distance Grabber

Last, let's include a final subtle game mechanic wherein the Distance Grabber's straight pointer is automatically turned off upon grabbing the Drill machine, which eliminates the need to turn it off manually. This makes sense as you've already grabbed onto an Interactable game object with your right hand and there is nothing more you can grab, so you may as well have the straight pointer turn off automatically. Let's set this up.

In the hierarchy, select the Toggle game object. Click the plus symbol located in the bottom right corner of the Activated event to add a new event listener. Now, select the Interactions Pointer Interactors, Distance Grabber Right game object and expand it until you locate its nested Pointer game object, as shown in Figure 15-9.

Now, drag and drop this Pointer game object into the newly added event listener box of the Activated event of the Toggle Action component of the Toggle game object. For the function, select Game Object, Set Active in the "Dynamic Bool" section, see Figure 15-9.

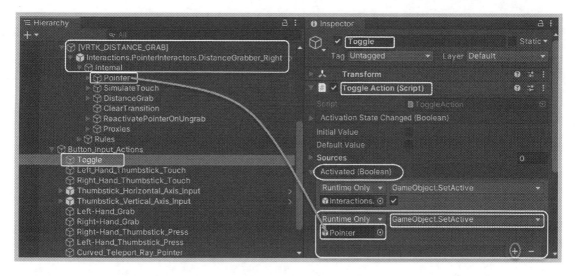

***Figure 15-9.*** *Forcibly activating the Pointer game object upon its parent
Interactions Pointer Interactors Distance Grabber Right game object being
activated*

This ensures that the Pointer game object is explicitly activated, which for some
bizarre reason, doesn't happen. In the case where once a grab has occurred, the
straight pointer on the Distance Grabber is automatically turned off, then subsequently
attempting to turn it on fails. Even though the Interactions Pointer Interactors, Distance
Grabber Right game object gets activated, its child Pointer game object remains inactive
for some inexplicable reason. Here you're forcibly activating this nested child Pointer
game object.

Next, select the Drill Machine in the hierarchy. In the Inspector, expand the Grabbed
event. Click the plus symbol located in the bottom right corner to add an event listener.
Now, drag and drop the Toggle game object from the hierarchy into the event listener
box for this Grabbed event. For the function, select Toggle Action Receive. You can leave
the box unchecked, as you simply want to toggle off the current state via the Toggle
Action component on the Toggle game object. This results in the Interactions Pointer
Interactors, Distance Grabber Right game object in the hierarchy being deactivated the
moment the grab occurs. Consequently, your Distance Grabber's straight pointer is
turned off, see Figure 15-10.

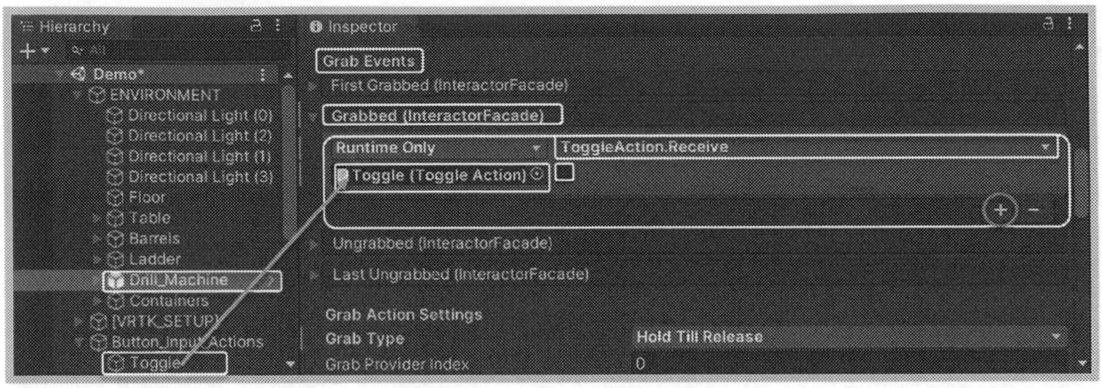

**Figure 15-10.** *Configuring the Drill machine's Grabbed event to toggle off the straight pointer on the Distance Grabber's when the Drill machine is grabbed*

Now, playtest your Demo scene using the Camera Rigs, Spatial Simulator via the keyboard and the Xbox controller. Ensure that you test using your VR headset using either the Camera Rigs, Unity XR or Camera Rigs, Oculus Integration setup. Note that you can toggle the Distance Grabber's straight pointer on and off as expected. Now, with your the straight pointer turned on, distance grab the Drill machine. You'll see that the moment the Drill machine has been grabbed, the straight pointer automatically gets deactivated.

# Summary

In this chapter, we found out about a new way of interacting with Interactable objects, the distance grab mechanic. You learned about and created one, offering you the projective ability to manipulate a physical object without physically interacting with it. We started by reviewing how distance grabbing works in the VRTK. We then went over the specific prerequisites for getting distance grabbing to work. We then learned how to set up our Distance Grabber, as well as a telekinesis grab. We saw that with just the blue reticle present, it becomes difficult to distance grab, so we set up a straight pointer that is immensely useful in grabbing Interactable objects from a distance. You learned how to adjust this straight pointer's grab distance. You then learned how to activate and deactivate the straight pointer using a button press. Finally, you learned how to automatically deactivate the straight pointer when a Interactable object grabbed from a distance reaches your hand.

# CHAPTER 16

# Snap Zones

In this chapter, we'll take a look at Snap Zones provided by the VRTK. A Snap Zone is a spatial zone that an Interactable object can be dropped into. You can create a lot of different behaviors by snapping objects together. Snapping objects together involves inserting one object into another. Here, we will be inserting an Interactable into a Snap Zone. Some real-life examples would be snapping a wheel onto a car, inserting a magazine into a weapon, inserting a USB stick into a USB port, inserting inventory into slots, and inserting weapons into weapon Holsters.

The VRTK provides you with an Interactions Snap Zone prefab to achieve snapping objects together. In this chapter, we'll create a few Tools to place our work tools in. These Tools will display the name of the tool they contain, using a Tooltip that you'll learn about later in this chapter. You'll also learn how to create Holsters that you can carry your work tools around with.

## Importing the Tool Holder UI Package and Setting Up Two New Work Tools

Let's begin by importing a simple UI that will serve as a Tool. The Tool has been created using Unity's UI elements. It is included as a Tool Holder UI Unity package that you need to download and import into your project. After you've done that, select the "Assets" folder in the Project tab, and you'll see the Tool Holder prefab you imported.

Now, drag and drop this Tool Holder prefab onto the Environment game object in the hierarchy, making it a child. Expand the Environment game object in the hierarchy, then select the Tool Holder game object, and right-click it. In the context menu that appears, select Prefab ➤ Unpack Completely. Now, double-click this Tool Holder game object to see it within your scene. You may need to rotate about with the Axis Gizmo

© Christopher Coutinho 2022
C. Coutinho, *Unity® Virtual Reality Development with VRTK4*, https://doi.org/10.1007/978-1-4842-7933-5_16

located in the upper-right corner of the scene tab to see this Tool Holder game object clearly. If you dig into the UI elements in the Inspector, you'll see that the tool holder is simply the letter *O*. There is nothing much to it, and it's not a configured Snap Zone yet.

To have Interactable objects snap into Snap Zones, you'll need to set up a tag for each Interactable object in the scene. Currently, you have just one Interactable object in the scene, which is the Drill Machine. Let's set up a tag for your Drill Machine.

Select the Drill Machine game object in the hierarchy, and you'll see that the Tag property in the Inspector has the value Untagged. Click this Tag's drop-down and select Add Tag. Expand the "Tags" section and click the plus symbol located in the bottom right corner. In the dialog box that pops up, set the New Tag Name property to Drill, and click Save.

You have now created a new tag, which you'll need to assign to your Drill Machine. To do so, click the Drill Machine game object in the hierarchy again. In the Inspector, click the Tag drop-down and select Drill as the tag for your Drill machine. You'll be using this tag name later.

Now, let's put two more work tools onto your worktable and set them up as Interactable objects. From within the Project tab, navigate to Assets ➤ Work Place Tools ➤ Prefabs. In the "Prefabs" folder, select the Axe and Hammer_01 prefabs, and drag and drop them onto the Environment game object in the hierarchy. Select the Hammer_01 game object and rename it "Hammer." Set its Transform, Position property values as follows: $X$ = -13.12; $Y$ = 0.744; and $Z$ = -4.25. You'll see that your Hammer is huge, so set the $X$, $Y$, and $Z$ Transform, Scale property values to 0.33.

With the Hammer game object selected in the hierarchy, right-click it, and in the context menu that appears, select Prefab ➤ Unpack Completely. Now, expand the Hammer game object in the hierarchy and select the Hammer_01_Handle child game object within it. In the Inspector, remove the Mesh Collider component and add a new Box Collider component instead. Ensure that this new collider encompasses the Hammer_01_Handle well. Now, select the Hammer_01_Top child game object and remove its Mesh Collider component as well. Add a new Box Collider component that encompasses the Hammer_01_Top well. Assign your Hammer a tag name, "Hammer."

Next, select the Axe game object in the hierarchy and set its Transform, Position property values as follows: $X$ = -12.57; $Y$ = 0.754; and $Z$ = -4.18. Set its Transform, Rotation, Z property value to 90. You'll see that your Axe is huge, so set the $X$, $Y$, and $Z$ Transform, Scale property values to 0.25.

With the Axe game object selected in the hierarchy, right-click it, and in the context menu that appears, select Prefab ➤ Unpack Completely. Now, expand the Axe game object in the hierarchy and select the Axe Handle child game object within it. In the Inspector, remove the Mesh Collider component, and add a new Box Collider component instead. Ensure that this new collider encompasses the Axe Handle well. Now, select the Axe Top child game object and remove its Mesh Collider component as well. Add a new Box Collider component instead, and ensure that it encompasses the Axe Top well. Assign your Axe the tag name "Axe."

Mesh Colliders are generally not performative. To aid in optimization, you're using Box Colliders on your Hammer and Axe game objects.

Now that you have your Hammer and Axe positioned and placed on your worktable with the proper setup for the collider, you need to convert your Hammer and Axe into Interactable game objects.

## Making the Hammer and Axe Interactable

In Chapters 7 and 8, we used a simple menu option to set up an Interactable game object. You can follow the same procedure we used there to make your Drill Machine interactable. However, here I will demonstrate a different way in which you can set up your Hammer and Axe to become interactable.

Select the Project tab and expand the "Packages" folder. Then, locate the Tilia Interactions, Interactables Unity package and expand it. Also expand its "Runtime" and "Interactables" folders, and select the "Prefabs" folder. In the right pane, you'll see the Interactions Interactable prefab. Drag and drop it onto your Environment game object in the hierarchy. Expand this game object and select the Interactions Interactable game object.

Ensure that the Interactable Facade component in the Inspector has been expanded. Scroll down until you see its "Grab Action Settings" section. For its Grab Type property, select the option Hold till Release. Set the Primary Action property's drop-down value within the "Primary Action Settings" section to Interactable Grab Action Follow. Ensure that the Follow Tracking property has been set to Follow Transform. Set the drop-down value for the Grab Offset property to Precision Point. Last, set the drop-down value for the Secondary Action Property in the "Secondary Action Settings" section to Interactable Grab Action Swap, see Figure 16-1.

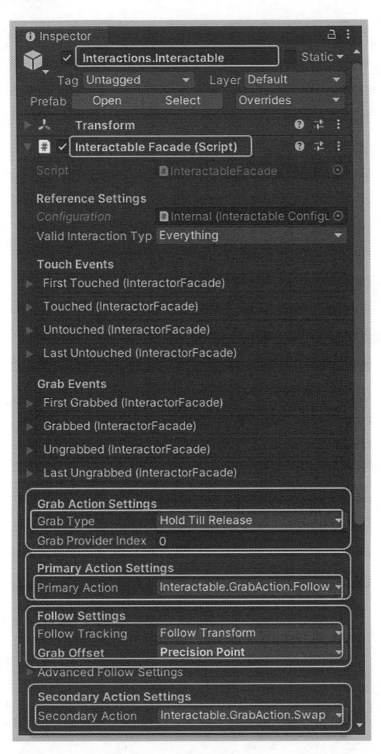

***Figure 16-1.*** *Setting up the Interactions Interactable game object*

Double-click the Interactions Interactable game object in the hierarchy to have it become visible in the scene view. You'll see that it is simply a white cube embedded in one of the Containers. If you look at the Transform component in the Inspector, you'll see that the Transform Position values for *X*, *Y*, and *Z* are set to 0. This Interactions Interactable white cube will serve as the base for converting your Hammer into an Interactable object, so you need to position it on the worktable.

Select the Hammer game object in the hierarchy and copy its Transform component by clicking the three vertical dots and selecting Copy Component from the context menu that pops up. Now, select the Interactions Interactable game object in the hierarchy. In the Inspector, click the three vertical dots located in the Transform component, and in the context menu that pops up, select the menu item Paste Component Values.

You have just repositioned the Interactions Interactable white cube so that it is sitting on your table on top of your Hammer.

With the Interactions Interactable white cube game object still selected in the hierarchy, duplicate it. You'll notice that the duplicated cube has the same Transform Position values as the original cube. This new duplicated cube will serve as the base for converting your Axe into an Interactable object, so you need to position it on the worktable to sit on top of your Axe.

Select the Axe game object in the hierarchy and copy its Transform component by clicking the three vertical dots and selecting Copy Component from the context menu that pops up. Now, select the Interactions Interactable (1) game object in the hierarchy. In the Inspector, click the three vertical dots located on the Transform component, and in the context menu that pops up, select the menu item Paste Component Values.

You have just repositioned the Interactions Interactable (1) white cube so that it is sitting on top of your Axe on the worktable.

Now, expand both game objects in the hierarchy: Interactions Interactable and Interactions Interactable (1). Then, expand their child Mesh Container game object until you see their nested Cube object. Select each Cube object in Interactions Interactable and Interactions Interactable (1) game objects and deactivate them. You'll immediately see that the white cubes sitting on top of the Hammer and Axe have disappeared.

Now, drag and drop the Hammer game object onto the Mesh Container child object of the Interactions Interactable game object, making it a child. Next, drag and drop the Axe game object onto Mesh Container child object of the Interactions Interactable (1) game object, making it a child, see Figure 16-2.

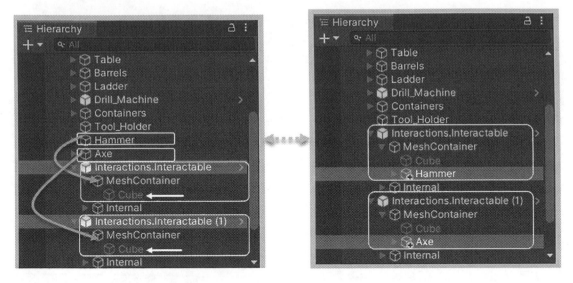

***Figure 16-2.*** *Making the Hammer and Axe game objects children of their respective Mesh Containers*

Ensure that the Transform component values for the nested Hammer and Axe game objects have been reset. This should happen by default.

Last, select the Interactions Interactable game object in the hierarchy and rename it "Hammer." Set its Tag property value to Hammer and its Layer property value to Interactable. Next, select the Interactions Interactable (1) game object in the hierarchy and rename it "Axe." Set its Tag property value to Axe and its Layer property value to Interactable. As mentioned earlier, all Interactable objects must have their Layer set to Interactable.

Now, playtest your *Demo* scene using your VR headset and ensure that you can grab all three Interactable game objects on the worktable. Note that you have set the Grab Offset property to Precision Point on the Axe and Hammer, so you should be able to grab any point on these Interactable game objects.

# Setting Up a Tool Holder Snap Zone

Let's now learn how to set up Snap Zones into which we can drop our work tools. We'll also find out how to use these Snap Zones as Holsters that move around with us, enabling us to carry our work tools around.

Select the Tool Holder game object available as a child of the Environment game object in the hierarchy.

In the Project tab, expand the "Packages" folder and locate the Tilia Interactions Snap Zone Unity package. Expand the package until you reach its "Prefabs" folder. Drag and drop the Interactions Snap Zone prefab from within this folder onto the Tool Holder game object in the hierarchy, making it a child. You'll immediately notice that your Snap Zone has been represented as a large cube.

Let's reduce the size of this Snap Zone first. With the Interactions Snap Zone selected in the hierarchy, expand its Snap Destination child game object and then expand the Destination Highlight game object, and from within this game object expand the Highlight Mesh Container game object. Now select the Default Highlight mesh child game object and look at the Inspector. As your Tool is circular, let's change the Mesh property to a sphere. Click the target-facing icon located on the right side of the cube mesh, and in the Select Mesh dialog that appears, choose Sphere. Expand the Mesh Renderer component and then its Materials property. You can change the material if you want to, but the default Snap Zone outline works excellently whenever a snappable object enters this Snap Zone. You'll notice that this sphere mesh is quite large, so let's scale it down. Select the Destination Highlight game object in the hierarchy and set its Transform Scale property values for *X* and *Y* to 0.2, and for Z to 0. Now when you zoom into your Tool Holder, you'll notice that the orange sphere mesh sits nicely in your circular Tool Holder.

Next, select the Activation Collision Area game object in the hierarchy. You need to scale down the Sphere Collider, which is currently huge compared to your Tool Holder. With the Activation Collision Area game object selected in the hierarchy, click the button beside the Edit Collider property in the Sphere Collider component of the Inspector. In the Scene tab, notice the massive size of the Sphere Collider. Scale it down by setting your Activation Collision Area game object's *X*, *Y*, and *Z* Transform Scale property values to 0.07. You'll see that the Sphere Collider now encompasses the sphere mesh well. You have now successfully set up your Snap Zone.

At this point, if you drop any of your Intractable tools into your Snap Zone, they'll expand to a gigantic size. However, you can easily control an object's size once it has been snapped into a Snap Zone by changing the scale values on the Destination Location child game object. To do so, select this game object in the hierarchy and set its *X*, *Y*, and *Z* Transform Scale property values to 0.2. Also set its Transform Rotation *Y* property value to 180.

Now, playtest your scene using your VR headset. Grab any tool from your worktable and approach the Tool Holder Snap Zone. Move the tool you're holding toward your Tool Holder Snap Zone. You'll immediately see that an orange circular outline displays within the inner bounds of your circular Tool Holder. This indicates that the Snap Zone is now ready to accept this Interactable tool game object. While the orange circular outline is displayed, let go of the tool. You'll see that it gets snapped into your Tool Holder Snap Zone. To remove this tool, grab it and pull it out of this Snap Zone. Try dropping other tools into this Snap Zone to ensure that they're all accepted. Note that a Snap Zone is meant to hold one Interactable object only.

You may have noticed an odd behavior happening with your Drill Machine: Whenever you grab it, the distance grab pointer is turned on. This is a side effect of setting up the distance grabber to turn off automatically once an Interactable game object is grabbed. You added this functionality in Chapter 15 when you set up the Grabbed event on the Drill Machine, which invoked the Toggle Action object and turned off the distance grab pointer. You can delete this Grabbed event on the Drill Machine if you feel the distance grab pointer showing is intrusive.

You may have also noticed that when you drop an Interactable game object into the Tool Holder Snap Zone, it instantly snaps into it. You can change this behavior so that the Interactable game objects you drop into your Snap Zone smoothly lerp into it. Select the Interactions Snap Zone child game object in your Tool Holder game object in the hierarchy. In the Snap Zone Facade component of the Inspector, locate the Transition Duration property. This property allows you to specify the duration over which an Interactable game object moves into a Snap Zone. Set the value for the property to 1.

Playtest your Demo scene using your VR headset. Grab any tool from your worktable and drop it into your Tool Holder Snap Zone. You'll now clearly see that it doesn't instantly snap into the Snap Zone but instead lerps smoothly into it.

Let's now create two new additional Tool Holder Snap Zones so that we have a Snap Zone available for each of our tools. In the hierarchy, select the Tool Holder game object and duplicate it twice. Then, select the Tool Holder (1) game object and expand its Rect Transform component in the Inspector. Set its Transform Position Z property value to -5. Next, select the Tool Holder (2) game object and expand its Rect Transform component in the Inspector. Set its Transform Position Z property value to -5.5, see Figure 16-3.

You'll now see three Tool Holder Snap Zones located on the left-hand side of your table. Playtest your scene once more using your VR headset, and drop each tool on your worktable into a separate Snap Zone. Note that you can drop any tool into any Snap Zone. There are no rules currently in place to ensure that a particular tool can only enter a specific Tool Holder Snap Zone.

*Figure 16-3.* *Setting up two additional Tool Holder Snap Zones*

## Setting Up Tooltips for Your Tool Holder Snap Zones

In this section, we'll create Tooltips for our Tool Holder Snap Zones. Whenever you drop an Interactable tool game object into one of your Tool Holders, the Tooltip beneath it will display the tool's name using its Tag property.

Let's set this up now. Select and expand the Environment game object in the hierarchy and create a new empty child game object and rename it "ToolTips." All Tooltips created during this project will reside in this ToolTips game object. From within the Projects tab, select the Tilia Visuals Tooltip, Unity package and expand it until your reach its "Prefabs" folder. Drag and drop the Visuals Tooltip prefab onto the ToolTips game object in the hierarchy and select it. Rename it "Tool Holder Tooltip." Set this game object's Transform Position values as follows: $X$ = -14.17; $Y$ = 0.93; and $Z$ = -4.5.

Also set its Transform Rotation Y value to 90. Now, duplicate this Tool Holder Tooltip game object twice, as you will be setting up a separate Tooltip for each Tool Holder. Select the Tool Holder Tooltip 1 game object in the hierarchy and change its Transform Position values to $X$ = -14.17; $Y$ = 0.93; and $Z$ = -5. Then, select the Tool Holder Tooltip 2 game object and change its Transform Position values to $X$ = -14.17; Y = 0.93; and Z = -5.5. Your Tooltips will now be aligned beneath their corresponding Tool Holders.

Select the Tool Holder Tooltip game object in the hierarchy. In the Tooltip Facade component of the Inspector, we now need to set up some properties. The Line Origin property specifies a line that will originate from the game object you provide as a value and go to the Tooltip. The Tool Holder Snap Zone game object in the hierarchy you created earlier sits directly above the Tool Holder Tooltip game object. You can have a line drawn from this Tool Holder game object going to the Tool Holder Tooltip game object by populating the Line Origin property of the Tool Holder Tooltip game object with its corresponding Tool Holder game object. With the Tool Holder Tooltip game object still selected, drag and drop the Tool Holder game object onto the Line Origin property parameter of the Tool Holder Tooltip game object.

The procedure for setting up the other two Tool Holder Tooltip game objects is similar. Select the Tool Holder Tooltip (1) game object and drag and drop the Tool Holder (1) game object onto the Line Origin property parameter of the Tool Holder Tooltip (1) game object. Then, select the Tool Holder Tooltip (2) game object and drag and drop the Tool Holder (2) game object onto the Line Origin property parameter of the Tool Holder Tooltip (2) game object. Figure 16-4 shows the Tool Holder Tooltip game object being set up.

Now, playtest the Demo scene using the Spatial Simulator and approach your Tool Holders. You'll see that each Tool Holder now features a thin black vertical line going from its center to its corresponding Tooltip. If you don't want this thin black line displayed, you can leave the Line Origin property value empty.

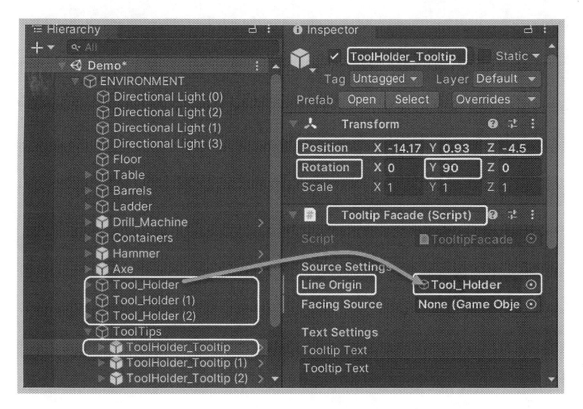

**Figure 16-4.** *Setting up the Tool Holder Tooltip game object's Line Origin property*

The Facing Source property determines which direction your Tooltip will face. Currently, if you approach your Tool Holders from the front, you can see their Tooltips display the default value Tooltip Text. If you approach them from behind, you won't be able to see the values displayed by the Tooltips beneath your Tool Holders. If you'd always like the values to be displayed by your Tool Holder Tooltips, you need to set this Facing Source property to your Headset Alias game object. The advantage of setting this up is that your Tool Holder Tooltips will always be facing you even if you're standing behind or beside your Tool Holders.

Expand the Camera Rigs Tracked Alias game object in the VRTK Camera Rigs Setup game object. Then, select all three *Tool* Holder Tooltip game objects in the ToolTips game object. Finally, drag and drop the Headset Alias game object from the Camera Rigs Tracked Alias game object into the Facing Source property parameter, see Figure 16-5.

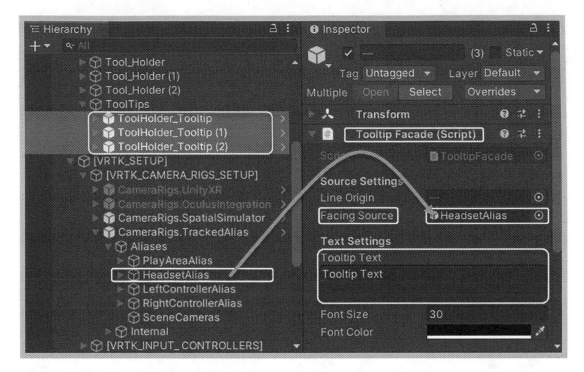

***Figure 16-5.*** *Setting up the Tool Holder Tooltip game object's Facing Source property*

Now let's clear out the default Tooltip Text value that exists in the Tooltip Text property. We'll be adding a Tooltip Text component to all our Tool Holder Tooltip game objects that displays the name of the Interactable game object that enters our Tool Holders Snap Zone.

To do this, ensure that you've selected all three Tool Holder Tooltip game objects in the hierarchy, as previously shown in Figure 16-5. In the Inspector, click the Add Component button and add the Tooltip Text component. The component will be added to each of your Tool Holder Tooltip game objects.

You'll see that the newly added component has a Tool Tip Facade property. You'll need to populate this property individually for each of the three Tool Holder Tooltip game objects. In the hierarchy, select the Tool Holder Tooltip game object. For its Tool Tip Facade property, drag and drop its Tooltip Facade component located immediately above the Tooltip Text component into the Tool Tip Facade property parameter, see Figure 16-6. The same procedure should be followed for setting up the other two Tool Holder Tooltip game objects.

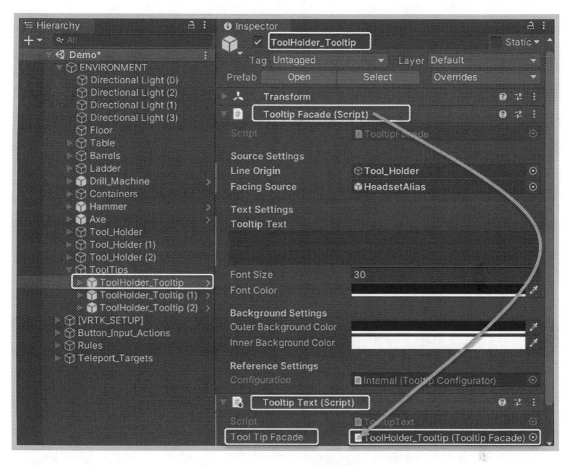

***Figure 16-6.*** *Setting up the Tool Holder Tooltip game object's Tool Tip Facade property*

Let's next set up the remaining two Tool Holder Tooltip game objects. In the hierarchy, select the Tool Holder Tooltip (1) game object. For its Tool Tip Facade property, drag and drop the Tooltip Facade component located immediately above its Tooltip Text component into the Tool Tip Facade property parameter of the Tooltip Text component. Next, select the Tool Holder Tooltip (2) game object. Here too, for its Tool Tip Facade property, drag and drop the Tooltip Facade component located immediately above its Tooltip Text component into the Tool Tip Facade property parameter of the Tooltip Text component.

As a final step, we need to set up event listeners against the Snapped and Unsnapped events for each of the three Tool Holder Interactions Snap Zone game objects. In the hierarchy, expand the Tool Holder, Tool Holder (1) and Tool Holder (2) game objects so that you can see both of their Interactions Snap Zone child game objects. Select all three of these child game objects. In the Inspector, expand the Snapped (Game Object) event in the "Zone Events" section and click the plus button to add an event listener to this Snapped event. Next, select and expand the Unsnapped (Game Object) event and click the plus button to add an event listener, see Figure 16-7.

***Figure 16-7.*** *Setting up Snapped and Unsnapped events against the Tool Holder Snap Zone game objects*

Now, select the Interactions Snap Zone game object, a child of the Tool Holder game object. Drag and drop the Tool Holder Tooltip game object from the hierarchy into the event listener boxes of both the Snapped and Unsnapped events. Note that the Tool Holder Tooltip game object connects to the Tool Holder Interactions Snap Zone game object. In the Snapped event function drop-down, select Tooltip text, Show Tooltip from within the "Dynamic Game Object" section of the context menu that pops up. Next, in the Unsnapped event function drop-down, select Tooltip text, Clear Tooltip from the "Static Parameters" section of the context menu that pops up.

You have now hooked up your Tool Holder Tooltip game object to your Tool Holder Snap Zone game object, see Figure 16-8. This means that whenever you drop (snap) one of your Interactable tools into this Tool Holder Snap Zone, the Tool Holder Tooltip beneath it will display the tool's name dropped into it. This is achieved using the tag name you assigned to the specific tool using the Show Tooltip method invoked in the Snapped event. When you pull out (unsnap) this Interactable tool from its Tool Holder Snap Zone, the Tool Holder Tooltip beneath it will be cleared using the Clear Tooltip method invoked in the Unsnapped event.

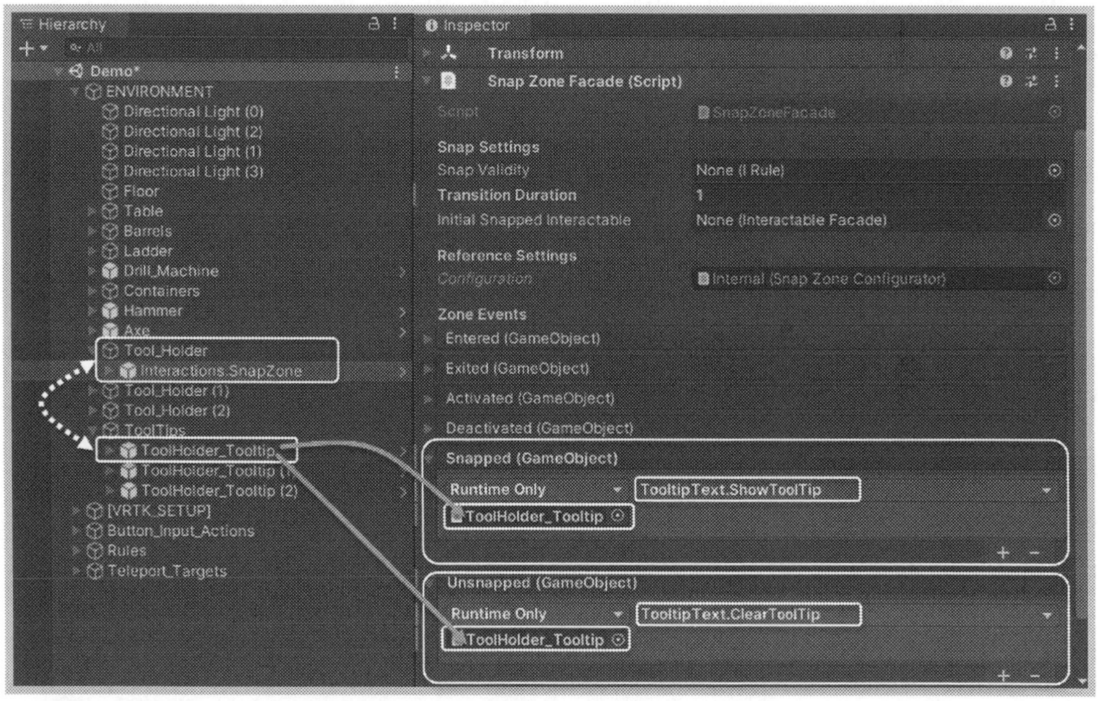

***Figure 16-8.*** *Setting up the appropriate tool name to show up whenever one of the work tools is dropped into the Tool Holder Snap Zone*

So far, we have set up our Tool Holder Snap Zone to display the name of the tool that's dropped into it. Let's now set up the other two available Tool Holder Snap Zones so that they function similarly.

Start by selecting the Interactions Snap Zone game object in the hierarchy, a child of the Tool Holder (1) game object. Then, drag and drop the Tool Holder Tooltip (1) game object from the hierarchy into the event listener boxes of both the Snapped and Unsnapped events. Note that the Tool Holder Tooltip (1) game object connects to the Tool Holder (1) Interactions Snap Zone game object. Now, in the Snapped event function drop-down, select Tooltip text, Show Tooltip from the "Dynamic Game Object" section of the context menu that pops up. Next, in the Unsnapped event function drop-down, select Tooltip text, Clear Tooltip from the "Static Parameters" section of the context menu that pops up. You have now hooked up your Tool Holder Tooltip (1) game object to your Tool Holder (1) Snap Zone game object.

Last, let's set up the Tool Holder (2) Snap Zone game object. Select the Interactions Snap Zone game object in the hierarchy, a child of the Tool Holder (2) game object. Drag and drop the Tool Holder Tooltip (2) game object from the hierarchy into the event listener boxes of both the Snapped and Unsnapped events. Note that the Tool Holder Tooltip (2) game object connects to the Tool Holder (2) Interactions Snap Zone game object. In the Snapped event function drop-down, select Tooltip text, Show Tooltip from the "Dynamic Game Object" section of the context menu that pops up. Next, in the Unsnapped event function drop-down, select Tooltip text, Clear Tooltip from the "Static Parameters" section of the context menu that pops up.

You have now hooked up your Tool Holder Tooltip (2) game object to your Tool Holder (2) Snap Zone game object. All three of your Tool Holder Snap Zones are now fully functional.

Now, playtest your Demo scene using your VR headset. Grab any tool from your worktable and drop it into any of your Tool Holders. You'll see that the Tooltip beneath the Tool Holder now reflects the name of the tool that was dropped into it. Also test this using the other two tools available to you, and you'll see that your Tool Holder displays the appropriate tool name. Interchange tools among the Tool Holders, and you'll see that the Tool Holders always reflect the correct name of the tool that was placed into them. Note that the moment you remove a tool from its Tool Holder, the Tooltip beneath it is cleared.

# Setting Up Rules to Restrict the Entry of Interactable Objects into Snap Zones

Currently, there are no restrictions to ensure that only specific tools can enter the Tool Holder Snap Zones. As things stand, any tool can be placed into any Snap Zone. Let's change this so that your Tool Holder Snap Zones won't accept the Drill Machine. The only tools you'll be able to drop into your Snap Zones will be the Hammer and the Axe. This can be easily set up by creating a Rule and assigning it to the Snap Validity property of each Tool Holder's Snap Zone. So far, you've created rules based on Layers only using the Any Layer component. Now that your Interactable game objects have been assigned Tags, you'll create a rule using the Any Tag Rule component provided by the VRTK.

Select and expand the Rules game object in the hierarchy, and create a new empty child game object and rename it "Snap Zone Valid Tags." This child game object will hold Interactable game object tags considered valid by a Snap Zone. An Interactable game object featuring any of these valid tags can be snapped into the Snap Zone. These valid tags will be held within the Any Tag Rule component, which must exist on the Snap Zone Valid Tags game object.

Let's set up a couple of components on the Snap Zone Valid Tags game object. In the hierarchy, ensure that this game object has been selected. Click the Add Component button and add the Any Tag Rule component to this game object in the Inspector. Expand this Any Tag Rule component, and you'll see that it contains a String Observable List property. You'll also see that you can't simply type in the Tag names for the Interactable game objects that you want your Snap Zones to accept, as this component doesn't accept all string values. The Any Tag Rule component will only accept a String Observable List, which is a collection of string values. You must ensure that you provide only this type of list as the String Observable List property parameter, see Figure 16-9.

*Figure 16-9. Adding the Any Tag Rule component to the Snap Zone Valid Tags game object*

Let's add another component to the Snap Zone Valid Tags game object. Click the Add Component button, and add the String Observable List component to this game object. This is the type of component that the String Observable List property of the Any Tag Rule component will accept (see Figure 16-9). Note that this String Observable List component accepts string values. Basically, this is another example of a level of indirection where one component connects to another, providing the required functionality.

Now, expand the String Observable List component and locate its Elements Size property. Set its property value to 2, as the Axe and the Hammer are the only two valid Interactable game objects allowed to enter a Snap Zone. You will be presented with two element slots upon changing the Size property to 2. In these slots, list the tags considered valid by your Tool Holder Snap Zones. For the Element 0 slot, type in the value "Axe." For the Element 1 slot, type in "Hammer." Ensure that the spelling of these values is the same as in the tag names assigned to these Interactable work tools. That's all the setup required against the String Observable List component.

You must now pass this String Observable List component as the parameter value to the String Observable List property in the Any Tag Rule component. Do this by dragging and dropping the String Observable List component from the Inspector onto the String Observable List property parameter in the Any Tag Rule component. You'll see that within the Any Tag Rule component, a size-two "Elements" section has been added that contains the elements you put in the String Observable List component.

Now your Snap Zone Valid Tags rule is ready to be applied to your Tool Holder Snap Zones, see Figure 16-10.

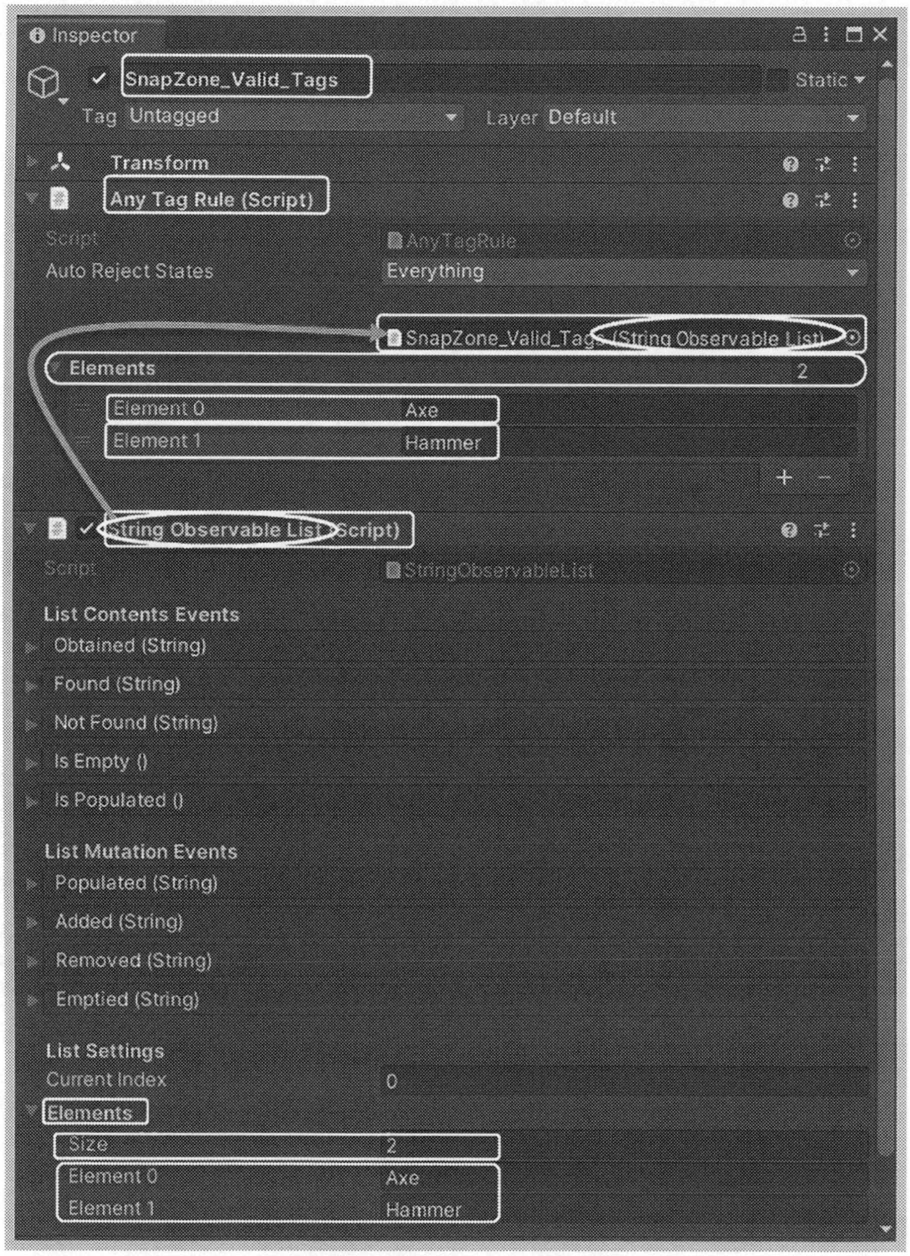

**Figure 16-10.** *Connecting the String Observable List component of the Snap Zone Valid Tags game object to the Any Tag Rule component*

Let's now assign this Snap Zone Valid Tags rule to the Snap Validity property of each of your Tool Holder Snap Zones. In the hierarchy, expand the Tool Holder, Tool Holder (1) and Tool Holder (2) game objects so that you have access to each of their Interactions Snap Zone child game objects. Then, select all three child game objects in the hierarchy. In the Snap Zone Facade component of the Inspector, locate the Snap Validity Property. Now, drag and drop the Snap Zone Valid Tags rule game object from the hierarchy into this Snap Validity property parameter, see Figure 16-11.

You have now told all three Snap Zones to only accept Interactable game objects tagged as either an Axe or a Hammer. As such, your Drill Machine no longer has any place to lodge itself in your Tool Holder Snap Zones.

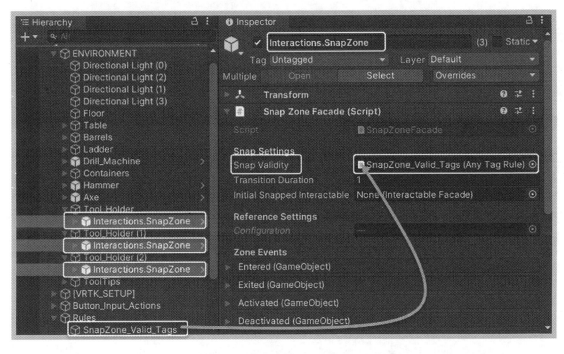

***Figure 16-11.*** *Setting up the Snap Validity property for all three Tool Holder Snap Zones with the Snap Zone Valid Tags rule*

Playtest your Demo scene using your VR headset. Grab the Drill Machine from your worktable and try to snap it into any of your Tool Holder Snap Zones. You'll see that it's no longer possible to lodge your Drill Machine into any of these Snap Zones. However, your Axe and Hammer can still be dropped into any of them.

We can take this further by creating three separate rules representing just one valid tag and attaching each rule to a Snap Zone. For example, we can apply an Axe rule to the Snap Zone closest to the table, then apply a Drill rule to the center Snap Zone, and then a Hammer Rule to the Snap Zone furthest from the table. This would ensure that your Drill Machine can only be lodged into the center Tool Holder Snap Zone, your Axe can only enter the Tool Holder Snap Zone closest to the table, and your Hammer is only allowed entry into the Tool Holder Snap Zone furthest from the table. I'll leave setting up these rules as an exercise for you to perform on your own.

## Setting Up Holsters That Move Around with the Player

So far, we've set up Snap Zones that can serve as inventory slots. In this section, we'll learn how to set up a Holster that stays with you as you move around. This Holster setup could be used in your next FPS game. The Holsters you set up here won't be able to carry weapons but will be used to carry your work tools. As we go through this setup, you'll learn to use a new VRTK prefab, the Mutator Object Follower.

Select and expand the Environment game object in the hierarchy, and create a new empty game object within it and rename it "Holsters." This will serve as the parent game object that will hold your Left and Right Holsters. Then, with the Environment game object expanded, select the Tool Holder game object and duplicate it twice. Rename the copied Tool Holder (3) game object "Left Holster" and the copied Tool Holder (4) game object "Right Holster." Now, select both of these game objects in the hierarchy and expand their Rect Transform component. Locate the Rotation property and set the Rotation X value to 90 and the Rotation Y value to 0. Also set the Scale property values for *X*, *Y*, and *Z* to 0.75.

Select and expand the Left Holster game object in the hierarchy and then select its Interactions Snap Zone child game object. In the Inspector, for the Snap Validity property, delete the rule that was previously set up. You'll find that you can't simply hit the Delete button to delete the rule placed here. You'll need to right-click the Snap Validity property text and select Revert from the context menu that pops up for it to be deleted.

Next, delete both the Snapped and Unsnapped events, as you won't be setting up any Tooltips for your Holster. Next, select and expand the Right Holster game object in the hierarchy and then select its Interactions Snap Zone child game object. Right-click the Snap Validity property text in the Inspector and select Revert from the context menu that pops up to have this rule removed. Then, delete both the Snapped and Unsnapped events, as you won't be setting up any Tooltips for this Holster. By getting rid of these rules for both the Left and Right Holsters, your Drill Machine can now be holstered.

Select the Left Holster game object in the hierarchy and change its Rect Transform position property values to Pos $X$ = -0.18; Pos $Y$ = 0; and Pos $Z$ = 0.15. Then, select the Right Holster game object and change these position property values to Pos $X$ = 0.18; Pos $Y$ = 0; and Pos $Z$ = 0.15. Now, drag and drop both Left and Right Holsters onto the Holsters game object you created, thereby making both the Left and Right Holsters children of the Holsters game object. Select the Holsters game object, and create a new child game object in it and rename it "Offset." This child game object determines which values your Holsters are to be offset from your Play Area Alias. Your Holsters will follow your Play Area Alias, see Figure 16-12.

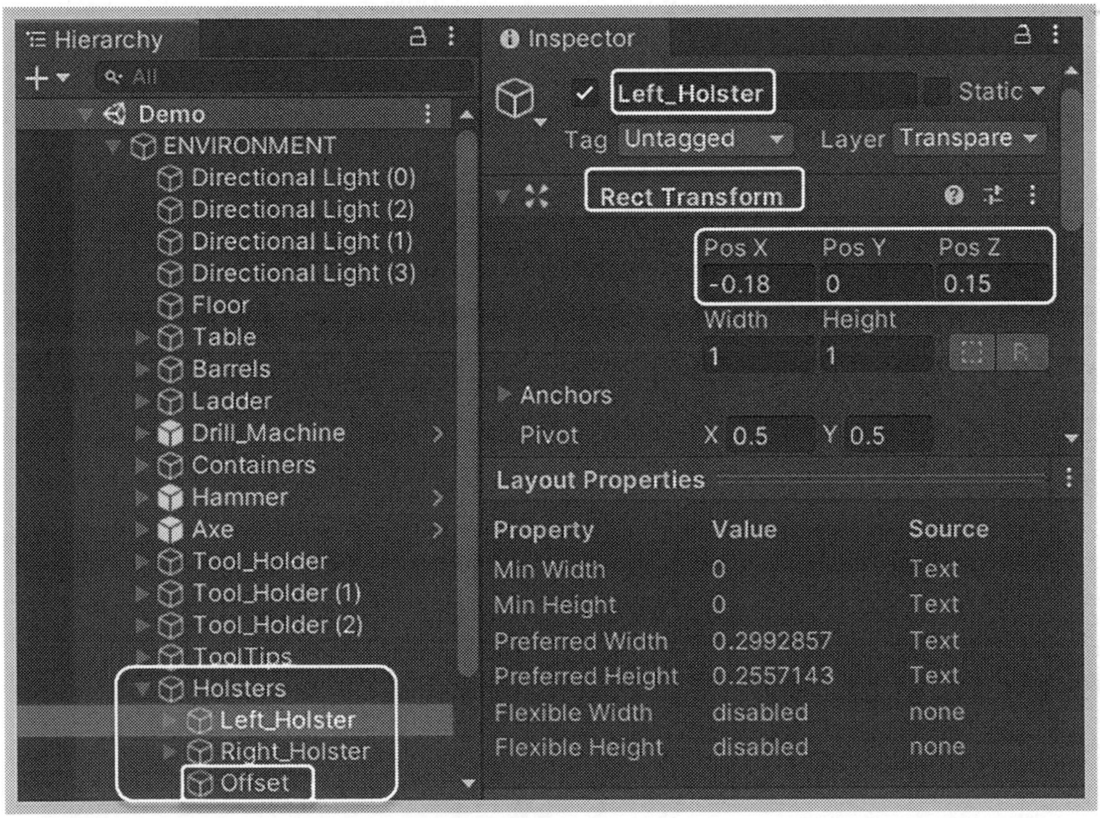

***Figure 16-12.*** *Setting up your Left and Right Holsters as children of the Holsters game object*

With the Holsters ➤ Offset game object selected in the hierarchy, let's set up its Offset game object Transform property values. For its Scale property, set the $X$, $Y$, and $Z$ values to 0.5. For its Position property, set the $X$, $Y$, and $Z$ values to $X = 0$; $Y = -0.3$; and $Z = 0.09$. These offset values have been obtained by seeing what suited you best while playing around with the VR headset. You may want to adjust these settings to your liking. You now have your Holsters all set up.

It's your Play Area Alias that is set up to move around in your VR world in the same way you move around. To have your Holsters follow you around, you need to connect them to your Play Area Alias. To make this connection, the VRTK provides you with a Mutators Object Follower prefab, avoiding the need to have one object serve as the parent to another. Let's set up this connection now.

In the hierarchy, select the VRTK SETUP game object, and create a new empty child object in it and rename it "Mutator Follower." Expand the "Packages" folder in the Project tab and locate the Tilia Mutators Object Follower package. Expand it until you reach its "Prefabs" folder. Now, drag and drop the Mutators Object Follower prefab onto the Mutator Follower game object in the hierarchy. With this game object selected in the hierarchy in the Inspector, ensure that its Object Follower component has been expanded. Set the Sources Elements property size to 1. You'll be provided with an Element 0 slot. The Sources Elements property represents the source game object that is followed around in the scene. In this case, that game object is the Play Area Alias. It moves around in the same way you do, and as you need your Holsters to follow you, they will need to follow the Play Area Alias.

From within the hierarchy, locate and expand the Camera Rigs Tracked Alias and then expand its Aliases game object until you see the Play Area Alias game object. Drag and drop the Play Area Alias game object into the Sources Element 0 slot you just created in the Object Follower component of the Mutators Object Follower, see Figure 16-13.

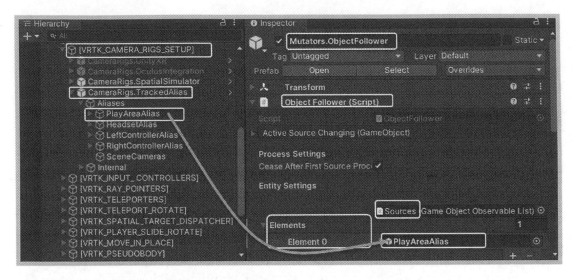

***Figure 16-13.*** *Setting the Sources Elements property of the Mutators Object Follower component to the Play Area Alias*

Next, set the Targets Elements property size to 1. You'll be provided with an Element 0 slot. The Targets Elements property represents the game object that should follow the source game object in the scene. The target here represents your Holsters, which need to follow the Play Area Alias. From the hierarchy, drag and drop the Holsters game object into the Element 0 slot, as shown in Figure 16-14.

Last, set the Target Offsets Elements property size to 1. You'll be provided with an Element 0 slot. The Target Offsets property represents an object that determines the values by which your Target object (Holsters) should be offset from its Source object (Play Area Alias). This property will contain the Offset game object, which is a child of your Holsters object. This Offset ensures that your Holsters will be positioned slightly in front of your Play Area Alias. From the hierarchy, drag and drop the Offset game object into the Element 0 slot, as also shown in Figure 16-14.

You have now connected your Holsters to your Play Area Alias.

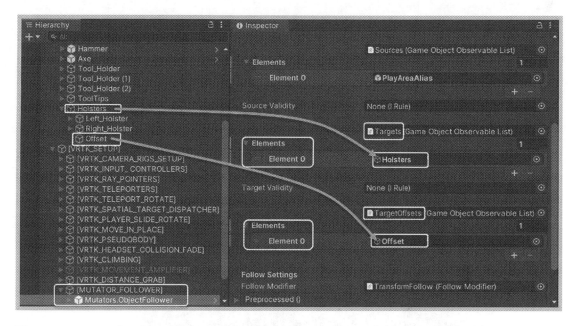

***Figure 16-14.*** *Setting the Targets Elements property of the Mutators Object Follower component to the Holsters game object and the Target Offsets Elements property to the Offset game object*

Note that, at this point, if you attempt to climb a Container with your Holsters empty, you'll be flung into the stratosphere upon reaching the top and releasing the grab hold on your VR controllers. This uncalled-for behavior happens because your Holster Snap Zones have their Layer set to Default, which collides with the Ignore Raycast Layer your Containers have been set to. You can check this out by navigating to Edit ➤ Project Settings ➤ Physics and looking at your Layer Collision Matrix settings.

However, if you have Interactable tools set up in your Holsters and then attempt to climb up any Container, you won't get flung into the stratosphere. This is because your Interactable tool game objects have been assigned to the Interactable Layer, and objects like the Containers have been assigned to the Ignore Ray Cast Layer. These Layers have been set up to ignore collisions. Look at the Layer Collision Matrix and you'll see that the box where the Ignore Raycast row intersects with the Interactable column has been unchecked, disallowing collisions between objects belonging to these Layers, see Figure 16-15.

To solve this problem, wherein you're climbing with empty Holsters, set the Layer for your Holsters to Transparent FX. In the hierarchy, select the Holsters game object and set the Layer to Transparent FX in the Inspector. Next, navigate to Edit ➤ Project Settings ➤ Physics in the main menu and scroll down to see the Layer Collision Matrix.

All the boxes are checked for the Transparent FX row, except for the fifth box, where the Transparent FX row intersects the Ignore Raycast column. By disabling collision between these Layers, you've ensured that your Holster Snap Zones, when empty, don't collide with climbable objects like the Containers and the Ladder, thus not yielding weird effects. Your Layer Collision Matrix at this point in the project should be set up as shown in Figure 16-15.

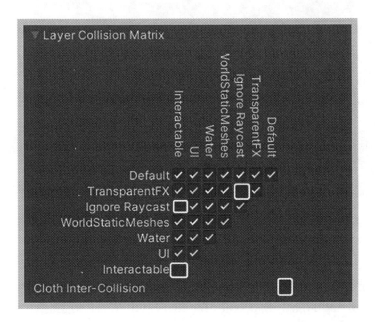

***Figure 16-15.***  *Layer Collision Matrix setup*

I have found the Layers in Unity 2020 to be plagued with technical bugs, so you need to test each time you change Layer collisions or create new Layers to ensure that they behave as they should. Looking at the Layer Collision Matrix in Figure 16-15, you'll be reminded that you disabled collisions between the Interactable and Ignore Raycast Layers. This is required when you use Holsters because the Interactable tools you drop into your Holsters could easily collide with your pseudo-body, which has its Layer set to Ignore Raycast. This may result in some jittering when you move as well as when you climb. To avoid this jittering, you have disabled collisions between game objects associated with these Layers.

However, this gives rise to another issue, where ideally, you wouldn't be allowed to grab any Interactable game object if using a previous version of the program, like Unity 2019. If you recall, in an earlier chapter I stressed the fact that your Example Avatar on both Interactors has its Layer set to Ignore Raycast by default. On account of this setting, your Example Avatar game objects on both hands shouldn't be able to collide with your Interactable tool game objects given the Layer Collision Matrix setup. Thus, you wouldn't be allowed to grab an Interactable game object in Unity 2019. However, this hasn't proven to be a problem with Unity 2020, as all this while you have had your Example Avatar game objects set to the Ignore Raycast Layer by default.

Suppose you happen to be using Unity version 2019, or a newer Unity 2020 LTS version, where the bug probably has been fixed. In that case, you may find yourself unable to grab onto an Interactable game object. To avoid being not being able to do this on account of the Layer Collision Matrix setup, you need to change the Layer for both your Example Avatar game objects to the Default layer. These game objects are available in your Interactions Interactor Right and Interactions Interactor Left game objects. Ensure that you set their Layer to Default. This ensures that regardless of the Unity version you're using, you can be assured that you'll always be able to grab an Interactable game object.

Playtest the Demo scene using your VR headset. You'll notice that both your Holsters are immediately visible and have been offset slightly in front of you. Slide around the scene, and you'll notice that the Holsters follow you around. Try climbing up a Container with your empty Holsters, and you should not be blasted off into the stratosphere. Approach the worktable and grab the Drill Machine and put it into one of your Holsters. Note that it's now allowed entry into your Holster Snap Zone. Grab any other tool from your worktable and put it into the other empty Holster. Grab the only tool left on the worktable with your hand. Slide around the scene and notice that you can now carry your tools with you. Finally swap tools between Holsters to ensure that any tool can be accommodated in any Holster. Last, with just two tools in Holsters and both your hands empty, approach one of the Containers and climb up. Here you added just two Holsters; however, you could add a third or even more to a limit, that makes sense. In an FPS game, you would ideally want two waist Holsters, as currently set up.

Additionally, you could provide your player with two shoulder Holsters in which it would be possible to stash a bow and possibly a rocket launcher. You could set up a Snap Zone in the vicinity of your player's head, allowing them the ability to put a hat or helmet onto their head. If you want to attach and detach magazines to weapons, you could use a Snap Zone to achieve this quickly. The possibilities are endless.

# Summary

In this chapter, we took a deep dive into setting up Snap Zones, a mechanic that is expected to be a part of any VR tool kit. We went over various scenarios where a Snap Zone could prove beneficial. We started the chapter by importing the Tool Holder UI package and setting up two new work tools. We then used a different approach to make the Hammer and Axe work tools interactable. We then set up three Tool Holder Snap Zones that served as inventory slots. You learned how to use the Tilia Visuals Tooltip Unity package to set up Tooltips for each of your Tool Holders. You learned about the Any Layer Rule component and used it to restrict particular Interactable game objects to the Tool Holder Snap Zones. Along the way, you learned about the String Observable List and the purpose it serves. We finally set up Holsters that follow you around, which will help you carry your work tools around the scene. We saw that there are certain oddities when working with Unity Layers and there's always the need to test how game objects assigned to different Layers interact. We wrapped the chapter up by testing the Demo scene using our VR headset and ensured that the Snap Zone mechanics we set up worked as desired.

# CHAPTER 17

# Creating Spatial 3D User Interface Game Objects

In this chapter, we'll learn to create User Interface game objects that accept input and communicate information. The UI is an integral part of any game. It informs players about their health and score, and helps control the game's workflow via menus and pause screens. In a non-VR game, the UI used is a Heads-Up Display, or HUD, which is placed over the top of the main screen and displays information to the player. This type of UI is known as a nondiegetic UI, meaning it doesn't exist in the game world. Nevertheless, it directly relates to what the player sees or interacts with inside the game. Unfortunately, this nondiegetic UI approach doesn't work well in VR, as the player can't focus on something so close to their eyes while trying to focus on the game. It's very distracting and uncomfortable, as it moves with the player's head as if it has been glued on. A better and more intuitive way to display the UI is to have it positioned in the game environment. This can be achieved by using Unity's UI and basing it on a world UI canvas. This approach is referred to as Spatial UI. However, with version 4 of the VRTK, you can create 3D spatial UIs using spatial buttons that can be interacted with via Interactors or pointers. In this chapter, we'll try out spatial 3D buttons, which exist as game objects in your VR world, using a spatial pointer. We've already encountered a straight object pointer when setting up our distance grab mechanic. We'll start out this chapter by adding a straight spatial pointer that can interact with spatial buttons made available to you in VRTK 4.

## Setting Up a Straight Menu Pointer

While setting up the distance grab mechanic, you may have noticed that a straight pointer casts a straight line (ray) from the palm of your hand either to its maximum specified length or until its pointer beam collides with a valid Interactable game object.

253

© Christopher Coutinho 2022
C. Coutinho, *Unity® Virtual Reality Development with VRTK4*, https://doi.org/10.1007/978-1-4842-7933-5_17

The Straight Spatial Menu Pointer you'll set up in this chapter is different from the one you set up for your distance grab mechanic in Chapter 15. The Straight Spatial Menu Pointer you'll set up in this chapter will be exclusively used for interacting with your Spatial 3D buttons. Also, a different button on your controller will be used to activate this pointer.

To activate the Straight Spatial Menu Pointer, we'll use the Start button on the Oculus left controller and the Top Menu button on the HTC Vive left controller. Even though the Xbox controller supports a Start button, we won't use it here, as the Key Code properties for the Start buttons on the Oculus Left Controller and the Xbox controller are the same. Both Start buttons use the Key Code Joy Stick Button 7. Attempting to use the Start button for both the Oculus and Xbox controllers would result in only the first listed controller button having this Key Code value function. To avoid this, we'll set up the Start Button against the Oculus controller and the Back button against the Xbox controller to activate the Straight Spatial Menu Pointer. To activate the pointer via a key press we'll use the *M* key on the keyboard. One thing to note is that when you press the Start button on the Oculus left controller, or the Top Menu button on the HTC Vive left controller, or the Back button on the Xbox controller, or the *M* key on the keyboard, the Straight Spatial Menu Pointer will be emitted from your right hand, not your left hand. If you are left-handed, though, you can change this.

Now, let's create a new Button Action game object that captures the *M* key press on your keyboard. Select and expand the Keyboard Input game object in the hierarchy. It's available in the VRTK INPUT CONTROLLERS game object. You already have Input Unity Input Manager Button Action game objects that capture your *Q*, *P*, *T*, and spacebar key presses. Duplicate the Input Unity Input Manager Button Action Q and rename it "Input Unity Input Manager Button Action M," which will capture the *M* key press. With the Input Unity Input Manager Button Action M game object selected in the hierarchy, locate its Key Code property in the Inspector and select the letter *M* from the drop-down. You now have a button action configured to capture the *M* key press.

Now, let's create a game object with a Boolean Action to capture all the button inputs just discussed. To do so, we'll select and expand the Button Input Actions game object in the hierarchy and create a new empty child game object in it and rename it "Spatial Menu Pointer Activator." With this child game object selected in the hierarchy, click the Add Component button in the Inspector and add a Boolean Action component to it and set the size of its Sources property to 4. We need to capture input button presses from four devices: the keyboard and Oculus, HTC Vive, and Xbox controllers. Ensure that you expand this Sources property so that its four element slots are visible.

With the Keyboard Input game object still expanded in the hierarchy, drag and drop the Input Unity Input Manager Button Action M game object from the hierarchy into the Element 0 slot of the Boolean Action component of the Spatial Menu Pointer Activator game object. Now, expand the Input Unity Input Manager X Box controller game object in the hierarchy and locate its Button Back Press [6] game object. Drag and drop the latter game object from the hierarchy into the Element 1 slot of the Boolean Action component's Spatial Menu Pointer Activator game object. Next, expand the Input Unity Input Manager Oculus Touch Left controller game object in the hierarchy and locate its Button Start Press [7] game object. Drag and drop the latter game object from the hierarchy into the Element 2 slot of the Boolean Action component of the Spatial Menu Pointer Activator game object. Last, expand the Input Unity Input Manager Open VR Left Controller game object in the hierarchy and locate its Left Button Primary Press [2] game object. Drag and drop the latter game object from the hierarchy into the Element 3 slot of the Boolean Action component of the Spatial Menu Pointer Activator game object. You have now channeled all input to activate the Straight Spatial Menu Pointer into the Spatial Menu Pointer Activator intermediary game object, see Figure 17-1.

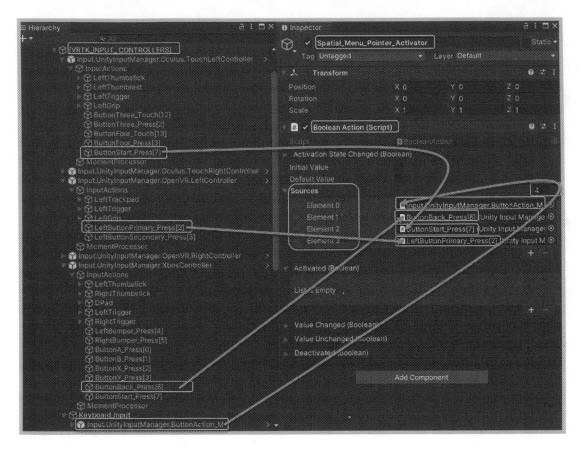

***Figure 17-1.*** *Spatial Menu Pointer Activator setup for capturing input from the controllers and keyboard*

In the hierarchy, select and expand the VRTK RAY POINTERS game object. All your ray pointers, whether straight or curved, will reside in this game object. Next, select the Project tab and expand the "Packages" folder. Locate the Tilia Indicators Object Pointers Unity package and expand it until you reach its "Prefabs" folder. Drag and drop the Indicators Object Pointers Straight prefab onto this game object and rename the Indicators Object Pointers Straight game object to "Indicators Object Pointers Straight Spatial Menu Pointer." With this pointer selected in the hierarchy, locate its Follow Source property in the Inspector.

Drag and drop the Right Controller Alias game object from the hierarchy into this Follow Source property parameter. This ensures that your Straight Spatial Menu Pointer will follow your Right Controller and emit from your right hand. This menu pointer will be deactivated by default, so you need a way to activate and deactivate its beam. This is where your Spatial Menu Pointer Activator intermediary game object comes in. It contains a Boolean Action component that emits either a True or False value. You'll hook up the Spatial Menu Pointer Activator to the Activation Action property of the Indicators Object Pointers Straight Spatial Menu Pointer game object. Thus, when the Spatial Menu Pointer Activator game object emits a True value, the Straight Spatial Menu Pointer will be activated and when it emits a False value, it will be deactivated. Drag and drop the Straight Spatial Pointer Activator game object from the hierarchy into the Activation Action property parameter of the Indicators Object Pointers Straight Spatial Menu Pointer game object, see Figure 17-2.

Now when the *M* key on your keyboard, the Start button on your left Oculus controller, the Back button on your Xbox controller, or the Top Menu button on your left HTC Vive controller is pressed, your Straight Spatial Menu Pointer will be displayed.

Playtest the Demo scene using the Spatial Simulator with the keyboard and Xbox controller. Note that pressing the *M* key or the Back button on your Xbox controller should activate your Straight Spatial Menu Pointer. Next, test using your VR headset. Press the Start button on your left Oculus controller or the Top Menu button on your left HTC Vive controller to activate your Straight Spatial Menu Pointer. Note that this menu pointer hasn't been set up as a toggle, so you'll need to keep the Start button, Back button, Top Menu button, or *M* key continually pressed to ensure that the pointer stays displayed. You could use the Toggle Action technique you learned about in Chapter 15 to have any of these buttons or keys function as a toggle that switches the pointer on and off. I'll leave this as an exercise for you to complete on your own.

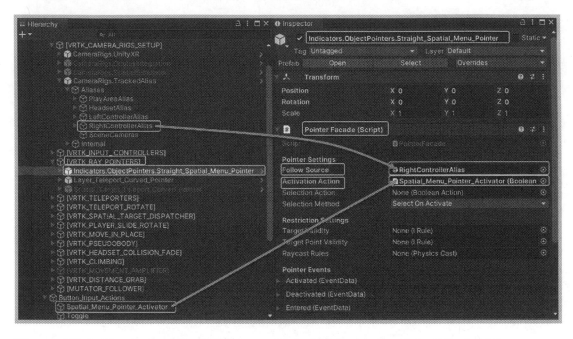

**Figure 17-2.** *Setting up the Indicators Object Pointers Straight Spatial Menu Pointer to be activated and deactivated on the press of a button*

# Setting Up Clickable Spatial 3D Buttons

In this section, we'll set up a clickable spatial 3D button that can be pressed using the Straight Spatial Menu Pointer you set up in the previous section. Let's begin.

You'll recall that when setting up your Teleport Targets in Chapter 9, you set up a Spatial Targets Dispatcher to work with your curved teleport pointer. As your Teleport Targets were spatial targets, they could receive any dispatched events from this dispatcher. When using spatial 3D buttons, the same analogy is applicable. Your Straight Spatial Menu Pointer can be connected to a Spatial Targets Dispatcher that is responsible for dispatching events to your spatial 3D buttons and your spatial Teleport Targets, as will be demonstrated. You already have a Spatial Targets Dispatcher in the hierarchy that can be used with your spatial 3D buttons.

When you point at your spatial 3D button using your Straight Spatial Menu Pointer, you would ideally want to be able to click this button to have an action occur. In the last section, we set up our Straight Spatial Menu Pointer to be displayed in the scene upon pressing a button. We now need a way of having this menu pointer register a click against a spatial 3D button in our scene. To invoke a selection (click) against a spatial 3D button, we'll first set up a clickable spatial 3D button. You can register a click against this button by either pressing the *Z* key on your keyboard or by pulling the trigger button of your Oculus, HTC Vive, or Xbox controller.

Let's begin by capturing a *Z* key press. The procedure is identical to that of capturing the *M* key press. In the hierarchy, expand the Keyboard Input game object, locate the Input Unity Input Manager Button Action M game object, and duplicate it, renaming this copied game object "Input Unity Input Manager Button Action *Z*." With this copied game object selected in the hierarchy, locate its Key Code property in the Inspector, and from the drop-down, select the letter *Z*. You have now captured the *Z* key press on the keyboard.

Next, let's create an intermediary game object into which we'll channel all button inputs that will result in a spatial 3D button being clicked. Select the Button Input Actions game object in the hierarchy and create a new empty child game object within it and rename it "Spatial Button Click." With this game object selected in the hierarchy, add a Boolean Action component to it. Set the Sources property size value to 4 for this component. You need to capture an input button press from four devices: your Oculus controller, HTC Vive controller, Xbox controller, and keyboard.

With the Keyboard Input game object still expanded in the hierarchy, drag and drop the Input Unity Input Manager Button Action Z game object from the hierarchy into the Element 0 slot of the Boolean Action component of the Spatial Button Click game object. Now, expand the Input Unity Input Manager X Box controller game object in the hierarchy and locate its Right Trigger Press game object. Drag and drop this Right Trigger Press game object from the hierarchy into the Element 1 slot of the Boolean Action component of the Spatial Button Click game object.

Next, expand the Input Unity Input Manager Oculus Touch Right Controller in the hierarchy and locate its Right Trigger Press game object. Drag and drop this game object from the hierarchy into the Element 2 slot of the Boolean Action component of the Spatial Button Click game object.

Last, expand the Input Unity Input Manager Open VR Right Controller in the hierarchy and locate its Right Trigger Press game object. Drag and drop this game object from the hierarchy into the Element 3 slot of the Boolean Action component of the Spatial Button Click game object.

You have now channeled all input for obtaining a spatial 3D UI button click, into the Spatial Button Click intermediary game object, see Figure 17-3.

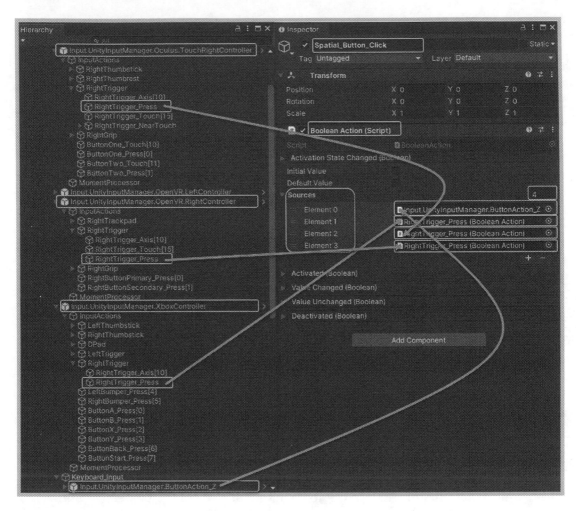

**Figure 17-3.** *Setting up the Spatial Button Click game object for receiving input from your controllers and keyboard*

To ensure that you can click your spatial 3D UI button, you need first to activate your Straight Spatial Menu Pointer. While it is active, point it toward this UI button, and either press the *Z* key on your keyboard or pull the trigger of your Oculus, HTC Vive, or Xbox controller.

Now, let's connect the Straight Spatial Menu Pointer to the Spatial Targets Dispatcher. You ideally have several spatial 3D buttons available in the scene, in which case you need to ensure that your Straight Spatial Menu Pointer is aware of each of them. This would be difficult to maintain, as each time you add a new spatial 3D button to your scene, you would need to manually link it to the menu pointer to make it aware of the new button. This is something it would be better not to be required to do.

This is where the Spatial Targets Dispatcher comes in, providing you with a level of indirection. Your Straight Spatial Menu Pointer only needs to know about this dispatcher, which itself knows about all the spatial 3D buttons in the scene. Any events fired by the dispatcher will be sent to all spatial 3D buttons and spatial targets in the scene.

Let's set this up now. From within VRTK RAY POINTERS in the hierarchy, select the Indicators Object Pointers Straight Spatial Menu Pointer game object. In the Pointer Facade component of the Inspector, expand the Enter, Exited, and Selected events. Click the plus symbol located in the bottom right corner of each event to add an event listener box to each. From the hierarchy, drag and drop the Indicators Spatial Targets Dispatcher game object into each of events' listener boxes.

For the function for the Entered event, select Spatial Target Dispatcher, Do Dispatch Enter from the "Dynamic Event Data" section of the context menu that pops up. For the function for the Exited event, select Spatial Target Dispatcher, Do Dispatch Exit from this section. For the function for the Selected event, select Spatial Target Dispatcher, Do Dispatch Select, see Figure 17-4.

Finally, you need to set up the Selection Action property to trigger the Selected event when it receives a True value. In the case of your spatial 3D buttons, a selection occurs when a button is clicked. You can ensure that this spatial 3D button click occurs in one of two ways: by pressing the Z key on the keyboard or by pulling the trigger of the Oculus, HTC Vive, or Xbox controller.

Now you have captured all these four button action inputs in the Spatial Button Click game object. All you have left to do is to drag and drop the Spatial Button Click game object into the Selection Action property parameter of the Indicators Object Pointers Straight Spatial Menu Pointer game object, as shown in Figure 17-4.

The Spatial Targets Dispatcher in your scene is now all set up to receive events triggered by your Straight Spatial Menu Pointer and send the appropriate methods to whichever spatial 3D button or Teleport Target is being pointed to in the scene.

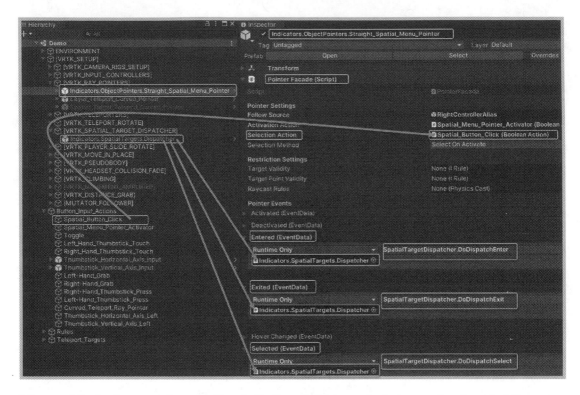

**Figure 17-4.** *Connecting the Straight Spatial Menu Pointer to the Spatial Targets Dispatcher*

Before you test your Straight Spatial Menu Pointer's clickable functionality, you need to add a clickable button to the scene. Select and expand the VRTK SETUP game object in the hierarchy, and create a new empty child game object in it and rename it "VRTK 3D SPATIAL UI BUTTONS." Select the Project tab, and expand the "Packages" folder until you locate the Tilia Interactions Spatial Button Unity package, and expand that until you reach its "Prefabs" folder. Drag and drop the Interactions, Spatial Buttons Click Button prefab onto the child game object in the hierarchy. All your spatial 3D UI buttons will be children of this VRTK SPATIAL 3D UI BUTTONS game object. If you don't have Text Mesh Pro installed, you will be prompted to import the TMP essentials. Go ahead and click the Import TMP Essentials button, and once it is done importing, close the TMP Importer dialog box. You don't need to import TMP examples and extras.

With the Interactions Spatial Button Click Button game object selected in the hierarchy, change its Transform, Position values as follows: $X$ = -14.52; $Y$ = 1.5; and $Z$ = -3.55. Your spatial 3D button has now been positioned above and to the left of the worktable.

Now, playtest your Demo scene using either the keyboard or Xbox controller with the Spatial Simulator, or you could playtest the scene with your VR headset. First, activate your Straight Spatial Menu Pointer, and while it is active, point it at the clickable button and either press the *Z* key on the keyboard or pull the trigger using either your Oculus, HTC Vive, or Xbox controller. You'll notice the button switches quickly to an activated green state, displaying the text ON before returning to its default state. Now, aim your Straight Spatial Menu Pointer toward one of your Teleport Targets and pull the controller's trigger or press the *Z* key on the keyboard. You will be teleported to that specific Teleport Target. The Spatial Targets Dispatcher sends its method calls to all Teleport Targets. As your teleport points and the teleport area are such targets, they are among those that receive these dispatched events. This is something you don't want happening when using your Straight Spatial Menu Pointer. In the next section, we'll go over how to get your Straight Spatial Menu Pointer to interact with only your spatial 3D buttons.

# Setting Up a Spatial Button Group

To ensure that our Straight Spatial Menu Pointer can only interact with your spatial 3D buttons, not any Teleport Targets, we'll set up a Spatial Button Group containing our clickable button. This group contains its Spatial Target Dispatcher, which you used to set up your clickable button in the last section, and will be connected to a Spatial Target Processor, a list of Spatial Target Dispatchers.

A Spatial Button Group allows you to compile your spatial 3D buttons. Each Spatial Button Group comes with a Spatial Target Dispatcher. You can set up different Straight Spatial Menu Pointers that can interact with different Spatial Button Groups if such a setup is required. However, what you want to achieve here is having your Straight Spatial Menu Pointer interact with the spatial 3D buttons only, not with any other Teleport Targets.

To have this happen, you'll first need to set up a Spatial Button Group. You'll then add all your spatial 3D buttons to this group. Note that, as previously discussed, each Spatial Button Group has a Spatial Target Dispatcher. You need to connect this Spatial Button Group, and its Spatial Target Dispatcher, to a new Spatial Target Processor game object that we'll explore in this section. Finally, instead of connecting your Straight Spatial Menu Pointer to the Spatial Target Dispatcher that currently exists, you'll connect the menu pointer to this new Spatial Target Processor game object.

Thus, your Straight Spatial Menu Pointer will now be talking to the Spatial Targets Processor. In turn, the Spatial Targets Processor will ensure that the events emitted by the Straight Spatial Menu Pointer are only redirected to the Spatial Target Dispatcher connected to this processor. As it is the Spatial Button Group, Spatial Target Dispatcher that is connected to the Spatial Target Processor, you can be ensured that the appropriate methods are dispatched only to the buttons contained in this Spatial Button Group. Let's implement this functionality so that you gain a better understanding of the connectivity involved here.

Select the Project tab and expand the "Packages" folder until you locate the Tilia Interactions Spatial Button Unity package. Then, expand it further until you reach its "Prefabs" folder. Drag and drop the Interactions Spatial Button Group prefab onto the VRTK SPATIAL 3D UI BUTTONS game object in the hierarchy. Rename the Interactions Spatial Button Group game object "Generic Spatial Button Group."

You now need to make your existing clickable spatial 3D button a child of this Generic Spatial Button Group game object by nesting it in its Buttons child game object. To do so, expand the Generic Spatial Button Group game object until its child game object, Buttons, is visible in the hierarchy. Then, drag and drop the Interactions Spatial Button Click button onto the Buttons child game object. Figure 17-5 shows how the Interactions Spatial Button Click button game object gets nested within Buttons.

***Figure 17-5.*** *The clickable 3D spatial getting nested in Buttons*

Now, select the Generic Spatial Button Group game object in the hierarchy and look at the Inspector. You'll see that this game object already contains a Spatial Target Dispatcher. It is this dispatcher that your Straight Spatial Menu Pointer will eventually use. However, your menu pointer will indirectly connect to the dispatcher via a Spatial Target Processor we'll set up now.

Select the VRTK SETUP game object in the hierarchy and create a new empty child game object in it and rename it "VRTK SPATIAL TARGET PROCESSOR." Now, select the Project tab, and expand the "Packages" folder until you locate the Tilia indicators Spatial Targets Unity package. Expand it further until you reach its "Prefabs" folder. Now, drag and drop the Indicators Spatial Targets Processor prefab onto the VRTK SPATIAL TARGET PROCESSOR game object in the hierarchy.

With the Indicators Spatial Targets Processor game object selected in the hierarchy, ensure that its Spatial Target Dispatcher Processor component has been expanded in the Inspector. Its Elements property size has been set to 1 by default, with an Element 0 slot also available. You'll need to expand the Elements property to see this slot. Drag and drop the Generic Spatial Button Group game object from the hierarchy into this Element 0 slot of the Spatial Target Dispatcher Processor component, as shown in Figure 17-6.

The Spatial Targets Processor is a list of Spatial Target Dispatchers whose responsibility is to pass data onto each active dispatcher in its list only, not all spatial targets in the scene. You can connect the Generic Spatial Button Group game object to the Spatial Targets Processor, as it has a Spatial Target Dispatcher within it, as circled in Figure 17-6.

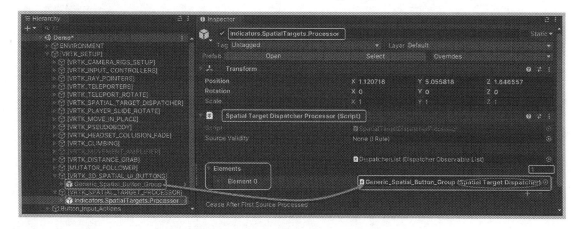

*Figure 17-6.* *Setting up the Spatial Targets Processor with a single Spatial Target Dispatcher that belongs to the Generic Spatial Button Group*

The Spatial Targets Processor will now dispatch data only to this Generic Spatial Button Group game object, which in turn will enlist the Spatial Target Dispatcher to send the data only to the buttons in this Generic Spatial Button Group. The last step in this process is to hook up the events of your Straight Spatial Menu Pointer to the newly added Spatial Targets Processor so that they call on this processor instead of calling on the Spatial Targets Dispatcher.

Select the Indicators Object Pointers, Straight Spatial Menu Pointer game object in the hierarchy. You'll notice that the event listener boxes for the Entered, Exited, and Selected events in the Inspector are still pointing to the Indicators Spatial Targets

Dispatcher, set up in the last section. You need to change this so that they point to your Spatial Targets Processor. To do this, with the Indicators Object Pointers, Straight Spatial Menu Pointer game object selected in the hierarchy, drag and drop the Indicators Spatial Targets Processor game object into each event listener box for the Entered, Exited, and Selected events. You'll notice that the relevant functions for each event listener in the Spatial Targets Processor are like those in the Spatial Target Dispatcher. You do need to set up these functions again.

For the Entered event's function, select Spatial Target Dispatcher Processor, Do Dispatch Enter from the "Dynamic Event Data" section. For the Exited event's function, select Spatial Target Dispatcher Processor, Do Dispatch Exit from the same section. For the Selected event's function, select Spatial Target Dispatcher Processor, Do Dispatch Select from this section, see Figure 17-7.

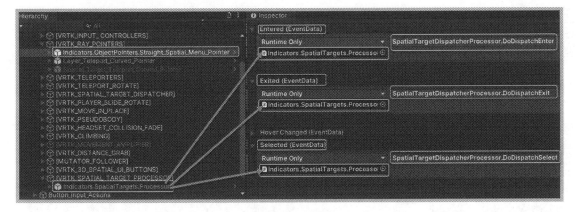

***Figure 17-7.*** *Connecting the Straight Spatial Menu Pointer to the Spatial Targets Processor*

Playtest the *Demo* scene using your VR headset. You'll notice that your clickable button still works in the same manner. Now, try using your Straight Spatial Menu Pointer to teleport onto any of your Teleport Targets. You'll find that it's not possible to teleport anymore using the Straight Spatial Menu Pointer, which can now only be used with your spatial 3D buttons.

# Changing the Appearance of Your Spatial Button

Your spatial buttons have specific Style properties whose appearance can be changed. These Style properties are available in the Spatial Button Facade component. In this section, we'll look at the various Style properties available for you to configure the look of your spatial buttons.

Select the Interactions Spatial Button Click Button game object, which is now nested in the Buttons game object of the Generic Spatial Button Group. In the Inspector within the Spatial Button Facade component of "Button Settings" section, you'll see several properties available for styling this button. A button can be in either of two primary states, Enabled or Disabled. Which state it's in is controlled by the Is Enabled check box, which is checked by default.

The Enabled Style Settings and Disabled Style Settings are used for the button's appearance. When the button is enabled, its Is Enabled property is checked, and when it is disabled, its Is Enabled property is unchecked.

First, let's explore the Enabled Style Settings, which comprise various states: Enabled Inactive, Enabled Hover, and Enabled Active. We'll begin by expanding the Enabled Inactive state. Although this state involves your button being enabled, because your Straight Spatial Menu Pointer isn't hovering over it, and it hasn't been selected (clicked on), it's in an enabled-but-inactive state by default. However, if you point your Straight Spatial Menu Pointer at it, you could transition it into the Enabled Hover or Enabled Active state.

In the Enabled Inactive state, you have some properties nested. The Is Applied check box indicates whether or not the properties you're about to set to define the style of the button should be applied when the button is in its Enabled Inactive state. If left unchecked, then you can manually style the internal elements of the button.

The first property you'll encounter for defining the style of your button when it's in an Enabled Inactive state is the Button Text property. This property refers to the text displayed when your button is in its Enabled Inactive state. Set the value in the text box for this property to Enabled Inactive State. The Font Size property determines the font size used to display the button text. Set its property value to 10.

The Font Color property determines the color of the font the button text will use. You can leave this as is. The Mesh Color property determines the color of the button's Mesh when your button is in its Enabled Inactive state. Clicking the View Enabled Inactive Container button will expand your clickable button in the hierarchy, highlighting its Mesh container. This is a shortcut for reaching the Mesh container of your button.

Expand this Mesh container game object, and select the Default Mesh child object. You'll see that the Mesh is a simple cube. You can change this into a sphere if you want your button to look more oval shaped or use any other Mesh in place of the cube. You can also change the Material for your button. The possibilities are endless for shaping your button.

Now, select the Normal Text child game object in the hierarchy. You'll see that the buttons use Text Mesh Pro, giving you a plethora of ways to change the look of your text. If you didn't have Text Mesh Pro installed already, you should have been prompted to install it when the Package Manager set up the Tilia Interactions Spatial Button Unity package. Figure 17-8 displays the properties of the Enabled Inactive state.

*Figure 17-8. Properties for the Enabled Inactive state*

Let's now move on to setting up the next state available as part of the Enabled Style Settings, the Enabled Hover state. Expand this state in the Inspector. In this state, your button is enabled and hovered over by your Straight Spatial Menu Pointer but hasn't yet been selected (clicked on); therefore, it is currently in an enabled-but-hovered-over state. You can transition into its Enabled Active state if you push your controller's trigger button while hovering over it.

In the Enabled Hover state, you have the same properties as you do in the Enabled Inactive state. You will, however, note that a different Mesh Color has been set up for this state. Change the Button Text property here to Enabled Hover State and set the Font Size property value to 10, as shown in Figure 17-9.

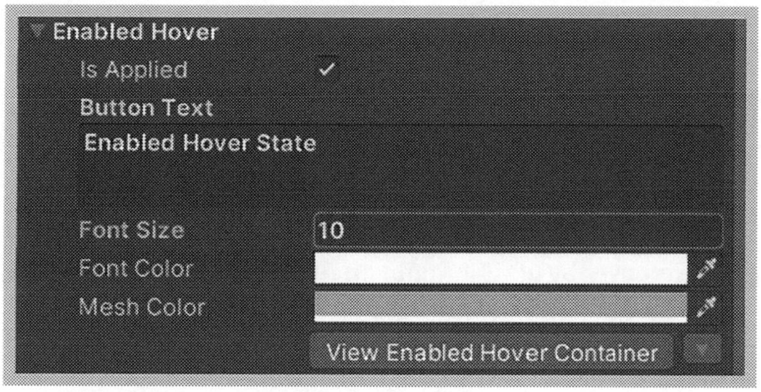

**Figure 17-9.**  *Properties for the Enabled Hover state*

Let's next explore the final state available in Enabled Style Settings, the Enabled Active state. In the Inspector, expand this state. Here, your button is enabled and selected (clicked on) by your Straight Spatial Menu Pointer, thereby transitioning you to the Enabled Active state.

In the Enabled Active state, you have the same properties available as you do in the Enabled Inactive and Hover states. You will, however, see that a different Mesh color has been set up here. Change the Button Text property to Enabled Clicked On. Also, set the Font Size property value to 10. Figure 17-10 displays the properties of the Enabled Active state.

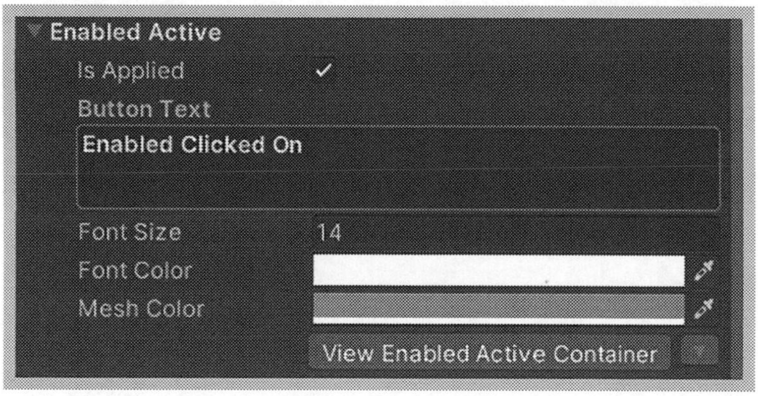

**Figure 17-10.**  *Properties of the Enabled Active state*

Let's now look at the second type of style settings available for your buttons: the Disabled Style Settings. These settings are applied to the button's appearance when the it is disabled; that is, when its Is Enabled property is unchecked. You'll notice that the Disabled Style Settings have only two states; namely, Disabled Inactive and Disabled Hover.

Begin by expanding the Disabled Inactive state. In this state, your button is disabled, as it isn't being hovered over by your Straight Spatial Menu Pointer; therefore, it's in an inactive state. However, you could transition this into the Disabled Hover state if you point your Straight Spatial Menu Pointer at it. You won't be able to click it to activate it, though, as its Is Enabled property is unchecked.

In the Disabled Inactive state, you have the same properties as you do in the Enabled Inactive and Hover states. You will, however, note that a different Mesh color has been set up for this state. Change the Button Text property here to Disabled Inactive State. Also, set the Font Size property value to 9. Figure 17-11 displays the properties of the Disabled Inactive state.

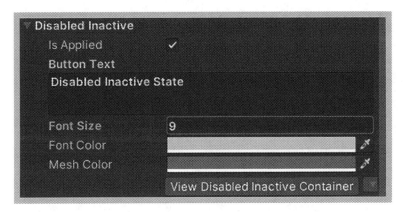

***Figure 17-11.*** *Properties of the Disabled Inactive state*

Last, expand the Disabled Hover state. In this state, your button is disabled, but it's being hovered over by your Straight Spatial Menu Pointer. Therefore, it's in a Hover state. Selecting (clicking) this button won't activate it, as its Is Enabled property is unchecked.

In the Disabled Hover state, you have the same properties available as you do in the Disabled Inactive state. You will, however, note that a different Mesh color has been set up for this state. Change the Button Text property here to Disabled Hover State. Also, set the Font Size property value to 9. Figure 17-12 shows the properties of the Disabled Hover state.

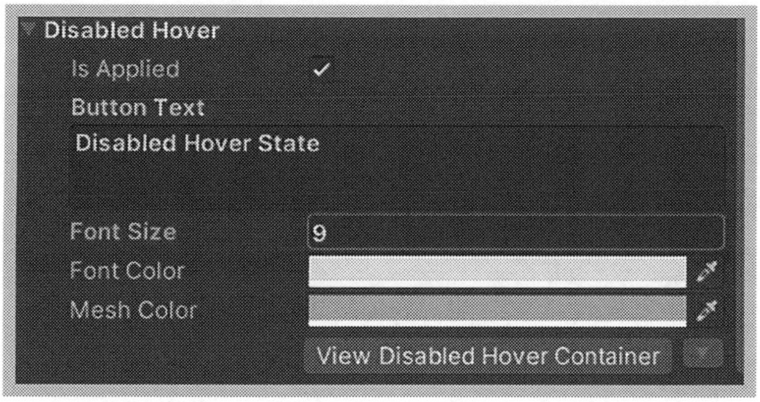

*Figure 17-12.* *Properties of the Disabled Hover state*

Last, note how different Mesh containers have been set up in the hierarchy for the different states your button could be in. You can view these different Mesh containers by clicking the View button in a given state.

Now, playtest your Demo scene using your VR headset. First, ensure that you have the button's Is Enabled property checked. You'll see that with this property checked, you can click the button and the new button text you set up will be displayed. Now, uncheck the Is Enabled property and playtest your Demo scene again. You'll find that you can hover over the button but can't click it.

# Creating a Spatial Toggle Button

A Toggle button allows the user to switch between the on and off states. It allows for situations where the button is in an activated/on/true state and a deactivated/off/false state. When clicked, a Toggle button will ideally go into the on/true state and stay in this state until it is clicked again, wherein it will go into the off/false state. You've worked with the Toggle Action component, which toggles a button's state from on to off, and vice versa. With your Straight Spatial Menu Pointer hovering over a Toggle button, a trigger press will activate the Toggle button and a subsequent trigger press will deactivate it.

Let's set up a Toggle button now. It needs to be placed in the Buttons child game object of the Generic Spatial Button Group game object. In the hierarchy, expand the Generic Spatial Button Group so that its child object, Buttons, is visible. In the "Packages" folder under the Project tab, locate the Tilia Interactions Spatial Buttons Unity package. Expand it until you reach its "Prefabs" folder. Drag and drop the

271

Interactions Spatial Button Toggle button prefab onto the Buttons game object that has been expanded in the hierarchy. This ensures that your Toggle button will now be contained in the Generic Spatial Button Group, see Figure 17-13.

***Figure 17-13.***  *The Interactions Spatial ButtonToggle button nested in the Buttons child object of the Generic Spatial Button Group*

Select this Interactions Spatial Button Toggle Button game object in the hierarchy and change its Transform Position property values to $X$ = -12.95; $Y$ = 1.5; and $Z$ = -3.55.

Now, let's set up the Button Text property for each of the three states in the Enabled Style settings. Set the Button Text property for the Enabled Inactive state to TOGGLE OFF; set this property for the Enabled Hover state to TOGGLE HOVER; and set this property for the Enabled Active state to TOGGLE ON. If you want to set up the states for the *Disabled Style Settings,* you could do this as well. We went over how to set these up in the previous section.

Playtest your Demo scene. You'll see that at the start, your Toggle button is in the Toggle Off state. Hover over the button using your Straight Spatial Menu Pointer and it will enter its Toggle Hover state. The moment you stop hovering over it, the button returns to its Toggle Off state. Now, click the Toggle button with your Straight Spatial Menu Pointer. The button will be activated, and its text will display, "Toggle On." The button will stay in this Toggle On state until it is clicked again. Finally, click the Toggle button again to have it return to its Toggle Off state.

# Creating Spatial Option Buttons

Option buttons allow you to provide multiple-choice options to the user, where only one of the Option buttons can be in an active/on state. Attempting to activate any other Option button in the group of Option Buttons will ensure that the currently activated Option button will be deactivated. We will create a new Spatial Button Group in this section and populate it with some Option buttons. This will require you to add the Spatial Target Dispatcher, available as part of this new Spatial Button Group, to your Spatial Targets Processor. You'll recall from Chapter 9 the section on Teleporting using Teleport Targets, that the Spatial Target Processor is a list of Spatial Target Dispatchers.

In the hierarchy, select and expand the VRTK SPATIAL 3D UI BUTTONS game object. Note that all your spatial buttons will reside in this game object. Expand the "Packages" folder in the Project tab and locate the Tilia Interactions Spatial Button Unity package. Expand it until you reach its "Prefabs" folder. Now, drag and drop the Interactions Spatial Button Group prefab onto the VRTK SPATIAL 3D UI BUTTONS game object in the hierarchy, and rename the Interactions Spatial Button Group game object "Option Buttons Group." Set its Transform Position property values as follows: $X = -11.4$; $Y = 1.5$; and $Z = -3.55$.

Now that you have another Spatial Button Group in the scene with its Spatial Target Dispatcher, you need to tell your Spatial Targets Processor about it. This is to ensure that when events are triggered via your Straight Spatial Menu Pointer, your Spatial Targets Processor knows that it must dispatch this data onward to this new Option Buttons Group.

In the hierarchy, select and expand the VRTK SPATIAL TARGET PROCESSOR game object, and select its child game object, Indicators Spatial Targets Processor. In the Spatial Target Dispatcher Processor component of the Inspector, increase the Dispatcher List, Element property's size value to 2, making an Element 1 slot available. Now, drag and drop the Option Buttons Group game object into this Element 1 slot. This ensures that your Straight Spatial Menu Pointer passes its event data across to the Spatial Targets Processor, which in turn will call on the Option Buttons Group, Spatial Target Dispatcher, see Figure 17-14.

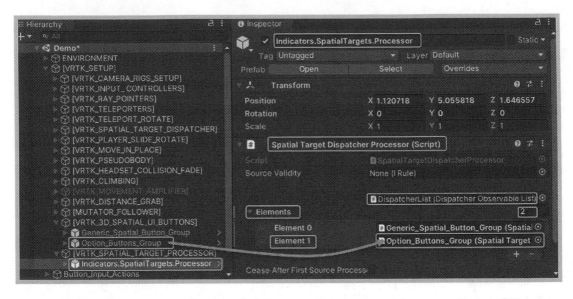

**Figure 17-14.** *Setting up the Spatial Targets Processor with a new Spatial Target Dispatcher that belongs to the Option Buttons Group*

Now, it's time to add some Option buttons to this Option Buttons Group. In the hierarchy, expand the Option Buttons Group so that its child object, Buttons, is visible. With the "Tilia Interactions Spatial Button Unity Package Prefabs" folder still expanded, drag and drop the Interactions Spatial Button Option Button prefab onto the Buttons child game object in the hierarchy. Rename this Option button "OPTION 1." Set this Option button's Transform Position Y property value to 0.35. In its Spatial Button Facade component, set the Button Text property for all available states in the Enabled Style Settings and Disabled Style Settings to OPTION 1.

Next, duplicate this OPTION 1 button game object in the hierarchy twice. Name the copied Option buttons "OPTION 2" and "OPTION 3," respectively. Select the OPTION 2 game object in the hierarchy, and ensure that its Transform Position Y property value is set to 0. In its Spatial Button Facade component, set its Button Text property for all available states in the Enabled Style Settings and Disabled Style Settings to OPTION 2.

Next, select the OPTION 3 game object in the hierarchy, and ensure that its Transform Position Y property value is set to -0.35. In its Spatial Button Facade component, set the Button Text property for all available states in the Enabled Style Settings and Disabled Style Settings to OPTION 3. Figure 17-15 shows your Option buttons nested in the Buttons child game object of the Option Buttons Group.

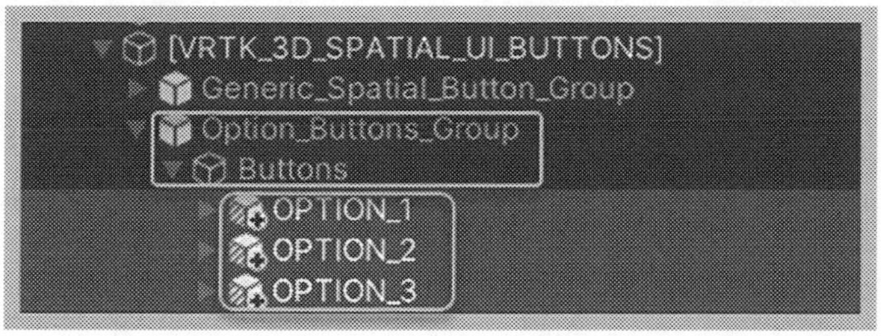

*Figure 17-15.* *The three Option buttons nested in the Buttons child game object of the Option Buttons Group*

Finally, you need to decide whether you want one of these Option buttons selected by default. Select the Option button's Group game object in the hierarchy. In the Spatial Button Group Manager component of the Inspector, you'll see the Active Button Index property, which allows you to specify one of the Option buttons as the default button.

If you don't want any of the Option buttons selected by default, ensure that the Active Button Index property value is set to -1. Setting this property value to 0 will ensure that the first Option button will be selected by default when your Option Buttons Group game object is enabled. If you want the last Option button to be selected by default, set the Active Button Index property value to 2. If you want the middle Option button to be selected by default, set this property value to 1.

For our purposes, let's set this Active Button Index property value to -1, as shown in Figure 17-16, so that no Option button is selected at startup.

*Figure 17-16.* *Setting the Active Button Index property for to -1, ensuring that no Option button will be selected by default*

Now, playtest your Demo scene using your VR headset and activate the Straight Spatial Menu Pointer. Point its beam at any unselected Option button and select it by pushing your controller's trigger button. You'll notice that the Option button you selected is now activated. Also, as all your Option buttons are within the same Spatial Button Group—namely, the Option Buttons Group—only one Option button can be activated at a time.

# Interacting Directly with VRTK's Spatial Buttons

In this section, we'll go over how to interact with your spatial 3D buttons using your hands, without the need for the Straight Spatial Menu Pointer. This provides you with a level of true immersion in VR. It opens a world of possibilities for UI interaction. You could create your own VR keyboard and interact with the buttons on it using your fingers, or you could have your UI pop up near yourself and then simply reach out with your hand and interact with its 3D buttons. In this section, we'll learn how to set this up.

In the hierarchy, select and expand the Buttons child game object in the Generic Spatial Button Group. Then, select the Interactions Spatial Button Click Button game object. In the Inspector, locate the Collision List, Element's property in the "Collision Settings" section and expand it. Set this element's property size value to 2, which will enable two element slots to be created. Now, from within the Camera Rigs, Tracked Alias game object in the hierarchy, drag and drop the Interactions Interactor Left game object into the Element 0 slot. Next, drag and drop the Interactions Interactor Right game object into the Element 1 slot.

You have now given your Interactions Spatial Button Click Button the ability to interact with the Interactors of your hands, see Figure 17-17.

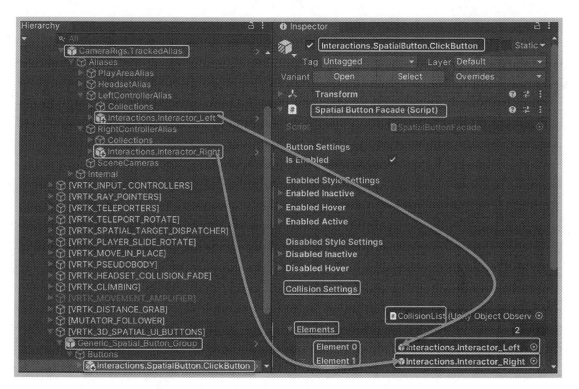

***Figure 17-17.*** *Setting up the Interactors Spatial Button Click Button to be able to interact directly with your hands*

Next, with the Buttons child game object still expanded in the Generic Spatial Button Group, select the Interactions Spatial Button Toggle Button game object. In the "Collision Settings" section of the Inspector, locate the Collision List, Element's property, and expand it. Set this element's property size value to 2, which will enable two element slots to be created. Now, from within the Camera Rigs, Tracked Alias game object in the hierarchy, drag and drop the Interactions Interactor Left game object into the Element 0 slot. Then, drag and drop the Interactions Interactor Right game object into the Element 1 slot.

You have now given your Interactions Spatial Button Toggle Button the ability to interact with the Interactors of your hands. You might have noticed that the procedure is like that for setting up the Interactions Spatial Button Click Button game object.

Next, you need to set up the three Option buttons to interact with your hands, too. The procedure here is the same. Unfortunately, you can't select all three Option buttons and set up their properties at the same time, so you need to set up each Option button's property one at a time.

In the hierarchy, expand the Buttons child game object in the Option Buttons Group, and select the OPTION 1 game object. In the "Collision Settings" section of the Inspector, locate the Collision List, Element's property and expand it. Set this element's property size value to 2, which will enable two element slots to be created.

Now, in the Camera Rigs, Tracked Alias game object in the hierarchy, drag and drop the Interactions Interactor Left game object into the Element 0 slot. Then, drag and drop the Interactions Interactor Right game object into the Element 1 slot.

You have now given your OPTION 1 Toggle Button the ability to interact with the Interactors of your hands. You might have noticed that the procedure is like that we used for setting up the Interactions Spatial Button Click Button game object. The procedure for setting up the Option buttons OPTION 2 and OPTION 3 is identical. I'll leave that as an exercise for you to complete.

Before playtesting the Demo scene, let's declutter the environment so that you can solely focus on interacting with your spatial 3D buttons using your hands. Expand the Environment game object in the hierarchy and deactivate the Table, Drill Machine, Hammer, and Axe game objects. This will allow you to walk straight toward your spatial 3D buttons and physically interact with them. Playtest the Demo scene using your VR headset. Approach the Option buttons. You will see that as you approach an Option button with your hand/finger, the button enters its hover state. On pushing your hand/finger further forward, the button is activated. Try activating each Option button, and note that the one you just used is deselected when you select a new button. Now, try interacting with the Toggle button and the Clickable button. You'll see that they both function similarly as they did when using the Straight Spatial Menu Pointer.

# Creating a Spatial Slider

A Slider is a control that lets the user select from a range of values by moving a knob control along a track. It allows you to display and utilize a numeric value within a predefined range. With the VRTK, you can easily create a Slider by using an Interactable game object in combination with a limited drive axis. In this section, we'll review how to use a linear drive to create a Slider control that displays the Slider's value, using a Tooltip as you move the Slider's knob around.

Select the VRTK SPATIAL 3D UI BUTTONS game object in the hierarchy, and create a new empty child game object within it and rename it "Slider." Set its Transform Position property values as follows: $X = -13.75$; $Y = 0.94$; and $Z = -3.55$. This will serve as the parent game object that will hold together the various game objects that comprise the Slider. Select the Slider game object, and create a new child cube game object within it and rename it "Slider Bar."

Set its Transform Scale property values as follows: $X = 1$; $Y = 0.01$; and $Z = 0.02$. Remove the box collider component on your Slider Bar.

In the "Packages" folder of the Project tab, select and expand the Tilia Interactions Controllable Unity package. Expand it until you reach its "Prefabs" folder and select the "Transform" folder within it. Drag and drop the Interactions Linear Transform Drive prefab onto the Slider game object within the hierarchy. You now have two child game objects in your Slider game object.

Instead of using the Linear Transform drive, we could have used the Linear Joint Drive available in the "Physics Joint" folder. However, the Linear Joint Drive uses Unity joints and works with Unity's physics system. For a Slider this simple, Unity joints and physics aren't required.

Now, expand the Interactions Linear transform Drive in the hierarchy until you reach its Mesh container and select the cube game object within it. You can reach the cube game object by navigating as follows: Interactions Linear transform Drive ➤ Internal ➤ Interactable Container ➤ Interactions Interactable ➤ Mesh Container ➤ Cube. This cube, which will serve as the knob of your Slider, is enormous, so change its Transform Scale property values to $X = 0.1$; $Y = 0.1$; and $Z = 0.1$.

The next step is to select the Interactions Linear Transform Drive game object in the hierarchy. In the Linear Drive Facade component of the Inspector, as shown in Figure 17-18, set the properties for the "Drive Settings" and "Target Value Settings" sections as follows:

- Set that the Drive Axis property to the X Axis, as your Slider knob will move horizontally.

- Check the box for the Move to Target Value property.

- Set the Target Value property to 0.

The following two settings in the "Step Settings" section ensure that your Slider knob starts in the 0 position of your Slider, which is also the position it will be moved to whenever you ungrab your Slider knob.

- Set the Step Range's Minimum value to 0 and Maximum value to 10.

This is the numerical range of your Slider. You now can't go below the 0 value or above the 10 value. Last, in the "Step Increment" section:

- Set the property value to 1.

This ensures that your Slider emits all the values between 0 and 10. If you set the Step Increment value to 2, the values emitted would be incremented by two. Thus, you would see the values 0, 2, 4, 6, 8 and 10 as you move the Slider knob.

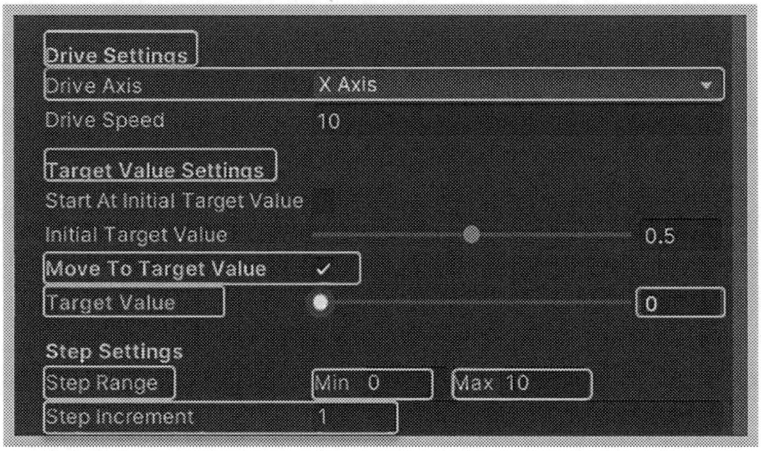

***Figure 17-18.*** *Choosing the Drive and Target Value settings for the Interactions Linear Transform Drive*

Now, you need to set up a visual Tooltip that displays the values of your Slider as you move its knob horizontally. In Chapter 16, we learned how to set up Tooltips, and the Tooltip we'll set up here will follow the same procedure.

In the hierarchy, expand your ToolTips game object, located in the Environment game object. Duplicate the Tool Holder ToolTip game object and rename it "Slider Tooltip." With this renamed game object selected in the hierarchy, set its Transform Position values as follows: $X$ = -13.75; $Y$ = 1.3; and $Z$ = -3.7.

You need to set up some properties in the Tooltip Facade component of the Slider Tooltip game object in the Inspector. The Line Origin property specifies that a line will originate from the game object you provide as a value to this property until the Tooltip. Drag and drop the Slider game object as the parameter value for this property. This ensures that a thin line will be drawn from the Slider to the Slider Tooltip game object. The Facing Source property determines which direction your Slider Tooltip should face. Since it would be good to always see the values displayed by your Slider, you should set this property to your Headset Alias game object. The advantage here is that your Slider Tooltip game object will always be facing you even if you're standing on the opposite side of your Slider. Drag and drop the Headset Alias game object into the Facing Source property parameter. Clear out any text in the Tooltip Text property. You'll be adding a Tooltip Text component to your Slider Tooltip game object that displays the Slider's value as you move the Slider's knob around the Slider.

Now that you have set up your visual Tooltip, the last step is to connect your Slider game object to the Slider Tooltip, so that whenever you move the Slider's knob, the Slider Tooltip display will be updated with the Slider's new value. In the hierarchy, select the Interactions Linear Transform Drive game object, and in its Linear Drive Facade component, expand the Step Value Changed event in the "Events" section. Click the plus symbol located in the bottom right corner of this event to add an event listener. Now, drag and drop the Slider Tooltip game object from the hierarchy into the event listener box of the Step Value Changed event. For the function, select Tooltip Text, Show ToolTip in the "Dynamic Float" section.

Playtest your Demo scene using your VR headset. Go to the Slider and grab its knob and slide it around. Notice how the Slider Tooltip changes its value when you move the knob. Now release the knob and note that it slides back to the zero position. Having your Slider knob slide back to the zero position is not always desirable. It would be a lot better if, after releasing your hold of the Slider knob, you could have it remain fixed at the point you released it.

In the hierarchy, ensure that the Interactions Linear Transform Drive game object has been selected. In the Linear Drive Facade component of the Inspector, locate the Move to Target Value property, and uncheck the check box.

Now, playtest your Demo scene again using your VR headset. Go to the Slider and grab its knob and slide it around. Note that you can grab your Slider's knob, move it around, and see the Slider Tooltip value change. Upon releasing the knob, it stays at the location where it was released, with the Slider Tooltip showing the Slider's value at that location. Also note that you can use any Mesh as your Slider's knob.

# Hacking Your Straight Spatial Menu Pointer to Interact with Your Slider

In the last section, we went over how you could interact with your Slider using your hands. In this section, we'll find out about an undocumented hack wherein you can have your Straight Spatial Menu Pointer interact with your Slider. Along the way, we'll set up a rule so that your Straight Spatial Menu Pointer is in an active state only when it's pointing at your spatial 3D buttons or the Slider's knob.

Let's begin by setting up this rule. It requires your spatial 3D buttons and the Slider's knob Layer property to be set to UI. In your Slider game object, select the Interactions Linear Transform Drive game object in the hierarchy. Then, in the Inspector, expand the Layer drop-down and select UI. When prompted to set the layer to UI for all child objects, select the button Yes Change Children. Next, select both the Generic Spatial Button Group and Option Buttons Group game objects. In the Inspector, expand the Layer drop-down and select UI. When prompted to set the layer to UI for all child objects, select the button Yes Change Children. This ensures that all your spatial 3D buttons and the Slider knob have their layer set to UI.

Now it's time to create a rule like the Teleport Layer rule we created in Chapter 9. Locate and expand the Rules game object in the hierarchy. Then, select the Teleport Layer rule within it and duplicate it. Rename this copied rule, game object to "UI Layer." Select this game object, and within the Inspector, ensure that its Any Layer Rule component has been expanded. Set its Layer Mask property to reflect the value UI only. Ensure that it doesn't state "Mixed," see Figure 17-19.

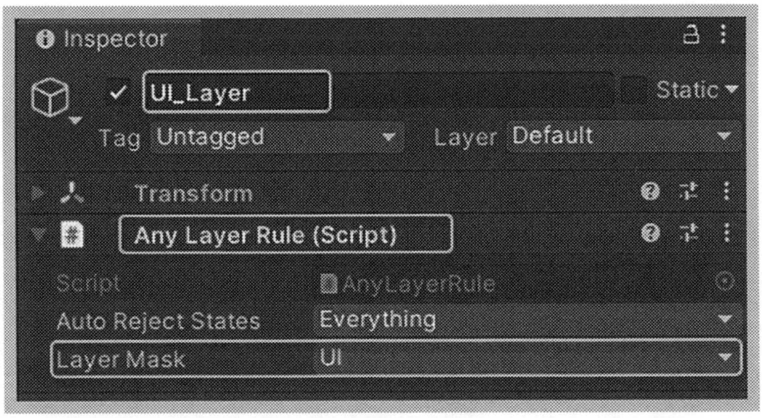

***Figure 17-19.***  *Setting up the UI Layer rule*

Now that your UI Layer rule has been set up, it needs to be hooked up to the Straight Spatial Menu Pointer, so that only when your pointer is aiming at a valid spatial 3D button or the Slider's knob will it display its active green beam.

In the hierarchy, select and expand the VRTK RAY POINTERS game object, and then select the Indicators Object Pointers Straight Spatial Menu Pointer game object. In the Pointer Facade component of the Inspector, locate the Target Validity property. Drag and drop the UI Layer game object from the hierarchy into this Target Validity property parameter, see Figure 17-20.

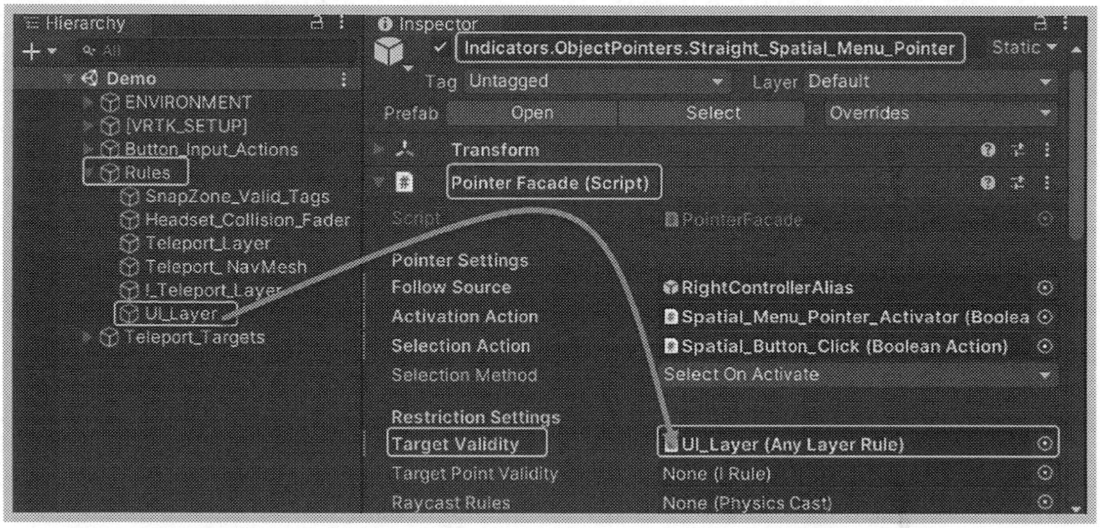

**Figure 17-20.**  *Hooking up the UI Layer rule to the Straight Spatial Menu Pointer*

The above UI Layer rule shown in Figure 17-20 ensures that the Straight Spatial Menu Pointer beam will assume its active green state only if the object it is pointing at complies with the rule that has been set up. In this case, the game object being pointed at must have its layer set as UI. If the game object being pointed at doesn't have its layer set to UI, the Straight Spatial Menu Pointer beam will turn red, indicating that you're pointing at an invalid game object.

Let's now hack the Straight Spatial Menu Pointer so that you can interact with the knob of the Slider using it. To have these components interact, you need to add an Interactor to the Spatial Pointers Cursor game object. You need to do this because your Slider knob is an Interactable game object, not a Spatial Target or a Spatial button. This menu pointer can only interact with Spatial game objects, not with any Interactable game objects.

Suppose you place an Interactor at the end of your Straight Spatial Menu Pointer. If you do this, you could aim this pointer toward the knob of the Slider and get the Interactor at the end to interact with the knob, which is an Interactable game object. This would be just like extending your hand, which has an Interactor game object, and having it interact with the Slider's knob. The critical point here is to figure out precisely where to place this Interactor so that it is at the very end of your Straight Spatial Menu Pointer. The valid sphere object on your Straight Spatial Menu Pointer represents its cursor and is its endpoint, so you need to be sure to set up your Interactor here.

In the hierarchy, select the Indicators Object Pointers Straight Spatial Menu Pointer game object and expand it until you reach its Valid Container game object, which contains the Valid Sphere game object that interests you. To reach this Valid Container game object, navigate as follows: Object Pointer Internal ➤ Elements ➤ Destination ➤ Elements Sphere ➤ Valid Container. In the Valid Container, you can now see the Valid Sphere game object. You'll make your Interactor a child of the Valid Container game object, thereby having it located at the same level as the Valid sphere green cursor game object.

From the Projects tab, expand the "Packages" folder. Locate the Tilia Interactions Interactables Unity package and expand its Runtime, Interactors, 'Prefabs' folder. Drag and drop the Interactions Interactor prefab onto the Valid Container game object in the hierarchy, making it a child.

For this Interactions Interactor game object, you need to set up the Grab Action property. This property requires a Boolean Action, which will initiate the Interactors grab mechanism when true.

Note that you currently have your controller's Trigger button set up so that when it's pulled, a button click action occurs against your spatial 3D buttons. Upon pressing the *Z* key on the keyboard, a spatial 3D button click is activated. To ensure that the Interactor positioned at the end of your Straight Spatial Menu Pointer can interact with the Slider knob, you can't use any of the button options you're currently using to interact with your spatial 3D buttons.

This means that you first need to decide which new button and key presses you'll use against the four devices you'll set up. You'll need to set up an intermediary game object to capture these button and key presses. Then you'll need to pass this intermediary game object, set up with a Boolean Action as the parameter value, to the Grab Action property of the Interactor residing in your Straight Spatial Menu Pointer.

You'll use the *B* button on your Oculus right controller, the *Y* button on your Xbox controller, the Top Menu button on your HTC Vive Right controller, and the *G* key press on your keyboard to capture these button/key press inputs. These inputs will initiate a grab against the Slider knob via the Straight Spatial Menu Pointer.

First, let's set up a button action to capture the *G* key press. Select and expand the Keyboard Input game object in the hierarchy, residing in the VRTK INPUT CONTROLLERS game object. Locate the Input Unity Input Manager Button Action Z game object within it and duplicate it. Rename this copied game object "Input Unity Input Manager Button Action G." In the Inspector, locate the Key Code property. Then, from the drop-down, select the letter *G*.

We have now captured the *G* key press that will be responsible for initiating a Grab action against the Slider's knob.

Let's now set up an intermediary game object to capture the button and key presses we just decided upon. These button and key presses will initiate a grab against the Slider knob via the Straight Spatial Menu Pointer. Select and expand the Button Input Actions game object in the hierarchy, and create a new empty child game object in it and rename it "Spatial Pointer Interactor Grab." With the Spatial Pointer Interactor Grab game object selected in the hierarchy, add a Boolean Action component to it. In this component, set the Sources property size value to 4. Drag and drop the Input Unity Input Manager Button Action G game object from the hierarchy into the Sources, Element 0 slot of this Boolean Action component.

Next, for the Oculus Touch right controller, drag and drop the Button Two Press [1] game object from the hierarchy into the Sources, Element 1 slot of the Boolean Action component. Then, for the Xbox controller, drag and drop the Button Y Press [3] game object into the Sources, Element 2 slot of the same component. Last, for the Open VR right controller, drag and drop the Right Button Primary Press [0] game object into the Sources, Element 3 slot of this component, see Figure 17-21.

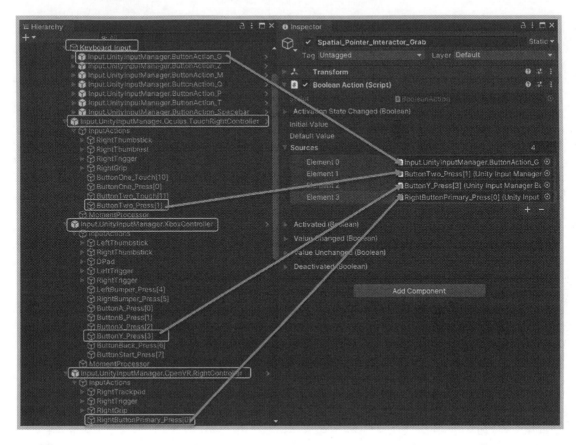

**Figure 17-21.** *Setting up the Spatial Pointer Interactor Grab intermediary game object to capture the input of the various button and key presses that are responsible for initiating a Grab action against the Slider's knob*

Now, select the Interactions Interactor game object that is nested in the Valid Container game object of your Indicators Object Pointers Straight Spatial Menu Pointer game object. Drag and drop the Spatial Pointer Interactor Grab game object from the hierarchy into the Grab Action property parameter of the Interactions Interactor game object, see Figure 17-22.

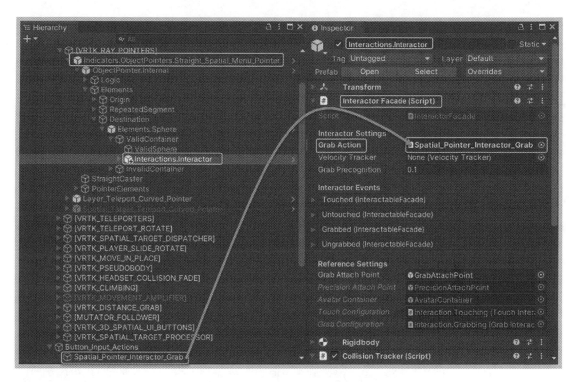

***Figure 17-22.*** *Setting up the Interactions Interactor Grab Action property with the Spatial Pointer Interactor Grab, Boolean Action game object*

Whenever you press the *G* key on the keyboard, the *Y* button on the Xbox controller, the *B* button on the Oculus right controller, or the Top Menu button on the right HTC Vive controller, the Interactions Interactor shown in Figure 17-22 will initiate a Grab action against the Slider's knob. You'll need to keep these buttons continually pressed as you move the Slider around.

Select the Interactions Linear Transform Drive game object from within the Slider game object in the hierarchy. Expand this Interactions Linear Transform Drive game object until you reach its Interactions Interactable game object. To reach this game object, navigate as follows: Interactions Linear Transform Drive ➤ Internal ➤ Interactable Container ➤ Interactions Interactable. Set the Grab Type property in the Inspector to Hold Till Release and the Grab Provider Index property value to 1, as shown in Figure 17-23.

***Figure 17-23.*** *Setting the properties in the "Grab Action Settings" section of the Interactions Interactable child game object in the Slider*

Next, select the Indicators Object Pointers Straight Spatial Menu Pointer game object in the hierarchy, and locate its Selection Action property. An important point to note about this property it that it has been set to Spatial Button Click. This property has no role to play when your Straight Spatial Menu Pointer interacts with your Slider's knob. The interaction occurring in this case is between the Interactor nested in your Straight Spatial Menu Pointer and the Slider knob, which is an Interactable. The Selection Action property, which holds the Spatial Button Click game object, is only used when your Straight Spatial Menu Pointer interacts with the spatial 3D buttons in your scene, initiating a pointer selection against them.

As you don't want the Example Avatar game object in your Interactions Interactor to show up at the end of your Straight Spatial Menu Pointer beam, you need to turn off its Mesh Renderer component. To do so, navigate to the Interactions Interactor game object in the Indicators Object Pointers Straight Spatial Menu Pointer game object, and locate and select its Example Avatar child game object in the hierarchy. In the Inspector, turn off the Mesh Renderer component, see Figure 17-24.

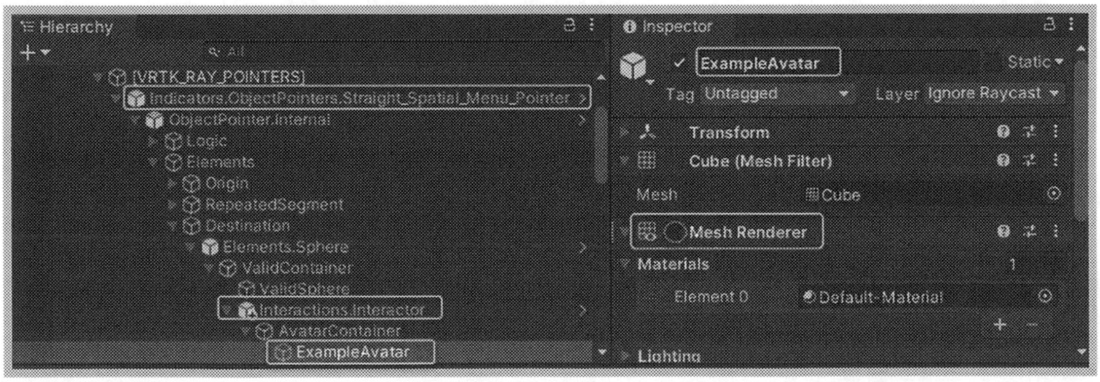

***Figure 17-24.*** *Deactivating the Mesh Renderer on the Example Avatar game object*

In the "Setting Up a Straight Menu Pointer" section of this chapter, you were asked to perform an exercise in which you set up your Straight Spatial Menu Pointer to work as a toggle by using a Toggle action. If you haven't completed that exercise yet, now is the time to do so. Otherwise, you may face difficulties in trying to keep the two buttons on your controllers pressed at the same time. One button displays your Straight Spatial Menu Pointer, and the other moves your Slider knob around while your Straight Spatial Menu Pointer is being pointed at it.

Let's implement and set up this Toggle now, in the event you have not done so yet. First, you'll need to set up a Toggle action to switch your Straight Spatial Menu Pointer on and off. In the hierarchy, select and expand the Button Input Actions game object. Locate the Toggle game object within it, and duplicate it and rename the copied game object "Toggle Menu Pointer."

In the Inspector, you'll see that your new Toggle Menu Pointer game object now has a Toggle Action component in it. Ensure you delete all the event listeners set up for the Activated and Deactivated events on this Toggle Menu Pointer game object.

Now, in the hierarchy, select the Indicators Object Pointers Straight Spatial Menu Pointer game object. In the Inspector, the Activation Action property determines whether or not the Straight Spatial Menu Pointer should be displayed. If a true value is emitted for this property, the Straight Spatial Menu Pointer will be turned on, and if a false value is emitted, it will be turned off. This enables the pointer to be toggled on and off.

Currently, this Activation Action property value has been set to the Spatial Menu Pointer Activator game object. This game object's responsibility is to emit a Boolean true or false value based on whether the *M* key on the keyboard, the Start button on the Oculus controller, the Back button on the Xbox controller, or the Top Menu button on the HTC Vive left controller is pressed. When any of these buttons is pressed, the Activation Action property will emit a true value, resulting in the Straight Spatial Menu Pointer beam being turned on. If none of these buttons are pressed, this property will emit a false value, resulting in the Straight Spatial Menu Pointer beam being turned off.

If you've attempted to test out your Straight Spatial Menu Pointer, you will have noticed that the moment you release your finger from the relevant controller button or key—be it the Start or Back button, the Top Menu button, or the M key—the Boolean Action component in the Spatial Menu Pointer Activator game object will emit a false value. When the Activation Action property receives this value, the Straight Spatial Menu Pointer beam is turned off. This forces you to make sure that the button responsible for displaying the Straight Spatial Menu Pointer is continually pressed down.

To ensure that your Straight Spatial Menu Pointer beam functions as a toggle, let's change the Activation Action property parameter value so that it points to your Toggle Menu Pointer game object. Drag and drop this game object from the hierarchy into this Activation Action property parameter. As this is a Toggle action, it will yield true or false value only. The Activation Action property can then use this Boolean value to display or hide the Straight Spatial Menu Pointer, see Figure 17-25.

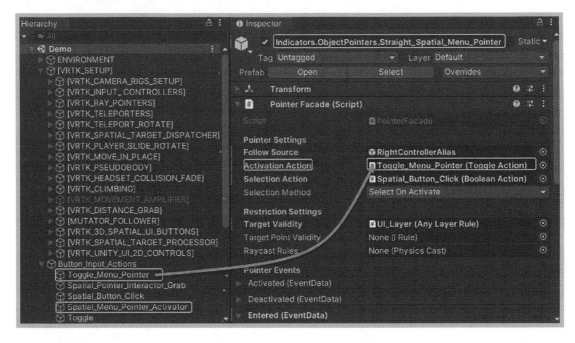

***Figure 17-25.*** *Changing out the Activation Action property parameter value for the Indicators Object Pointers Straight Spatial Menu Pointer game object to enable the Straight Spatial Menu Pointer to function as a toggle*

Now, select the Spatial Menu Pointer Activator game object in the hierarchy. Note that its Boolean Action component checks for button presses responsible for activating the Straight Spatial Menu Pointer. Whenever one of these button presses occurs, you need to tell your Toggle Menu Pointer game object, connected to the Activation Action property shown in Figure 17-25, to assume an active/on/true state. This ensures that the Activation Action property will activate your Straight Spatial Menu Pointer.

Also, when the button that toggles on your Straight Spatial Menu Pointer is pressed again, you need to let your Toggle Menu Pointer game object know that it should assume an inactive/off/false state. This ensures that your Activation Action property will deactivate your Straight Spatial Menu Pointer.

Letting your Toggle Menu Pointer game object know that it is in either the on or off state can be easily achieved by asking the game object to receive the State that it should be in, depending upon whether one of the buttons responsible for toggling the pointer on and off was pressed or not. To achieve this, we'll have our Spatial Menu Pointer Activator game object convey a true or false value to our Toggle Menu Pointer.

Select the Spatial Menu Pointer Activator game object in the hierarchy. Within its Boolean Action component, expand the Activated event. Click the plus symbol located in the bottom right corner of this event to add an event listener. Then, drag and drop the Toggle Menu Pointer game object from the hierarchy into the event listener box of this event. For the function, select Toggle Action, Receive from the "Dynamic Bool" section, see Figure 17-26.

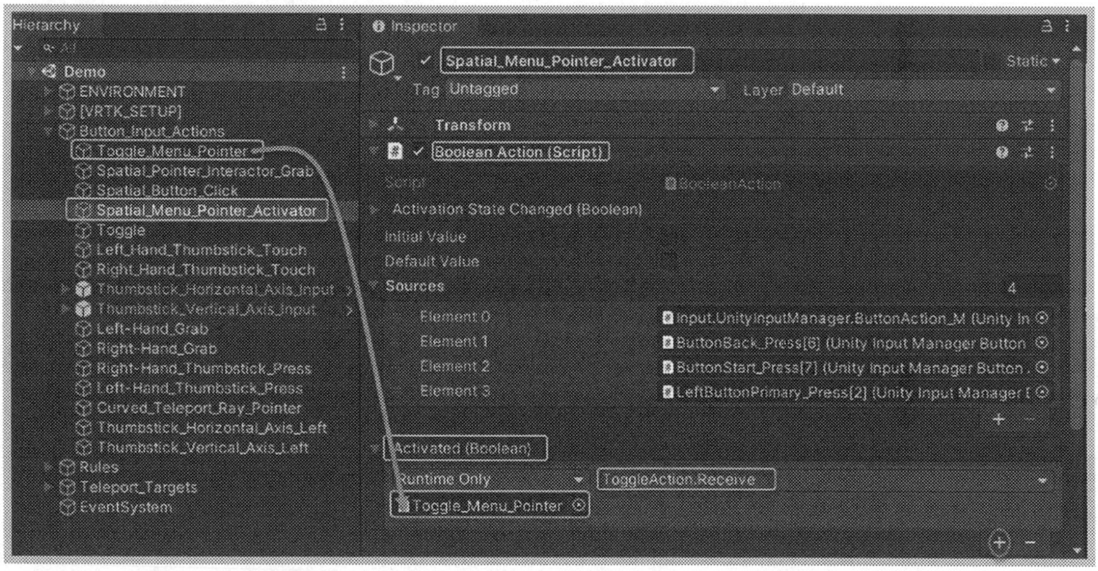

***Figure 17-26.*** *Having the Toggle Menu Pointer game object receive a true or false value whenever one of the buttons listed in the Sources dropdown is pressed*

Essentially, we've achieved the following: Whenever a button responsible for toggling our Straight Spatial Menu Pointer on and off is pressed, our Spatial Menu Pointer Activator captures this button press Boolean value. The activator then asks the Toggle Menu Pointer to receive this captured Boolean value. The Boolean value is then passed to the Activation Action property shown in Figure 17-25. This results in toggling the Straight Spatial Menu Pointer on and off, which is the effect we set out to achieve.

Having completed this exercise, let's now playtest our Demo scene using our VR headset. First, activate your Straight Spatial Menu Pointer (which should now be functioning as a toggle after completing the previous exercise). Then, with your pointer beam displayed, aim it toward your Slider's knob. The beam should turn green, indicating its active state.

Now while continually pressing down on the *B* button of your Oculus right controller, or the Top Menu button on the HTC Vive right controller, or the *Y* button on the Xbox controller, or the *G* key on the keyboard, move the Slider's knob around.

You have just performed a spatial pointer Interactor grab against the Slider's knob.

When you release any of these buttons or keys, the Interactor at the end of your Straight Spatial Menu Pointer might not always immediately perform an ungrab. To completely release your Interactor's hold on the Slider knob, you need to explicitly press and release the appropriate button on the keyboard or controller a second time while your pointer is still aiming at the Slider's knob.

Finally, test your spatial 3D buttons by pointing at them and pushing the Trigger button of your controller. Don't forget to activate the Table, Drill Machine, Hammer, and Axe game objects.

# Summary

This chapter has been all about creating Spatial 3D User Interface game objects. VR uses a diegetic UI approach instead of the nondiegetic UI used in non-VR games, wherein the UI is referred to as a "Heads-Up Display." A diegetic UI can be created using Unity's UI, which is based on a world space UI canvas. This approach is commonly referred to as Spatial UI. With VRTK 4, you're provided the ability to create spatial 3D user interfaces using spatial 3D buttons without the need to deploy Unity's UI elements.

We started this chapter by learning to create a Straight Spatial Menu Pointer that would serve as a menu pointer that could interact with our spatial 3D buttons. We went on to set up the very first clickable spatial 3D button in our scene. You learned to register a click against this spatial 3D button using a key press or your controller's trigger button. We then connected the Straight Spatial Menu Pointer to the Spatial Targets Dispatcher, which already existed in the hierarchy. We next saw that this pointer is able to interact with the spatial 3D button. It also enables you to teleport around the scene using the Teleport Targets available, which is something you didn't want your pointer to achieve.

To circumvent this uncalled-for behavior, we went on to set up a Spatial Button Group and a Spatial Targets Processor. This group contains a Spatial Target Dispatcher.

You learned that you would need to add all your spatial 3D buttons to this group for your Straight Spatial Menu Pointer to only interact with this group and the buttons it contains. You also found out that you needed an intermediary Spatial Targets Processor to talk to your Straight Spatial Menu Pointer. In turn, this processor would dispatch this pointer's events to the various Spatial Target Dispatchers listed within it only. With this setup, you were ensured that your Straight Spatial Menu Pointer wouldn't interact with any spatial Teleport Targets in the scene.

We proceeded to learn how to change the appearance of our spatial 3D buttons and the various states our 3D buttons could be in. After that, we created a spatial Toggle button. VRTK 4 also allowed us to create spatial Option buttons using the Spatial Button Group prefab, where only one button could be selected from a group of buttons.

We set up an exciting mechanic where we could use our hands to interact directly with the VRTK's spatial 3D buttons. You learned about some examples where this approach would be highly beneficial.

We then created a Spatial Slider that you could interact with directly using your hands. We also delved a bit into working with the VRTK-provided linear transform drive and explored some of its properties. We'll delve deeper into working with the VRTK's linear and angular drives in a later chapter. We also learned to set up a visual Tooltip to display your Slider's value as you move your Slider's knob around.

Last, we learned to hack our Straight Spatial Menu Pointer so that it could interact with our Slider. You set up a new rule so that your pointer would only be in an active state when it is pointing at the spatial 3D buttons or the Slider's knob. We set the Layer property of these spatial game objects to UI to enable these spatial game objects to adhere to the UI Layer rule we set up. We finally tested our spatial 3D buttons using our VR headset to ensure that all the interactions work using the Straight Spatial Menu Pointer and our hands.

# CHAPTER 18

# Using Unity's UI Controls with the VRTK

This chapter is about setting up the VRTK to work with Unity's UI system and controls. In the last chapter, we reviewed the VRTK's spatial 3D UI controls. If you've used version 3.3.x of the VRTK in the past, you probably noticed that in some instances you were provided with a menu layout that includes the commonly used Unity UI controls. This menu layout is based on a Unity World Space UI canvas. To use Unity's UI system in VR, you need to similarly base it on a World Space UI canvas.

## Downloading and Importing Unity Package Files

For this chapter, there are two associated Unity package files that you need to download and import into your project. Both files are available to you as part of the downloads included with this book. First, download the "Tilia_Unity_UI" Unity package file and import it into your project. This is the core package that enables VRTK 4 to interact with Unity's UI system.

---

**Note**  The developers of VRTK 4 didn't create the "Tilia_Unity_UI" Unity package file. This package file is a port of the original VRTK 3.3.0 UI system with some additional tweaks and fixes added that enable it to work with VRTK 4. It was ported for use with VRTK 4 by an individual in the VRTK community. It could take a while for this import to complete.

---

The second file you need to download is the "UI Menu Elements 2D" Unity package file, a skeletal menu layout built using various Unity UI controls. In its current state, it can't interact with any VRTK menu pointers. In this chapter, we'll set up the required

C. Coutinho, *Unity® Virtual Reality Development with VRTK4*, https://doi.org/10.1007/978-1-4842-7933-5_18

menu pointer and connect it to various components to get the menu working in your VR scene. Further updates could be made to the "Tilia_Unity_UI" package in the future, so it would be good to periodically visit the following GitHub page to check for any updates: https://github.com/studentutu/Tilia.UnityUI.

Once you've imported the "Tilia_Unity_UI" package file into your project, select the "Assets" folder. In it, you'll notice a new "Tilia_Unity_UI" folder containing the required prefabs and scripts to get VRTK 4 working with Unity's UI system. After you've imported the "UI Menu Elements 2D" package file into your project, you'll see that a UI Elements 2D prefab has been added to your "Assets" folder.

# Setting Up the UI Elements 2D Skeletal Menu

In this section, we'll create a new game object in VRTK SETUP that will be home to your skeletal menu structure. To start, select the VRTK SETUP game object in the hierarchy, and create a new empty child object in it and rename it "VRTK UNITY UI 2D CONTROLS."

Then, drag and drop the UI Elements 2D prefab from the "Assets" folder onto the VRTK UNITY UI 2D CONTROLS game object, making it a child. With the UI Elements 2D game object selected in the hierarchy, right-click it and select the menu item Unpack Prefab Completely from the context menu that appears.

Double-click this UI Elements 2D game object to have it obtain focus in the scene. You'll see that it has already been positioned to the right of the table.

# Setting Up a Straight 2D UI Menu Pointer

You'll need to set up a new menu pointer that exclusively interacts with your UI Elements 2D game object: the Straight 2D UI Menu Pointer. This is a dedicated menu pointer that you'll need to activate if you intend to use this 2D UI menu system. In this case, your Indicators Object Pointers Straight Spatial Menu Pointer will need to be deactivated when you activate the Straight 2D pointer, as both menu pointers can't function together.

In the hierarchy, select the Indicators Object Pointers Straight Spatial Menu Pointer game object and duplicate it and rename the copied game object "Indicators Object Pointers Straight Unity UI." Now, deactivate the Indicators Object Pointers Straight Spatial Menu Pointer.

Select the Indicators Object Pointers Straight Unity UI game object in the hierarchy. In the Inspector, delete the Entered, Exited, and Selected events by clicking the minus symbol in the bottom right corner of each event. You'll notice that these events point to the Indicators Spatial Targets Processor, which you won't be addressing with your 2D UI menu system. The rest of the properties on the Pointer Facade will remain the same.

The Indicators Object Pointers Straight Unity UI game object is a copy of the Indicators Object Pointers Straight Spatial Menu Pointer game object. It contains the Interactor game object you added for interacting with the Slider's knob. This game object isn't required by your Indicators Object Pointers Straight Unity UI game object, which will only be interacting with Unity's 2D UI controls, so you need to get rid of this nested Interactor game object.

In the hierarchy, ensure that the Indicators Object Pointers Straight Unity UI game object has been selected. Expand it until you reach its Valid Container game object, which you can do as follows: Expand Object Pointer Internal, then expand Elements, next expand Destination, followed by expanding Elements Sphere, and finally expand Valid Container. In the Valid Container game object, you'll see the Interactions Interactor game object. Select it in the hierarchy and delete it.

# Having the 2D UI Menu Pointer Interact with the 2D UI Menu System

You now need to set up the Indicators Object Pointers Straight Unity UI game object to interact with the UI Elements 2D game object and its controls. Select the Indicators Object Pointers Straight Unity UI game object in the hierarchy and expand it until you reach its Points Renderer game object. To reach the Points Renderer game object, navigate as follows: Expand Object Pointer Internal, then expand Logic, next expand Points Handler, and finally select the Points Renderer game object.

In the Assets folder, expand the "Tilia_Unity_UI" folder, then expand its "Runtime" folder, followed by expanding its "Shared Resources" folder, and finally double-click its "Prefabs" folder. You'll see that there exists a [L_R]_Points Renderer UI Pointer prefab in this "Prefabs" folder. Drag and drop this prefab onto the Points Renderer game object selected in the hierarchy. With the [L_R]_Points Renderer UI Pointer game object selected in the hierarchy, look at the Inspector. It has been fitted with two components, a VRTK 4 UI Pointer component and a VRTK 4 Ui to Pointer component. Because the names of these components sound similar, you need to ensure that you set up the correct component, as will now be discussed.

Let's first set up the properties in the VRTK 4 UI Pointer component. In this component, locate the Activation Button property. Drag and drop the Toggle Menu Pointer game object from the hierarchy into this Activation Button property parameter. This activates and deactivates your Indicators Object Pointers Straight Unity UI menu pointer beam. Then, drag and drop the Spatial Button Click game object from the hierarchy into the Selection Button property parameter. This allows you to execute a click at your menu pointer's target position by either pulling the trigger button on your controller or pressing the Z key on your keyboard. For the Click Method property, select Click On Button Down from the available drop-down list. The Custom Origin property determines where your menu pointer will originate from. For the value for this property, you'll use your Right-Hand Interactor, as the pointer beam needs to originate from your right hand. Drag and drop the Interactions Interactor Right game object from the hierarchy into the Custom Origin property parameter, see Figure 18-1.

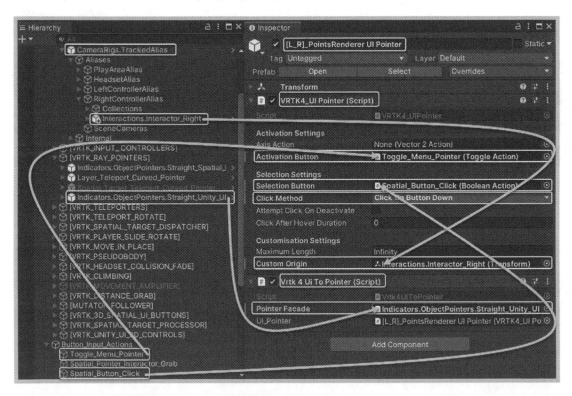

***Figure 18-1.*** *Setting up the properties on the VRTK4 UI Pointer and VRTK 4 Ui To Pointer components of the [L_R]_Points Renderer UI Pointer game object*

Let's next set up the properties in the VRTK 4 Ui to Pointer component. For its Pointer Facade property, drag and drop the Indicators Object Pointers Straight Unity UI game object into this parameter.

You now have set up your Indicators Object Pointers Straight Unity UI pointer to interact with only your UI Elements 2D game object, which has been created using Unity's UI controls, see Figure 18-1.

Next, you need to ensure you have at least one Unity UI Event System active in your scene. Select the Demo game object in the hierarchy and right-click it. From the context menu that pops up, navigate to Game Object ➤ UI ➤ Event System. Note that Unity won't allow you to add another Event System to your scene as long as one already exists.

After that, you need to add the VRTK 4 Player Object component onto the Interactions Interactor Right game object. Select this game object in the hierarchy, and click the Add Component button in the Inspector and add the VRTK 4 Player Object component to it. You'll need to configure two properties for this component. For the Object Type property, set its drop-down value to Pointer. For the Pointer Reference property, drag and drop the [L_R]_Points Renderer UI Pointer game object from the hierarchy into this Pointer Reference property parameter, see Figure 18-2.

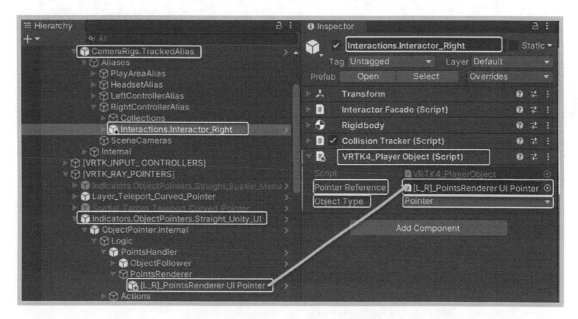

***Figure 18-2.*** *Setting up properties for the VRTK4 Player Object component that has been added to the Interactions Interactor Right game object*

Finally, you need to set up the skeletal UI Elements 2D game object so that it's able to interact with the Indicators Object Pointers Straight Unity UI Menu Pointer you've created. Select this game object in the hierarchy, and expand it and select the UI Menu child game object in it. Then, add two new components, Graphic Ray Caster and VRTK 4 UI Canvas, to the selected UI Menu game object in the Inspector. If you click the Canvas component in the Inspector, you'll see that its Render Mode property has been set to World Space. For any new canvas you may set up from scratch, its Render Mode property must be set to World Space to use it in VR. Looking at the hierarchy, you'll also see that various Unity UI controls have been created for you to utilize as part of this UI Elements 2D game object, see Figure 18-3.

***Figure 18-3.*** *Adding the VRTK 4 UI Canvas and Graphic Ray Caster components onto the UI Menu child game object of the UI Elements 2D game object*

This is all the setup required to have your *UI Elements 2D* game object interact with your *Indicators Object Pointers Straight Unity UI* menu pointer.

Now, playtest your scene using your VR headset. Activate the straight Unity UI menu pointer and point it at your UI Elements 2D menu. Pull on the Trigger button to use the various UI controls available in this UI Elements 2D menu. Note that you can't use this straight Unity UI menu pointer to interact with any of your spatial 3D UI buttons.

# Summary

In this chapter, we went over how to implement Unity's UI controls in our VRTK project. We began by downloading and importing two essential Unity package files into the project. The "Tilia_Unity_UI" package is the core package that enables VRTK 4 to interact with Unity's UI system. We then imported the UI Elements 2D skeletal menu containing the most widely used Unity UI controls. We set up a new Straight 2D UI Menu Pointer to interact with the Unity UI Elements 2D skeletal menu. To do this, we had to deactivate our Indicators Object Pointers Straight Spatial Menu Pointer, as both menu pointers can't function together. You then learned how to configure various components to enable your UI Elements 2D skeletal menu to work with your Straight 2D UI Menu Pointer. Last, it was noted that to set up a Unity UI canvas for use in VR, its Render Mode property must be set to World Space.

# CHAPTER 19

# Angular Drives

In this chapter, we'll get to know the Angular Drive prefab provided in the VRTK. We'll also implement three common examples of its use. In the process, you'll create a Steering Wheel, a Door, and a Lever. Angular Transform Drives and Angular Joint Drives can be thought of as controllable mechanisms that provide you with both physics- and nonphysics-based angular Interactable controls that can be used with a wide variety of game objects. Ideally, you'll want to use the nonphysics-based linear/angular Transform Drive prefabs wherever possible, as the physics-based linear/angular Joint Drives rely heavily on Unity's joints. If you intend to build multiplayer games, it's best to keep joints to their bare minimum.

## Setting Up a Steering Wheel

We'll start our exploration of Angular Joint Drives by setting up a Steering Wheel in VR that you can rotate around using your hands. A Steering Wheel can be created using an Angular Transform Drive prefab. The Steering Wheel will rotate around a central hinge point. Whenever the item's Angular Transform Drive value changes, an event can be triggered notifying the car's axle of the change in value. The car's wheels could then be aligned accordingly.

Let's begin setting up this Steering Wheel game object. As one of the features available to download with this book, you've been provided with a Unity package file named "Steering Wheel." This package file contains a prefab that comprises a Mesh for your Steering Wheel and a Box Collider that's already been set up.

To begin the setup, download the "Steering Wheel" Unity package file and import it into your project. Once imported, you'll have access to the Steering Wheel prefab in the "Assets" folder. If you open this prefab, you'll see that it comprises a Steering Wheel mesh, a couple of materials, and a Box Collider. Select and expand the Environment game object in the hierarchy, and create a new empty child object and rename it

© Christopher Coutinho 2022
C. Coutinho, *Unity® Virtual Reality Development with VRTK4*, https://doi.org/10.1007/978-1-4842-7933-5_19

"Steering Wheel." Your Steering Wheel will be placed on top of your worktable. Select the Steering Wheel game object in the hierarchy and set its Transform Position values as follows: $X = -11.94$; $Y = 0.775$; and $Z = -4.33$. Note that you won't see the Steering Wheel yet, as it still isn't hooked up.

Next, select the "Packages" folder in the Project tab and expand it until you reach the Tilia Interactions Controllables Unity package. Then, expand it further until your reach its *Prefabs, Transform* folder. Then, drag and drop the Interactions Angular Transform Drive onto the Steering Wheel game object in the hierarchy. A large white cube will now be sitting on your worktable, and you'll soon replace this cube mesh with a Steering Wheel mesh.

Now, expand the Interactions Angular Transform Drive in the hierarchy until you reach its Interactions Interactable game object and then expand that, too. You can reach this Interactions Interactable game object by navigating as follows: Internal ➤ Interactable Container ➤ Interactions Interactable, see Figure 19-1.

You'll see that Interactions Interactable game object contains a Mesh Container game object, which in turn holds your white cube that needs to be replaced with the Steering Wheel. Note that by nesting the Interactions Interactable game object in the Interactions Angular Transform Drive, you've been automatically provided the ability to interact with its Mesh without having to explicitly add an Interactable game object yourself.

Select the Interactions Interactable child game object in the hierarchy and look at its Interactable Facade component in the Inspector. Locate its Follow Tracking property and note that it has been set to Follow Transform Position Difference Rotate. This property setting is what allows you to rotate your Steering Wheel around smoothly, see Figure 19-1.

Now, select the Cube child game object in the Mesh Container game object, as shown in Figure 19-1, and deactivate it. Next, drag and drop the Steering Wheel prefab from your "Assets" folder onto the Mesh Container game object, making it a child. If you look at your worktable now, there will be a Steering Wheel sitting on it.

Now that we've set up the proper Mesh for the Steering Wheel, let's explore some of the Interactions Angular Transform Drive properties.

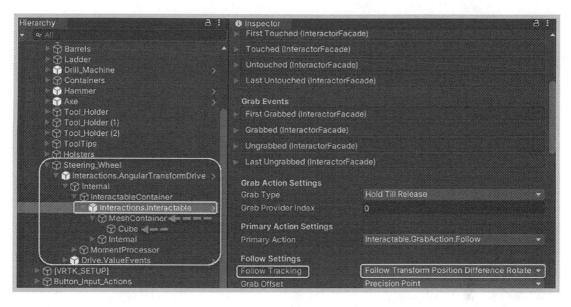

***Figure 19-1.*** *Accessing the Interactions Interactable game object, noting the setting for its Follow Tracking property*

In the hierarchy, select the Interactions Angular Transform Drive game object, and in the Inspector, ensure that the Angular Drive Facade component has been expanded. Locate the Drive Axis property and set this to Y Axis, see Figure 19-2.

| Drive Settings | |
|---|---|
| Drive Axis | Y Axis |
| Drive Speed | 10 |

***Figure 19-2.*** *Setting the Drive Axis property of the Steering Wheel sitting on top of the table to the Y Axis*

Now if you click on your Steering Wheel, you'll notice that its green y axis (outlined with a red oval in Figure 19-3) is pointing upward. Your Steering Wheel needs to rotate around this upward-pointing y axis. If the Steering Wheel were placed on dashboard of a car, then you would need to rotate it around its forward-pointing z axis. However, since it's sitting on a table, you will need to rotate it around its upward-pointing y axis, see Figure 19-3.

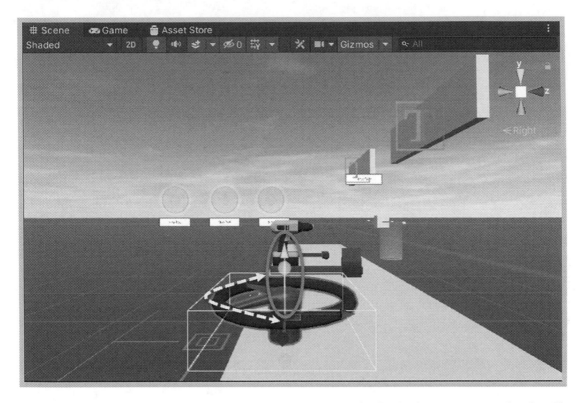

***Figure 19-3.*** *Upward-pointing green y axis around which the Steering Wheel will rotate. The dual-facing dashed arrow indicates the directions in which the Steering Wheel can rotate*

All the other properties in the Angular Drive Facade component of the Interactions Angular Transform Drive game object can be left at their default values. One important property to note is the Drive Limit, whose minimum and maximum values have been set to -180 and 180 by default. Having the Drive Limit property set to these values ensures that you can't turn your Steering Wheel a full 360 degrees, but only 180 degrees (i.e., in a semicircle). That's all the setup required to use your Steering Wheel.

Now, playtest the Demo scene using your VR headset. Note that you can grab your Steering Wheel and smoothly spin it around. Also note that it won't spin beyond 180 degrees when being turned either left or right. You can efficiently perform a Snap Grab action with either hand against your Steering Wheel, thanks to the Secondary Action property setup on the Interactions Interactable, which has been set to Interactable Grab Action Swap.

Before setting up a Door in the next section, let's set the Layer for the Steering Wheel game object to Interactable. Select the Steering Wheel game object in the hierarchy, and in the Layer drop-down of the Inspector, select the value Interactable. When asked whether to also set the Layer to Interactable for all child objects, select the button Yes, Change Children. Last, disable your Holsters game object.

## Setting Up a Door

In this section, we'll create a Door that will rotate around a given hinge point on its frame. Doing this allows us to simulate a Door that can be opened and closed. To set up this mechanism, you'll use an Angular Joint Drive prefab that uses Unity joints. Along the way, you'll also learn about a new VRTK prefab, the Collision Ignorer.

As part of downloads available with this book, you were provided a Unity package file named "Door and Frame." It contains one prefab: a Door Frame and a single Door model (an .FBX file). Download this "Door and Frame" package file and import it into your project. Once imported, you'll have access to the Door Frame and the single Door prefab as an .FBX file in the "Assets" folder. This prefab has been created using three unity cube objects, resizing them appropriately, and setting up their position. These settings ensure that the Door aligns within the Door Frame well. A simple dark-brown wood material has been applied to this Door Frame.

Let's begin by setting up the Door Frame. Select and expand the Environment game object in the hierarchy. Then, drag and drop the Door Frame prefab from the "Assets" folder onto the Environment game object in the hierarchy, making it a child. Note that your Door Frame has been positioned beside your Tool Holders. Expand this Door Frame game object in the hierarchy, and you'll see that it contains three cubes representing the top, left, and right frames that make up your Door Frame.

Next, expand the "Packages" folder in your Project tab, locate the Tilia Interactions Controllables Unity package, and expand it until you reach its "Prefabs" folder. This time around, select and expand the "Physics Joint" folder. Now, drag and drop the Interactions Angular Joint Drive prefab onto the Door Frame game object in the hierarchy, making it a child. You'll notice that a giant white cube has filled your Door Frame.

With your Door Frame game object expanded, select the Interactions Angular Joint Drive and expand it until you reach its Mesh Container. Expand that, too, until you can see its Cube game object and rename it "Door," see Figure 19-4.

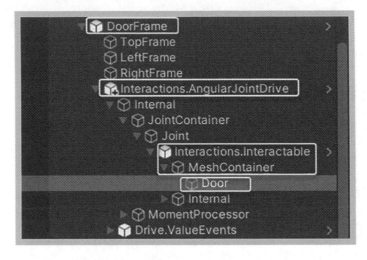

*Figure 19-4.* *Locating the Cube game object in the Interactions Angular Joint Drive and renaming it "Door"*

With the newly renamed Door game object selected in the hierarchy in the Inspector, expand its Mesh Filter and Mesh Renderer components. In the "Assets" folder, expand the "Single Door Model" .FBX file. With the Door game object still selected in the hierarchy, drag and drop Wooden Door from within the Single Door Model into the Mesh property parameter. Then, drag and drop Room Door from the Single Door Model into the Materials Element 0 slot. In the Scene view, you'll see that the Door has been positioned in a sleeping position. We will fix this next, see Figure 19-5.

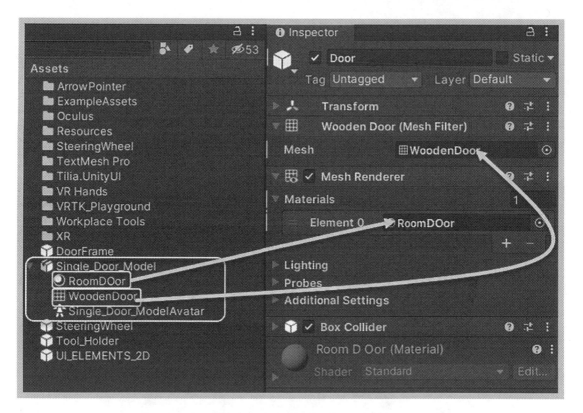

***Figure 19-5.*** *Populating the Mesh Filter and Mesh Renderer properties to have the Door displayed instead of the white cube*

In the Inspector, with the Door game object still selected in the hierarchy, set its Transform Position property values as follows: $X$ = 0.453; $Y$ = 0.17; and $Z$ = -0.028. Then, set its Transform Rotation property values to $X$ = -90; $Y$ = 0; and $Z$ = 0. Last, ensure that the Transform Scale property values for $X$, $Y$, and $Z$ are set to 1. You'll notice that the Door now fits in its Door Frame perfectly, see Figure 19-6.

With the Door game object still selected, expand its Box Collider component and click the Edit Collider button in it. You'll see that the Box Collider for the Door game object isn't even close to encompassing the entire Door; you need to ensure that it encompasses the Door completely. You could go about adjusting this yourself, but it would be quite tedious, so I'll provide you with the values that would make for a suitable fit.

Set the Center property values of the Box Collider component on your Door to $X$ = -0.45; $Y$ = -0.028; and $Z$ = -0.006. Set its Size property values to $X$ = 0.933; $Y$ = 0.172; and $Z$ = 2.327. Now click the Edit Collider button in the Box Collider component again, and you'll see that your Box Collider now encompasses your Door completely, see Figure 19-6.

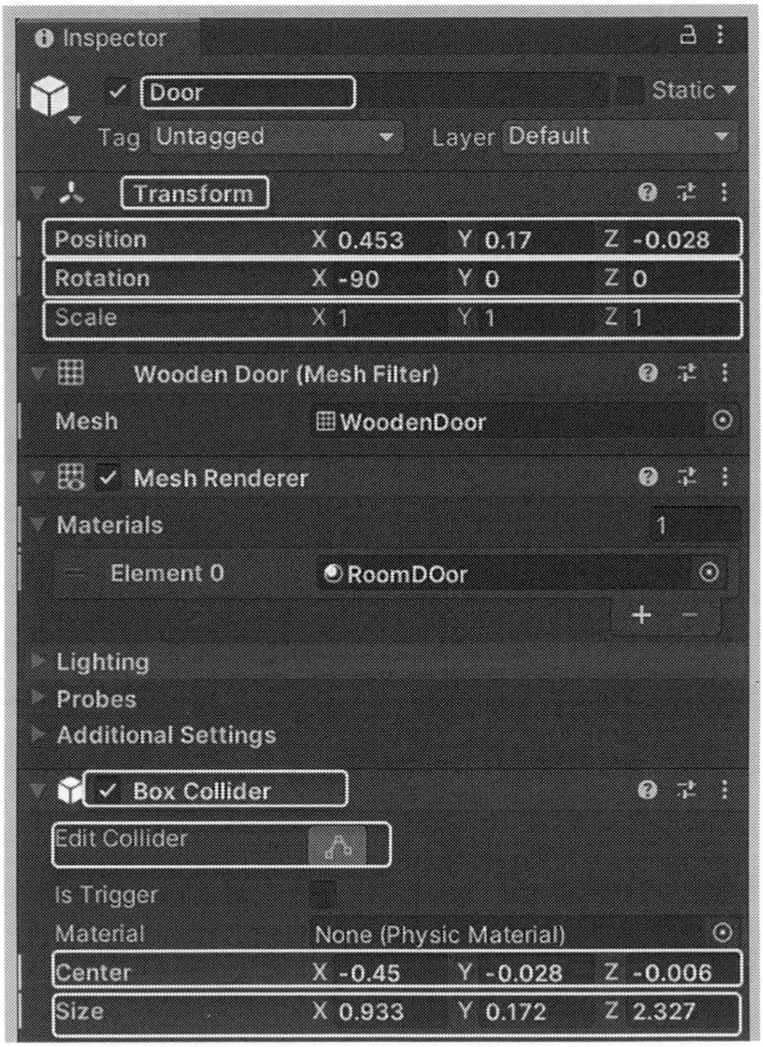

***Figure 19-6.*** *Setting up the property values for the Transform and Box Collider components of the Door game object*

By rotating your Door with the Transform values set in Figure 19-6, your Door handle is now located beside the left Door Frame. The Door, in this case, must now be hinged onto the right Door Frame and rotate around it. It's important to note this fact, as you'll need to set the Hinge Location property value appropriately, as we'll see shortly. Now, select the Interactions Angular Joint Drive in the hierarchy, and in the Inspector locate its Drive Axis property. Set this property to Y Axis, as this is what your Door will need to rotate around. Next, in the "Limit Settings" section, set the Drive Limit Min and Max values to –120 and 120. This ensures that your Door won't rotate a full 360 degrees around its right Door Frame, to which it will be hinged. Now, for the Hinge Location property, set the X value to 0.45 to ensure your Door is hinged onto its right Door Frame. Here, you're setting the Hinge Location against the right Door Frame so that it is slightly on the inside of the door at 0.45. If you select the game object Right Frame from within the Door Frame game object in the hierarchy and look at its Transform Position X property value, you'll see that it has been set to 0.5, see Figure 19-7.

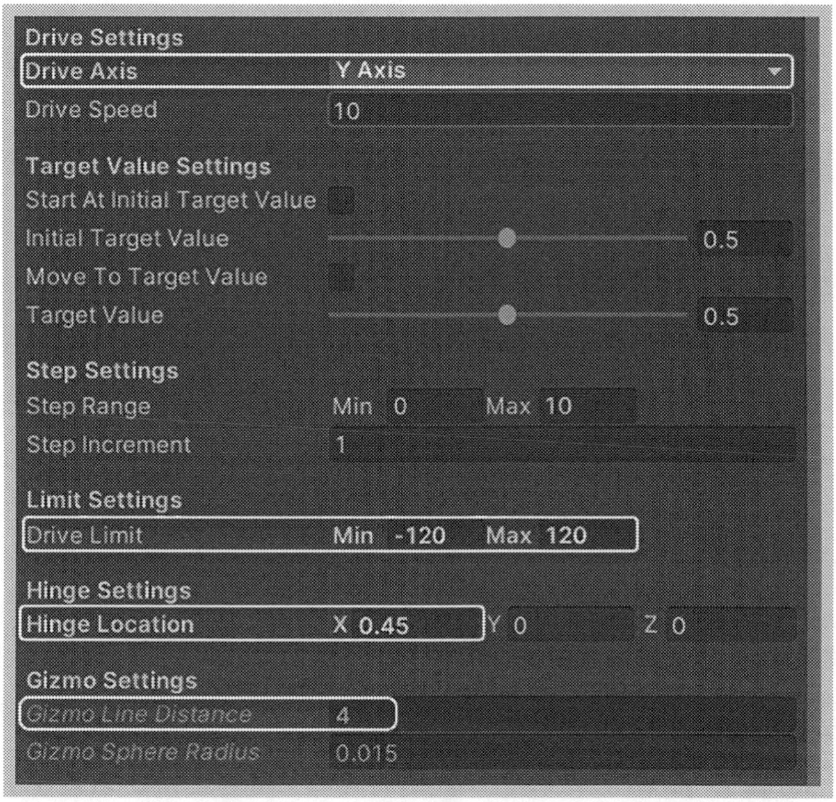

*Figure 19-7.* Setting up property values in the Angular Drive Facade component of the Interactions Angular Joint Drive game object

To be able to view the y axis that your Door will rotate around, first ensure in the Scene view that the Gizmos button on the Title Bar has been toggled on. Then, in the Angular Drive Facade component, with the Interactions Angular Joint Drive still selected in the hierarchy, scroll down to the "Gizmo Settings" section and set the Gizmo Line Distance property value to 4, as shown in Figure 19-7. Now, look at your Door Frame in the Scene view, and you will notice that there exists a thin yellow vertical line passing through your right Door Frame. This represents the y axis that your Door will rotate around, constrained to the Drive Limit, Min, and Max values that you've set, see Figure 19-8.

***Figure 19-8.*** *The Gizmo Line Distance property showing a thin vertical line passing through the right Door Frame, representing the y axis that the Door will rotate around*

If your Door has its Handle located next to the right Door Frame, you'll need to hinge your Door against the left Door Frame. In this case, your Hinge Location X value would need to be set to -0.45, as the Transform Position X value of the Door's Left Frame game object is equal to -0.5. It's essential to keep this concept in mind when working with Doors that have a Handle.

Playtesting your Demo scene at this point will result in the Door being hurled away into the stratosphere. This is on account of the Box Collider on the Door colliding with the Box Colliders on the Door Frame. You could use the Layer Collision Matrix to avoid these colliders from colliding with each other. However, the VRTK provides you with a Collision Ignorer prefab, which you can use to have all the colliders on the Door Frame ignore the collider on the Door. Let's set this up now.

Expand the "Packages" folder in the Projects tab and locate the Tilia Mutators Collision Ignorer Unity package. Expand it until you reach its "Prefabs" folder. Drag and drop the Mutators Collision Ignorer prefab onto the Door Frame game object in the hierarchy, making a child of it. Select this Mutators Collision Ignorer game object in the hierarchy, and ensure that its Collision Ignorer component has been expanded in the Inspector. Set its Sources Elements size property value to 3. This will provide you with three element slots. Drag and drop the Top Frame game object from within the Door Frame game object in the hierarchy into the Element 0 slot. Then, drag and drop the Left Frame game object into the Element 1 slot. After that, drag and drop the Right Frame game object into the Element 2 slot, see Figure 19-9.

Within this Collision Ignorer component, under Targets, set the Elements size property value to 1, and you'll be provided with an Element 0 slot. Drag and drop the Interactions Angular Joint Drive game object from the hierarchy into this slot. This Collision Ignorer setup ensures that your Targets, Door collider will no longer collide with the Source, Door Frame colliders. You have now set up a Door that can be opened and closed, see Figure 19-9.

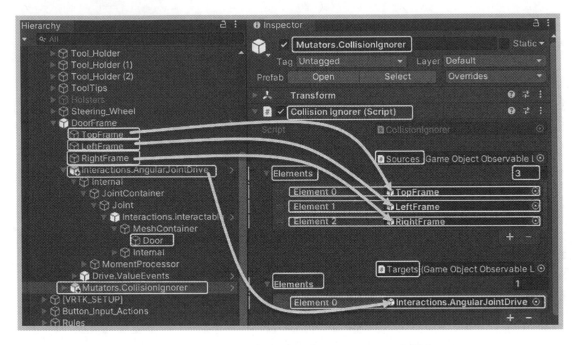

***Figure 19-9.*** *Setting up property values for the Mutators Collision Ignorer game object*

Now, playtest the Demo scene using your VR headset. Walk up to the Door and either pull or push it to open it. You'll notice that doing either of these things won't force the Door past the Min and Max rotation values that you set as part of its Drive Limit property.

Under normal conditions, you would want a Door that when pushed or pulled would move only until it gets to its closed position and then remain shut. Most real doors don't revolve past their closed position and can only be opened and shut from one side. We'll now configure the Door further so that reproduces these conditions, so that will be more realistic to how a door actually works.

Expand the Door Frame game object in the hierarchy and select the Interactions Angular Joint Drive game object. In the Inspector, in the Angular Drive Facade component of the "Target Value Settings" section, check the box for the Start At Initial Target Value property and set the Initial Target Value property to 0.5. This ensures that when your scene starts up, your Door will be in its closed position. If you want your Door to start in an open position, where it is perpendicular to the Door Frame, then set this Initial Target Value property to 0.25, see Figure 19-10.

***Figure 19-10.*** *Choosing properties in Target Value Settings that ensure that the Door is shut at scene startup*

Next, in the "Step Settings" section, set the Min and Max values of the Step Range to 0 and 1. Also, set the Step Increment value to 0.5. This will not play any part in setting up your Door currently, but it will be helpful if you want to check if a specific target value has been reached, as the Step Range will now increase in increments of 0.5, moving from 0 to 0.5 and finally to 1. Here, the 0 step value represents the Door being rotated -120 degrees, which makes it entirely open; a step value of 0.5 represents the Door being at 0 degrees, in which case it is entirely shut; and a step value of 1 reflects the Door being rotated 120 degrees, which means it is entirely open facing the opposite side, see Figure 19-11.

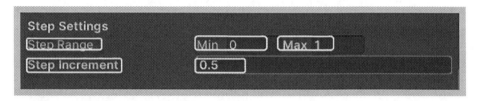

***Figure 19-11.*** *Setting up properties within the Step Settings section*

Next, we need to set up the Started Moving event, which is fired whenever your Door starts moving as a result of pulling or pushing it. Within the Angular Drive Facade component of the Interactions Angular Joint Drive game object, locate and expand the Started Moving event. Click the plus symbol located in the bottom right corner of this event to create an event listener. Drag and drop the Interactions Angular Joint Drive game object from the hierarchy into the event listener box of this event.

For the function, select Angular Drive Facade, and in the context menu that appears, select Set Drive Limit Maximum from the "Static Parameters" section. Set the value for this function's parameter to 0. This ensures that whenever the Door starts moving after you pull or push it, its Drive Limit Max value will immediately be set to 0, according to which the Door will now revolve only between its Drive Limit Min value of -120 degrees and its newly set Drive Limit Max value of 0 degrees. It will stop at this zero-degree Drive Limit Max value, which represents the Door being in the shut position, see Figure 19-12.

Last, select the Door game object in the hierarchy and set its Layer to Interactable.

***Figure 19-12.*** *Setting up the Started Moving event to ensure that when the Door is pulled or pushed, it doesn't move beyond its shut position*

Playtest your Demo scene using your VR headset. Approach the Door, which is currently in a closed position, and pull its Handle to open it. With your Door open, push it to slam it shut. Note that your Door no longer goes past its closed state. Now, approach the Door from the opposite side, and grab its Handle and attempt to pull it open. You'll find that it can't be pulled open from the other side. Simply push the Door and you'll see that it swings open.

You now have a Door that can be opened and closed realistically.

# Setting Up a Lever

In this section, we'll create a Lever that will rotate around an x axis hinge point. We'll use an Angular Joint Drive prefab to set this up. One everyday use of a Lever would be for a gearbox within a car. As part of the downloads for this book, you were provided a Unity package file named "Lever" containing a VR Lever prefab. Download the "Lever" file and import it into your project. After you're done, you'll have access to the VR Lever prefab in the "Assets" folder.

Select and expand the "Environment" folder in the hierarchy. Then, from within the "Assets" folder, drag and drop the VR Lever prefab onto the Environment game object in the hierarchy, making it a child. Note that a Lever has been positioned on your worktable. Select this VR Lever game object in the hierarchy, right-click it, and then select *Prefab, Unpack Completely* from the context menu that pops up. Expand this VR Lever game object in the hierarchy, and you'll see that it contains two child game objects, a Handle and a Container. The Handle represents a lever that can be grabbed and moved forward and backward, while the Container represents the gearbox within which the Handle sits.

Expand the "Packages" folder in the Project tab, locate the Tilia Interactions Controllables Unity package, expand it until you reach its "Prefabs" folder, and then select the "Physics Joint" folder. Now, drag and drop the Interactions Angular Joint Drive prefab onto the VR Lever game object in the hierarchy, making it a child. You'll notice that a large white cube has encompassed your VR Lever.

With your VR Lever game object expanded, select the Interactions Angular Joint Drive and expand it until you reach its Mesh Container. Expand this Mesh Container game object until you can see its child Cube game object and deactivate it. Drag and drop the Handle game object onto the Mesh Container, making it a child. Select this game object, and ensure that its Transform Position property values for *X*, *Y*, and *Z* are set to 0. Make sure that its Transform Rotation property values for *X*, *Y*, and *Z* are also set to 0. Leave the Transform Scale property values at their default. Last, set the Layer for this Handle game object to Interactable and apply this Interactable Layer to its child objects as well when prompted.

Select the Interactions Angular Joint Drive game object in the hierarchy, and within the Inspector, set its Transform Position Y value to 0.6. This ensures that your Lever Handle will be moved up slightly and sit well in its Container, see Figure 19-13.

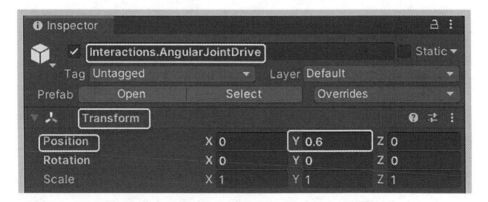

***Figure 19-13.*** *Setting up the Transform Position Y value for the Lever Handle*

Within the Angular Drive Facade component, ensure that the Drive Axis property is set to X Axis, as your Lever needs to rotate around its x axis. Then, check the Start At Initial Target Value box and set the Initial Target Value property to 0.5. This will ensure that your Lever is centered within its gearbox container at the start. Set the Step Range Min value to 0 and the Step Range Max value to 1. Set the Step Increment property to 0.5.

It's not required that you set up these values. However, doing do will be helpful if you plan to use some of the available events to pass these values across to other components. In the "Limit Settings" section, set the Drive Limit Min property value to -45 and the Drive Limit Max property value to 45.

Last, you need to set the Hinge Location property value to -0.6. This ensures that the hinge is placed at the bottom of the Lever rod, see Figure 19-14.

You'll notice that the Interactions Angular Transform Drive game object, which contains the Lever Handle, was set up with its Transform Position Y value at 0.6. If the Hinge Location Y value were set to a positive 0.6, your hinge would be placed at the top of your Lever Handle and the Lever would rotate around the Lever knob instead.

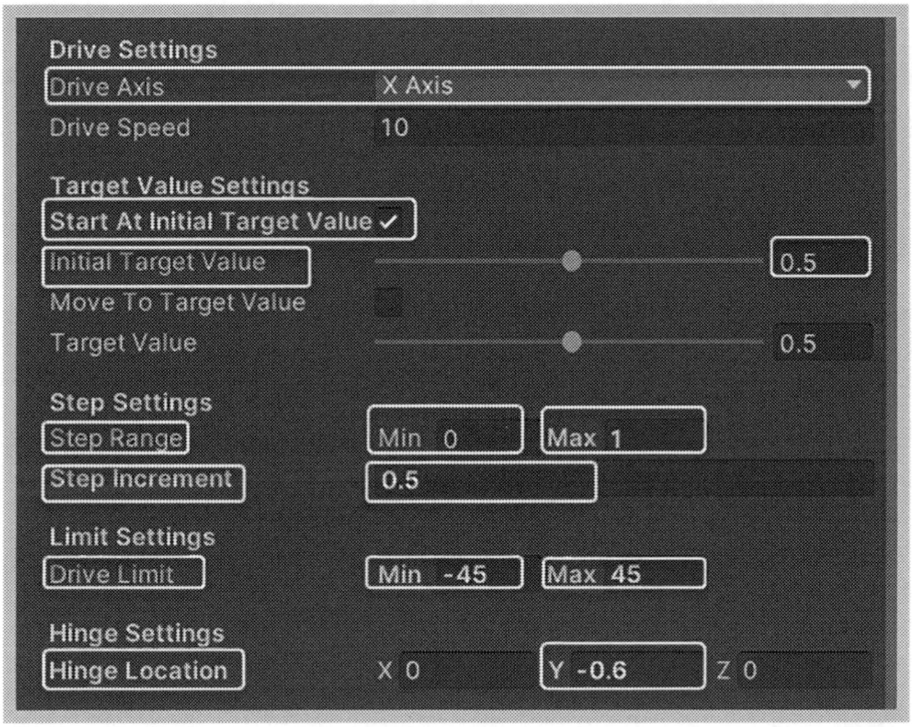

***Figure 19-14.*** *Setting up property values in the Angular Drive Facade component of the Interactions Angular Transform Drive game object*

Last, let's add a Collision Ignorer component to the VR Lever so that collisions between the VR Lever Container game object and the VR Lever Handle, which resides in the Interactions Angular Transform Drive, are ignored. Expand the "Packages" folder in the Projects tab, locate the Tilia Mutators Collision Ignorer Unity package, and expand it until you reach its "Prefabs" folder. Then, drag and drop the Mutators Collision Ignorer prefab onto the VR Lever game object in the hierarchy, making a child of it. Select this Mutators Collision Ignorer game object in the hierarchy and ensure that its Collision Ignorer component has been expanded in the Inspector. Set its Sources Elements size property value to 5, which will provide you with five element slots. In the hierarchy, expand the Container game object, a child of the VR Lever. Drag and drop each Base game object into each of these element slots, see Figure 19-15.

Within this Collision Ignorer component, under Targets, set the Elements size property value to 1, and you'll be provided with an Element 0 slot. Drag and drop the Interactions Angular Joint Drive game object from the hierarchy into this 0 slot, as shown in Figure 19-15. The Collision Ignorer setup now ensures that your Targets, Handle collider will no longer collide with the Source, VR Lever Container colliders.

You've now set up a Lever that can be used in your next car-racing game.

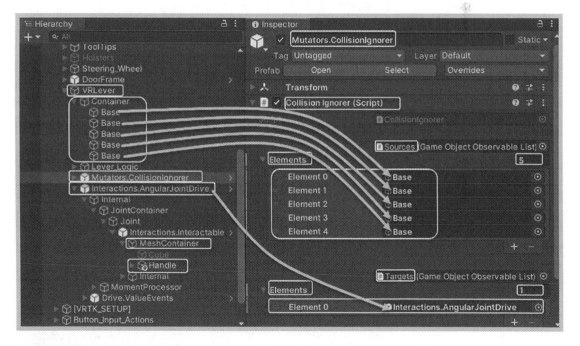

***Figure 19-15.*** *Setting up property values for the Mutators Collision Ignorer game object*

Playtest the Demo scene using your VR headset. Approach the Lever and note that its is centered in your gearbox at the start. Grab the Lever knob and push it forward to see it rotate forward smoothly. Now pull on the Lever knob, drawing it back. Note that it stays within the Drive Limits setup.

While playtesting the Demo scene, you might have noticed that the Lever at times continues to move upon being released. This behavior is ideally not something you would want to have happen. It's an uncalled-for action that happens because of the Rigidbody, Angular Drag value being set too low. Let's fix this now.

From within the VR Lever game object, select the Interactions Angular Joint Drive, and from within that, select Interactions Interactable. Now, in the Interactable Facade component of the Inspector, locate the Last Ungrabbed event and expand it. Note that within its event listener box for the function Rigidbody, Angular Drag, the parameter value has been set to 0.01 by default. This Angular Drag value is minimal, which causes not enough angular Drag to be applied to the Lever to stop it from moving. Change this value to 5000 or any other large value.

Now, playtest the Demo scene and you'll see that the moment you release the Lever, it no longer continues to move, as the higher Angular Drag Value has kicked in, see Figure 19-16.

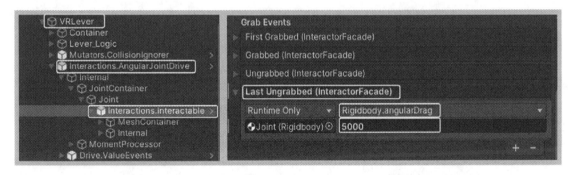

***Figure 19-16.*** *Increasing the Angular Drag Value to 5000 in the Last Ungrabbed event*

Last, select the Interactions Angular Joint Drive game object in the hierarchy. Ensure that your Gizmos button has been toggled on. In the Angular Drive Facade component of the Inspector, scroll down to the bottom and locate the "Gizmo Settings" section. Set the value of the Gizmo Line Distance property to 2. Now look closely at your Lever game object in the Scene view, and you'll see a horizontal line gizmo representing the X-Axis hinge, which your Lever Handle will rotate around, see Figure 19-17.

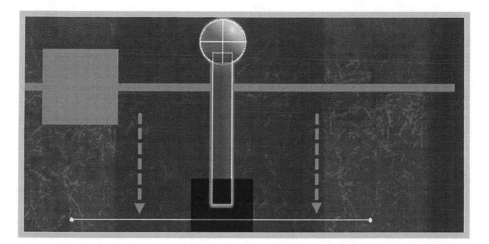

**Figure 19-17.** *The Gizmo Line Distance property showing a thin horizontal line that represents the X axis that the Lever will pitch around*

# Angular Joint Drive and Logic Objects

In this section, we'll take a deep dive into the Interactions Angular Joint Drive and examine some of its Internal events that might be helpful when building your game or application. We'll look at the Minimum Reached, Midpoint Reached, and Maximum Reached event objects. These events are triggered when the Target Value property in the Angular Drive Facade component of the Interactions Angular Joint Drive reaches either its Minimum, Midpoint, or Maximum value. To see these events in action, we'll create some Lever logic, wherein your Lever will initially be allowed to rotate from its central position in a forward direction only, allowing you to push it forward and pull it back. However, when pulled back, it will rotate back to its central position only. We'll then set up the Lever so that it rotates between its central position in a reverse direction only, so that you may pull the Lever back. However, upon attempting to push it forward, it will rotate only to its central position. Finally, we'll set up the Lever to work like it does in automatic transmission for a car and allow the Lever to be moved between three positions: forward (drive), central (neutral), and backward (in reverse). To verify that the appropriate events are being called, we'll examine the Min and Max values for the Dive Limit . Let's begin setting this up.

First, select the VR Lever game object in the hierarchy, and set its Transform Rotation *Y* value to 0. This ensures that moving the Lever forward 45 degrees represents the Lever in its forward/drive, fully rotated state; moving it 0 degrees represents the Lever in its central/neutral position; and moving it back 45 degrees represents the Lever in its backward/reverse, fully rotated state.

Then, with the VR Lever game object selected in the hierarchy, expand the Interactions Angular Joint Drive and Drive Value events. In these events, expand both Event Outputs and Internal In Event Outputs, and you'll find the Minimum Reached, Midpoint Reached, and Maximum Reached event objects, using which you'll hook up your Lever logic. The Maximum Reached event is triggered when the Target Value property reaches a value of 1, representing the Lever in its forward/drive state. The Midpoint Reached event is triggered when the Target Value property reaches a value of 0.5, representing the Lever in its central/neutral position. The Minimum Reached event is triggered when the Target Value property reaches a value of 0, representing the Lever in its backward/reverse state. The Lever will start in the central/neutral position, with its Drive Limit values set to Min = -45 and Max = 45.

The first piece of Lever logic we'll set up will only allow the Lever to rotate from its central position forward and vice versa. To achieve this, you need to ensure that during runtime, when the Maximum Reached event is triggered, the Drive Limit Min value to is set to 0 and Drive Limit Max value is set to 45. This will ensure that the Drive can rotate 45 degrees forward from its central position. By setting the Drive Limit Min value to 0, you have ensured that it will only rotate to its central position when you pull back on the Lever Handle.

Let's implement this logic now. Select the VR Lever game object in the hierarchy, and create a new empty child game object and rename it "Lever Logic." Then, select this Lever Logic game object, and create a new empty child game object and rename it "Lever Max Reached." Select this Lever Max Reached game object in the hierarchy, and in the Inspector, add a new component, Empty Event Proxy Emitter. Expand this Emitted event and click the plus symbol in its bottom right corner twice to add two event listeners. Now, drag and drop the Interactions Angular Joint Drive game object into both of these event listener boxes.

For the function of the first event listener, select Angular Drive Facade, Set Drive Limit Minimum from the drop-down, and set its value to 0. For the function of the second event listener, select Angular Drive Facade, Set Drive Limit Maximum from the drop-down, and set its value to 45, as shown in Figure 19-18.

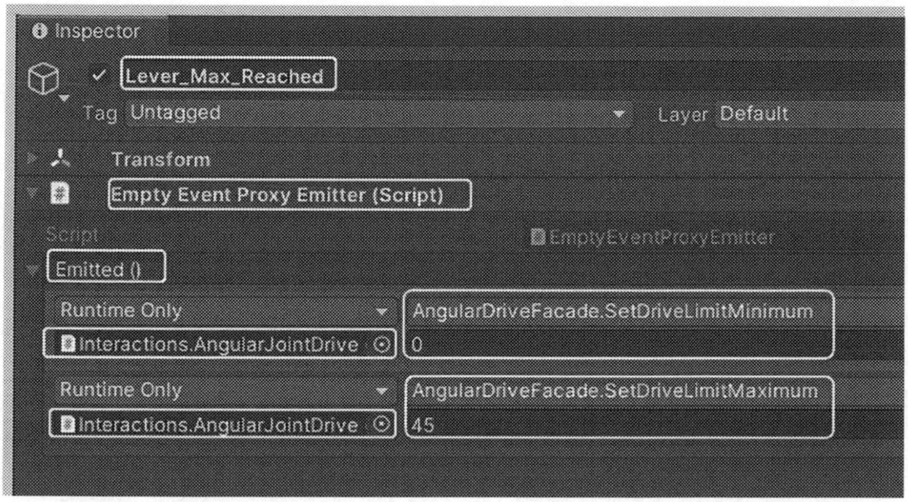

***Figure 19-18.*** *Setting up the Empty Event Proxy Emitter component on the Lever Max Reached game object*

When your Lever Max Reached, Empty Event Proxy Emitter is invoked via the Maximum Reached event, the logic you've set up will ensure that your Lever will only be able to rotate between its central and forward positions. Note that the VRTK has allowed you to place your logic in a game object, which does away with the necessity of writing code.

Now you need to hook up the Lever Max Reached game object to the Maximum Reached event. Select the Maximum Reached event in the hierarchy. In the Inspector, locate and expand its Activated (Boolean) event. Click the plus symbol located in the bottom right corner of this event to add an event listener. Now, drag and drop the Lever Max Reached game object into this event listener box. For the function, select Empty Event Proxy Emitter Receive from within the "Static Parameters" section, see Figure 19-19.

We have now ensured that the moment we push the Lever forward, the Maximum Reached event will be triggered as soon as its Target Value property reaches 1. It will, in turn, invoke the logic we've built within the Lever Max Reached game object. Our Drive Limit Min and Max values are set appropriately when this Lever Max Reached logic is executed, allowing the Lever to rotate only between its central and forward positions.

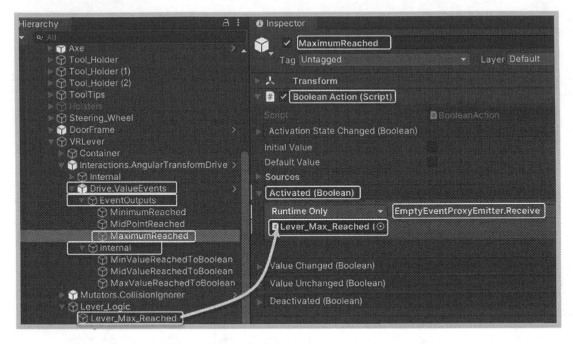

***Figure 19-19.*** *Setting up the Maximum Reached event to invoke the Lever Max Reached logic object*

Now let's work on setting up the second phase of Lever logic, where we'll allow our Lever to rotate from its central position in a reverse direction. When pushed forward from its reversed position, it will rotate forward to its central position only. To achieve this, you need to ensure that when the Minimum Reached event is triggered, the Min and Max Values for the Drive Limit are set to -45 and 0. This will guarantee that the Drive can rotate in reverse from its central position to -45 degrees. Also, by setting the Drive Limit Max value to 0, you have ensured that when you push the Lever forward from its reversed position, it will rotate only up to its Max value 0, which is its central position.

The overall steps we'll follow to implement this second phase of Lever logic are like those we performed when setting up the Lever Max Reached logic. However, the logic that will be built into a new Lever logic game object will be different, and the event we'll now use to invoke this logic is the Minimum Reached event. Let's implement this logic now.

Select the Lever Logic game object in the hierarchy, and create a new empty child game object in it and rename it "Lever Min Reached." Select this child game object in the hierarchy, and in the Inspector, add a new component to it called Empty Event Proxy

Emitter. Expand its Emitted event, and click the plus symbol located in its bottom right corner twice to add two event listeners. Now, drag and drop the Interactions Angular Joint Drive game object into both of these event listener boxes.

For the function for the first event listener, select Angular Drive Facade, Set Drive Limit Minimum from the drop-down, and set its value to -45. For the function for the second event listener, select Angular Drive Facade, Set Drive Limit Maximum from the drop-down, and set its value to 0, see Figure 19-20.

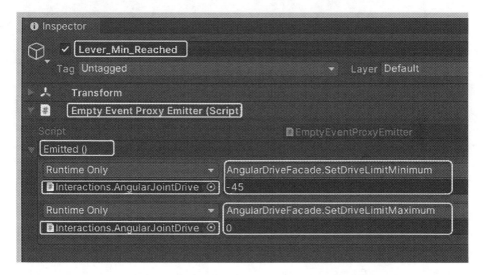

***Figure 19-20.*** *Setting up the Empty Event Proxy Emitter component on the Lever Min Reached game object*

When your Lever Min Reached, Empty Event Proxy Emitter is invoked via the Minimum Reached event, the logic you have set up will ensure that your Lever will only be able to rotate between its central and rearmost positions. Note how the VRTK allows you to place your logic in a game object, doing away with the necessity of writing code.

Now you need to hook up the Lever Min Reached game object to the Minimum Reached event. Select the Minimum Reached event in the hierarchy. In the Inspector, locate and expand its Activated (Boolean) event. Click the plus symbol located in the bottom right corner of this Activated (Boolean) event to add an event listener. Now, drag and drop the Lever Min Reached game object into this event listener box. For the function, select Empty Event proxy Emitter Receive() from within the "Static Parameters" section, see Figure 19-21.

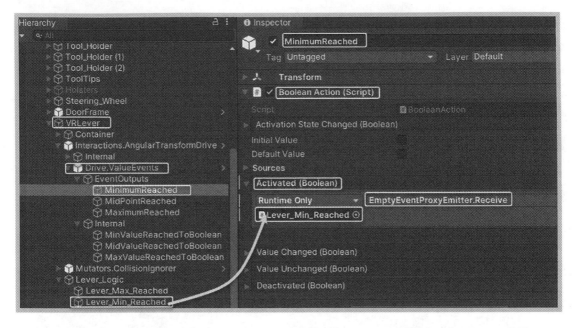

***Figure 19-21.*** *Setting up the Minimum Reached event to invoke the Lever Min Reached logic object*

You've now ensured that after you pull your Lever back, as soon as its Target Value property reaches 0, the Minimum Reached event will be triggered. This, in turn, will invoke the logic you've built in the Lever Min Reached game object. The Min and Max values for your Drive Limit are set appropriately when this Lever Min Reached logic is executed, allowing the Lever to rotate only between its central and rearmost positions.

Before testing the Demo scene, we may need to tweak some essential values for triggering the Minimum, Maximum, and Midpoint reached events. I have noted that the positive bounds limits set up by default, which are essential to triggering events previously discussed, may need some tweaking with my testing. With their default values, they do not trigger events appropriately. I have gone through a trial-and-error phase of tweaking these numbers to get these events to work well with my Oculus Quest. If you find the default values aren't working out well with your own testing, I'd suggest updating these values.

Select and expand the Internal game object in the hierarchy, a child of the Drive Value Events game object. Then, select the Min Value Reached to Boolean game object in the hierarchy, and locate its Positive Bounds property in the Inspector. Set the property's Min value to 0 and its Max value to 0.1, as shown in Figure 19-22.

***Figure 19-22.*** *Tweaking the Min and Max values of the Positive Bounds property for the Min Value Reached to Boolean game object*

Now when the Target Value is anywhere between 0 and 0.1, it will be considered that the minimum value has been reached. I personally found the default value settings too close in number, due to which the minimum value was rarely reached. As a result, the Min Reached event would be triggered only occasionally.

Next, select the Mid Value Reached to Boolean game object in the hierarchy, and in the Positive Bounds property of the Inspector, set the Min value to 0.47 and the Max value to 0.53, as shown in Figure 19-23. Here, too, I found the default range of values to be too close, because of which several Midpoint Reached events never got triggered.

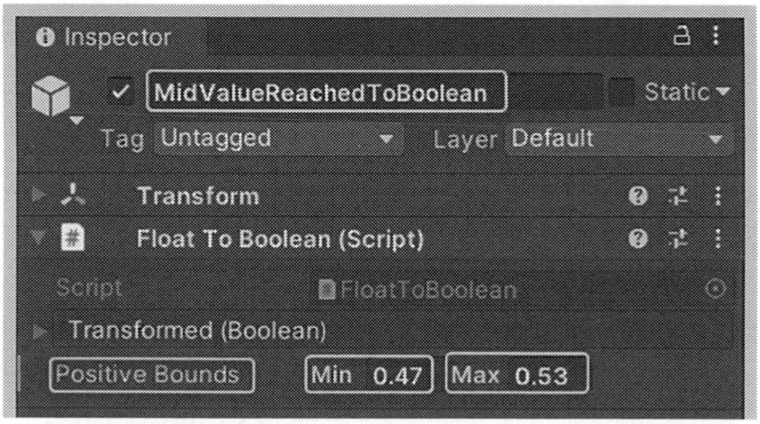

***Figure 19-23.*** *Tweaking the Min and Max values of the Positive Bounds property for the Mid Value Reached to Boolean game object*

Last, select the Max Value Reached to Boolean game object in the hierarchy, and in the Positive Bounds property of the Inspector, set the Min value to 0.85 and the Max value to 1, as shown in Figure 19-24. Here, too, I expanded the range limit so that the values were not too close in number, as the default values resulted in the Maximum Reached event not being triggered every single time. You may need to play around with these values to reach a sweet spot that works well for your own VR device.

**Figure 19-24.** *Tweaking the Min and Max values for the Positive Bounds property for the Max Value Reached To Boolean game object*

Now, playtest the Demo scene using your VR headset, and watch as the Drive Limit values change in the Inspector. In the hierarchy, select the Interactions Angular Joint Drive, and in the Inspector, scroll down until you can see its Drive Limit property. Then, press the Play button in the Unity editor to playtest your scene. When your scene starts playing, you'll see that your Drive Limit values start at Min = -45 and Max = 45. This indicates that you can now move your Lever either forward or backward.

Approach the Lever and grab it, then push it forward. Ensure that you push it all the way forward so that you see the change in the Drive Limit values in the Inspector. When you look at these values, you'll see that they are now at Min = 0 and Max = 45. Now, grab the Lever again and attempt to pull it back. You'll find that you can't pull it back past its central position because your Drive Limit Min value is set to 0.

Now, exit playtest mode, so that you can validate that you're able to pull the Lever back to its rearmost position. Press the Play button in the Unity editor to playtest the Demo scene again. When your scene loads, you'll see that your Drive Limit values start as Min = -45 and Max = 45, which indicates that you can now move your Lever backward.

Approach the Lever and grab it, then pull it back far enough to see a change in the Drive Limit values in the Inspector. When you look at these values, you'll see that they are now set at Min = -45 and Max = 0. Now, grab the Lever again and attempt to push it all the way forward. You'll find that you can't push it past its central position because your Drive Limit Max value is set to 0.

Now, let's use the Midpoint Reached event. In it, when you reach the Midpoint, the *Drive Limit's Min* value is set to -45 and *its Max value* to 45. This allows the Lever to rotate from its forward/drive position to its central/neutral position, from which it can rotate either to a backward/reverse position or to a forward/drive position. This is ideally how you would want the automatic transmission of your car to function—having the Lever move from neutral either forward or backward, and having it pause for a moment when it reaches neutral, rather than simply moving past its central/neutral position.

The only slight modification we will add here is to ensure that when our Lever is in its central/neutral position, it will halt there for a moment before its Drive Limit values are changed to Min = -45 and Max = 45. This results in providing you with a clean gear shift, from drive to neutral, followed by a short pause, and then allowing you to shift either forward or backward. Let's implement this logic now.

Select the Lever Logic game object in the hierarchy, and create a new empty game object and rename it "Lever Mid Reached." Select this empty game object in the hierarchy, and in the Inspector, add a new component called Empty Event Proxy Emitter. Expand its Emitted event, and click the plus symbol in its bottom right corner twice to add two event listeners. Now, drag and drop the Interactions Angular Joint Drive game object into both these event listener boxes.

For the function for the first event listener, select Angular Drive Facade, Set Drive Limit Minimum from the drop-down, and set its value to -45. For the function for the second event listener, select Angular Drive Facade, Set Drive Limit Maximum from the drop-down, and set its value to 45. This ensures that the Lever can be rotated either forward or backward when it's in the central/neutral position. Now, your Lever Mid Reached game object contains logic that will be executed when the Lever reaches its central/neutral position, see Figure 19-25.

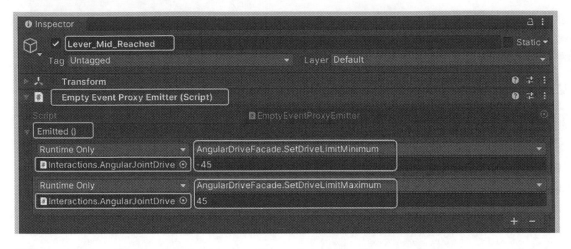

***Figure 19-25.*** *Setting up the Empty Event Proxy Emitter component on the Lever Mid Reached game object*

Now, select the Lever logic game object in the hierarchy, and create another new empty game object and rename the empty game object "Neutral State." With this game object selected, click the Add Component button in the Inspector and add the Wait For Seconds Realtime Yield Emitter component. Set its Seconds To Wait property value to 5. This may be a large value, but it's suitable for testing purposes. You can always reduce the value once you test to ensure everything works well.

Next, expand the Yielded event and click the plus symbol in the bottom right corner to add an event listener. Then, drag and drop the Lever Mid Reached game object from the hierarchy into this event listener box. For the function, select Empty Event Proxy Emitter, Receive(), as shown in Figure 19-26. Now, whenever the Neutral State game object is invoked, its Yielded event will be triggered after five seconds have elapsed.

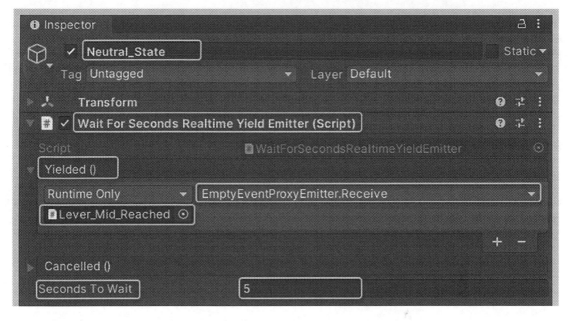

***Figure 19-26.*** *Setting up the Wait for Seconds Realtime Yield Emitter component on the Neutral State game object*

Last, select the *Midpoint Reached* event game object in the hierarchy, and in the Inspector, expand the Activated (Boolean) event. Click the plus symbol located in the bottom right corner to add an event listener. Drag and drop the Neutral State game object into this event listener box. For the function, select Wait For Seconds, Realtime Yield Emitter, Begin() from the "Static Parameters" section, see Figure 19-27.

With this setup, whenever your Lever reaches its Midpoint, the Midpoint Reached event will be triggered. This, in turn, will invoke the logic you've built in the Neutral State. The Yielded event, within the Neutral State, is triggered after five seconds has elapsed since invoking the Neutral State. The Lever Mid Reached logic is then executed, setting the Drive Limit's Min value to -45 and its Max value to 45.

You have now successfully hooked up your Lever Mid Reached game logic to the Midpoint Reached event.

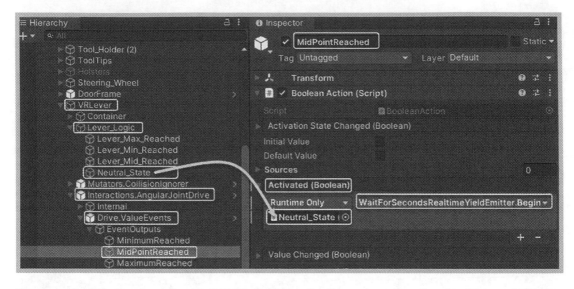

***Figure 19-27.*** *Setting up the Midpoint Reached event to invoke the Neutral State logic object*

Now, playtest the *Demo* scene, and you'll see that you can move the Lever more realistically across the drive, neutral, and reverse modes. When in the central/neutral state, look at the Drive Limit values in the Inspector. You should find that your Drive Limit property has its Min set to -45 and its Max set to 45 if the Lever is centered and perfectly perpendicular. These values are set the moment the Midpoint Reached event is triggered. As stated earlier, you may need to further tweak the Min and Max values of the Positive Bounds property for the Min Value Reached To Boolean, Mid Value Reached To Boolean, and Max Value Reached To Boolean game objects to reach a sweet spot that works well for you. Getting these settings accurate is vital to ensuring that your events are triggered successfully.

In this section, we've delved deeper into dealing with some of the internal events provided by the VRTK. We also learned to build and link up simple game logic objects without writing any code.

# Summary

This chapter has been all about using the Angular Drives provided by the VRTK. We learned to implement both an Angular Transform Drive and an Angular Joint Drive. We first set up a Steering Wheel that uses the VRTK's Angular Transform Drive. You learned to set up various properties against this Angular Transform Drive and were introduced to the Drive Limit and Drive Axis properties. We went over how to set up a realistic Door that can be opened and closed. We used the Angular Joint Drive that uses Unity's joints. You were introduced to the Hinge Location and Gizmo Line Distance properties. We reviewed setting up a Mutators Collision Ignorer prefab instead of using Unity's Layer Collision Matrix. We became familiar with how to use the Start at Initial Target Value and Initial Target Value settings to have our Door start out in a shut state. We then went over the Step Range and Step Increment properties and saw how to sync them up with the Drive Limits' permissible angle range. You learned to use the Started Moving event, which gets triggered when your Door begins to move. Finally, we playtested the Demo scene to ensure that the Door functions as desired. We then created a Lever that uses an Angular Joint Drive. We set up a Mutators Collision Ignorer here, too, and worked with the properties we used when creating our Door. You learned to use the Last Ungrabbed event to increase the Angular Drag against our Lever. We then explored the Angular Joint Drive value events and learned how to create logic game objects that did away with the necessity to write code. We learned to use the Minimum Reached, Midpoint Reached, and Maximum Reached event objects provided by the VRTK. We created four logic game objects that help track whether the Lever is in a drive, neutral, or reverse state. Along the way, we reviewed how to use two new VRTK-provided components: the Empty Event Proxy Emitter and the Wait for Seconds Realtime Yield Emitter. Finally, you learned to tweak the Positive Bounds' Min and Max values for the Min Value Reached to Boolean, Mid Value Reached to Boolean, and Max Value Reached to Boolean objects to reach a sweet spot that works for our Lever.

# CHAPTER 20

# Linear Drives

In the previous chapter, we learned about the VRTK's Angular Drives. In this chapter, we'll get familiar with the VRTK's Linear Drive and implement two examples of its use. You'll recall that we've already used the Linear Transform Drive when we created the Slider game object in Chapter 17. In this chapter, however, we'll be using the Linear Joint Drive to set up a Drawer, and we'll then again use the Linear Transform Drive to set up a Push button. A Linear Drive is a controllable mechanism that provides you with physics- and nonphysics-based linear Interactable controls. These controls can be used with a wide variety of game objects. Ideally, you'll want to use the nonphysics-based linear/angular transform drive prefabs wherever possible. The physics-based joint drives rely heavily on Unity's joints, and if you intend to build multiplayer games, it's best to keep joints to a bare minimum.

## Setting Up a Drawer

Let's begin by moving the Steering Wheel to the opposite side of the worktable so that there's enough space to also place the Drawer on the table. From within the Environment game object in the hierarchy, select the Steering Wheel and change its Transform Position values to $X = -14$; $Y = 0.775$; and $Z = -4.33$. This ensures that your Steering Wheel is placed on the other side of the worktable beside the Lever, which now clears sufficient space to place the Drawer on the table.

As part of the downloads that came with this book, you were provided with a Unity package file named "Drawer," which contains one prefab, the Drawer game object. Download this "Drawer" package file and import it into your project. Once that's done, you'll have access to the Drawer Cabinet prefab in the "Assets" folder. In the hierarchy, select and expand the "Environment" folder. Then, from within the "Assets" folder, drag and drop the Drawer Cabinet prefab onto the Environment game object in the hierarchy, making it a child. Note that the Drawer Cabinet has now been positioned on your

C. Coutinho, *Unity® Virtual Reality Development with VRTK4*, https://doi.org/10.1007/978-1-4842-7933-5_20

worktable. Select this Drawer Cabinet game object in the hierarchy, right-click it, and go to *Prefab, Unpack Completely* in the context menu that pops up. Expand this game object in the hierarchy, and you'll see that it contains five child box game objects that make up the outer Container that holds the Drawer. It also contains a separate Drawer child game object that is made up of individual parts that constitute the actual Drawer.

Next, select the Project tab and expand the "Packages" folder. Locate the Tilia Interactions Controllables Unity package, expand it until you reach its "Prefabs" folder, then expand its "Physics Joint" folder. Drag and drop the Interactions Linear Joint Drive prefab onto the Drawer Cabinet game object in the hierarchy, making a child of it. You will notice that a giant white cube has encompassed your Drawer.

With the Drawer Cabinet game object expanded, select the Interactions Linear Joint drive, and expand it until you reach its Mesh Container. Expand the Mesh Container until you see its Cube game object and deactivate this game object. Now, drag and drop the Drawer game object from the hierarchy onto the Mesh Container, making it a child, see Figure 20-1.

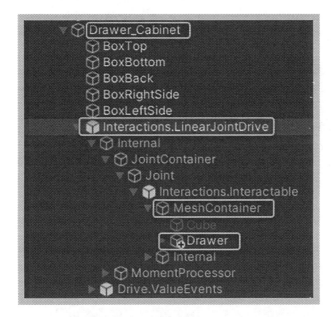

***Figure 20-1.*** *Deactivating the Cube game object and making the Drawer game object a child of the Mesh Container*

Select the Interactions Linear Joint Drive game object in the hierarchy, and in the Inspector, ensure that the Linear Drive Facade component has been expanded. Set its Drive Axis property to Z Axis, as your Drawer needs to move forward and backward.

Check the box for the Start at Initial Target Value property. Set the Initial Target Value to 1, ensuring that the Drawer starts in a closed position. Last, set the Drive Limit value to 0.4, see Figure 20-2.

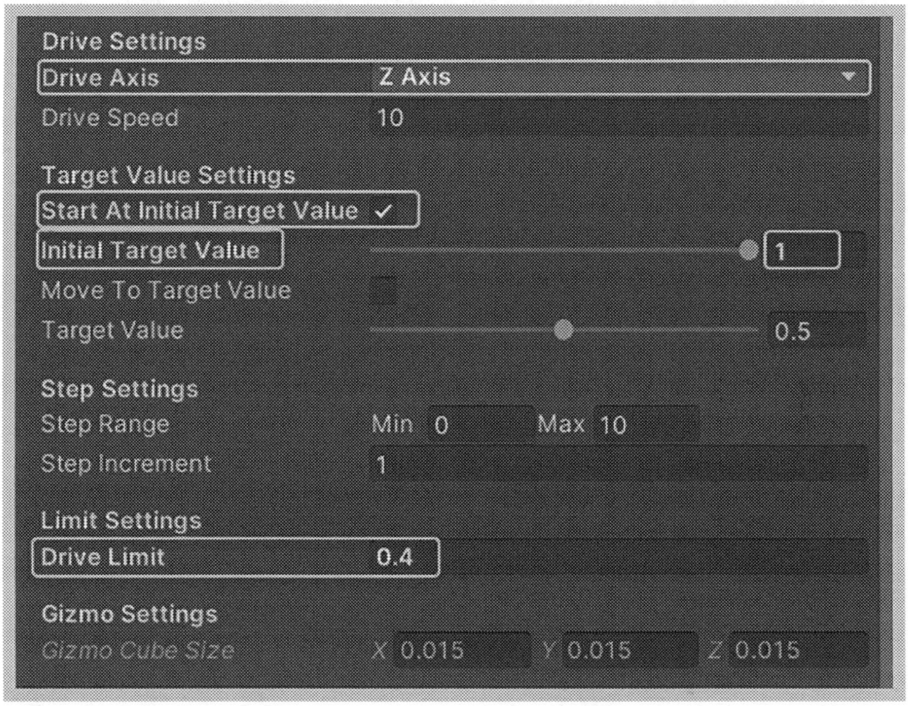

**Drive Settings**
- Drive Axis — Z Axis
- Drive Speed — 10

**Target Value Settings**
- Start At Initial Target Value ✓
- Initial Target Value — 1
- Move To Target Value
- Target Value — 0.5

**Step Settings**
- Step Range — Min 0   Max 10
- Step Increment — 1

**Limit Settings**
- Drive Limit — 0.4

**Gizmo Settings**
- Gizmo Cube Size — X 0.015   Y 0.015   Z 0.015

***Figure 20-2.*** *Setting up the properties of the Linear Drive Facade component of the Drawer*

Now, playtest the Demo scene using your VR headset. Approach the Drawer, and grab its Handle and pull it open. Then, push its Handle to close it. You'll see that your Drawer now opens and closes smoothly in a realistic way. That's all the setup required to get a Drawer working in VR.

## Setting Up a Push Button

In this section, we'll go over how to set up a Push button that will be pressed down upon being touched and will automatically spring back up upon being released. We'll create this Push button using a Linear Transform Drive, and along the way, we'll set up a couple of events.

As part of the downloads that came with this book, you were provided a Unity package file named "Button." This file contains one prefab, the Push Button game object. Download this "Button" package file and import it into your project. Once that's done, you'll have access to the VR Button prefab in the "Assets" folder.

From within the "Assets" folder, drag and drop the VR Button prefab onto the Environment game object in the hierarchy, making it a child. Select this VR Button game object in the hierarchy and set its Transform Position values as follows: $X$ = -13.32; $Y$ = 0.74; and $Z$ = -4.37. You'll see that the button has now been positioned on your worktable.

With the VR Button game object selected in the hierarchy, right-click it, and from the context menu that pops up, select *Prefab, Unpack Completely*. Expand this VR Button game object in the hierarchy, and you'll see that it contains two child game objects, a Button and a Container, both of which have been fitted with Box Colliders. Now, from within the Project tab, expand the "Packages" folder, locate the Tilia Interactions Controllables Unity package, and expand it until you reach its "Prefabs" folder and then expand its "Transform" folder. Drag and drop the Interactions Linear Transform Drive prefab onto the VR Button game object in the hierarchy, making it a child. You'll notice that a giant white cube has encompassed your VR Button.

With the VR Button game object expanded, select the Interactions Linear Transform Drive, and expand it until you reach its Mesh Container. Then, expand the Mesh Container until you see its Cube game object and deactivate this game object. Drag and drop the Button game object, a child of the VR Button game object, from within the hierarchy onto the Mesh Container, making it a child, see Figure 20-3.

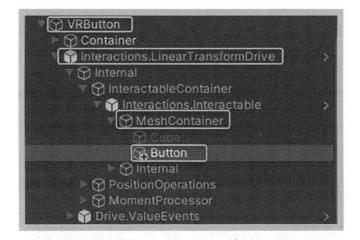

***Figure 20-3.*** *Deactivating the Cube game object and making the Button game object a child of the Mesh Container*

Now, select the Interactions Linear Transform Drive game object in the hierarchy, and within its Linear Drive Facade component, set up the following features: Set the Drive Axis property to Y Axis, as your button will be pressed down. Check the box for the Start At Initial Target Value property. Set the Initial Target Value property to 1. Check the box for the Move to Target Value property. Set the Target Value property to 1. Set the Drive Limit property to 0.15. These settings will ensure that your button starts in an unpressed state, see Figure 20-4.

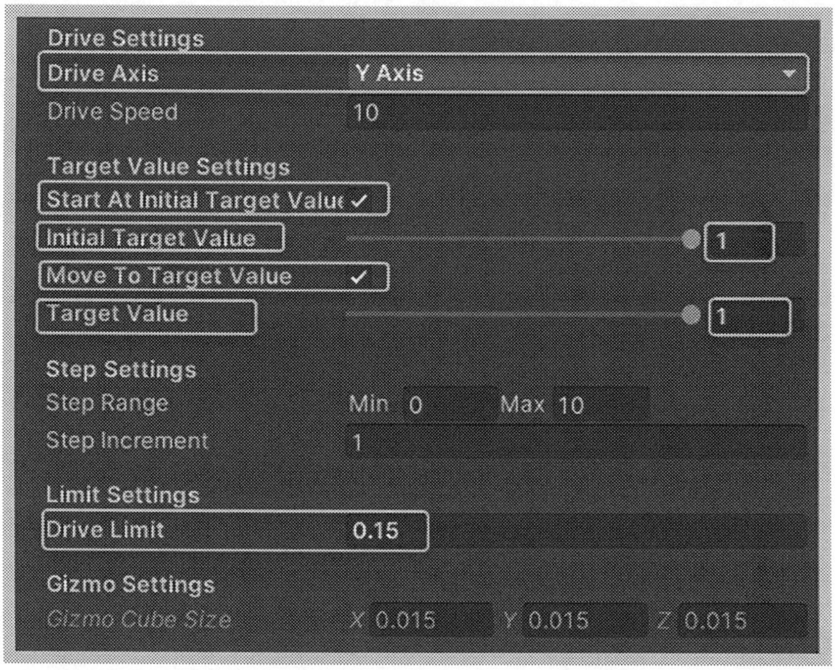

***Figure 20-4.*** *Setting up properties of the Linear Drive Facade component of the Push button*

When your button encounters a collision with your Interactor or some other game object, you want the button to be pressed down. Then, you want it to immediately pop back up once it's no longer colliding with your Interactor. To achieve this, we'll use the First Touched event, available in Interactions Interactable, whose Mesh Container the Button game object is nested in.

In the hierarchy, select the Interactions Interactable game object, and in the Interactable Facade component of the Inspector, select and expand the First Touched event. Click its plus symbol to add an event listener to it. Then, drag and drop the Interactions Linear Transform Drive into this event listener box. For its function, select Linear Drive Facade, Float Target Value, and set the value in its text box to 0, see Figure 20-5.

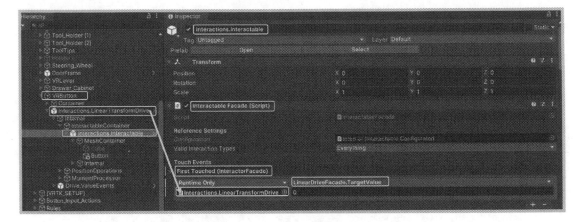

***Figure 20-5.*** *Setting up the First Touched event in for the Push button in Interactions Interactable. The Linear Drive Facade, Target Value has been set to the value 0*

By setting the Target Value property to 0, as shown in Figure 20-5, you have ensured that the Push button will go fully down when any Interactor touches it. You also need to make sure that the button springs back up once the Interactor stops touching the button. You will see that achieving this is easy; all you need to do is set up the Last Untouched event in the Interactable Facade component. Let's set this up now.

In the Interactable Facade component of the Inspector, expand the Last Untouched event and click the plus symbol in its bottom right corner to add an event listener. Now, drag and drop the *Interactions* Linear Transform Drive into this event listener box. For its function, select Linear Drive Facade, Float Target Value and set the value in its text box to 1. By setting the Target Value to 1, you have ensured that your button will spring back up once your *Interactor* (hand) stops touching it, see Figure 20-6.

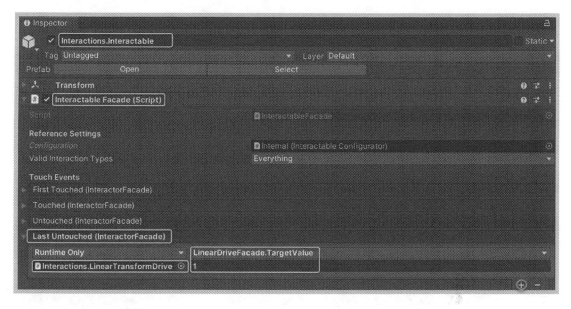

***Figure 20-6.*** *Setting up the Last Untouched event for the Push button in Interactions Interactable. The function Linear Drive Facade, Target Value has been set to the value 1*

Last, let's add a Mutators Collision Ignorer prefab to the VR Button so that collisions between its Container parts colliders and the button collider are ignored. Select the "Packages" folder from within the Project tab, locate the Tilia Mutators Collision Ignorer Unity package, and expand it until you reach its "Prefabs" folder. Now, drag and drop the Mutators Collision Ignorer prefab onto the VR Button game object in the hierarchy.

Select this Mutators Collision Ignorer game object in the hierarchy, and within the Inspector, set the Sources Elements property size value to 5, which will make five element slots available. In the hierarchy, expand the Container game object that is a child of the VR button game object, and drag and drop each of its Edge and Bottom child game objects into each of the five available element slots. Next, in the Inspector, set the Targets Elements property size value to 1, which makes an Element 0 slot available. Drag and drop the Interactions Linear Transform Drive into this slot.

You have now ensured that your Buttons Box Collider will not collide with the colliders of its Container, see Figure 20-7.

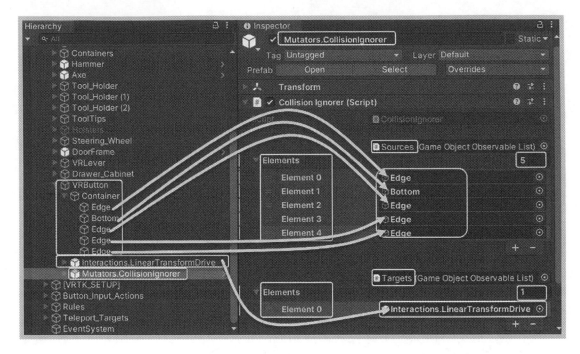

***Figure 20-7.*** *Setting up the Mutators Collision Ignorer on your VR button*

Now, playtest the Demo scene using your VR headset. Approach the Push button on the worktable and push down on it with your hand. You'll find that it gets pressed down and immediately springs back up upon being released.

# Summary

In this chapter, we learned all about using Linear Drives provided by the VRTK. We learned to implement both a Linear Joint Drive and a Linear Transform Drive. We started by setting up a Drawer, for which we used a Linear Joint Drive. You probably noticed that setting up the Drawer was like setting up the Lever in Chapter 19. After that, we tested the Drawer in VR. Next, found out how to set up a more involved Push button, but nothing that was too challenging to achieve. We set up this Push button using a Linear Transform Drive, putting in place two new properties: the Move to Target Value and the Target Value properties. We also set up the First Touched and Last Touched events so that the button would push down and spring back up automatically. Finally, we playtested the *Demo* scene to ensure that the Push button worked as it was meant to.

# CHAPTER 21

# Tips, Tricks, and Recipes

In this chapter, we'll learn some valuable tips and tricks to address common game play scenarios. The sections in this chapter can be thought of as quick recipes designed to teach you specific mechanics and provide you with some neat tips and tricks. You'll learn to implement the following game mechanics:

- Creating realistic physical hands

- Implementing haptic feedback

- Highlighting Interactable game objects

## Adding Realistic Physical Hands

In this section, you'll learn to set up realistic hand collisions for your avatar hands. Currently, the way your hands are set up, they pass through game objects without colliding with them, which is not very realistic. Whenever your hand encounters an Interactable game object, it should be allowed either to grab it or, if your intention isn't to grab the object, to collide with it, allowing you to push the object around. You'll learn to set this up by using the VRTK's Trackers Collider Follower prefab.

In the hierarchy, select the VRTK SETUP game object, and create a new child game object and rename this new child game object "VRTK COLLIDER FOLLOWER." Then, expand the "Packages" folder in the Project tab, locate the Tilia Trackers Collider Follower Unity package, and expand it until you reach its "Prefabs" folder. Drag and drop the Trackers Collider Follower prefab onto the VRTK COLLIDER FOLLOWER game object in the hierarchy. Rename this Trackers Collider Follower game object "Trackers Collider Follower Right," as this collider follower will track the Interactor on your right hand.

© Christopher Coutinho 2022
C. Coutinho, *Unity® Virtual Reality Development with VRTK4*, https://doi.org/10.1007/978-1-4842-7933-5_21

With the Trackers Collider Follower Right game object selected in the hierarchy, ensure that the Inspector's Collider Follower Facade component has also been expanded. Now, drag and drop the Right Controller Alias game object from the hierarchy into the Tracking Settings Source property parameter, as shown in Figure 21-1. This ensures that the Trackers Collider Follower Right game object will follow your Right Controller (your right hand) around.

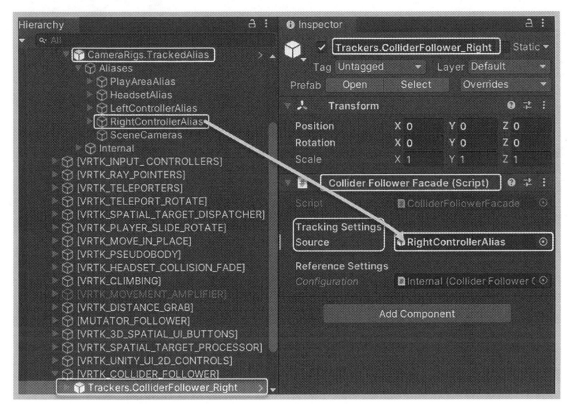

***Figure 21-1.*** *Setting up the Trackers Collider Follower Right game object*

Then, expand the Trackers Collider Follower Right game object in the hierarchy and select the Collider game object. You'll notice that it contains a Sphere Collider component that is currently huge and not positioned well enough to encompass your right hand. You need to update the Sphere Collider property so that it maps your right hand well. In the Sphere Collider component, change the values for its Center property to X = 0.02; Y = -0.02; and Z = 0.015. Also, set the Radius property to 0.04, see Figure 21-2.

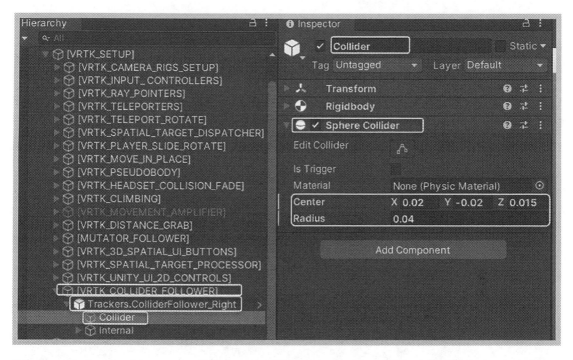

***Figure 21-2.*** *Setting up the Sphere Collider component of the Collider game object*

Now, playtest the Demo scene, and select the Scene tab in the Unity editor. Double-click the Collider game object in the hierarchy and you should be able to see your right hand in the Unity editor. Click the Edit Collider button in the Sphere component of the Collider game object and ensure that your Sphere Collider is encompassing your right hand well. Adjust the collider properties further if required.

You also need to ensure that as soon as your Right Controller's Grab button is pressed, the Trackers Collider Follower Right game object will be deactivated. This will guarantee that there's no conflict between grabbing an Interactable and interacting with it by pushing it around.

You'll need to hook up your Right Controller's Grip button so that as soon as it's pressed, the Trackers Collider Follower Right game object will be deactivated. This will ensure that you can't push your Interactable game objects around when you're in Grab mode. Similarly, the moment you ungrab an Interactable game object, the Trackers Collider Follower Right game object will be activated. This ensures that you can push the Interactable game objects around again when you're not in grabbing mode.

Let's set this up now. Expand the Buttons Input Actions game object in the hierarchy, and select the Right-Hand Grab game object. In the Inspector, you'll see that the *Activated* and Deactivated events for this Right-Hand Grab game object have an animator action setup.

Click the plus symbol located in the bottom right corner of the Activated event to add a new event listener. Then, drag and drop the Trackers Collider Follower Right game object into the event listener box for the Activated event. For the function, select Game Object, Set Active from the "Static Parameters" section, and leave the check box unchecked. When you press your Right Controller's Grip/Grab button, your Trackers Collider Follower Right game object will be deactivated, see Figure 21-3.

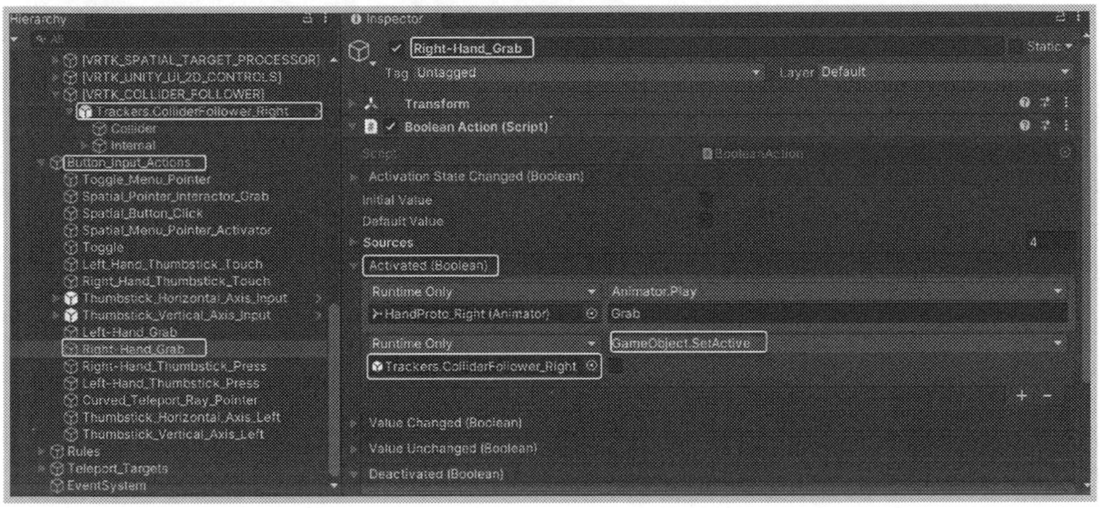

***Figure 21-3.*** *Setting up the Activated event against the Right-Hand Grab game object*

Next, you need to set up the Deactivated event. Click the plus symbol located in the event's bottom right corner twice to add two new event listeners to it. Drag and drop the Trackers Collider Follower Right game object into the first event listener box. For the function, select Game Object, Set Active from the "Static Parameters" section and ensure that you check its check box. Then, drag and drop the Trackers Collider Follower Right game object into the event listener box for the second Deactivated event listener. For the function, select Collider Follower Facade, Snap to Source from the "Static Parameters" section. This ensures that the moment you release the Grip button on your Right Controller, you'll be able to push Interactable game objects around, see Figure 21-4.

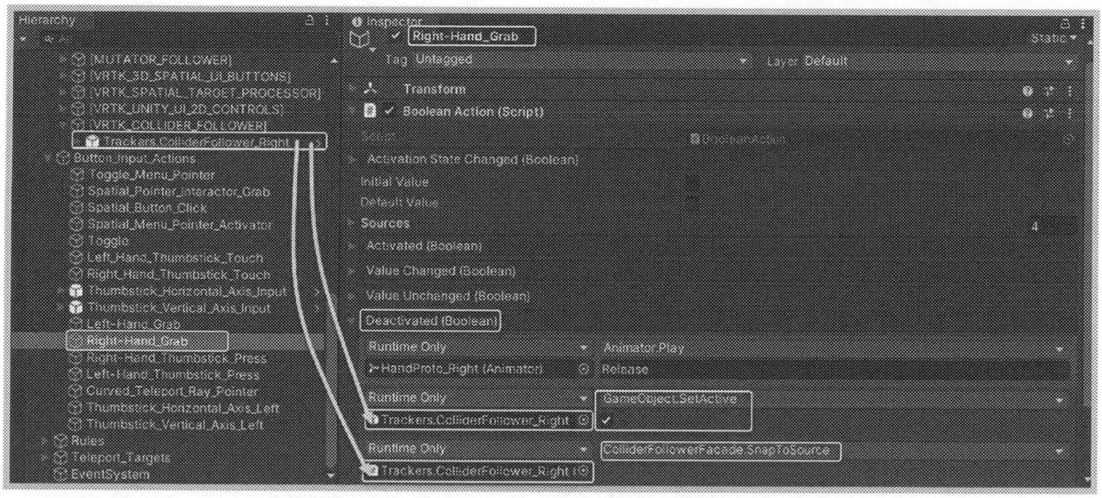

***Figure 21-4.*** *Setting up the Deactivated event against the Right-Hand Grab game object*

Playtest the Demo scene using your VR headset. Approach the worktable and push the Hammer, Axe, and Drill Machine around with your open hand. You'll find that these objects are easy to push around. Now, press the Grip button on your Right Controller so that your hand forms a clenched fist, and then approach any of the Interactable game objects on the worktable. Try pushing around any Interactable game objects using your right hand with your fist clenched and the Grip button on your Right Controller still pressed. You won't be able to push these Interactable game objects around with your hand in this position. Last, try grabbing an Interactable game object, and note that you can grab it as before, as discussed in Chapter 8. Now, set up a Trackers Collider Follower Left game object for your Left Controller following these same steps. I will leave this as an exercise for you to complete on your own.

As the last step, you need to avoid any uncalled-for jittering behavior that may arise when the Trackers Collider Follower Right game object that is now following your right hand encounters your pseudo-body. In the hierarchy, select the Collider game object, nested within the Trackers Collider Follower Right game object, and set its Layer property to Transparent FX in the Inspector.

Now, from the main menu, select *Edit ➤ Project Settings* to open the Project Settings dialog. From within the left pane, select Physics. Then, scroll down within the right pane until you see the Layer Collision Matrix. Here, ensure that the check box at the intersection of the Transparent FX row and the Ignore Raycast column has been unchecked, as shown in Figure 21-5.

347

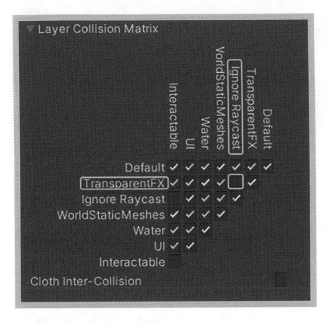

***Figure 21-5.*** *Ensuring that the check box at the intersection of the Transparent FX row and Ignore Raycast column is unchecked*

You can now be assured that the collider following your right hand won't be able to interact with your pseudo-body but will be able to interact with Interactable game objects.

Set this up for your Trackers Collider Follower Left game object, too.

# Obtaining Haptic Feedback

In this section, we'll become familiar with how to obtain haptic feedback against our Left and Right Controllers whenever we grab an Interactable game object. Note that the haptic feedback provided against the Unity XR Rig is not great, so minimal feedback will be obtained when using the Unity XR Rig.

To get started, expand the "Packages" folder in the Project tab, and locate the Tilia Output Interactor Haptics Unity package and expand it until you reach its "Prefabs" folder. Now, drag and drop the Output Interactor Haptics prefab onto the VRTK SETUP game object in the hierarchy and select it. Ensure that the Interactor Haptics Facade component has been expanded in the Inspector.

We now need to set up the properties available in the "Linked Settings "section. Drag and drop the Camera Rigs, Tracked Alias game object from the hierarchy into the Tracked Alias property parameter. Then, drag and drop the Interactions Interactor Left game object from the hierarchy into the Left Interactor property parameter. Last, drag and drop the Interactions Interactor Right game object from the hierarchy into the Right Interactor property parameter. In the "Haptic Settings" section, set the Intensity property value to 1, as shown in Figure 21-6.

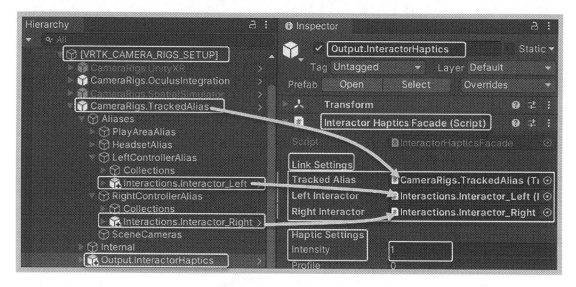

***Figure 21-6.*** *Setting up the Link Settings and Haptic Settings properties for the Output Interactor Haptics game object*

Now, select the Interactions Interactor Left game object in the hierarchy, and in the Inspector, expand the Grabbed event in the "Interactor Events" section. Click the plus symbol in the bottom right corner of this event to add an event listener. Drag and drop the Output Interactor Haptics game object from the hierarchy into this event listener box. For the function, select Interactor Haptics Facade, Perform Default Haptics (Interactor Facade). Then, drag and drop the Interactions Interactor Left game object from the hierarchy into the text box below the function drop-down, see Figure 21-7.

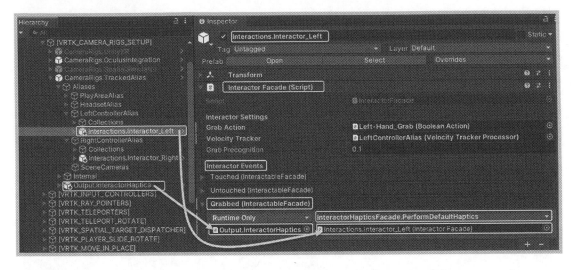

***Figure 21-7.*** *Setting up the Interactions Interactor Left game object to receive a haptic pulse*

Then, select the Interactions Interactor Right game object in the hierarchy, and in the Inspector, expand the Grabbed event in the "Interactor Events" section. Click the plus symbol in the bottom right corner of this event to add an event listener. Drag and drop the *Output Interactor Haptics* game object from the hierarchy into this event listener box. For the function, select Interactor Haptics Facade, Perform Default Haptics (Interactor Facade). Last, drag and drop the Interactions Interactor Right game object from the hierarchy into the text box below the function drop-down, see Figure 21-8.

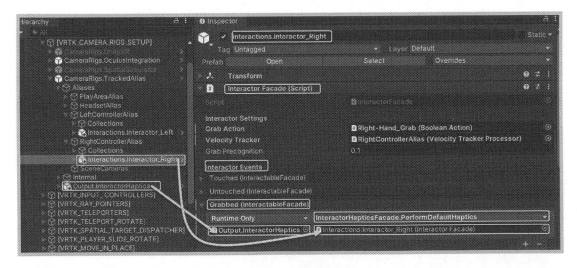

***Figure 21-8.*** *Setting up the Interactions Interactor Right game object to receive a haptic pulse*

Now, whenever you grab an Interactable game object using your right hand, your Right Controller will emit a short haptic pulse. A similar haptic pulse will be emitted by your Left Controller when you grab an Interactable game object with your left hand.

# Highlighting Interactable Game Objects

The VRTK provides you with some very basic shaders that you can use to highlight your Interactable game objects upon touching them. It lets you provide the player with a visual cue indicating that an Interactable game object has been touched. To achieve this, we'll use one of the six shaders provided by the VRTK. Of course, if you have access to a better-quality shader, you could use that one instead. To achieve this highlighting, the VRTK provides you with a Tilia package called Tilia Visuals Interactable Highlighter Unity. In this section, we'll have the Hammer game object get highlighted when either of your hands encounters (touches) it.

To set this up, expand the "Packages" folder in the Project tab, and locate the Tilia Visuals Interactable Highlighter Unity package and expand it until you reach its "Prefabs" folder. In the hierarchy, select the VRTK SETUP game object and expand it. Then, drag and drop the Visuals Interactable Highlighter prefab onto the VRTK SETUP game object in the hierarchy and select it.

In the Inspector, ensure that the Interactable Highlighter Facade component has been expanded. Then, in the hierarchy, expand the Environment game object and locate the Hammer game object. Drag and drop the Hammer game object from the hierarchy into the Interactable property parameter. This lets the Interactable Highlighter Facade know that the Hammer Interactable game object should be highlighted upon being touched. For the Highlight Material property, click the target icon in its text box to display the Select Material dialog. Double-click on a material of your choice to serve as the highlight for the Hammer. I've selected the material Ambisonic Object, see Figure 21-9.

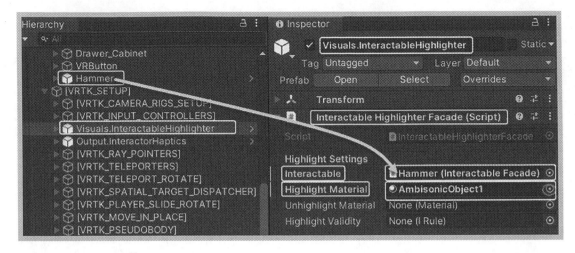

***Figure 21-9.*** *Setting up the Visuals Interactable Highlighter to get highlighted the Hammer upon being touched*

Now, test the Demo scene using your VR headset. Approach the Hammer and touch it with either your left or right hand, and you'll see that the chosen Ambisonic Object material immediately gets highlighted on the Hammer. When you actually grab the Hammer, the highlight disappears. Using the Visuals Interactable Highlighter prefab makes it extremely simple to highlight your Interactable game objects. You now need to set up the Axe game object to be highlighted upon being touched. I'll leave this as an exercise for you to complete.

# Summary

In this chapter, you learned a few tips and tricks that can be used within any of your VR games or apps. We started by going over how to set up realistic physical hand collisions against our avatar hands. We achieved this by using the VRTK's Trackers Collider Follower prefab. We saw how to get the Sphere Collider to encompass our right hand well. We then set up the Activated and Deactivated events to activate and deactivate the Trackers Collider Follower. Finally, we set up the Layer Collision Matrix so that the game objects assigned to the Transparent FX and Ignore Raycast layers wouldn't collide with each other. In the next section of the chapter, we became acquainted with how to obtain haptic feedback against our controllers upon grabbing an Interactable game object. This was made possible using the VRTK's Output Interactor Haptics prefab. We learned to set up several properties against this prefab. We also learned to set up the Grabbed event on the Interactions Interactor Left and Right game objects, allowing your controllers (Interactors) to receive haptic feedback. Last, we found out how to have an Interactable game object get highlighted upon touching it using the VRTK's Visuals Interactable Highlighter prefab. Here, we selected the Interactable object we wanted to highlight and provided it with a suitable highlighting material. We ended the chapter by testing this highlighting mechanic.

# CHAPTER 22

# Minigame

In this final chapter, we'll create a small minigame without writing a single line of code. The game will be a simple ball rolling–style game, where the objective will be to roll a ball down a garden path, collecting strewn objects until the time runs out. It won't be a full-blown ball-rolling puzzle game, but you could easily achieve one by further coding simple mechanics if you want to. You could have the ball grow in size as the player picks up objects, or you could have the player start out by picking up medium-sized objects until the Ball has grown to a specific size, at which point the player will graduate to picking up larger objects and then complete the level.

In this chapter, you'll learn to develop the core mechanic of having a ball roll around and pick up objects. You'll also set up a timer that counts down the seconds you have left to complete the level, and when it reaches zero, it won't allow you to roll the ball any further. We'll use the Slide movement mode of locomotion to move through the scene. This will be implemented using our Left Controller's Thumbstick, as we set up in Chapter 10, "Seamless Locomotion." Our Right Controller's Thumbstick will be used to control the Ball, allowing it to move forward, backward, left, and right. The Countdown Timer will be set up as a spatial UI Tooltip that will display the seconds you have remaining to collect all objects win the level. Along the way, you'll learn how to set up a Moment Processor and an event that will be called once a specific time interval has elapsed.

We'll also use the VRTK's Input Combined Actions Axes to Vector 3 Action prefab to roll the Ball around by adding force to the Ball's rigid body. Attempting to achieve this realistic ball movement without using the VRTK-provided Input Combined Actions Axes to Vector 3 Action prefab would require you to write math-intensive code involving vectors and trigonometry. But thanks to this VRTK prefab, you don't need to code this pretty complicated stuff yourself.

© Christopher Coutinho 2022
C. Coutinho, *Unity® Virtual Reality Development with VRTK4*, https://doi.org/10.1007/978-1-4842-7933-5_22

# Importing the Base Unity Package

We'll use the same VR Playground project here, as it already comprises all the required Tilia Packages and the entire VRTK SETUP created with this book. In this case, we'll utilize only those prefabs required to build our minigame.

As part of the downloads that come with this book, you've been provided a Unity package file called "Garden Path" that you need to download and import into your project. Note that it may take a while to import. Once the import is complete, select the "Assets" folder and then navigate to and expand the "Garden Environment" folder and then expand the "Game" folder within it. Now, launch the Garden scene. You may need to rotate your garden path around in the scene view so that it's facing forward, as shown in Figure 22-1.

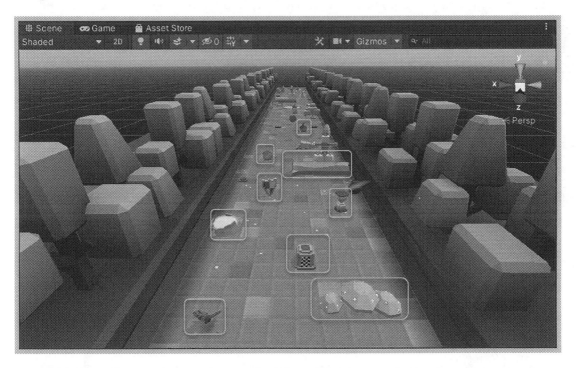

***Figure 22-1.***  *The garden path populated with 37 game objects*

The garden path you see in Figure 22-1 has been populated with 37 game objects that the player needs to pick up by rolling a Ball onto them. Some of these game objects have a basic animation on them and some don't. However, each game object on the garden path is fitted with either a Sphere or Box Collider. The colliders on the game objects have both been set up as a Trigger. Setting them as a Trigger is vital to the development of the core game mechanic. Select any game object from within the Scene tab, and in the Inspector, you'll see that the Is Trigger property in its collider component has been checked, as shown in Figure 22-2.

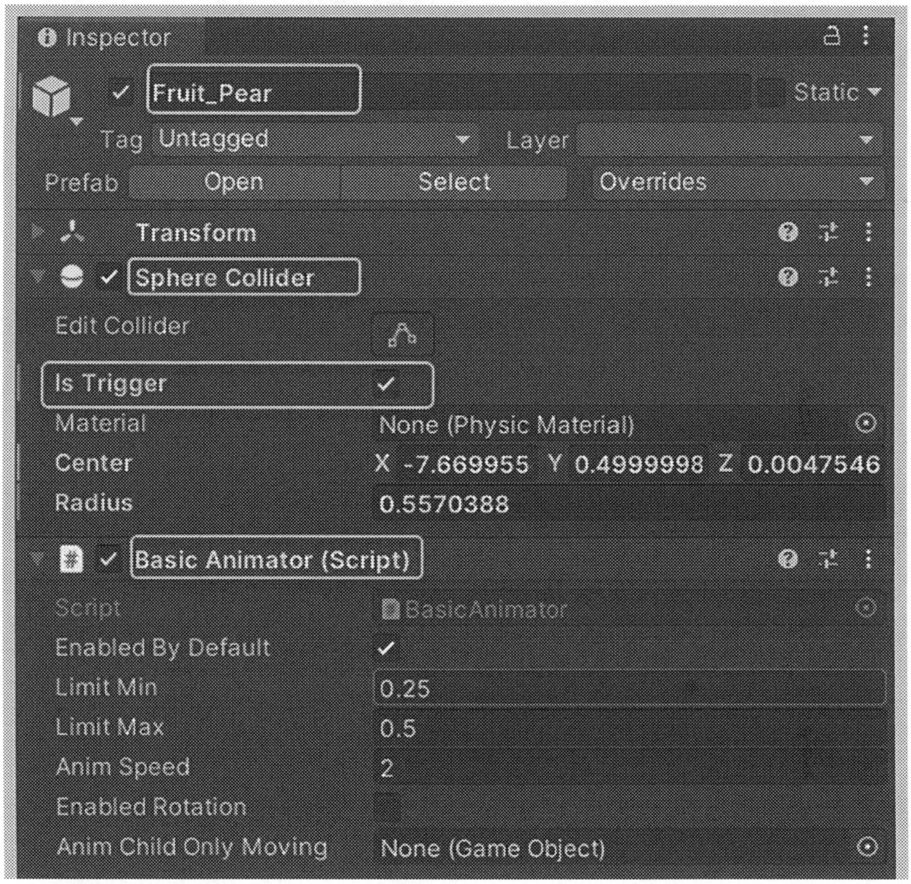

**Figure 22-2.** *The Fruit Pear game object's Basic Animator component with its Sphere Collider's Is Trigger property checked off*

Now, you need to create a new Tag named Grabbable that will be used to identify grabbable game objects in the Scene. From the main menu, go to Edit ➤ Project Settings, and from the pane on the left, select the item Tags and Layers. Expand the "Tags" section and click the plus symbol in its bottom right corner. For the New Tag Name property, type in "Grabbable," and click save. Now, close the Project Settings dialog, see Figure 22-3.

**Tags and Layers**

▼ Tags

| | |
|---|---|
| Tag 0 | Drill |
| Tag 1 | Axe |
| Tag 2 | Hammer |
| Tag 3 | Grabbable |

***Figure 22-3.*** *Creating the Grabbable tag in Tags and Layers*

We next need to set up the VRTK-provided Collision Tracker component on each of the 37 obstacle game objects in your garden path. Let's first set up this component on the Fruit Apple obstacle. To do so, expand the Environment game object in the hierarchy, then select the Fruit Apple game object, and in the Inspector, click the Add Component button and add a new Collision Tracker component. Set its Emitted Types property to Trigger. Set its States to Process property to Enter, which indicates that you're looking for an On Trigger Enter Collision to occur against your Fruit Apple Obstacle. Once this On Trigger Enter state has been reached, the Collision Started Event listed in the "Collision Event" section will be triggered. Here you need to set the Fruit Apple obstacle game object's Tag value to Grabbable. Let's set this up.

Click the plus symbol located in the bottom right corner of the Collision Started Event to add an event listener. Then, drag and drop the Fruit Apple obstacle game object into this event listener box. For this function, select Collision Tracker, String, Tag. In the text box below, type in "Grabbable." Ensure that you spell it exactly as shown in Figure 22-3.

We have now ensured that the moment the Ball collides with the Fruit Apple obstacle, its Tag will be set to Grabbable, as shown in Figure 22-4. The Collision Tracker component works like the On Trigger event that you use in coding to determine if one object has collided with another and what action should be taken in response. With the Collision Tracker component placed in each obstacle game object, the moment the Ball collides with any obstacle, its Collision Tracker component's Collision Started event will be triggered, setting the Tag of the obstacle that collided with the Ball to Grabbable. This Tag value is later used by a rule that allows the obstacle to attach itself to the Ball, as we will see shortly.

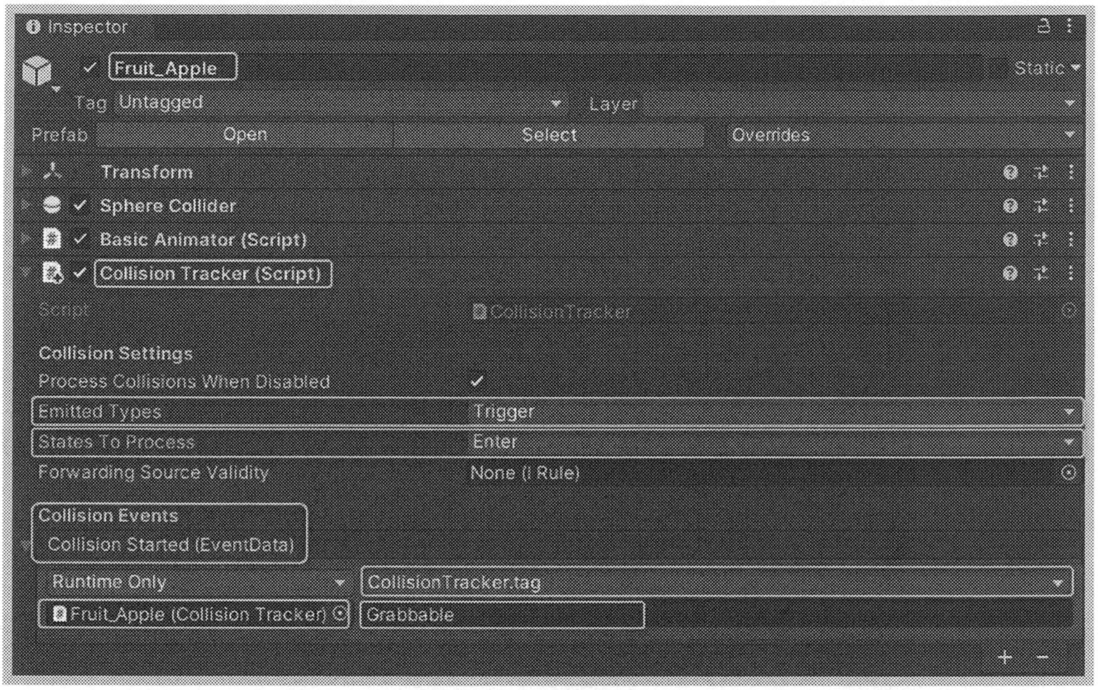

**Figure 22-4.** *Setting up the Fruit Apple obstacle game object with a Collision Tracker component*

Now it's time for to set up the Collision Tracker component on the remaining 36 obstacle game objects in the Scene. With the Fruit Apple game object still selected in the hierarchy, copy its Collision Tracker component from within the Inspector. Select all the remaining obstacle game objects in the hierarchy, starting with Fruit Orange and going all the way down to Gate (3). Then, click the vertical ellipsis button next to the Transform component, and in the context menu that pops up, select Paste Component as New. This will set up the Collision Tracker component for each of the obstacle game objects you selected, see Figure 22-5.

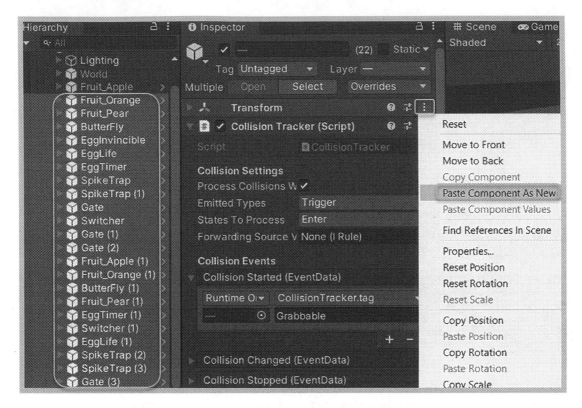

**Figure 22-5.** *Setting up the Collision Tracker for 22 of the 36 obstacle game objects*

Now, in the Environment game object, expand the World game object and then expand Map Objects. It is within Map Objects that the remainder of your obstacle game objects reside. Select only those obstacle game objects that are active, as they are the ones available in the Scene. In total, there are 14 active obstacle game objects in Map Objects that you need to select. Once you have selected all of them, click the vertical ellipsis button next to the Transform component. In the context menu that appears, select Paste Component as New. This will set up the Collision Tracker component on these remaining 14 obstacle game objects, see Figure 22-6.

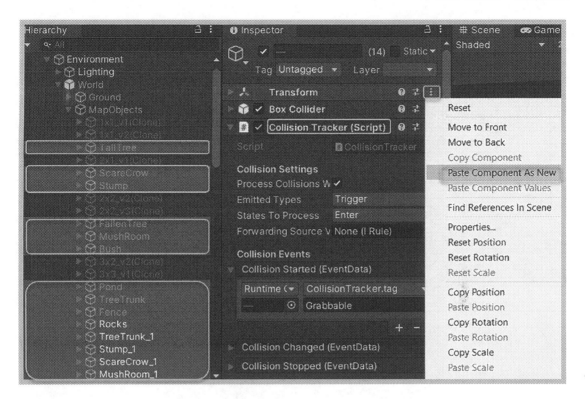

*Figure 22-6.* *Setting up the Collision Tracker on the remaining 14 obstacle game objects*

You may have noticed that you've also been provided with the Ball game object as a sphere in the hierarchy. Click on this Ball game object, and in the Inspector, you'll see that its Transform Scale valuesc have been set to 0.5 across all axes. Also, a Football Net material has been applied to it, giving it a netted ball effect. It has been fitted with a Sphere Collider, which is not a Trigger, whose Radius of 0.5 ensures that it encompasses the Ball well. It also has a Rigidbody component with a Mass of 1 and a Drag and Angular Drag of 0.5. The Use Gravity property has been checked, and the Collision Detection property has been set to Continuous, as shown in Figure 22-7. This is the basic setup you've been provided.

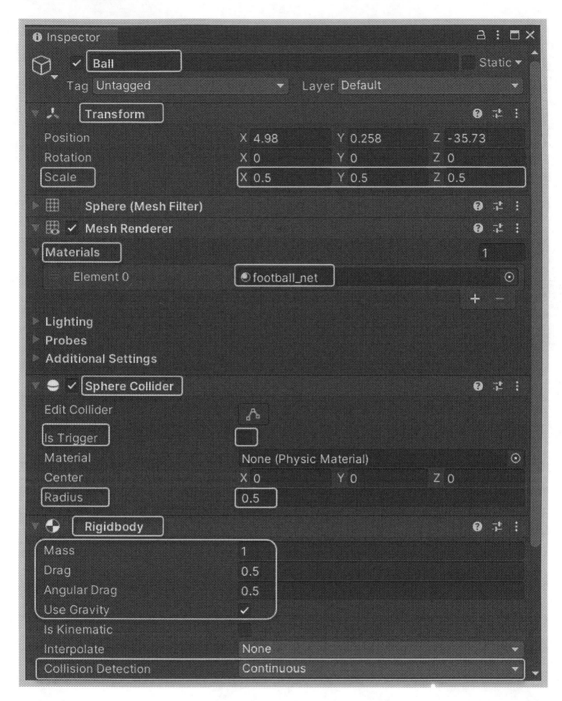

***Figure 22-7.*** *Exploring the setup of the Ball game object*

# Setting Up the VRTK Prefabs

In this section, we'll create prefabs of certain game objects in the Demo scene that are required by the Garden scene to set up its VR functionality. Let's start by launching the Demo scene and creating a new folder in the "Assets" folder and naming it "Prefabs." Then, with the Demo scene open, expand the VRTK SETUP game object, and drag and drop its child game object, VRTK CAMERA RIGS SETUP, from within it to the newly created "Prefabs" folder. You now have a VRTK CAMERA RIGS SETUP prefab that can be used in any other scene of your project.

Next, let's create the remaining prefabs that will be required in the Garden scene of our minigame. With the VRTK SETUP game object still expanded, locate the VRTK INPUT CONTROLLERS game object in the hierarchy and drag and drop it into the "Prefabs" folder. Then, drag and drop the VRTK PSEUDOBODY game object into this folder. Select the VRTK PSEUDOBODY prefab in the same folder, and click the Open Prefab button in the Inspector. With this prefab opened, select the Trackers Pseudo Body game object in the hierarchy. In the Inspector, you'll see that the property values for its Source, Offset, and Ignored Game Objects (Elements 0 through 5) have been lost. You'll need to set these up again once you drop this prefab into the Garden scene, see Figure 22-8. This is because Unity won't allow you to reference scene game objects in a prefab. These are all the prefabs required from within VRTK SETUP for the Garden scene.

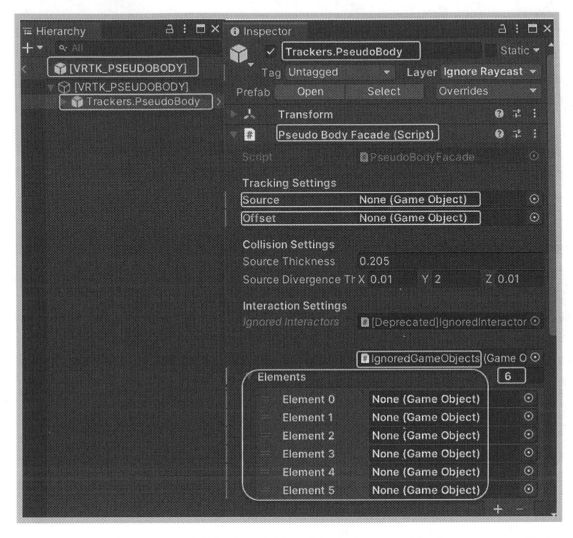

***Figure 22-8.*** *The VRTK PSEUDOBODY prefab with several broken property links*

Within the Demo scene, select and expand the Button Input Actions game object in the hierarchy. Drag and drop the Thumbstick Horizontal Axis Input game object into the "Prefabs" folder. When asked whether you want to create an original prefab or a variant of this prefab, select Original Prefab. Then, drag and drop the Thumbstick Vertical Axis Input game object into the "Prefabs" folder. When asked whether you want to create a new original prefab or a variant of this prefab, select Original Prefab.

Then, click either the Thumbstick Vertical Axis Input or Thumbstick Horizontal Axis Input prefab in the "Prefabs" folder, and then click the Open Prefab button in the Inspector. You'll see that the Activated event settings have been lost. You'll need to recreate both of these prefabs once you drop them into the Garden scene, see Figure 22-9. All this Activated event did was to play the Teleporting animation that goes with the Hand Proto Left game object.

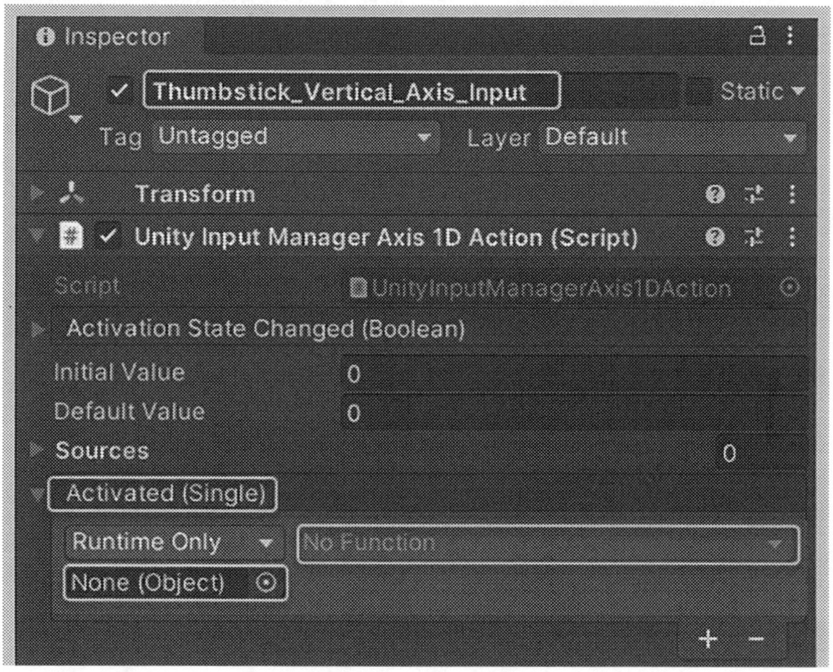

**Figure 22-9.** *The Thumbstick Vertical Axis Input prefab with its Activated event broken*

Finally, as we'll be using just one of the Slide movements for locomotion, we'll set up this locomotion method from scratch directly in the Garden scene. Let's start setting up the various VRTK prefabs in the Garden scene.

Launch the Garden scene. With the Garden game object selected in the hierarchy, navigate to the Assets ➤ "Prefabs" folder, and drag and drop in the VRTK CAMERA RIGS SETUP prefab. With the VRTK CAMERA RIGS SETUP game object selected, set its Transform Position property values as follows: $X = 5$; $Y = 0$; and $Z = -38$. This ensures that you start out positioned behind the Ball.

Now, expand the VRTK CAMERA RIGS SETUP game object in the hierarchy and deactivate the Camera Rigs, Oculus Integration and Camera Rigs, Spatial Simulator game objects. Activate the Camera Rigs, Unity XR game object. By setting this up , you can test your game using either your Oculus or HTC Vive headset.

After that, ensure that you have the Garden game object selected in the hierarchy, and then drag and drop in the VRTK INPUT CONTROLLERS prefab. You'll need to unpack the VRTK INPUT CONTROLLERS game object before deleting some of its child game objects. Expand this game object and delete the child game objects Mouse Input, Keyboard Input, and Input Unity Input Manager Xbox Controller, as you'll be targeting only the Oculus and HTC Vive controllers.

Next, drag the VRTK PSEDUDOBODY prefab into the hierarchy, making it a child of the Garden game object. Expand the VRTK PSEDUDOBODY game object in the hierarchy, and select its Trackers Pseudo body child game object. You need to set up all its missing property values in the Inspector. For its Source property, drag and drop in the Headset Alias game object. For its Offset property, drag and drop in the Play Area Alias game object. For the Ignored Game Objects, Element 0 property, drag and drop in the Interactions Interactor Left game object. For the Ignored Game Objects, Element 1 property, drag and drop in the Interactions Interactor Right game object. For the Ignored Game Objects, Element 2 property, drag and drop in the Custom Hand Left game object. For the Ignored Game Objects, Element 3 property, drag and drop in the Hand Proto Left game object. For the Ignored Game Objects, Element 4 property, drag and drop in the Custom Hand Right game object. Finally, for the Ignored Game Objects, Element 5 property, drag and drop in the Hand Proto Right game object, see Figure 22-10.

Your pseudo-body has now been set up.

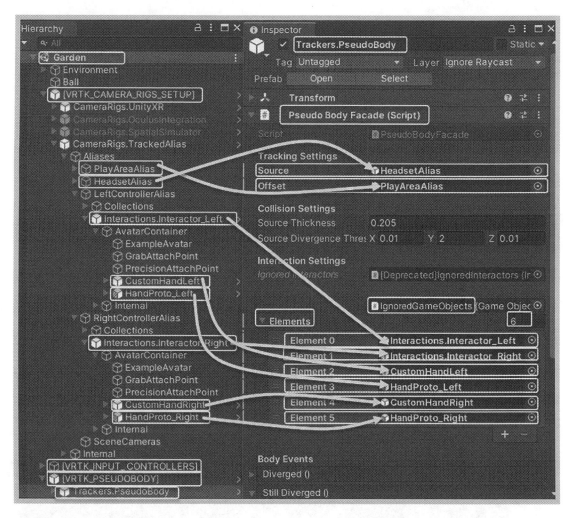

**Figure 22-10.** *Setting up the missing properties for the Trackers Pseudo Body game object*

Next, with the Garden game object selected, drag and drop the Thumbstick Horizontal Axis Input and Thumbstick Vertical Axis Input prefabs into the hierarchy, as shown in Figure 22-11.

***Figure 22-11.*** *The Garden game object with its nested child game objects*

Then, select both the Thumbstick Horizontal Axis Input and Thumbstick Vertical Axis Input game objects in the hierarchy, and populate their Activated event in the Inspector. Following that, drag and drop the Hand Proto Left game object into this event listener box. For the function, select Animator, Play String from within the "Static Parameters" section. Type "Teleporting" into the box below that, as shown in Figure 22-12, to specify that this is the animation that needs to play.

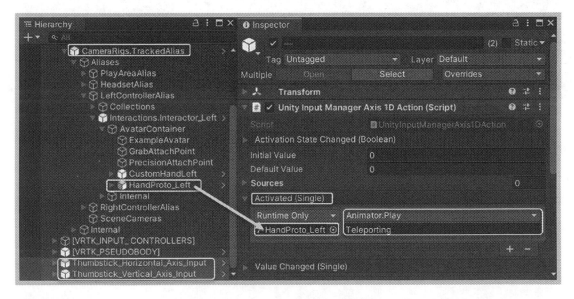

***Figure 22-12.*** *Setting up the Activated event for the Thumbstick Horizontal Axis Input and Thumbstick Vertical Axis Input game objects*

Next, in the "Packages" folder of the Project tab, locate the Tilia Locomotors Axis
Move Unity package and expand its "Runtime/Prefabs" folder. Drag and drop the
Locomotors Axis Move Vertical Slide Horizontal Snap Rotate prefab into the hierarchy,
making it a child of the *Garden* game object.

Now, select the Locomotors Axis Move Vertical Slide Horizontal Snap Rotate game
object in the hierarchy, and let's set up its properties in the Inspector. Drag and drop the
Thumbstick Horizontal Axis Input game object into the Horizontal Axis property of its
Axis Move Facade component; drag and drop the Thumbstick Vertical Axis Input game
object into the Vertical Axis property of this component; drag and drop the Play Area
Alias game object into its Target property; drag and drop the Headset Alias game object
into its Forward Offset property; drag and drop in the Headset Origin game object into its
Rotation Pivot property; and finally, Drag and drop the Scene Cameras game object into
its Scene Cameras property.

You now have your Sliding locomotion set up, see Figure 22-13.

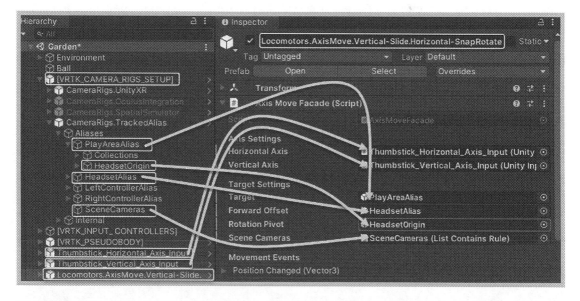

***Figure 22-13.*** *Setting up the Locomotors Axis Move Vertical Slide Horizontal
Snap Rotate game object*

We now need to capture button input actions for the horizontal and vertical
movements of our Right Controller's Thumbstick. This will enable us to move the Ball in
different directions during game play. We'll capture these inputs for the Oculus and HTC
Vive controllers.

To do this, with the Garden game object selected, let's create a new empty game object in the hierarchy and rename this game object "Thumbstick Horizontal Axis Right." Then, let's add a Float Action component to this game object, and set its Sources size property to 2, which will provide you with two Element slots. Now, select the Thumbstick Horizontal Axis Right game object in the hierarchy, and duplicate it and rename the copied game object "Thumbstick Vertical Axis Right."

Now, expand the VRTK INPUT CONTROLLERS game object in *the* hierarchy, and then expand the Input Unity Input Manager Oculus Touch Right Controller game object until you reach its Right Thumbstick game object, which you need to expand, too. You'll be capturing input for the horizontal and vertical axis movement of the Right Thumbstick.

Next, expand the Input Unity Input Manager Open VR Right Controller game object until you reach its Right Trackpad game object, which you also need to expand. You'll be capturing input for the horizontal and vertical axis movement of the Right Trackpad.

Now, in the hierarchy, select the Thumbstick Horizontal Axis Right game object. Drag and drop the Right Thumbstick Horizontal Axis [4] game object from the hierarchy into the Element 0 slot. Then, drag and drop the Right Trackpad Horizontal Axis [4] game object into the Element 1 slot, as shown in Figure 22-14.

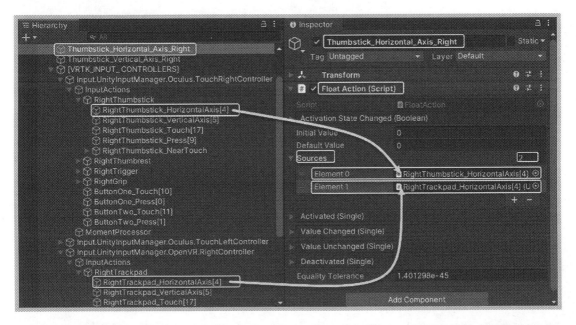

***Figure 22-14.*** *Setting up the Thumbstick Horizontal Axis Right intermediary game object*

Now, in the hierarchy, select the Thumbstick Vertical Axis Right game object. Drag and drop the Right Thumbstick Vertical Axis [5] game object from the hierarchy into the Element 0 slot. Then, drag and drop the Right Trackpad Vertical Axis [5] game object into the Element 1 slot, see Figure 22-15.

You now have two intermediary game objects that capture the horizontal and vertical axis movements the Thumbstick and Touchpad. You'll use values for this movement to move the Ball in different directions during the game.

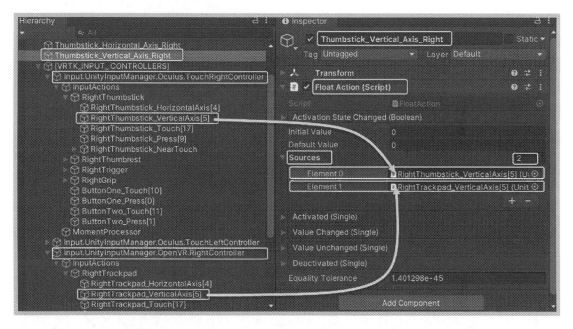

***Figure 22-15.*** *Setting up the Thumbstick Vertical Axis Right intermediary game object*

# Enabling Obstacle Objects to Attach to the Ball

Upon rolling the Ball onto any obstacle game object in the Scene, you must ensure that the object attaches itself to the Ball. To achieve this behavior, we'll set up a Mutators Object Follower. You'll recall that we learned to use the Mutators Object Follower prefab when we had our Holsters follow our Play Area Alias. We also used the Offset Object property to offset the Holsters a bit in front of the Play Area. We'll apply the same strategy here, with the Ball becoming the Source game object and each of the 37 obstacle game objects becoming a Target of the Mutators Object Follower prefab. Each of these 37 game objects contains a child Offset game object that has been assigned a random Transform

Position value. Each child Offset game object with an assigned Transform Position value allows each obstacle game object to attach itself to the Ball in a slightly different position.

Let's set this up now. Expand the "Packages" folder in the Project tab, locate the Tilia Mutators Object Follower Unity package, and expand it until you reach its "Prefabs" folder. Drag and drop the Mutators Object Follower prefab into the hierarchy, making it a child of the Garden game object, and rename the Mutators Object Follower game object, "Mutators Object Follower Obstacles."

With the Mutators Object Follower Obstacle game object selected in the hierarchy, ensure that its Object Follower component has been expanded in the Inspector. Set its Sources Elements property size to 1, which will provide you with an Element 0 slot. Then, drag and drop the Ball game object from the hierarchy into this slot. The Ball is now the Source object that the obstacles will follow, see Figure 22-16.

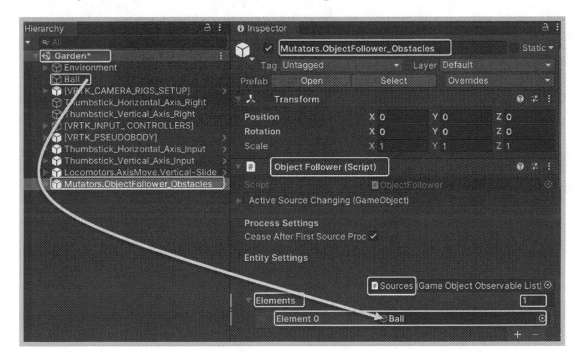

***Figure 22-16.*** *Setting up the Source game object (Ball) for Mutators Object Follower Obstacles*

With the Mutators Object Follower Obstacles game object still selected in the hierarchy, set the Targets Elements property size to 37. This will provide you with 37 Element slots. Also, set the Target Offsets Elements property size to 37. This will provide you with 37 Element slots. Note that you now have 37 target obstacle game objects in the Scene. Each has its own Offset child game object.

You now need to populate all 37 Element slots with the obstacle game objects in the hierarchy. Note that you should only use the obstacle game objects that are activated, as those that are deactivated haven't been configured with the necessary components. Twenty-three of these obstacle game objects are available as children of the Environment game object, and you can find the remaining 14 by navigating to Environment ➤ World ➤ Map Objects, see Figures 22-5 and 22-6 earlier in this chapter.

For each obstacle game object you populate the Targets Elements list with, you should also populate the Target Offsets Elements list with the corresponding obstacle Offset child game object. This way, you'll ensure that you don't match one obstacle game object with a different Offset obstacle game object. Figure 22-17 shows 18 of the Targets Element list slots populated with obstacle game objects. You'll need to populate this list with all 37 obstacle game objects.

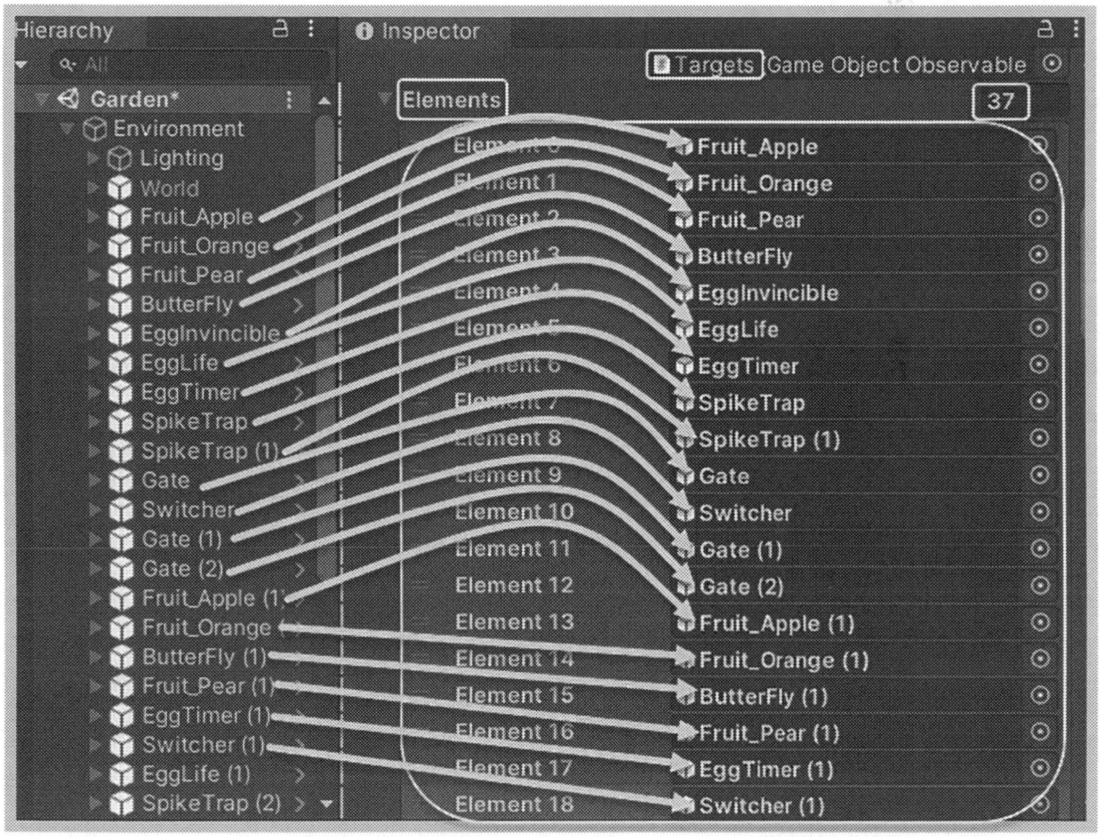

***Figure 22-17.*** *The Targets Elements List populated with the obstacle game objects*

Figure 22-18 shows 8 Target Offsets Elements list slots populated with the obstacle game objects Offset child game objects. You will need to populate this list with all 37 Offset child game objects.

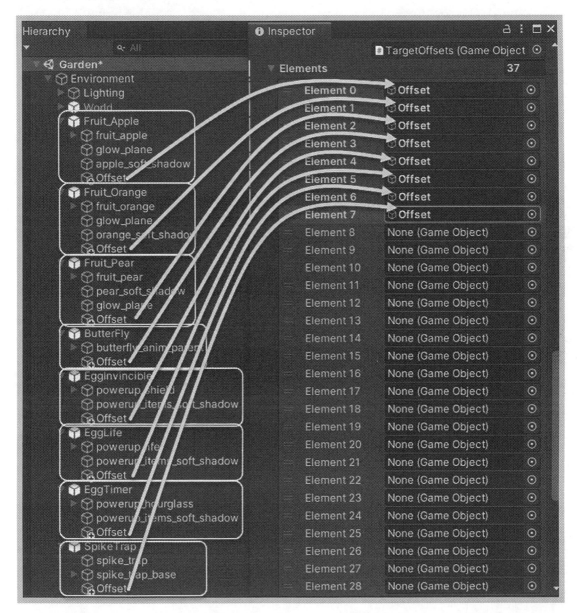

***Figure 22-18.*** *The Target Offsets Elements List populated with each obstacle game objects, nested Offset child game object*

We now need to set up a Rule that defines which target obstacles will be considered ready to be attached to the Ball. You have assigned a Collision Tracker component to each obstacle game object in the Scene. Whenever the Ball collides with an obstacle, the Collision Started event in the Collision Tracker component for that specific obstacle gets triggered, setting the obstacle's Tag to Grabbable.

The Rule that you'll create as part of the Target Validity property of the Mutators Object Follower Obstacles game object will only allow an obstacle game object whose Tag is set to Grabbable to be attached to the Ball when the Ball collides with the obstacle. According to this Rule, when the Ball collides with an obstacle whose Tag is set to Grabbable, it will be attached to the Ball. It will then begin to follow the Ball using the Offset that was created.

Let's set up this Rule now. In the hierarchy, with the Garden game object selected, create a new empty child game object and rename it "Attach Rule." Select the Attach Rule game object, and in the Inspector, add two new components to it: the Any Tag Rule component and the String Observable List component. We've already used both of these components in Chapter 16, when we set up the Snap Zone Valid Tags rule game object in the Demo scene.

Drag and drop the String Observable List component from the Inspector onto the String Observable List property parameter in the Any Tag Rule component. Set the Attach Rule (String Observable List)'s property size to 1 for the latter component. This will provide you with an Element 0 slot, in which you should type in the value "Grabbable," see Figure 22-19.

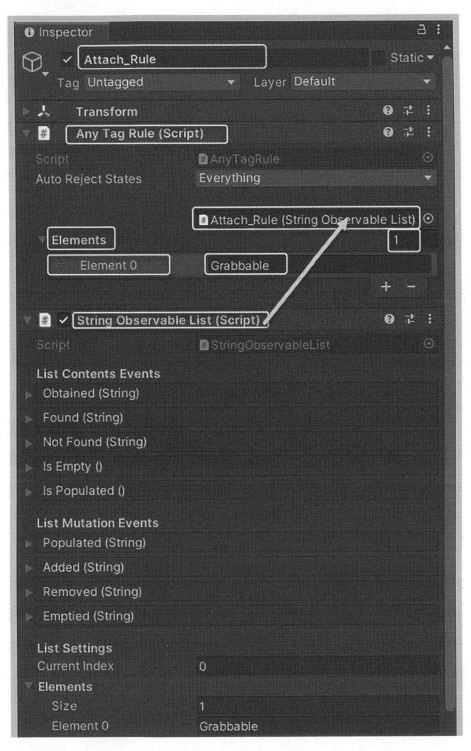

***Figure 22-19.*** *Setting up the Attach Rule game object*

Now that we've created the Rule, we need to apply it to the Target Validity property of the Mutators Object Follower Obstacles game object. To do so, select this game object in the hierarchy. Then, locate the Target Validity property in the Inspector. Drag and drop the Attach Rule game object from the hierarchy into this Target Validity property parameter, as shown in Figure 22-20.

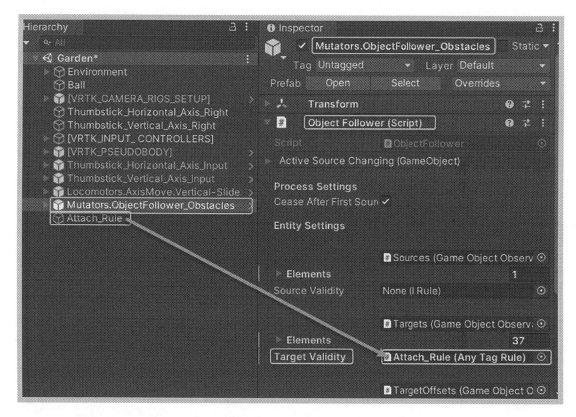

***Figure 22-20.*** *Setting up the Target Validity property to reference the Attach Rule that allows only game objects tagged as Grabbable to be attached to the Ball*

The Attach Rule will now only allow any of the 37 listed target obstacle game objects to attach themselves to the Ball. The concerned obstacle Tag is set to Grabbable when the Ball collides with it, and it is then that the obstacle attaches itself to the Ball.

# Getting the Ball to Roll About Freely

In this section, we'll set up the Right Controller Thumbstick to control the Ball's movement, wherein the player will be allowed to roll the Ball forward, backward, left, and right. The Left Controller Thumbstick is responsible for controlling the player's movement and rotation.

To achieve realistic Ball movement, we'll use a physics force against the Ball Rigidbody with the Input Combined Actions Axes to Vector 3 Action prefab. Attempting to achieve such realistic Ball movement without using this VRTK-provided prefab would require us to write math code involving Vectors and Trigonometry. But thanks to this VRTK prefab, we're not required to write any such math code. Let's begin setting this up now.

From within the Project tab, expand the "Packages" folder, locate the Tilia Input Combined Actions Unity package, and expand its "Prefabs" folder. Drag and drop the Input Combined Actions Axes to Vector 3 Action prefab into the hierarchy, making it a child of the Garden game object. With the Input Combined Actions Axes to Vector 3 Action game object selected in the hierarchy, ensure that its Axes to Vector 3 Action component has been expanded in the Inspector. Scroll down to the "Axis Settings" section, where you'll need to set up some properties.

Locate the Lateral Axis property, and drag and drop the Thumbstick Horizontal Axis Right game object into this property parameter. The Lateral Axis (x axis) is responsible for capturing the left and right movement of the Thumbstick. You'll recall that the Thumbstick Horizontal Axis Right returns a float value between -1 and 1 when you push your Thumbstick either left or right, see Figure 22-21.

Then, do the same for the Longitudinal Axis property, dragging and dropping the Thumbstick Vertical Axis Right game object into its property parameter. The Longitudinal Axis (z axis) captures the forward and backward movement of your Thumbstick. The Thumbstick Vertical Axis Right returns a float value between -1 and 1 when you push your Thumbstick either forward or backward, see Figure 22-21.

As these lateral and longitudinal axes values are too small to have any real impact on the movement and rotation of the Ball, we'll use the Multiplier property in conjunction with the Time Multiplier property to obtain a vector value that will be applied as the force to the Balls Rigidbody. Set the $X$ and $Z$ values of the Multiplier property to 100. Leave its $Y$ value at 1, as you haven't specified anything for the Vertical Axis property since you don't want your Ball moving up and down.

Next, set the Time Multiplier property to Delta Time. This ensures that value of each axis will be computed based on the time elapsed since the last update frame only; otherwise, you would encounter an incredibly fast-moving Ball. The settings for your Dead Zone can be left as is, or you could fine-tune them to your liking, see Figure 22-21.

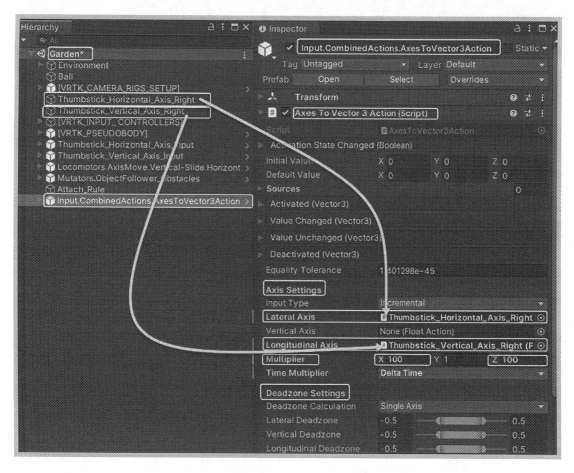

***Figure 22-21.*** *Setting up the Input Combined Actions Axes to Vector 3 Action*

Last, we need to set up the Value Changed event of the Axis to Vector 3 Action component, which is triggered whenever you move the right Thumbstick around. Expand the Value Changed event, and click the plus symbol located in its bottom right corner to add a new event listener. Then, drag and drop the Ball game object into this event listener box. For this function, select Rigidbody, Add Force from within the "Dynamic Vector 3" section. The Lateral and Longitudinal Axis values, combined with the Multiplier and Time Multiplier, are fed as a Vector 3 to the Value Changed event, which then uses this Vector 3 value to apply force to the Ball Rigidbody, which gets the Ball to move, see Figure 22-22.

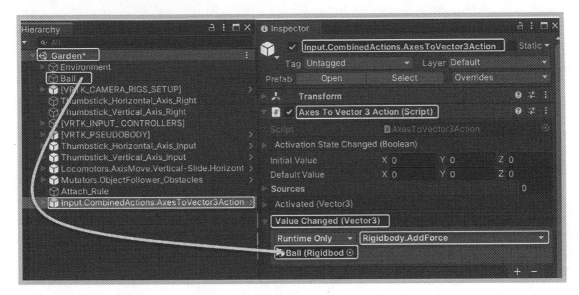

***Figure 22-22.*** *Setting up the Value Changed event*

Using the Input Combined Actions Axes to Vector 3 Action, we've taken axis input data from our Thumbstick and converted it into movement and rotational information that the Ball can use. All the math involved in obtaining this information has been encapsulated into the VRTK's Axes to Vector 3 Action component.

Now, playtest the scene using your VR headset and roll the Ball around. Note the fluidity of the Ball movement, as physics has been applied to it. Approach one of the obstacles, and roll the Ball onto it. You'll see that it attaches itself to the Ball. We're now able to collect obstacles in our game.

# Spatial Tooltip to Display Countdown Timer

In this section, we'll learn to set up a Countdown Timer for our minigame. This timer counts down the seconds you have left to complete the level, and upon the timer reaching zero, you're no longer able to roll the Ball any further. This Countdown Timer will be displayed in the world using the Visuals Tooltip prefab provided by the VRTK. You could quickly write a Countdown Timer script yourself. The reason for setting up a

Countdown Timer here is mainly to learn how to use the Moment Processor available with VRTK. Once you wrap your brain around this setup, you'll find yourself using the Countdown Timer in several situations. Let's begin.

First, let's set up the Visuals Tooltip that will be used to display the Countdown Timer. You already learned how to set this up when you created the *Slider* and *Snap Zone* inventory slots.

From within the Projects tab, expand the "Packages" folder and locate the Tilia Visual's Tooltip Unity package. Expand its "Prefabs" folder, and drag and drop the Visuals Tooltip prefab into the hierarchy, making it a child of the Garden game object. Rename this Visuals Tooltip game object "Visuals Tooltip Timer."

With this game object selected in the hierarchy, add the Tooltip Text component to it in the Inspector. Then, drag and drop the Tooltip Facade component into the Tool Tip Facade property parameter of the Tooltip Text component. Next, in the Tooltip Facade component, set the Facing Source property to the Headset Alias game object. Leave the Line Origin property empty. Set the Font Size to 50, as shown in Figure 22-23.

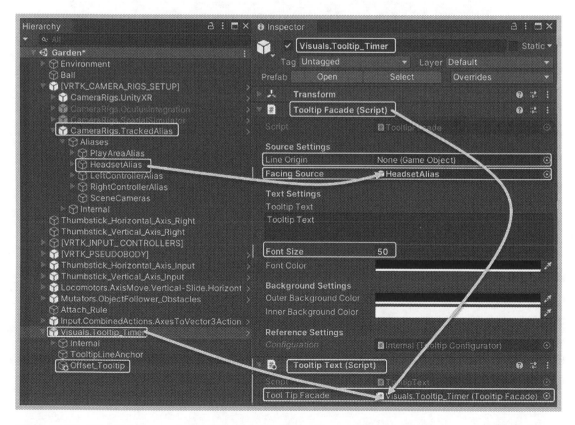

***Figure 22-23.*** *Setting up the Visuals Tooltip Timer game object*

Now, with the Visuals Tooltip Timer game object still selected in the hierarchy, create an empty child game object within it and rename this child game object "Offset Tooltip." Your Tooltip will follow your Play Area Alias, and this Offset Tooltip game object will allow you to offset the Tooltip timer a certain distance forward from the Play Area Alias. Select the Offset Tooltip game object in the hierarchy, and set its Transform Position property values as follows: $X = 0$; $Y = -0.75$; and $Z = 2$. Last, set its Transform Rotation $Y$ value to 180. You can fine-tune these values to your liking if you wish, see Figure 22-24.

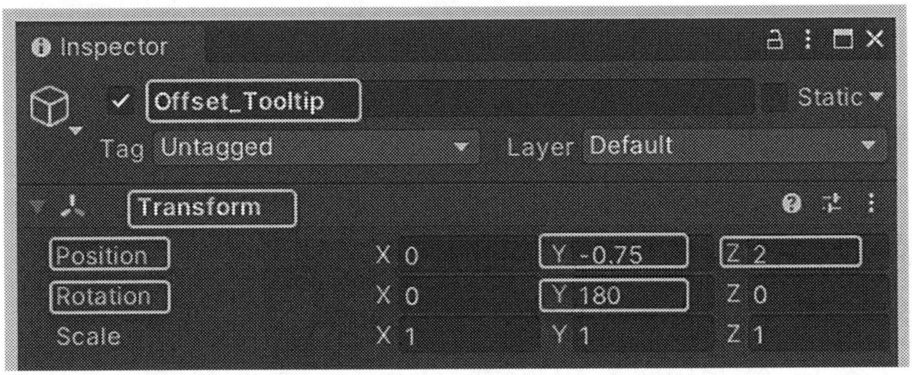

***Figure 22-24.*** *Setting up the Transform Position and Rotation values for the Offset Tooltip game object*

Now that our Visuals Tooltip Timer game object has been set up, we need to set up a Mutators Object Follower so that the Visuals Tooltip Timer game object can follow the Play Area Alias around at the given Offset distance. Let's do this now.

Select the "Packages" folder in the Project tab, and locate the Tilia Mutators Object Follower Unity package and expand it until you reach its "Prefabs" folder. Drag and drop the Mutators Object Follower prefab into the hierarchy, making it a child of the Garden game object. Rename this Mutators Object Follower game object "Mutators Object Follower Tooltip." With this game object selected in the hierarchy, ensure that its Object Follower component has been expanded in the Inspector. Set its Sources Elements property size to 1. This provides you with an Element 0 slot. Drag and drop the Play Area Alias game object from the hierarchy into this slot. The Play Area Alias is the Source Object that the Visuals Tooltip Timer game object will follow. Now, set the Targets Elements property size to 1. This provides you with an Element 0 slot. Drag and drop the Visuals Tooltip Timer game object into this slot. Next, set the Target Offsets Elements property size to 1. This provides you with an Element 0 slot. Drag and drop the Offset Tooltip game object into this 0 slot.

We have now set up the Visuals Tooltip Timer game object so that it is always positioned in front of us as we move around in the Scene, see Figure 22-25.

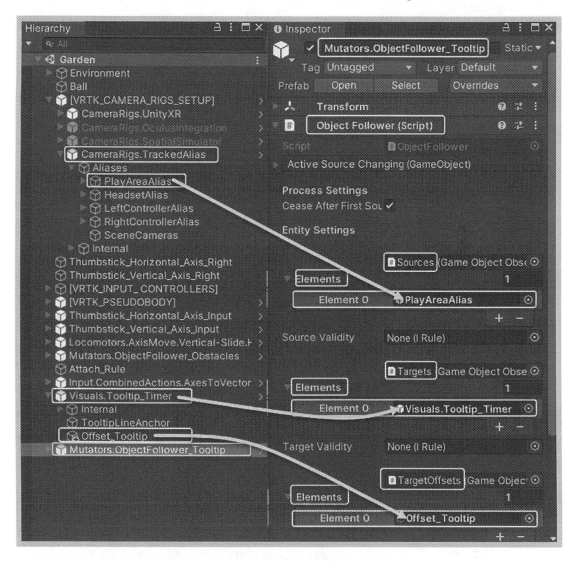

***Figure 22-25.*** *Setting up the Mutators Object Follower Tooltip game object to have the Visuals Tooltip Timer game object follow the Play Area Alias around at a predefined Offset distance*

# Setting Up the Countdown Timer and Moment Processor

The VRTK provides you with a Countdown Timer component that can be used to create a seconds countdown. Once this Countdown Timer reaches zero, you can perform an action. That action is to deactivate the Ball so that the player can no longer roll it farther. First, we'll set up the Countdown Timer game object and then we'll set up the two supporting objects needed to get a Moment Processor working. Let's begin.

In the hierarchy, with the Garden game object selected, create a new empty game object and rename it "Timer." Within the Inspector, add two new components to this Timer game object: Countdown Timer and Any Action.

With the Countdown Timer component expanded, set the Start Time property to 300 seconds. This allows the player five minutes to collect all obstacles in the level. You can adjust this Start Time property value to your liking, but note that its value should be in seconds.

Then, expand the Completed event, and click the plus symbol located in the bottom right corner to add a new event listener. Drag and drop the Ball game object into this event listener box. For this function, select Game Object, Set Active, and ensure that the check box below is left unchecked. This ensures that once your Countdown Timer has completed (i.e., reached 0), the Ball will be immediately deactivated and you'll no longer be able to move the Ball any farther, as the time allotted to complete the level will have elapsed.

Next, expand the Remaining Time Emitted event, and click the plus symbol in the bottom right corner to add a new event listener. Drag and drop the Visuals Tooltip Timer game object into this event listener box. For thus function, select Tooltip Text, Show Tooltip from the "Dynamic Float" section, see Figure 22-26.

The Remaining Time Emitted event will be triggered whenever the Countdown Timers, Emit Remaining Time method is invoked. This method passes a float value of the seconds remaining to the Remaining Time Emitted event, which in turn passes this value to the Show Tooltip method, displaying the seconds remaining on the Tooltip. The Countdown Timers, Emit Remaining Time method will be invoked via the Moment Processor, which we'll set up shortly.

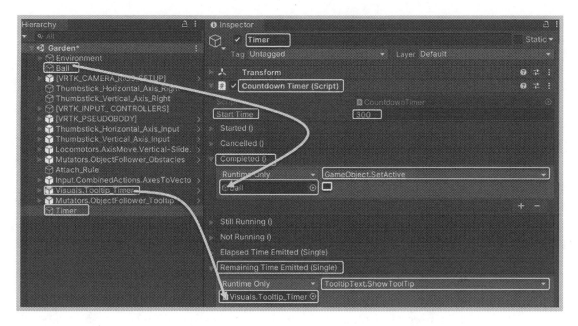

**Figure 22-26.** *Setting up properties and events on the Countdown Timer component of the Timer game object*

To get the Countdown Timer mechanism working, you first need to tell the Timer to begin counting down. You'll start the Countdown Timer by calling its Begin method via the Any Action component's Activated event. This component can be used to execute any possible action. Here, you'll utilize it to execute the Countdown Timer's Begin action.

For the Timer game object, ensure that the Any Action component has been expanded in the Inspector. To get the Countdown Timer to start counting down, expand the Activated event in the Any Action component and click the plus symbol in the bottom right corner to add a new event listener. Drag and drop the Timer game object from the hierarchy into this event listener box. For this function, select Countdown Timer, Begin from the "Static Parameters" section, see Figure 22-27.

Now, the moment the Any Action component's Initial Value property is true, the Activated event in it will be triggered and the entire countdown mechanism will roll into motion. You need to ensure that this component is in a true state when the game starts so that the countdown mechanism can start rolling. Check the box for the Initial Value property in the Any Action component to set it to true, as shown in Figure 22-27.

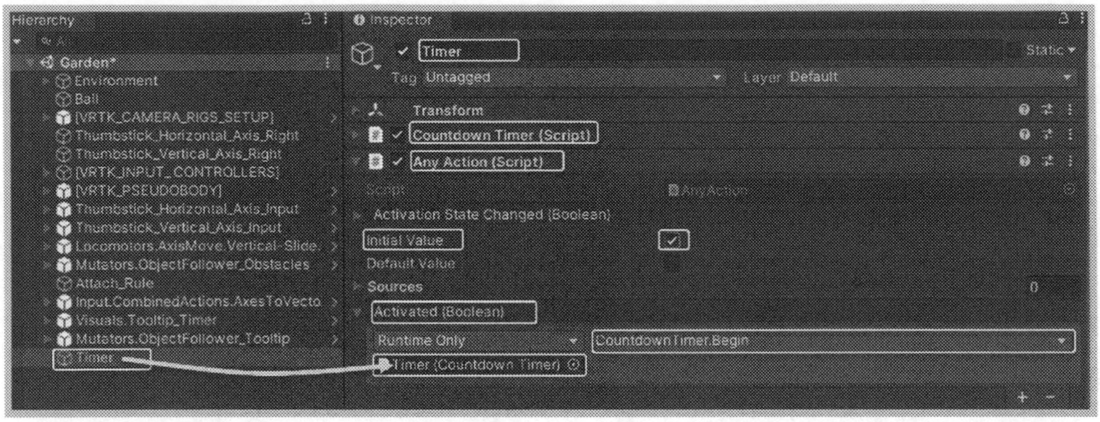

***Figure 22-27.*** *Setting up the properties and events in the Any Action component of the Timer game object*

Now that we've made the Countdown Timer functional, it needs to be polled repeatedly at a fixed interval—say, every half a second—so that at this given interval, the time remaining can be displayed via the Visuals Tooltip Timer game object. If you were writing your script, you could easily achieve this using Unity's Update method. However, the VRTK provides you with a Moment Processor that functions like Unity's Update method and can be used to call another Process repeatedly whenever a specific time interval has elapsed. We'll use the Moment Processor to call the Countdown Timer Process after every half a second has elapsed. Let's set up the Moment Processor game object first.

In the hierarchy, with the Garden game object selected, create a new empty game object and rename it "Moment Processor." Add two new components to the Moment Processor game object in the Inspector: the Moment Processor and the Moment Process Observable List. In the Moment Processor component, set the value for the Process Moment property to Update. This ensures that the processes you invoke, like processing a code block in Unity's Update method, will be done in Update. Now, drag and drop the Moment Process Observable List component into the None (Moment Processes Observable list) text box in the Moment Processor component, as shown in Figure 22-28.

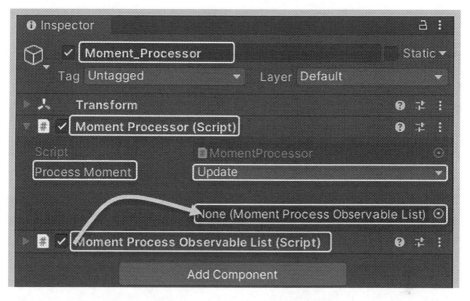

***Figure 22-28.*** *Dragging and dropping the Moment Process Observable List component into the None (Moment Process Observable List) text box as you set up the properties for the Moment Processor game object*

In the Moment Processor component, set the Moment Processor, Elements property size to 1, which will provide you with an Element 0 slot. Drop a Moment Process that will be processed every Update into this slot, see Figure 22-29.

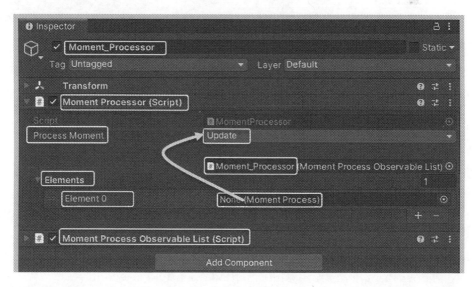

***Figure 22-29.*** *Element 0 slot requiring a Moment process to be dropped in that will be processed on every Update*

Let's now set up a Moment Process that can be processed on every Update. In the hierarchy, with the Garden game object selected, create a new empty game object and rename it "Process Every Half Second." With this game object selected in the hierarchy in the Inspector, add two new components: the Moment Process and the Event Process.

Drag and drop the Process Every Half Second game object from the hierarchy into the Source property of the Moment Process component. You'll be prompted to choose between a Moment Process and an Event Process. Select Event Process, as it is an event that you will execute as part of the Moment Process, see Figure 22-30.

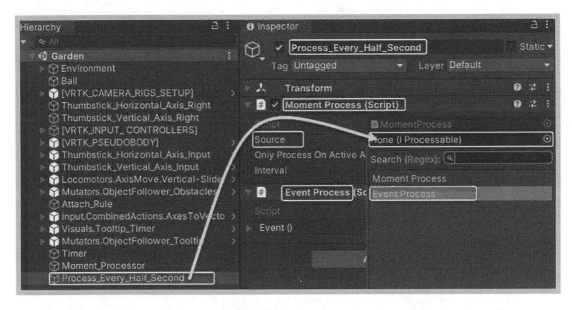

***Figure 22-30.*** *Dragging and dropping the Process Every Half Second Game object into the Source property of the Moment Process component presents a dialog box where you will select Event Process*

Set the value of the Interval property to 0.5, as shown in Figure 22-31, so that the Event Process you'll set up will be called only every half a second, not every time an Update runs. In the Event Process component of the Process Every Half Second game object, expand the Event drop-down and click the plus symbol in the bottom right corner to add a new event listener. Drag and drop the Timer game object from the hierarchy into this event listener box. For the function, select Countdown Timer, Emit Remaining Time, as shown in the figure. Here, setting the Interval to 0.5 means that it will call the Countdown Timer Emit Remaining Time method every half a second.

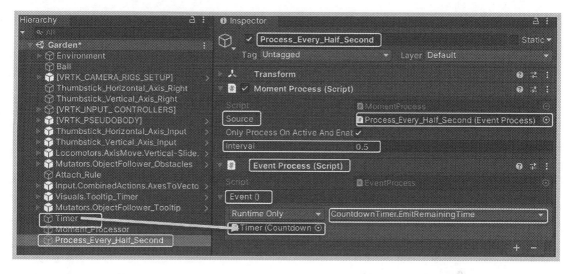

**Figure 22-31.** *Setting up Event () in the Event Process component*

Last, select the Moment Processor game object in the hierarchy. In its Moment Processor component, locate Moment Process Observable List, Elements, Element 0 slot. Drag and drop the Process Every Half Second game object from the hierarchy into this slot.

We have now provided the Moment Processor with a Moment Process that will be executed during an Update process, and we've set up the Moment Processor so that the Countdown Timer is fully functional, see Figure 22-32.

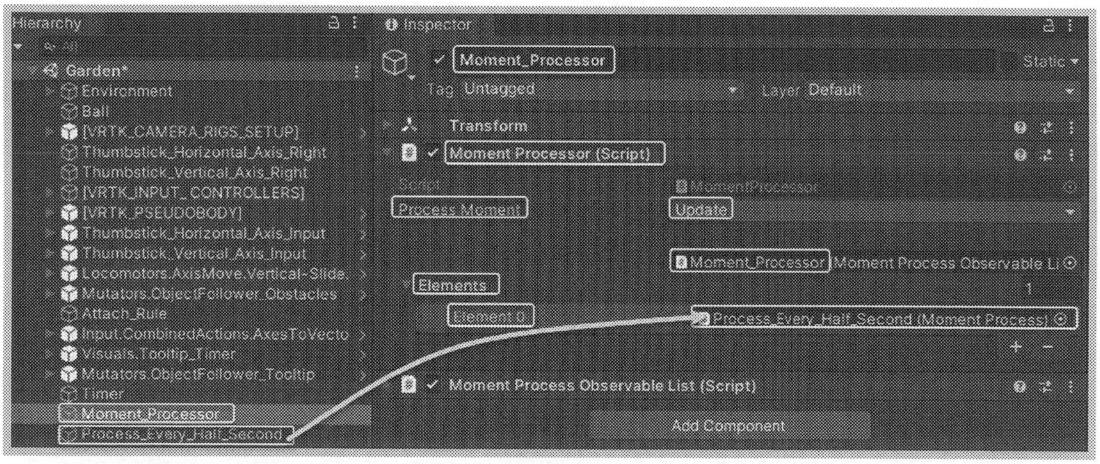

**Figure 22-32.** *Adding the Process Every Half Second Moment Process game object to the Moment Processor Moment Process Observable List, Elements, Element 0 slot*

If you found setting up all these connections to be a mind bender, let me summarize how all the connections you hooked up and synced together got the Countdown Timer to work. Let's start with the Moment Processor that runs processes assigned to it, every Update. Every Update, the Moment Processor will run the only Moment Process you have assigned—Process Every Half Second, see Figure 22-32.

The Process Every Half Second (Moment Process), shown in Figure 22-32, suggests that when it's invoked, a half a second must have elapsed before it triggers the Event Process component's Event () event. At that point, it will execute the Countdown Timer, Emit Remaining Time metho

The moment the Countdown Timer, Emit Remaining Time method is invoked, the Timer game objects, Remaining Time Emitted event will be triggered. The triggering of this event results in the Visuals Tooltip Timer game object displaying the floating-point value—or the time in seconds remaining as per the Countdown Timer—getting passed to it. Look back at Figure 22-26.

Figure 22-33 shows an image summarizing the entire Countdown Timer process workflow. Before playtesting the minigame, ensure that the Oculus-provided Custom Hand Right and Custom Hand Left are deactivated, and that the Hand Proto Right and Hand Proto Left are activated. Then, playtest your minigame using your VR headset. Use the Left Controller to move within the game world and the Right Controller to roll the Ball onto the obstacle game objects strewn around the garden path. Note how they attach themselves to the Ball when it collides with them. See how many obstacles you can gather in the five minutes of game play allotted, and, if required, increase the Countdown Timer component's Start Time property value.

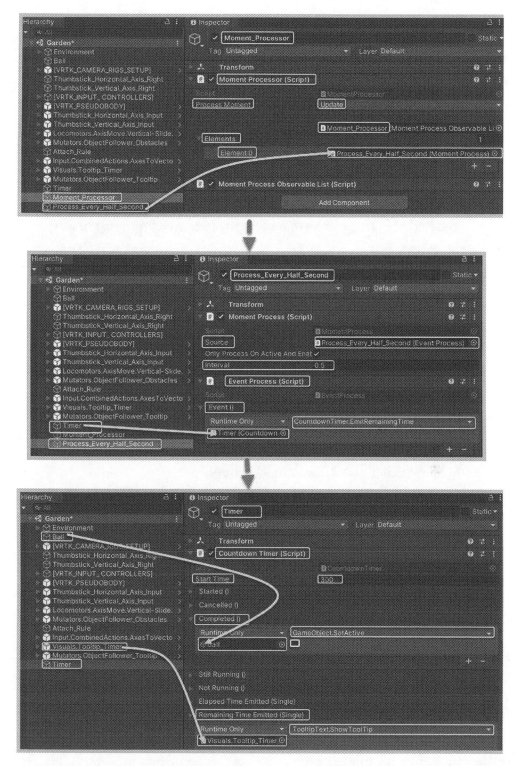

**Figure 22-33.** *The Countdown Timer's process workflow*

# Enhancing the Minigame

Now that we've created our minigame without having written a single line of code, let's now enhance this simple minigame further by writing small snippets of code to achieve the following:

- Increase the Ball scale factor by 0.1 every time the player attaches an obstacle to it.

- Set up a Game Manager to keep count of the number of obstacles collected. Once a certain number of obstacles have accumulated, or the Ball has attained a specific size, the player can progress to the next level.

- Use another Tooltip that displays an incremental count of the number of obstacles being attached to the Ball.

- Assign categories to the obstacles, such as small, medium, and large, and then ensure that a certain number of small obstacles have been attached before allowing the player to capture the medium- and larger-sized obstacles.

- Add some sound effects, preferably different types, for the different unique obstacle game objects attached to the Ball.

- Add an overall musical theme to the game.

# Summary

In the final chapter of this book, we have created a minigame without writing a single line of code, using several mechanics we learned about throughout the book. We learned how to create a Countdown Timer and set up a Moment Processor. We also learned to use a critical VRTK prefab, Input Combined Actions Axes to Vector 3 Action, to roll the Ball around by adding force to its Rigidbody, thereby avoiding the need to write math code involving Vectors and Trigonometry. We used the Collision Tracker component to set up Source, Targets, and Target Offset game objects that allowed obstacle game objects to attach themselves to the Ball. We set up a Spatial Tooltip to display the game's Countdown Timer. We utilized the VRTK-provided Countdown Timer to count down time in seconds, ensuring that once the timer reaches zero, the game ends and the player isn't allowed to move the Ball any farther. You learned to set up the Input Combined Actions Axes to Vector 3 Action prefab to allow the player to move the Ball realistically around the garden path. You also learned about the Countdown Timer's Completed and Remaining Time Emitted events. In the last section of the chapter, we set up a Moment Processor and used its Update process moment to call another Process repeatedly whenever a specific time interval has elapsed. Along the way, we became familiar with how to use the Moment Process and Event Process components. We wrapped up the chapter by testing our minigame using our VR headset and, finally, were provided some tips on enhancing this minigame by adding some simple mechanics.

# Index

## A

Activated and Deactivated events, 346
Activated Boolean, 68
Activated event, 77, 385
Activation Action property, 122, 289, 290
Active Button Index property, 275
Active Input Handling, 21
Alias game object, 163, 344
Ambisonic Object, 351
Amplified movement, 207
Android SDK, 14
Android tab, 19
Angular Drag, 361
Angular Drive Facade
    component, 311, 318
Angular drives, 102
Angular Joint Drives
    Box Collider component, 310
    Door Frame, 307, 308, 314
    dual-facing dashed arrow, 306
    Follow Tracking property, 305
    Lever, 316, 317, 320
    Logic objects, 321, 322, 324, 326, 329
    Mesh Filter, 309
    Started Moving event, 316
    Steering Wheel, 303–305
    Step Settings, 315
Animator, 346, 368
Animator component, 56, 70
Animator Play string, 136, 161
Any Layer Rule component, 126
Any Tag Rule component, 243, 375

API Compatibility Level, 21, 22
Apply Destination Rotation
    property, 128, 142
Arm-Swinging Locomotion, 175
Arm-swinging movement, 171
Attach Rule game object, 375
Avatar, 161
Avatar Container game object, 57
Avatar cuboid objects, 83
Axe game object, 229, 278
Axes to Vector 3 Action component, 166
Axis gizmo, 93
Axis Move Facade
    component, 160, 163, 369
Axis Move Unity package, 160
Axis Move Vertical Slide Horizontal Snap
    Rotate prefab, 369
Axis Name property, 158
Axis Settings heading, 160, 378
Axis to Angle Action component, 140
Axis to Vector 3 Action component, 379

## B

Begin method, 385
Bezier Pointer, 121
Boolean action, 58
Boolean Action component, 84, 119,
    255, 289
Boolean Action Sources property, 120
Box Collider component, 91, 103, 310
Bumper, 84
Button Text property, 272

© Christopher Coutinho 2022
C. Coutinho, *Unity® Virtual Reality Development with VRTK4*, https://doi.org/10.1007/978-1-4842-7933-5

# T

# W